How to
BUY STOCKS

EIGHTH EDITION # How to BUY STOCKS

by LOUIS ENGEL

and HENRY HECHT

Little, Brown and Company

BOSTON   NEW YORK   TORONTO   LONDON

To Olive Tamborelle,
Reference Librarian Extraordinaire
and Wonderful Friend
whose skill and willingness to dig up sources
were invaluable in the preparation of this edition
as was proved only too well
when she was untimely taken from us

—H.H.

Eighth Edition

Library of Congress Cataloging-in-Publication Data

Engel, Louis, 1909—
    How to buy stocks / by Louis Engel and Henry Hecht.—8th ed.
        p.   cm.
    Includes index.
    ISBN 0-316-35380-9 (pb)   ISBN 0-316-19956-7 (hc)
        1. Securities.   2. Investments.   I. Hecht, Henry R.   II. Title.
HG4521.E6   1994
332.63'2—dc20   93-47215

10 9 8 7 6 5

MV-NY

Published simultaneously in Canada
by Little, Brown & Company (Canada) Limited

PRINTED IN THE UNITED STATES OF AMERICA

Contents

Foreword to the Original Edition

This book is based on a very simple premise: that the stock market is going up.

Tomorrow? Next month? Next year?

Maybe yes, maybe no. Maybe the market will be a lot lower than it is today.

But over any long period of time — 10 years, 20 years, 50 years — this book assumes that the market is bound to go up.

Why?

Because it always has.

Because the market is a measure of the vigor of American business, and unless something drastic happens to America, business is going to go on growing.

Because prices of food and clothing and almost everything else in this country — including stocks — have steadily gone up as the buying power of the dollar has gone down. That's a trend that isn't likely to be reversed.

And so these are the reasons why the author is sold on the value of investing, of buying stocks for the long pull — and not for a quick profit tomorrow.

There's nothing hidden about this prejudice. You'll see it when you read the book. And you will find other prejudices, other opinions, despite an earnest effort to focus this book strictly on facts — the facts about investing that have been obscured all too long by double talk, by financial jargon, and by unnecessary mystery.

Of course it can be said that there are no facts when you get beyond the simple business of adding one and one. That's true. So let's say that here are the facts as the author sees them — and as plainly as he can state them.

He has only one hope: that they will add up to good common sense in your own mind.

LOUIS ENGEL

Foreword to Current Edition

I first met Lou Engel in 1947, soon after he had become Merrill Lynch's first advertising director and I had latched on to a junior writer's position on the company's business news magazine, *Investor's Reader*. Our offices were located on an isolated expansion floor, and we both tended to work late. When we stopped to chat in the evening hours, Lou showed me some of the groundbreaking educational advertisements he was preparing. Against the conventional wisdom, which demanded splashy, eye-catching displays, Lou's ads filled the page with text — but it was text that in a lively, never condescending style explained the fundamentals of investing so that a reader totally unfamiliar with the subject could understand what it was all about.

The overwhelming response to these ads led Lou to plan the book that became *How to Buy Stocks* — and it was greeted with the same enthusiasm by Americans who knew they should invest for their future, and wanted a simple guide on how to do it.

By now this book has continued to fulfill its mission for more than four decades, and, as a longtime disciple of Lou's, I'm honored by the assignment to prepare this new edition for the investor of the 1990s. This is the most thoroughgoing revision yet — as it would have to be to cover all the new investment opportunities and procedures that have evolved in recent years. But the basic principles that Lou Engel espoused and explained are as valid today as when he first typed them. I've done my best to stay true to the premise (and also the style) that made his book a best-seller over the decades: Investment is everybody's business, and it's a business everybody can understand when it's presented in lively, easy-to-read language.

Each time I glance over the roster of "Acknowledgments" Lou Engel included in his earlier editions, I'm struck by how many names — both at the firm we both served and throughout Wall Street — were friends and associates who also were repeatedly helpful to me in my career as financial writer and editor. And surely I, too, owe them a debt for their fine contribution to the earlier editions on which I now have been able to build.

Working on the present edition, I've been blessed by the generous cooperation of countless men and women — including, I'm happy to report, quite a few of Lou Engel's earlier helpers who were still ready to share their knowledge this time around.

Among those whose information, ideas, and other support helped me prepare this book are Kelly Aherne, Mary Amberg, Margaret M. Andretta, Richard Bernstein, Nina Brill, Paul Bruehl, James E. Carlson, Joan Caron, Dominic Carone, Joan Christensen, Thomas L. Chrystie, Fran Connors, Paul Critchlow, Linda Danatzko, William DeMeo, Andrew Dickson, Robert J. Farrell, John Feeley, Michael R. Feigeles, Terry Ferraro, Kathy Fitzpatrick, Betsy Flagler, Robert Flynn, Glenn Fowler, Vincent Galbo, Mary Galvin, Randy Gretz, Lorraine Hanley, Fred Harbus, Betty Hart, Robert Heady, Kathy K. Hecht, Enno Hobbing, Richard Hoenig, Clark Hooper, Betty Hope, Lindsey Howes, Rita Hughes, Mark Hulbert, Joseph Hunt, Patricia Hussey, Roger Ibbotson, Teresa Jasko, Malin Jennings, Dwight Johnson, Kenneth A. Johnson, Steve Jones, Martin E. Kaplan, Richard Kaplin, William Katchin, William J. Kehoe, John F. Kelly, Joseph Kenrick, Richard Kreuder, Daniel Lalima, Jack W. Lavery, George T. Lee, Ed Levine, Robert Lewton, Perrin Long, James H. Lorie, Terry Maguire, Barbara Maher, Vernon Martens, Carol Martz, Philicia Matthews, James E. May, Richard T. McCabe, Sue McCabe, Mary McCue, Anna Merjos, Betsy Metz, Stuart Meyerhart, Kate Michel, Lee Mitgang, Maureen Mooney, Carlos Morales, Steven R. Narker, Dorothy Nelsen-Gille, James Noone, Andrew

Nybo, Tony Onofrio, Margaret Pacey, Chuck Parnow, H. William Peterson, Joseph M. Petri, Gerald M. Richard, John Riley, Thomas R. Robinson, Jack W. Roehrig, Chris Rohan, Gary Rosenfeld, Greg Russo, Robert Salerno, Arthur Samansky, Barbara Samuelson, Karen Sanantonio, Robert Shabazian, Howard Silverblatt, Carolyn Simpson, Rhonda Singer, Martin Skala, Everett Smith, Bart Sotnick, James Spellman, Richard Spiegelberg, Kenneth Spirer, John Sprung, William B. Stannard Jr., Debbie Stevens, Frank Teixeira, Kitty Thomas, Gary Tuttle, Robert G. Volpe, Joseph Vuolo, Walter Wager, Louis Wald, James Walsh, Robert Wenick, Bill Wilde, and Arthur Zeikel.

My sincere gratitude to all — very much including those who, through my negligence in recording, are left nameless here.

Special thanks are due to Jane Keen, a onetime associate of Lou Engel's and later a stellar editor for me at *Investor's Reader,* who persuaded me to undertake this project; to John A. Fitzgerald, retired vice president for corporate communications at Merrill Lynch, Professor Edwin J. Perkins of the University of Southern California, and my son, Neil Hecht, a CPA and corporate controller, who each read my entire first draft and offered invaluable suggestions; to my computer professional sons Peter and Andrew Hecht and Merrill Lynch vice president Kevin Zuccala, whose combined efforts repeatedly saved my manuscript and worksheets from electronic disaster; and to my able, patient, and encouraging series of editors at Little, Brown — Ellen Denison, Debra Roth, Becky MacDougall, Jordan Pavlin, and copy editor Michael Mattil.

Henry R. Hecht

A Note on How to Read This Book

Many people are afraid to buy stocks because they think investing is a complicated business.

If it were really complicated, more than 51 million Americans wouldn't own stocks, as they did as of 1990.

Actually, investing only *sounds* complicated, and that is because it uses a lot of unfamiliar words. The words themselves stand for very simple things.

Winston Churchill once said, "Old words are best, and old words when short are best of all." This book tries to use old, short words instead of Wall Street jargon. It seeks to explain the technical words of the securities business by explaining the things they stand for. In other words, each term is explained in *context* as the story of investing unfolds. You won't find a glossary or any long list of definitions anywhere in this book.

In telling the investment story, the book begins with the common words in the business — *stock, share, capital* — and just to be sure that the reader realizes he has encountered a technical term, possibly new to him, the word is italicized the first time it is used. And to be further sure there is no misunderstanding or confusion, no technical term is used until the reader comes logically upon it in the development of the whole thesis.

If the reader has by any chance forgotten the meaning of a particular word, all he has to do is refer to the index and look back in the book to that page on which the word is first used.

Here, then, is the story of investing told in terms that the author believes everyone can understand — himself included.

How to
BUY STOCKS

CHAPTER 1

What Investment Means to You

THIS is a book about how to make your money earn more money for you by investing it.

It is not a book about how to make a fortune in the stock market. If there were any certain way to do that, all the brokers in the world, the "experts" who are supposed to know more than most people about the market, would be multimillionaires. Needless to say, most are not.

This is a book about investing. Primarily, it's about investing in stocks and bonds — directly or through mutual funds and also through some of the fancy new ways of combining or "packaging" these basic investment building blocks. Such investment is a way of putting your extra money to work so that in the long run it will earn a good return for you — either in the form of a regular income from dividends and interest, or in the form of a profit resulting from growth in value, or a combination of both.

Most people, if they have anything left at all after paying their bills, will think first of putting that extra money into a savings account and perhaps into life insurance. Nobody can quarrel with such a prudent course. These forms of saving are essential if people are going to protect themselves properly against the always unpredictable emergencies of life.

But today millions of people have come to regard *securities* — stocks and bonds in all their varied and continually evolving forms — as a sound and attractive means of investment.

In their broadest sense, securities are certificates that represent your participation in an investment activity — a *negotiable* participation, which means you are able to buy or sell your interest in that investment. The variety of securitized investment choices has grown explosively since this book was first written — to include money funds and all kinds of specialized mutual funds, Ginnie Maes, options, financial futures, limited partnerships, to name just a very few.

And it's a safe bet you'll be offered still more choices tomorrow. Throughout the financial services industry, everyone is busily developing new investment products tailored to meet the endless variety of investor needs — needs that themselves are constantly changing and growing. Many are designed to open up to individuals of moderate means participation in investments long regarded as the preserve of institutions or others who buy or sell at a million-dollar clip.

In increasing numbers, people have been introduced to securities investing through retirement programs — often Individual Retirement Accounts (technically, and on your tax return, the "A" in IRA stands for "Arrangement") or 401(k) and 403(b) plans sponsored by their employers. This trend seems bound to accelerate as people become more and more aware that Social Security and company pensions alone won't suffice to sustain the lifestyle they want.

Of course, there's a risk in buying stocks and bonds — and for most people it's a far bigger risk than it needs to be, because they've never taken the time to study securities or find out how to invest in them wisely.

But it should never be forgotten that there's some risk in any form of investment. There's a risk in just having money. Indeed, having money is a double-barreled risk. The one risk — that your dollars might actually, physically be lost (theft, fire) or diminished (unprofitable investment) — is always evident. The other — never so apparent — is the risk that the money you save today may not buy as much at some future time if prices of food and clothing and almost everything else continue to go up, as indeed they have over most any long period of years. The person who simply hoards extra dollars — puts them in a vault or buries them in the ground — may avoid that first *evident* risk, of physical loss, but can never sidestep the *unseen* risk, the risk of *inflation*. For instance, an inflation rate of 5% a year means that one of today's dollars will buy only 50¢ worth of goods and services 14 years from now.

So every decision you make about what to do with your extra money should take into consideration those two kinds of risk: the evident and the unseen.

Naturally, you must also consider the return you hope to realize on your money. In most forms of investment, the greater the return you try to get, the greater the risk, the *evident* risk, you must be prepared to take.

If you put your money in a savings account, it's almost impossible to lose any of it because Uncle Sam insures your savings for up to $100,000 in one bank. But interest on most passbook and other "plain vanilla" accounts has averaged 5% or less a year over the past 10 years, and in early 1994 you'd be lucky to get 3%. (Keep in mind that *all* interest rates have fluctuated widely during the past few decades, hitting long-term highs in the early 1980s and lows in the 1990s.) Your money, or capital, will grow only through the reinvestment of the interest you get. Especially as you have to pay income tax on the interest, the basic savings account provides little protection against the *unseen* risk of inflation.

If you maintain the minimum balance set by your bank, you may be able to get better value from interest-bearing checking accounts (which had been banned since the Depression but were gradually brought back over the past two decades). These accounts often pay as much or even a bit more than a savings account, and may meet your check-writing needs as well.

The highest-yielding savings accounts are the so-called *Money Market Deposit Accounts* (or Money Market Accounts), which let you write three checks a month, along with unlimited direct withdrawals. Their yields fluctuate more frequently, reflecting general trends in money rates, and at times have run several percentage points above the plain savings-account rate. Many newspapers regularly publish tables of typical rates.

You may be able to get a still higher return by putting your money in various bank time deposits, especially in the form of *Certificates of Deposit* (CDs), though after you've paid taxes on the interest, even these more generous yields often keep the return on your invested capital not that much above inflation. Rates earned on CDs depend on the amount of money you deposit and the length of time you agree to leave it with the bank — and, of course, the current level of interest rates in general. Also, there's often a considerable difference among the rates offered by various banks, so it pays to shop. As compiled by the *Bank Rate Monitor* of North Palm Beach, Florida, the national annual average rate of 6-month CDs fluctuated from 6.58% for 1987 to 8.57% for 1989. After falling to 2.80% in December 1993, it had moved up to 2.99% by April 1994. The average yield for 5-year CDs rose from 1987's 7.86% to 8.57% for 1989, hit a 4.66% low in November 1993 and was at 4.96% by April 1994.

Whatever the level of rates, normally the longer the term, the higher the yield. However, note that for 1989, both the 6-month and 5-year CDs averaged an identical 8.57%. In fact, for part of that year, the short-terms actually yielded more than the longer maturities. That's called an *inverse yield curve* and happens when investors, fearing the general level of interest rates will be declining, are willing to accept a little lower rate as long as they can "lock in" that rate for several years ahead.

In a CD your money is tied up for the length of time specified in the deposit contract. You can't get at it, either for emergencies or to take advantage of other developing investment opportunities, without incurring the "loss of interest" penalties that most of these time deposits stipulate for premature withdrawal.

You can also buy insured bank CDs through many securities brokers, who can normally give you the pick of favorable rates. What's more, these brokers usually stand ready to buy back the CDs at the prevailing market level — but remember that, if interest rates have risen since you bought the CD, the "prevailing market" price will have gone down. And while the issuing bank paid a fee to the broker for selling its CD (so there was no extra cost to you), when you sell rather than wait for your certificate to mature, you must expect to be charged the equivalent of a broker's commission.

Moving away from bank savings, you can invest your spare cash in *money market funds*, frequently just called "money funds." (They're explained in more detail in chapter 19.) Their current yield is usually better than the rate then offered on short-term time deposits. Of course, by definition, time deposits promise you a set rate for the duration of your CD, while money fund rates keep changing — up or down. Money funds, which have become enormously popular since the late 1970s, are nothing more than a pooling of enormous amounts of money from thousands of individual investors for investing in a wide range of short-term money market instruments — such as U.S. Treasury bills and corporate IOUs — with various maturity dates. Thus, there is always a steady stream of cash flowing into, and back through, these funds to guarantee that individual investors can get any or all of their money out anytime they want to. Money market funds are a good way to keep cash reserves or to "park" cash while you are waiting to make a longer-term investment. They offer you ready access, great flexibility, and continuous earnings on your money.

(Incidentally, during times of low general interest rates, such as prevail in the early 1990s, the rate *differential* between plain savings accounts and other short-term savings instruments, such as Money Market Deposit Accounts and money funds, tends to shrink; normally, the difference, or spread, widens again when the overall interest level rises.)

Despite some well-publicized problems of a few companies, life insurance is also generally safe — as *insurance*, that is, as protection for your family. But the familiar "ordinary life" policy, on which you pay regular premiums while the policy slowly builds up cash value, fails to protect you against the *unseen* risk of inflation. The money you can get by cashing in such a policy when you retire is not likely to buy as much as you could have bought with all the money you paid out in premiums over the years.

Here, too, there have been important changes, and today a number of investment-oriented insurance policies are available that may suit your purpose (see chapter 38). On the other hand, there are those who recommend buying the cheapest available term insurance (which builds up no investment value whatever) and using what you save in premiums to make direct investments on your own.

What else might you do with your money? Well, you might invest in real estate. As a general rule, real estate prices are likely to rise if the prices of other things do. So there, you say, you can find protection against that *unseen* risk. Yes — provided you don't get trapped with high debt in a period (however temporary) of huge oversupply of properties — a condition that can lay low even some of the most astute professionals. Further, keep in mind that even in good times, it's far from a sure thing. You can succeed, provided you buy the right piece of property at the right time and at the right price, and provided you're just as lucky when you sell it. Provided, too, that all the taxes you pay while you own the property don't eat up your potential profit. And provided you cope with all the unpredictable actions of local zoning and assessment boards.

Buying your own home has generally proved an excellent investment. Even with occasional periods of weakness, it's likely to remain so. But watch out when you buy other property. Here the *evident* risks are so great that for the average person with only a little extra money and even less spare time, taking a "plunge" in real estate tends to be just that — not an investment but a speculation. However (as noted in chapter 19), a great variety of instruments, from Real Estate Investment Trusts to limited partnerships, have been developed to offer a securitized participation managed by professionals. That still leaves lots of risk — so, if you look into these ventures, make sure you weigh carefully the particular risks, costs, and quality of management.

Then, too, you can invest in some of the "hard asset" areas that became popular as inflation hedges. You can buy gold or silver. But they and all other investment metals are expensive to store and earn no dividends at all to help pay for their keep. You could buy gems or coins or stamps. But they require a great deal of expertise and are characterized by exorbitant retail markups, which discount a significant percentage of their potential appreciation right off the bat. You could buy art or antiques. But they're not the most portable of assets for apocalypse-minded investors. And they're very difficult to liquidate in times of down markets.

And then, you can invest in stocks and bonds. That's what banks, insurance companies, pension funds, and other big institutional investors do with at least part of the money entrusted to them, to help earn the funds they need to meet their obligations to their customers and beneficiaries. During the post–World War II era, many of these institutions have moved heavily into stocks.

Why?

Because, over the years, the record shows that the average stock has paid a better return and provided a better balance of protection against both evident and unseen financial risk than any other form of investment.

The stockholders of America are the people who own much of America's business — virtually all its more important business. As that business has grown, stockowners have prospered. As it continues to grow, they will continue to prosper.

Not all of them have prospered all the time. Of course not. But most of them have prospered most of the time. Some have made millions, and some have gone broke, just as some companies have succeeded and some have failed. But over the years, the average investor has generally earned a significant return on his or her money. Most times, investors have been able to sell their stocks at a profit, especially if held a long time. Thus they have protected their money against the unseen risk of inflation.

Data compiled by Ibbotson Associates of Chicago show that over the 68-year span from 1926 through 1993, total returns on common stocks, as measured by the Standard & Poor's index, exceeded the rise in the consumer price index by a ratio of better than three to one. What's more, during the 59 possible ten-year holding periods over those 68 years, common shares outpaced consumer prices in all but eight.

Every investor must of course keep in mind there's no simple cut-and-dried formula for success — in investing or any other aspect of life. A prudent course is to work out a plan for *asset allocation* appropriate for you at each particular time. It means placing varying proportions of your assets into stocks, bonds, cash reserves (hopefully earning their keep in money funds or savings instruments), insurance products, and perhaps, if that's your inclination, limited amounts into such specialized and riskier areas as real estate and "hard assets."

It's very important to keep a watchful eye on your investments and on your investment plan. You'll want to vary the proportions allocated to different assets to reflect changes both in market and economic conditions and in your own situation. The investment climate has changed significantly over the years — for instance, bonds are relatively more attractive than they were 30 years ago — and it will inevitably continue to change. Furthermore, investors have had to cope with a long string of drastic revisions in the tax laws. And, again, there are many more investment vehicles now available to every type of investor than when this book was first written. But none of this alters the basic principle that a sound program of regular, steady investing in our free enterprise system is likely to pay handsome returns over time.

That's why — directly, or through mutual funds or some of the specialized instruments now available — millions of people are investing, millions who had never given securities much thought. And they find that it pays to know something about the fundamentals of the business. So . . .

CHAPTER 2

What You Should Know about Common Stocks

THERE'S nothing commonplace about *common stock*. It's the number-one security in our system, basic to all corporate business and to our whole free enterprise system. If you own a *share* of stock in a company, you own part of that company. You and the other shareholders own the company in common.

How does common stock come into being?

Assume for the moment that you've invented a fine new collapsible metal fishing rod. You've got your patents, and you're convinced there is a splendid market for your pocket fishing pole.

You're all ready to begin production, except for that one essential: *capital*. You haven't got the money to rent a small factory, buy the necessary machinery, and hire labor and salespeople. You think you could get your business under way for $200,000.

You don't want to start out in debt, so you decide to form a company and sell shares in the venture. You file the necessary incorporation papers as required by your state law, and the Pocket Pole Company, Incorporated, comes into being.

In setting up that company, you might find 20 people, each of whom was willing to put up an even $10,000 of *venture capital*. In that case, you'd have to issue and sell only 20 shares of stock at $10,000 apiece. Then every person who bought such a share would own ¹⁄₂₀ of the company.

But one person might be willing to put $20,000 or even $50,000 into your Pocket Pole Company, while another person could only afford to invest $1,000. So instead of issuing twenty shares of stock at $10,000 each, you decide it's better to put a lower price on every share of stock and sell more shares. Such a plan would be more attractive to the people who might be interested in buying the stock, because if they ever had to sell it, they would probably find it easier to dispose of lower-priced shares. After all, more people can spare $100 than can afford to invest in a $10,000 unit.

So you finally decide to issue 20,000 shares at $10 apiece. Taken collectively, those shares would represent the common stock issue of the Pocket Pole Company.

By selling the 20,000 shares at $10 apiece, you raise your $200,000 capital. The Pocket Pole Company is in business. Actually, of course, you might well think of Pocket Pole as *your* business. So when setting up the company, you might bargain with the other stockholders to let you acquire a stock interest in the company at little or no cost to yourself. But for purposes of simplicity, let's assume that you simply buy your stock like any other stockholder.

Every person who owns a share of Pocket Pole stock is a stock-holder in the company. They are shareowners, part owners. How big a part of the company they own depends on how many shares they buy in relation to the 20,000 that were sold and are now *outstanding*. If they buy one share, they own $1/20,000$ of the company. If they buy 200 shares, they own $1/100$, or 1%, of the company. As evidence of their ownership, a *stock certificate* is issued to each stockholder showing the number of shares owned.

Suppose, when the stock is all sold, the company has 50 stock-holders on its books. Now it would be difficult to operate Pocket Pole if all 50 of them had to be consulted about every major decision — whether to buy this lathe or that one, whether to price the product at $40 or $50.

So the stockholders elect a *board of directors* to oversee the operations of the company. How is the board picked? By the stockholders, on the basis of the number of shares of stock each one owns. If there are five persons to be elected to the board, each for a set term, anyone who owns one share of stock will, as a matter of general practice, be allowed one vote for each of the five vacancies, and anyone who owns 10 shares will have 10 votes for each vacancy.

Some corporations allow *cumulative voting*. In that case, if five directors are to be elected and you own ten shares, you have 50 (5 × 10) votes and you can cast all 50 for a single director, rather than 10 each for five different people. The idea is that if you or your group owns a substantial block of the company, though not a majority, you should still be able to get some representation on the board.

Once elected, the board of directors elects its own *chairman*, and is responsible for managing the affairs of the Pocket Pole Company. In most instances, board members can't give their full time to the job of running the company, so they pick a *chief executive officer* (or CEO) to be the working head of the company. In many companies these days, the chairman serves as fulltime CEO; in others the top post is held by the president, who, like all major officers, is officially elected by the board. Such officers may or may not be members of the board. But they are responsible to the full board, and periodically — perhaps once a month or once a quarter — the officers report to the board on the progress of the company and their conduct of its affairs.

At the end of each year, Pocket Pole management, with the approval of the board of directors, puts out an *annual report*, which is distributed to all stockholders. It contains the formal financial statements, certified by Pocket Pole's independent auditors, which report how much the company earned and what its assets and liabilities are. In other sections of the report, management usually presents its review of the year and explains its concept of the company.

Directors must also call an *annual meeting*, open to all the stockholders. Top management usually presents a "State of the Company" review and entertains questions from the owners of the business, the stockholders. Any stockholder can speak out at the meeting. Individual stockholders may even make a motion that the board adopt some policy or procedure that they think is an improvement on present practice. If the motion is in order, it will be submitted to the stockholders for a vote. In most instances, such issues are decided by simple majority vote, with each stockholder being allowed one vote for each share owned.

The legal business of annual meetings also usually includes election of directors and often ratification of important corporate actions such as pension and benefit plans or changes in the corporate charter. Since most stockholders cannot (or choose not to) attend the annual meeting, they are usually asked to sign a paper that authorizes one or more of the officers or directors to act as their *proxy*, or representative, and vote on their behalf. That's why these papers are called *proxies*. A *proxy statement* sent each shareholder before the meeting outlines the business to be transacted and must give the holders an opportunity to vote their proxies for or against each of the directors and for or against various proposals which management or shareholders plan to bring up at the meeting.

Sometimes a dissident group of stockholders will propose a rival slate of directors in opposition to those picked by the management. In such a fight, each side will try to get signed proxies from the stockholders favoring its slate. This is called a *proxy fight*.

In addition to the regular meetings of the board or the annual meeting of the stockholders, special meetings of either group may be called to deal with special problems.

Why should people invest money in the Pocket Pole Company? Because they think it has a good product and one that is likely to make money. If it does, they as part owners stand to make money. This can happen in two ways: through the payment of *dividends*, and through an increase in the value of Pocket Pole stock.

Let's look at the dividend picture first. Suppose in the first year, after paying all bills and taxes, the company has *earnings*, or profits, of $20,000, or 10% on its $200,000 *capitalization*, the money that it raised by selling 20,000 shares of common stock. (As we'll see later, a company's capitalization also includes any other stock and bond issues, as well as the portion of earnings that's retained to further build up the company.) Such a 10% return would be a handsome profit for a new company, but not impossible.

It would then be up to the board of directors to decide what to do with that profit. It could pay it all out to the stockholders in dividends. Or it could vote to keep every penny of it in the company treasury and use it to buy more machinery to make more pocket poles and earn more profits the following year. Most new companies follow the latter course — figuring that the owners' money is most prudently devoted to building up the company during its early years. But let's say Pocket Pole's board wants stockholders to receive a concrete token of the company's success. It might vote to pay out $5,000 in dividends and plow the other $15,000 back into the business. Such reinvested money is called *retained earnings*.

Now if the board has $5,000 for dividends and 20,000 shares of stock outstanding, the dividend per share will be $0.25. That's what the shareholder with one share of stock gets, while the shareholder with 10 shares gets $2.50, and the shareholder with 100 shares gets $25. For all of them this would represent a 2.5% return on their investment, regardless of the number of shares they own, since they each paid $10 a share.

But there's another intangible return that they would get on their money. Presumably the $15,000 that the board decided to retain and plow back into the business will serve to increase the value of every person's share in the company — their *equity* in the company, as it's called.

If an original share of stock in Pocket Pole was fairly valued at $10, each of the 20,000 shares might now be considered to be worth $10.75, since the company now has an extra $15,000 in the business besides the original capital of $200,000. That, in any case, would now be the *book value* of each share of Pocket Pole. To calculate book value, you (1) take the total *assets* of the company — everything it owns: its plant, machinery, and inventory of products; (2) subtract its *liabilities* — the sum total of what the company owes; and then (3) take the resulting figure (called *shareholders' equity*) and divide it by the number of shares outstanding.

If the company continues to earn good money and if the directors continue, year after year, to put a major portion of those earnings back into the company, Pocket Pole's assets might well double in comparatively few years without a corresponding increase in its lia-bilities. That, in turn, would bring a very substantial increase in the book value.

A number of astute securities analysts consider book value an im-portant tool in finding stocks that are undervalued, or overvalued, by the market. But remember it's only a *tool* — and not the *only* one, either. And then you must know just what's behind the figures in a particular company. We're not talking here of occasional instances of "aggressive accounting" that counts some rather doubtful assets or minimizes some serious liabilities. Rather, it's the fundamental issue of placing a realistic value on different assets. For instance, a lumber company may own vast tracts of timber it acquired generations ago for a fraction of their current value — but it's the original cost that's on the books. Similarly, a department store may own downtown property that has multiplied in value. On the other hand, the assets of some big manufacturing companies include factories and machines that no longer can produce competitively. And then there are service com-panies where, as the head of one advertising agency once said, "most of our assets go down the elevator each afternoon at five."

One concept of book value is that it represents what the owner of a share of stock could expect to get if the company were *liquidated* — if it went out of business and sold off all its property. But when a trou-bled company is in liquidation, it can rarely get full value for the prop-erty it must dispose of. On the other hand, as we saw in recent years, when large companies are "restructured" with many divisions sold off or taken over by an eager buyer, the price realized by stockholders can often be far above the nominal book value.

So, to repeat, book value can be a helpful guide. But don't neglect the basic investment considerations: the earning power of the com-pany and its growth prospects (which, of course, will influence its fu-ture book value).

Another term you may run across is *par value*. For common stocks, it has no investment significance whatever. Par (or stated) value is the amount at which each share is entered on the account books. Some such figure is needed as one part of a corporate balance sheet, and, especially in the past, companies often set par at the price at which stock was initially offered. Thus, when Pocket Pole started, it might have set $10 as the par value of a share, so 20,000 shares times $10 would make up its initial *paid-in capital* of $200,000 — a figure that hasn't changed, even while the accumulation of retained earnings over the years steadily increased *total* equity and book value.

In fact, par value is a term so generally misunderstood and useless from an investment standpoint that many companies today either do not set any such value on their stock, in which case it is known as *no-par stock*, or they fix the par value at $1 or even less, a figure so low that it could not possibly be misinterpreted as an indicator of the stock's real value.

Well, then, how *do* you know what a share of stock is really worth — Pocket Pole stock or any other?

There's only one answer to that. Bluntly, *a share of stock is worth only what somebody else is willing to pay for it when you want to sell it.*

If the product isn't popular and sales suffer, if the cost of wages and raw materials is too high, if the management is inefficient, Pocket Pole or any other company can fail. And if it goes into bankruptcy, your stock can become worthless.

That's the dark side of the picture. That's what can happen if the risk you assumed in buying a stock proves to be a bad one.

But if Pocket Pole proves to be a successful company, with a consistent record of good earnings, then your stock is likely to be worth more than the $10 you paid for it. Perhaps a good deal more.

And that is the other way in which a stockholder expects to make money on an investment. Not just through dividends, but also through an increase in the value of the stock — or, rather, an increase in the price that somebody else will pay for it. This is known as *price appreciation*. In fact, especially in developing companies like Pocket Pole, price appreciation — which results in *capital gains* when you sell your securities for more than what you paid for them — is the prime objective of most stockholders.

The price of a stock, like the price of almost everything else in this world, is determined by supply and demand: what one person is willing to pay for a stock and what another one is willing to sell it for, what one person bids and another asks. That's why stocks always have a *bid* and an *asked* (or *offered*) price. And don't forget that the particular dollar price at which a stock is quoted won't by itself tell you whether or not it's a good investment. Some people think that a low-priced stock is a good buy because it is cheap, and they shy away from a high-priced stock because they think it is expensive. That isn't necessarily so. The stock of one company may sell at a low price simply because it has a large number of shares outstanding — because the whole pie has been cut up into lots and lots of little pieces — while the stock of another equally good company may sell at a high price because that stock hasn't been cut up into so many pieces; that is, there are relatively fewer shares outstanding.

National preferences play a role, too, in whether companies go for relatively few high-priced or many low-priced shares. Among major American companies, the heaviest concentration of stock prices tends to be in the $20-to-$60 range. In Great Britain, where stocks are quoted in pence rather than pounds, many blue-chip stocks trade in the 200-to-800-pence range and only a handful sell above 1,000 pence (£10 or about $17). Meanwhile, in Germany, leading stocks are quoted at several hundred and even thousand marks (i.e., well over $100 and up). In Japan, the great majority of leading stocks have been selling under 3,000 yen (not quite $30) but some trade at well over 10,000 yen. Nippon Telephone (NTT) set a record for a major stock at its 1987 peak when it sold at over 2 million yen (then more than $15,000). Though badly hurt in the severe Japanese market slump, its low in 1992 was still an awe-inspiring 453,000 yen (about $3,700) a share.

This, in brief, is the story of common stock — what it is, how it comes into being, what it means to own it.

American Telephone & Telegraph, General Motors, and International Business Machines have their many millions of shares of stock held by anywhere from three-quarter million to three million shareholders. But in these giant corporations, each share of stock plays precisely the same role as a share of stock in our Pocket Pole Company.

And each stockholder has the same rights, privileges, and responsibilities.

There is only one significant difference between buying a share of Pocket Pole and investing in a share of AT&T, GM, or IBM. These big companies have been in business for many years. You know something about them and the reputations they enjoy. You know how good their products or services are. You can examine their financial history, see for yourself how the prices of their stocks have moved over the years and what kind of record they have made as far as earnings and dividends are concerned. And on the basis of such information you can form a more reliable judgment about whether the stocks of these companies are overpriced or underpriced.

In contrast, people who buy stock in our Pocket Pole Company have nothing to go on other than their own estimate of how good a product the company has, how big its sales are likely to be, and how capable the management may prove itself. There are no benchmarks to guide them, no past records on which to base an appraisal of the future.

In the eyes of some purists, the Pocket Pole stockholders don't fully qualify for the term *investor*. To them, an investor is a person who is willing to take a moderate risk for the sake of earning a moderate return; such investors tend to put their money in better-known, more established companies. And when people buy stock in a brand-new company such as Pocket Pole, they usually aren't investing in it; they're speculating in it.

But hold on. By traditional definition, a *speculator* is a person willing to take a big risk in the hope of making a big profit in a relatively short period of time. This hardly fits the people who put their money into Pocket Pole, who must take a longer view. So, at the least, you have here another class of speculators — *venture capitalists* who risk (speculate with) their money to get new ventures going in the hope of realizing large returns when the venture proves itself.

And some of today's wisest market analysts feel the old conservative definitions are far too narrow and not appropriate for today's more sophisticated investor. To them, the true investor buys value and has the patience to let the market reflect it, but is certainly not limited to mere "moderate" returns.

In any case, American business needs these different risktakers. Without the speculator and venture capitalist, new business wouldn't be born, nor would many an old business be tided over a rough spot. Without the investor, a company would not have the capital to carry on, much less grow and expand.

CHAPTER 3

How and Why New Stock Is Sold

LET'S assume that the years are good to our Pocket Pole Company. It continues to grow. The original collapsible fishing pole has proved a best-seller, and the company now has a full line of models. Solid growth year after year has lifted earnings close to $100,000 and enabled the management to put the stock on a regular dividend basis of $1 a year per share, or 25¢ a quarter. In several good years the directors even declared *extra dividends*, one of 25¢ and two of 50¢ a share.

Now the company feels that the time has come to plan a major expansion. It could sell twice as many pocket poles, make twice as much profit, if only it had a bigger factory. So the board of directors decides to expand the plant. That means it will need more machinery, a larger workforce, and, above all, more money — a lot more money than it has in the company treasury. Problem: how to get $500,000.

Of course, in today's financial world, $500,000 is pretty small change — but let us stick to a small scale to make it easier to grasp just how a small company like Pocket Pole goes about its business. Then you can simply multiply the scale and get a general idea of how the billion-dollar companies operate.

Let's assume Pocket Pole's directors had been brought up in the pay-as-you-go school and didn't want to borrow for the project.

So how else to raise the money?

Maybe the present stockholders would like to put more money into the company. And maybe there are other people who would like to invest in a nice thriving little business like Pocket Pole. There's an idea.

So the board of directors proposed that the stockholders authorize the company to issue 20,000 additional shares of stock; 10,000 shares to be sold at once, and the remaining 10,000 to be held in reserve for "other corporate purposes" — maybe another stock sale down the road or perhaps an acquisition. Each of the new shares of stock will carry with it the same rights and privileges as an original share.

The stockholders readily approved this proposal, though some wondered why the company couldn't create a second class of common stock. The present stock could become *Class A stock*, retaining all rights and privileges; the new shares might be designated *Class B stock* and would receive the same dividends but would not carry any voting privileges. That, it was argued, would keep control of the company in the hands of the original stockholders.

At one time quite a number of companies, particularly family-controlled enterprises, instituted such *classified stock* setups where one class of common has all or most of the voting power. However, such arrangements have become increasingly unpopular with investors, who feel the two-class system could entrench inefficient management, limit their stock's marketability, and restrict opportunities to realize the maximum potential of their shares. Indeed, the New York Stock Exchange "as a matter of general policy" for many years refused to list nonvoting common stocks. Some modifications were adopted in 1989, generally regarded as a competitive response to more aggressive listing efforts by the American Exchange and other markets. Meantime, the Securities and Exchange Commission promulgated a "one-share, one-vote" rule that would apply to all markets, but implementation has been blocked by a 1990 Federal Appeals Court decision. The huge takeover wave of the later 1980s, which made even the largest corporations vulnerable to being bought out, then led many managements to study possible defenses against what they considered raids threatening the true interests of their "stakeholders" — a term often meant to include employees, customers, and communities as well as stockholders. A few companies successfully asked their stockholders to approve a two-class arrangement to strengthen their hand against possible hostile takeovers.

All in all, though, Pocket Pole management felt it was in the company's and stockholders' interest to broaden the market for the stock. They also noted that Pocket Pole management, employees, and associates would continue to hold a large portion of the stock.

The board had considered the advisability of selling the stock through a *rights offering*, a once-popular procedure under which the new shares would be offered first to existing stockholders, and at a slight discount from the prevailing market price. Since Pocket Pole had 20,000 shares outstanding and wanted to sell an additional 10,000, you would get the right to buy one new share for every two shares you owned. Technically, you would get one *right* for every share you owned, and it would take *two* rights to buy one new share. If the existing shares were currently trading in the market at about $50, the *exercise price* at which you could buy the new stock might be set at $47.50. You would normally have two weeks to exercise your rights — or to sell them to someone who wants to buy Pocket Pole stock and will pay you for the right to do so at the discount price.

Many companies used to turn to rights offerings whenever they wanted to sell additional stock. Here they had a group already interested in the company, a convenient audience. In many cases, the company charter or state law required *preemptive rights* — the legal term for giving current holders first crack at the new shares. But in recent years rights offerings have become rare. Companies found them costly to administer; besides, the increasingly dominant institutional investors display little interest in the rights system. Thus, most companies now go for a straight public stock offering — and that's what Pocket Pole decided to do.

Sometimes companies issue another type of certificate that entitles whoever holds it to buy a share of stock. Called *warrants*, these certificates (which can be freely traded) can be exercised not just during a quick two-week period but for a number of years and sometimes with no expiration date whatever. However, while rights offer you a chance to buy stock at a discount, when a warrant is issued, its *exercise price* is invariably set significantly higher than the price at which the underlying stock is then trading. In other words, the stock must move up in price before it's worth exercising the warrant privilege. Warrants are issued mostly in connection with mergers, corporate restructurings, or bankruptcy reorganizations as a way to let the warrant recipient participate in a future resurgence of the company.

Meet the Investment Banker

When a company such as Pocket Pole offers stock, how is the sale handled? Perhaps we should first note that, to keep our story simple, we've implied that Pocket Pole sold its initial stock to a small group of family, neighbors, and friends. That, of course, is how many budding entrepreneurs first incorporate their small businesses — and they may then turn to local banks for added capital, often by borrowing on their homes, their cars, their personal credit. But when they want or need a broader capital base and a wider circle of stockholders with the ready ability to buy or sell the shares, they normally seek out the services of an *investment banker*.

Investment bankers specialize in raising the kind of money that business needs for long-term use, usually in amounts many times what Pocket Pole is looking for here.

Before committing itself to *underwrite* an issue of common stock, or any other security, an investment banking firm must conduct a thorough, painstaking investigation of all aspects of the company, utilizing the help of outside accountants, engineers, and/or other needed specialists. Underwriting means the investment banker will buy all the new stock from the company, then resell it at a set price per share to individual buyers. Once the offering is over and the stock is in public hands, regular trading begins in the over-the-counter market or on one of the exchanges, and the stock's price will be determined by the market forces under the law of supply and demand — how much buyers will pay and how much the sellers want for the stock they own.

Of course, supply and demand is also very much on the mind of the investment bankers when they set the offering price of the security. It's particularly crucial when the company does not already have actively traded stock to serve as a guide — in short, when it's an *initial public offering* or IPO. Such pricing is indeed a fine art. The investment bankers must carefully weigh all the investment aspects of the company, the going market price for similar companies, as well as the immediate status of the general market. They seek to price the issue so it will readily find buyers while getting as good a price as reasonably possible for the company.

Especially in times of general market strength, there is often a wild rush to buy the new stocks of companies in the glamour industries of the moment — which, in the past, have included electronics, waste disposal, biogenetics, and many, many others. Such "hot issues" often rise to a quick premium over the offering price as buyers seek far more shares than are offered. It's quite risky to "chase" the stock up this high-premium ladder, because in all too many cases the stock soon drops back as enthusiasm wanes. Over the longer term, while some of the new companies (like our Pocket Pole) do quite nicely, others encounter great difficulties and quite a few go under.

An IPO isn't necessarily a young company just making its public debut. In one of the biggest stock offerings ever, Ford Motor Company "went public" in 1956 when the Ford Foundation sold some of its holdings, and there have been many IPOs of well-known family-held companies since. Also, today's active corporate restructurings have led to many corporate owners *spinning off* or selling major enterprises that are part of their holdings. In fact, there are quite a few examples of companies that had been prominent in the stock market, were bought up in a merger or acquisition, and, after some further changes, were brought public again. All are considered IPOs, because at the time of the new offering, no stock is in public hands.

In bringing out an issue, the investment banking firm generally chooses to share the risk and effort with other investment bankers, who join in forming an *underwriting group* or *syndicate* under its management. That's especially true if the stock is for a company new to or little known in the market, the *lead manager* knows participation by more underwriters will encourage wider distribution and a greater following in the *aftermarket*, the everyday buying and selling of shares once they are in public hands.

For the risk that the investment bankers assume in underwriting an issue of common stock, the risk that they may not be able to resell the entire issue they have bought, they expect to make a profit greater than on a routine brokerage transaction. The costs depend primarily on the nature of the marketing effort involved. Those costs might run anywhere from 3% to 10% of the final selling price, and they are wholly paid by the seller (the company issuing the stock or the family or major existing owners that are offering some of their holdings). The buyers get such stock at the stated offering price, free of all commission cost or other charges.

On some issues, such as cheap mining or oil stocks offered at a dollar or two a share, the investment banker's charges might even run as high as 20 percent. That's because these *penny stocks* can usually be sold only through a costly merchandising effort.

On any new issue, a third to a half of the total commission might go to those who underwrite it, with the manager of the group getting an extra fee for its services, and the balance going to the other brokerage firms that merely help distribute the issue.

When a company wants to raise capital by selling a new securities issue, it usually shops around for an investment banker that provides the best advice as well as the best terms and the lowest total cost for handling the new issue. Once an investment banker is selected, the relationship is naturally apt to develop into a close one. If the company needs to raise additional capital at some future time, it will often seek out the same investment banker — especially in the case of smaller and mid-sized companies without their own large, high-priced financial staff.

After Pocket Pole raised the needed capital, it quickly moved ahead with its expansion. Still, there was delay in construction and sizable expenses to gear up for the expanded production and marketing efforts. And just then a recession caused many people to delay buying recreational equipment. So, for the first time, Pocket Pole faced a severe decline in profits. It earned just $45,000 for the year, or $1.50 for each of the 30,000 shares now outstanding compared with the previous year's $5 on the 20,000 shares then outstanding. Still enough to cover the $1 dividend, but with cash needs for the business high, was it prudent to pay out that much?

No one suggested that directors omit or *pass the dividend* ("pass" here is used in the sense of bidding in a bridge game, not as in passing a legislative resolution). But a majority of directors felt cutting back temporarily to 50¢ a share would free more cash to support operations and be in the stockholders' best long-term interest.

Still, many stockholders would be unhappy for now. To ease their disappointment, the board decided to utilize some of the 10,000 new shares that had been authorized but not issued. The directors took 3,000 of those shares and distributed them without any charge among the owners of the 30,000 outstanding shares on the basis of $\frac{1}{10}$ of a share of new stock for every single share that a stockholder owned.

Actually, this *stock dividend* did nothing to improve the lot of any individual stockholder. The holders were not one penny richer, nor did they actually own any greater proportion of the company. Someone who had one share before the stock dividend owned $\frac{1}{30,000}$ of the company. Now with 1.1 shares out of the 33,000 outstanding, that stockholder still owns exactly $\frac{1}{30,000}$.

Yet, to many stockholders, those extra shares are welcome as a token of future prospects, as well as a means of current flexibility. Those dependent on regular cash proceeds from their investment could sell the additional shares to get current cash while retaining the same number of shares they had before. Those that held on to the extra stock found a small measure of immediate comfort in that, instead of being fully cut in half to 50¢, their dividend income now was 55¢, since they owned 1.1 shares for each old share previously held. And in addition to the psychological pleasure most people seem to get from holding a greater number of shares, they counted on bigger returns when the company got rolling again.

That, happily, is exactly what happened. Pocket Pole earnings quickly recovered to $115,000, or $3.50 per share — a new record in total profits, though per-share earnings were not yet back to the high of two years earlier when fewer shares were outstanding. Plenty good enough for directors to agree they could prudently restore the old $1 dividend. To the stockholder who held 1.1 shares, that meant an annual dividend income of $1.10.

The momentum continued, and within a few years earnings had doubled to $7 per share and the stock was frequently quoted in the $80-to-$90 range. Surprisingly, some stockholders complained that it was too high priced. Why? They felt it inhibited potential buyers and so the stock couldn't be sold as easily.

So the company decided to *split* the stock on a three-for-one basis. That meant stockholders would now own three new shares for every old one they owned — the total common stock capitalization was increased from 33,000 shares to 99,000. Again, as in the case of the stock dividend, the split created no new intrinsic value for any stockholder, and each holder continued to own exactly the same proportion of the company as before. If a share of the old stock was quoted at $90, theoretically, each of the new shares should have been worth about $30. But since the stock was now in a more popular price range and the split had drawn more market attention to the company, the stock was now fetching a bit more than that.

Even in well-known companies where there is already a huge supply of shares, many individual stockholders often greet splits with enthusiasm. Psychologically, they like to hold more shares, they prefer the lower price range, and they figure the directors' action means that things are going well. While studies on how splits affect stock prices are inconclusive, more often it's the old stock that goes up when a split is thought likely; by the time the actual split takes place, the impact may already have been felt.

To make historical comparisons possible, whenever there's a stock split, the past per-share figures for that company are *adjusted*. Thus, the records would now show that, just before the split, Pocket Pole's shares sold around $30 on an adjusted basis (one-third the actual $90), and the $7 earnings on the old shares would be shown as $2.33, because that's what was earned on each of today's shares.

In fact, such adjustments are also made for stock dividends. So since each original share of Pocket Pole has by now turned into 3.3 shares (one multiplied by 1.1 for the 10 percent stock dividend, and then by 3 for the 3-for-1 split), you'd divide the $10 initial offering price by 3.3 and find that if you were an original shareholder you paid just $3.03 for each of today's shares. In short, your fishing pole investment reeled in quite a catch.

CHAPTER 4

What You Should Know about Preferred Stocks

SO far, with its new plant and its new machinery, the Pocket Pole Company had achieved its rapid growth through internal expansion — building up its own facilities and organization. Now another opportunity presented itself. The Rapid Reel Company, a well-known competitor owned and operated by a single family, could be acquired for $750,000. It was, the Pocket Pole directors agreed, a good buy at that price. But where could they get the $750,000?

Negotiations with the president of Rapid Reel revealed that he was anxious to retire from business. He planned to invest whatever he got from the sale of the company so that it would yield him and his family a safe, reasonable income. Further, it was evident that he had a high regard for the management of Pocket Pole and was favorably impressed with the company's prospects. Here was the basis for a deal.

So the directors of Pocket Pole proposed that they take over Rapid Reel as a going concern and merge it into their company. How would they pay for it? By issuing *preferred* stock in the Pocket Pole Company and giving it to the owners of Rapid Reel in exchange for their company.

This preferred stock is to carry a specific dividend that will have to be paid every year on every share before any dividends can be paid to common-stock holders. To make the deal as attractive as possible for the owners of Rapid Reel, the company was willing to pay a good dividend — 10%, or $10 on each of the 7,500 shares of $100 par value preferred stock to be issued. This stock would normally be designated a 10 percent preferred; were the issue instead no-par, it would be called $10 preferred, so you'd know what the promised dividend is.

Directors can pass, or omit, a preferred stock dividend when they feel their company's available cash resources (or lack thereof) make it advisable. But they will be even more reluctant to do so than in the case of common stock. It would not just be a blow to the company's reputation, but would incur a future obligation. Most preferred stocks are *cumulative preferred*. That means if Pocket Pole fails to pay the full $10 dividend in any year, the right to the unpaid amount will *accrue* to the preferred-stock holders, to be paid (in addition to the current dividend) as soon as the company is able. If the company could not make the payments on the preferred for a period of years, the payments would keep accruing during all that time and the entire *arrears* would have to be paid in full before the holders of common stock could get as much as a dime in dividend payments.

Occasionally, *accrued dividends* pile up in bad years to a point where it seems impossible for a company to pay them off. In such a situation the company may attempt to negotiate a settlement with the preferred holders on the basis of a partial payment, or offer an exchange for a new security (often common). However, some companies have paid off arrears totaling several hundred dollars a share in accumulated back dividends.

Of course, if a company fails, the stock might be wiped out. But even in that dire eventuality, preferred-stock holders normally have at least some preferential protection. They are guaranteed that, should it ever be necessary to liquidate the company, they would have a prior claim on the company's assets — once all debts are taken care of.

The Pocket Pole and Rapid Reel negotiators agreed to another widely used protective provision. Should the company ever fail to pay the preferred dividend for eight consecutive quarters, the preferred holders would have the right to elect two directors to the board.

On the other hand, it was agreed that (again as with most preferreds) this would not be an issue of *participating preferred*. Consequently, the holders of the preferred would not participate, beyond the stipulated dividend payment, in any of the extra profits the company might earn in good years. Even if earnings were so good that dividends on the common stock doubled or trebled, the holders of the preferred would still get just their $10 a share and no more. Furthermore, they would have no participation in company affairs and no voting rights except on matters that might adversely affect the rights guaranteed them as preferred-stock holders (e.g., establishment of a new, more senior class of preferred).

Although the terms of this issue might be regarded as fairly typical, there is no such thing as a standard preferred stock. About the only common denominator of all such issues is the guarantee that the owner will be accorded a preferential treatment, ahead of the common-stock holder, in the payment of dividends and in the distribution of any assets that might remain if the company were liquidated. That's why it is called preferred stock. And such preferential treatment is why its price usually doesn't fluctuate, either up or down, as much as the price of a company's common stock — though the preferred stock's price will reflect movements in the general level of interest rates.

Preferreds can be used, as in the case of Pocket Pole, to acquire another company. But most are issued simply to raise more capital for expansion or improvements at a time when the company does not want to enlarge its common-stock capitalization, or might have difficulty finding enough willing buyers for the common.

Another kind of preferred stock is *convertible preferred*. That's what Pocket Pole used the next year to acquire Fishing Supplies Corporation. Since the preferred stock issued the owners of Rapid Reel had been granted prior claim to earnings and assets, this issue would have to be a *second preferred*, ranking behind that *first preferred* issue. So, to make it more attractive to the Fishing Supplies owners, Pocket Pole, in addition to promising to pay $8 in dividends a year, threw in a conversion privilege. The recently split Pocket Pole common stock was quoted at around $32 a share. The conversion clause might provide that every share of the new Pocket Pole 8%, $100 par convertible second preferred could be exchanged for 2.5 shares of

Pocket Pole common stock at any time during the next five years (most conversion privileges are permanent, but some, as in this Pocket Pole preferred, have a limited life). Sometimes the conversion privilege is expressed the other way around; that is, the preferred is said to be "convertible at $40" (2.5 common shares × $40 conversion price = the $100 preferred par value). Obviously, there would be no advantage to the preferred-stock holders making such a swap unless the common stock advanced in price to at least $40.

What makes a convertible popular with many investors is that they can count on regular annual income — though usually at a slightly lower rate than would be offered by a similar-quality straight preferred, and with a little less protection — while also being able to profit if the price of the common stock shoots up.

The price of a convertible is apt to fluctuate more than the price of other preferreds because the convertible's value is tied to the price of the common stock of the company. This has its good and bad points. If the company does well and the price of its common stock rises, the holder of a convertible preferred will find a corresponding increase in value for that stock, since it can be exchanged for the common. Suppose, for instance, Pocket Pole common soars to $50. Since each share of your convertible preferred can be turned into 2.5 shares common, the conversion value of your preferred is now $125. On the other hand, if the price of the common declines, the convertible preferred is apt to suffer too. This is because one of the features that was counted on to make it attractive has suddenly lost something of its value. However, your convertible stock's fall will be cushioned to some extent by your continued right to the $8 dividend.

Most preferreds carry a provision that permits the company to *call*, or redeem, the issue and pay it off, generally at par (or stated) value, plus a small premium. A company will usually exercise this right if it thinks it can replace the outstanding issue with a less expensive form of financing. Often, especially at times of high interest rates, there is a *call protection* of several years, so that investors buying the new issue are assured they'll receive the promised rate of return for at least that much time. In the case of convertible securities, companies may call the preferred stock in order to force conversion into common stock, streamlining their capitalization. This tactic, of course, only works when the common stock has risen above the conversion price ($40 in the Pocket Pole example). If a call occurs, any neglectful preferred-stock holder who fails to convert (or sell to someone who will) by the deadline loses the valuable conversion premium and gets only the stipulated redemption price of the preferred.

Pocket Pole, aided by its bunch of acquisitions, was on its way to becoming a big business. And in the next 10 years, with booming sales, it strode forward along that path with seven-league boots.

It bought the little Nylon Line Company for cash. Then it bought the Sure-Fire Rifle Company by authorizing additional common stock and arranging to trade the Sure-Fire stockowners one share of Pocket Pole for every three shares of Sure-Fire that they owned.

Finally, it acquired control of Camping Supplies, Incorporated, again on a *stock-swapping* basis. The Camping Supplies owners negotiated an *earn-out* provision under which the ultimate amount of Pocket Pole stock they receive will be adjusted, based on the next three years' earnings performance of the Camping Supplies unit within the Pocket Pole operation.

Now, with a full, well-rounded line of fishing, hunting, and camping supplies, backed by an aggressive advertising and merchandising campaign, the company decided to experiment with its own retail outlets. In a few years, these grew into a small chain of sporting-goods stores, known as the Rod & Reel Centers.

With sales and earnings multiplying, the directors decided it was time for another stock split, this time 2-for-1. They also proposed a change in the corporate name to Rod & Reel, Incorporated — deemed more appropriate since most fishermen consider the fishing "pole" passé. Consequently, the company issued new certificates: two shares of Rod & Reel common stock for every single share of the old Pocket Pole stock.

The split of the common also affected the $8 convertible preferred. The preferred was not split, but, like virtually all convertibles, it carried a provision protecting its holders against *dilution*. Thus, when the common stock was split 2-for-1, each preferred share became convertible into 5 new Rod & Reel common shares, the equivalent of the 2.5 shares agreed to at the time the convertible preferred was issued.

This is the story of Rod & Reel, Incorporated, formerly Pocket Pole Company, Incorporated. It is a success story, as it was meant to be, enabling us to show the various kinds of stock operation that may mark a company's growth. But for that matter, it is no more a success story than the real-life stories of International Business Machines, McDonald's Corporation or Walt Disney Company, or any of hundreds of other companies in which the original investors (or venture capitalists) have seen the value of their stockholdings multiplied 10, 20, even 100 times over.

CHAPTER *5*

What You Should Know
about Corporate Bonds

WHEN this book was first written, only people with substantial sums or special conservative needs were considered likely bond investors. These days, however, nearly all investors should at least consider placing part of their holdings in bonds — quite possibly through the use of bond funds, which give you greater diversification and flexibility than buying a specific corporate bond.

In any case, every intelligent investor should know something about bonds, because they are an important part of the investment picture.

Bonds represent borrowed money, which the company issuing them is obligated to repay. That's why they are called *obligations*. While there are many types of obligations — issued not only by corporations but also by governments — the term *bond market* is generally used for *debt instruments* that mature more than a year from now, while the *money market* concerns itself with debt due to be repaid in a year or less.

The easiest way to understand bonds is to turn again to a micro-example; when, say, Rod & Reel was looking for $10 million of new capital — a greater sum than it had ever had to raise before.

It needed that money because, after years of rapid if sometimes haphazard growth, it saw the need to pull operations together in an efficient new plant with fully modernized equipment and to finance expansion of its retail chain. In the long run, the $10 million would unquestionably prove to be money well spent.

But how do you, as company treasurer, come up with the money?

Your regular commercial bank is one option. While you've turned to it mostly for such month-to-month credit needs as financing your raw materials or the receivables from your customers, many banks have moved beyond these traditional roles to supply intermediate and even long-term financing. However, as you explore possibilities, you will want to call in your investment banker. (You established an investment banking relationship when you brought out your stock issues and negotiated some of your acquisitions.)

The investment banking firm knows your company and its needs, as well as the current market for different securities. So it can propose and discuss a number of financing alternatives.

Often a company seeking money may prefer to get it without obligating itself to pay any set return on the money. In short, it wants *equity capital* — capital representing ownership in the company, especially common stock. But selling more common stock would *dilute* the equity of Rod & Reel's present stockholders, because the expected growth in earnings and net worth would have to be divided among a greater number of shares. The investment banker may well suggest an issue of intermediate or long-term debt as the best alternative for the company at this time.

The person who buys stock in a company actually buys a part of that company. The person who buys a company's bonds simply lends money to the company. Each bond is an agreement on the part of the company to repay at a specified time the face value of the bond — usually $1,000 — and in most cases to pay a set annual rate of interest from the day the bond is issued to the day it is redeemed.

While stockholders may hope for steadily increasing dividends on their stock as their company prospers, bondholders expect only to earn a fixed return on their investment in the form of interest payments.

Even more important, if a company is successful, the stockholder can hope to make a substantial profit because the price of the stock should go up. The bondholder cannot share that hope. Market price appreciation for a company's bonds is usually limited, regardless of how successful the company may be. However, price changes sparked by interest rate fluctuations can be quite dramatic in an era of interest volatility.

On the other hand, if the bondholders can't expect to gain as much on invested capital, neither do they run the risk of losing as much. The investment is much better protected, thanks to the fact that bonds do represent debt. If the company is dissolved, the debt it owes its bond-holders, like any other debt it owes, such as for labor and materials, must be paid before the stockholders, either common or preferred, can get a nickel out of what's left of the company. The claims of bond-holders come first, then those of the preferred-stock holders — and last, the common-stock holders.

The comparatively smaller element of risk in corporate bonds has historically made them a popular form of investment with institutional investors. This is the principal market that investment bankers look to when underwriting a corporate bond issue. Very often, they may suc-ceed in selling an entire bond issue to just one or two large institu-tional customers, such as an insurance company or a retirement fund. When there is no public offering, the deal is known as a *private place-ment*.

Bond mutual funds and unit investment trusts (another form of pooled investment) have also become important sources of demand for corporate bonds, buying on an institutional scale and then provid-ing individual investors a participation in a diversified bond portfolio.

Because the institutional market for bonds has over time been such a good market, underwriting and selling commissions are usually much lower on an issue of bonds than on an issue of stock.

From a company's point of view, a bond issue entails one obvious disadvantage: the interest represents a fixed charge that has to be met in bad times as well as good. By contrast, stockholders don't have to be paid dividends when the company is tight for money — and even in good times, there is no binding obligation. And bonds must be paid off when they come due, while stocks can remain outstanding forever.

So why would a company that has a choice opt for a bond issue? Because, in its financial plans, it expects that it can earn a substantially greater profit on the additional capital raised through the bond issue than it will have to pay out in interest on it. Moreover, bond interest payments are an expense item deducted from a company's earnings before it pays its federal income tax on those earnings, whereas dividends are paid out of what is left after a company has paid its income taxes. Thus, it actually costs a company less to pay a given amount of money to bondholders than it does to pay the same amount of money to stockholders. This advantage is compounded over the years if earnings and dividends keep growing while the interest paid the bondholders remains fixed.

Much like individuals seeking a personal loan from their bank, companies borrowing through bonds would prefer to get the money without putting up their property as collateral. That's why the Rod & Reel treasurer, once a bond issue was suggested, proposed that the company issue $10 million of debentures.

A *debenture* is a bond that is backed only by the general credit of the corporation. No specific real estate or property stands as security behind it. It is, in effect, a giant-sized IOU. Debentures are the most common type of bond issued by big, well-established industrial companies. But at Rod & Reel, investors might want more specific security.

One possibility therefore was a *first mortgage bond* — the kind of bond that is secured by a mortgage on all of a company's property; sometimes even on all property that it might later acquire. Industrial bonds of this type have long been considered to be among the highest-grade security investments. They offer the investor an undisputed first claim on company earnings and the greatest possible safety. The claims of the holder of such a first mortgage take absolute precedence over the claims of all other owners of the company's securities, including the holders of debentures, *second mortgage bonds*, or any other *junior debt* instruments that may be issued.

To ease debenture holders' concern that the company might later issue a mortgage bond that would outrank them, debenture issues often carry a *negative pledge* clause that promises the company will not pledge any property or collateral ahead of the debentures in any future borrowing.

The characteristics of some industries lend themselves to specialized borrowing arrangements. For instance, the railroads often use *equipment trust* obligations to buy freight cars, locomotives, and other such equipment. The equipment trusts mature *serially*. That is, they are typically divided up into 15 series, with one series coming due in each of the next 15 years. In effect, the railroad is buying on the installment plan, with the equipment itself serving as the guarantee for repayment.

In general, of course, it's always important to look past the particular security at the underlying value of the investment. Thus, a junior bond in a top-quality blue chip company may be a much safer, and higher-rated, investment than a fully secured first mortgage bond in an untried or struggling company.

For Rod & Reel, with a good record and fine prospects but as yet only a brief market history, the investment banker suggested a debenture with a convertible provision. The *debt service requirement* — the amount Rod & Reel will need each year to pay interest on its debt, and also to pay off any portion of the principal that may come due during the year — would probably be considerably lower than with a straight bond, thus protecting the cash flow the company needs to support its growth.

There are many *convertible bonds* on the market, and their terms vary widely. But like convertible preferred stocks, all convertible bonds offer the owners the privilege of converting their bonds into a specified number of shares of common stock. Most buyers purchase convertibles primarily as a longer-term investment in the common stock; they get steady interest income while waiting for the conversion to become worthwhile. What's more, because of that interest income, you enjoy some "downside protection" in case of a stock price slide. The issuing company also tends to look at a convertible as, in effect, a deferred common stock issue — and at a higher price than it could obtain from an immediate stock sale, since the conversion price is always set higher than what the common stock sells for at the time the convertible is issued.

Sophisticated bond buyers know well that you don't get something for nothing in a security, any more than in any other kind of merchandise. So the conversion "sweetener" is normally "paid for" through a lower interest rate and a rank that is subordinate to the claim of senior bonds. But that's a trade-off both issuer and buyer often find attractive.

Next, Rod & Reel's treasurer wanted to know what rate of interest the company might have to pay. That depends on many factors: the financial strength and earnings prospects of the company, the type and particular terms of the security being offered, current supply and demand for that kind of security — and the general level of interest rates at the time of the offering. While the investment banker had followed Rod & Reel's progress, it still had to conduct a thorough new investigation before underwriting another securities issue.

Before a new bond issue is floated, Moody's Investors Service and Standard & Poor's Corporation, the two most prominent organizations in the field of securities research and statistics, are asked to assign a quality rating. Most times the two companies agree on the ratings. But they don't quite agree on the form of the designation. Thus, Moody's grades bonds (downward in quality) as Aaa, Aa, A, Baa, Ba, and so on down to C ("extremely poor prospects"). Standard & Poor's prefers capital letters, using AAA, AA, A, BBB, etc., and may further refine the rating with a plus or minus.

As might be expected, each step down in the ratings generally requires the company to pay a higher interest rate. Ratings down to Baa qualify as *investment grade*. Aside from the prestige involved, some portfolios and trusts are required to keep most or all of their investments in securities with these ratings. In the 1980s, a big market developed for bonds that could not achieve that high a rating but still were considered of fair, if more or less "speculative," quality (often in the Ba or B category); such bonds carry significantly higher interest rates to offset the perceived higher risk. These securities (as well as even riskier bonds rated in the C's) are formally described as *high-yield bonds*, but more popularly known as *junk bonds*.

Public attention centers on the huge issues of junk bonds floated in connection with corporate takeovers and restructurings; however, over the years, a far larger number of issues have been brought out to finance the operations of companies too small, young, or little known to attain investment grade ratings — companies often very much like Rod & Reel.

But the wild junk-debt binge of the second half of the eighties loaded down many substantial companies with more debt than they proved able to handle. Numerous borrowers defaulted and this in turn caused major distress for many lenders, including S&Ls and some insurance companies. Prices of virtually all junk bonds plunged. More recently, a rebound from those super-depressed levels by companies able to weather the storm has resulted in sizable gains for certain junk bond indexes. But it's a very high risk area, and any investors who feel they can afford (and have the temperament to be comfortable with) some speculation in junk bonds should exercise extreme caution.

As for the interest rate a borrower has to pay (and that's true of individuals and governments as well as of corporations), again, it's not just a question of quality, but also of timing. Thus, in 1920, Aaa or AAA bonds paid over 6%, while in 1945 they were paying only 2.5%. By the early 1960s, Aaa bonds were in the 4% to 5% range, in the mid-1970s over 8%, and at the height of the tight-money binge in 1981 just about 15%. In the early nineties, the top-rated corporate bonds' yields were a more moderate 9.7% to 6.8%.

When money is "tight" and general interest rates go up, bond interest rates tend to go up, too. This can lead to a situation in which investors figure bonds promise a better return than the total return they are likely to get from a stock portfolio; thus they are tempted to shift to the "safer" investment for a time.

The shifting trends in interest rates help determine not only the rate a company must promise to pay when it issues a new bond, but also the market price of bonds already outstanding. That's easy to understand. No one is going to pay face value for an old bond with an interest rate of 6% at a time when a new bond of equal quality offers an interest rate of 12%.

How does the market adjustment process work? It helps to understand the terminology used in connection with bond interest. The interest rate of a bond is frequently referred to as the *coupon rate*. The term derives from the detachable coupons, one for each six months of the bond's life, that were traditionally attached to each bond certificate. Coupons were needed because in the past nearly all bonds were not registered as to ownership but were *bearer bonds*. The bonds were the property of the bearer — whoever possessed the certificates at a given time. The bondholder would clip each coupon as it came due and present it for payment. However, nearly all bonds issued in recent years are *registered bonds* — registered in each owner's name, just like stocks, with semiannual interest checks sent automatically to the registered owners.

The coupon rate is set at the time the bond is issued. If Rod & Reel, or any other company, sells 9% debentures due to be repaid in 2010 (the market would call them 9s of 2010), it is obligated to pay $90 a year interest on each $1,000 bond until 2010. Should the going rate for issuing similar-quality debentures rise to 12% or even 15%, management could congratulate itself on having financed at a favorable time — much as you would be happy with a 9% mortgage when new ones run around 12%. But suppose interest rates fall to 6%; Rod & Reel would still have to shell out $90 a year — unless and until it has the right to call or redeem the old issue. Most bonds (like preferred stocks) come with call provisions that give the company the right to pay them off before maturity. But in many cases holders are protected against early calls, sometimes for as long as 10 years.

If it has the right to call the issue, the company may try to pay it off by selling a new, lower-coupon bond; that's called *refunding*. In the case of a convertible bond, a redemption call is usually intended to force the holders to convert their bonds into common stock.

Now, how does the bondholder — or someone contemplating the purchase of an already outstanding bond — look at the coupon rate? Well, if you're going to get $90 a year in a period of 12% interest, you might think that the bond is worth only $750 to you (12% of $750 = $90). Indeed, if you paid $750 for the bond, 12% would be your *current yield* — the direct annual cash interest you earn on the amount invested. Or, if interest rates were falling, a 6% current yield would place a theoretical $1,500 value on a bond paying $90 a year.

But haven't you left out another factor? In time, the bond is to be paid off at face value. So, if the market value were actually $750 for the $1,000 bond, you could count on a $250 appreciation in the bond's value over the rest of its life. As a very rough rule of thumb, you could just divide this $250 by the remaining life; if it's 20 years, you figure you'd get about $12 a year atop the $90 interest. That would make a total of $102 on a $750 investment or about 13.6%.

The actual calculation of such a *yield to maturity* — the compounded annual interest you can expect if you buy the bond today, counting both (1) the semiannual interest payments during the remaining life of the bond, and (2) the capital gain or loss you will realize when the bond is finally paid off at par — is more sophisticated. It has to allow for a uniform percentage (rather than a uniform dollar amount) of increase in the value of the bond — or, as the experts say, the discounted present value of the interest and principal you'll get in the future. So you'd go to prepared tables or, more likely today, to a computer. You'd find that to get a 12% yield to maturity on a 9% bond with 20 years of remaining life, you'd pay about $775. Of course, if interest rates have fallen and the same bond sells at a premium, you must allow for this premium to evaporate over the remaining life of the bond, so the bond's price would be about $1,340 to give you a 6% yield to maturity. If the bond can be called, you should figure not just the yield to maturity but the yield to the earliest call date.

The yield to maturity (or call) is a key factor in determining the market price of a bond. And it's important to keep in mind the mathematical fact that a *rise in yields brings a decline in the bond price*, while *falling yields mean higher bond prices*. So the bigger and more frequent interest rate shifts of the past 20 years have led to unprecedented volatility in the once staid, slow-moving bond market.

Look, for instance, at the top-rated 5½% debentures due in 1997 that American Telephone & Telegraph issued in 1967. In the early years these bonds reached a high of 103⅝. (While stocks are quoted in dollars per share, bond quotations are in percent of par or face value; thus 103⅝ means the price of a standard $1,000 bond was $1,036.25.) But as interest rates soared, the price of these Telephone debentures plunged, to a low of 42 in 1981. That provided a yield to maturity of 14.8%. By 1991, these bonds had recovered to around 92, reflecting a yield to maturity of 7.15%. The price of the bond had more than doubled in 10 years. That's in addition to the $55-a-year cash interest — by itself a fat 13% annual yield for anyone who bought at the 1981 low. By early 1993 (now a "short-term" bond with only four years till maturity) it had risen further to around 100 (i.e., par), so anyone buying at that point got both a *current* and *to-maturity* yield of 5.5%. Then, in September 1993, the bond's life ended a bit prematurely — it was called and redeemed at par.

If you expect interest rates to fall, there's an advantage in purchasing a low-coupon bond, preferably with maturity well in the future, selling at a steep discount. (You don't have to worry about such a bond being called, as might happen with a higher-coupon bond that could be pushed to a premium above par by lower interest rates.) If the rate does fall, the rise in the market price of the bond can be expected to reflect the adjustment in the yield structure — not just for the current year but for the entire remaining life of the bond. (After all, the name of the game is yield to maturity.) Of course, this also works in reverse — in a period of rising rates, long-term bonds tend to decline more sharply. In brief, the longer the maturity, the greater the likely fluctuations both up and down.

Such volatility is especially marked in so-called *zero coupon* bonds. These bonds pay no current interest at all; the way you get your income is that the "zeroes" are sold at a deep discount from the face value at which they are paid off. That's the system used for half a century now on the U.S. government's Series E and EE Savings Bonds. A few corporate bond issuers adapted the zero idea in the late 1970s, but more recently most of the action on zeroes has moved into the government and municipal bond areas.

An advantage of zeroes is that, if you just want to build up income for the future, the appreciation in value during the life of the bond gives you a known interest rate, continually reinvested till maturity.

But because there's no current income at all, the market value of zeroes fluctuates more sharply than regular bonds; that might be a problem if you want to get out before maturity. Also — and here the treatment differs from the EE bonds — the IRS will assess you for the *"phantom interest,"* the imputed income that a zero generates each year. What these fancy terms mean is you have to pay tax annually even if you only get your income at maturity. So *taxable* zero-coupon bonds are more attractive in tax-exempt accounts, such as retirement plans.

Whether a bond or stock investor, you will want to look at the makeup of a company's capitalization: the relative size of its debt, preferred stock, and (common) stockholders' equity. When a company has a substantial amount of bonds or preferred stock outstanding in relation to the common's equity, the common stock is said to have *high leverage.* Any increase or decrease in the company's operating earnings will have a proportionately far greater impact on the earnings (and quite likely the price) of the common stock. Here's why: Suppose a company is obligated to pay $4 million in bond interest and pre-ferred dividends every year. If it has earnings of $5 million before paying such *fixed charges*, it has $1 million left for the common-stock holders. If the pre-charge earnings rise to $6 million, there will be $2 million available for the benefit of the common-stock holders. Thus, just a 20% increase in earnings before fixed charges doubles the earn-ings for the common; a 50% increase before charges would raise com-mon earnings 3.5-fold. This is because, no matter what the company earns, the holders of the bonds and preferred stock still receive only the prescribed $4 million.

Of course, if the company's pre-charge earnings declined from $5 million to $4 million, there would be no earnings at all available to the common-stock holders — that is, a 20% drop in pre-charge earnings translates into a 100% drop in common earnings. And should pre-charge earnings slip further to $3.5 million, the common holders would be faced with a half-million-dollar deficit on their stock. With fluctuations in operating results having such magnified effects on earnings available to the common-stock holders, it's easy to understand why prices of high-leveraged stocks are likely to fluctuate more drastically than those of stocks in companies with relatively small amounts of bonds and preferred stocks outstanding.

Clearly, almost by definition, high leverage maximizes the opportunities for multiplying the value of an equity investment but at the same time it steps up the risks. And, among the many investment decisions facing them, prudent investors must determine the degree of risk with which they are comfortable.

CHAPTER 6

How New Issues Are Regulated

WHENEVER a company like Rod & Reel wants to raise capital by floating a new issue of stocks or bonds, it must comply with the federal law that governs the sale of any such issue offered to the public.

In the boom days of the twenties, many a new stock was sold with few facts and lots of glittering promises. In 1933, Congress changed all that. It passed the *Securities Act of 1933*, widely known as the *Truth in Securities Act*. The next year it followed up with the *Securities Exchange Act of 1934* and set up the *Securities and Exchange Commission* (SEC) to administer both laws.

No one, least of all the SEC, will argue that the passage of laws and the establishment of a vigilant watchdog agency has ended abuse in the securities markets. In fact, during the past few years, the SEC has been engaged in unraveling some of the biggest securities law violations ever. In turn, of course, we must recognize that "biggest ever" in good part reflects: 1) the growing size of the economy and the financial markets, and 2) a continuous upgrading of standards — what might have been shrugged off 40 or 20 years ago is not acceptable today.

Nor was there a totally uncontrolled wilderness before the New Deal laws came along. The New York Stock Exchange, whatever its preoccupation with preserving the prerogatives of a "private club" for much of its long history, repeatedly came up with regulations aimed at making listed companies and stock traders toe the line. For instance, as early as 1869 it insisted that corporations maintain an independent transfer agent to issue stock certificates. That was aimed at financiers and entrepreneurs who doubled as printing press operators and engaged in a practice picturesquely termed *watered stock*.

That graphic expression had its origin in the practice of feeding cattle large quantities of salt on their way to market and then giving them a big drink of water just before they went on the weighing scales.

As applied to securities, the phrase describes stock issued with an inflated value — generally, fraudulently inflated. For instance, an unscrupulous operator might pay only half a million dollars for all the stock of a company, then print an additional half-million dollars' worth of stock certificates, without benefit of stock split or advising anyone of the change in capitalization. He might then sell the entire issue to an unsuspecting public and pocket a half-million dollars' profit. Or, after he sold half the stock and got his cost back, he might keep the remaining shares and thus own a half interest in the company at no cost to himself.

Also, even before World War I, many states began to enact so-called *blue sky laws*, which attempted to put some controls and supervision on securities offered within their borders.

But while the move toward better market supervision and investor protection is an ongoing and never-ending effort, the enactments of the early thirties undeniably marked the real watershed.

Before a company makes a *public offering* of new stocks or bonds, the SEC requires *full disclosure* of all the pertinent facts. This is done through a lengthy *registration statement* that the company must file with the SEC. In it, the company sets forth all the pertinent data concerning its financial condition: its assets and its liabilities, what it owns and what it owes. It must furnish its profit-and-loss record for the past several years, and the market price and dividend record of stock already outstanding. It must describe all outstanding issues of its securities as well as details of the new securities to be issued and their offering terms. Then it must show a *pro forma* capitalization — what the capitalization will look like once the new securities are issued. Similarly, it must recalculate earnings per share based on the new capitalization. The company must also list all its officers and directors, together with the salaries of the CEO and the four next-highest-paid officers. It must also reveal the identity of anyone who holds more than 5% of any of its securities issues, as well as the ownership of such securities by its executive management. Finally, it must provide a detailed description of its business, with financial results of the major operating sectors.

The SEC staff reviews the material submitted and often — especially with companies just entering the market — requests additional information or clarification. Assuming the data appear to be complete and accurate, the SEC then gives a green light to the new issue. But this *does not mean that the SEC passes any judgment whatsoever* on the quality of the securities, how good or bad they may be for any investor.

The Securities and Exchange Commission also sees that the information that is filed with it is made available to any possible buyer of the new issue. A company is required to put all the essential facts into a printed *prospectus*. Every securities dealer who offers the new stock or bond for sale must give a copy of that prospectus to everyone who buys the new issue and also to anyone who might request a copy. This requirement is generally binding on newly public companies or others not already subject to SEC reporting requirements for 40 days after the new issue is offered for sale; this requirement is cut to 25 days if the company obtains immediate listing on a stock exchange or Nasdaq.

Before the price is set on a new issue, a preliminary draft of the prospectus is usually printed up. Such drafts are known as *red herrings*, because they must carry on their face a warning printed in red ink to the effect that the prospectus has not yet been reviewed by the SEC. The red herring name was considered apt by some early observers of the regulatory process because various issuers in their initial submissions to the SEC have been tempted to try to get away with little more than outright sales promotion, designed not so much to divulge information as to distract the reader from facts about the new issue that the SEC might regard critically.

The prospectus is usually about 50 to 60 pages long, sometimes even longer. But some well-established companies, notably utilities, that can meet certain high standards of financial responsibility have for years been permitted by the SEC to use a *short-form prospectus* on bond issues. In 1970 the commission relaxed its rules and extended the short-form privilege to stock issues of companies that were already subject to regular SEC filings, had a strong financial position, and had a record of consistent earnings over a period of years. And in a significant rule change in 1983, the SEC permitted major companies on which extensive financial information has already been publicly available for a period of time to utilize *shelf registrations* — a generalized filing covering a specified amount of securities (mostly bonds) that can be offered "from time to time." When the company thinks the time is right for an offering, it files the appropriate details and can come to market promptly without the normal registration wait. In 1992 the shelf registration rules were further liberalized, and it's possible to make a filing covering both debt and equity securities.

During the period when a new issue is under prospectus regulation, no broker or dealer can provide the public with any additional information or opinion about that new issue or any outstanding issue related to it. The broker is free to publish the prospectus or a detailed summary of it as an advertisement. But apart from that, the only kind of permissible advertising for the issue is the so-called *tombstone* announcement. This is an advertisement in which no information is provided beyond the name of the issue, its price, its size, and the names of the underwriters and dealers who have it for sale. And above even this austere announcement the underwriters usually insert a precautionary note to the effect that the advertisement is not to be interpreted as an offer to buy or sell the security, since such offer is made only through the prospectus.

Sometimes you may see in the *Wall Street Journal* or one of the large metropolitan newspapers a tombstone ad announcing a new issue and stating that the issue has already been completely sold. You may well wonder why such an ad appears. The answer is simple. Underwriting houses are proud of their financing activities, and when they have managed to place all of a given issue even before the ad can hit the paper, they go ahead and publish the new-issue advertisement as a matter of prestige. It is a good piece of public relations for both the underwriter and the company whose offering has been sold.

Even if a company satisfies all the requirements of the Securities and Exchange Commission on a new issue, the company's regulatory task may not end there, in view of the blue sky laws of the individual states. There's sufficient variance from state to state to cause a good deal of extra legal and administrative expense in filing the necessary forms to comply with the various state laws. And while the federal objective is full disclosure so investors have the facts to make up their own mind, many states have a "merit" system under which issuers must convince state regulators that the stock or bond meets certain standards if they want to offer it in that state.

All told, preparing a new issue for sale can be a very expensive undertaking. The bill for preparing the necessary forms and printing a prospectus can run into the hundreds of thousands of dollars. Fees for lawyers and accountants can add a lot more to this bill.

However, the federal law, as well as most state laws, provides an "out" for little companies like Rod & Reel. For instance, if the new issue has a value of not more than $5,000,000, the company need file only a short registration form with the SEC. This is known as a *Regulation A* filing. Companies using it can satisfy the requirements of the law by distributing an *offering circular* instead of a full prospectus. And, as noted, if the new issue can be structured as a private placement rather than as a public offering, it doesn't even have to be registered with the SEC, no matter what its size. While a private placement usually can be purchased by no more than 35 persons, this limit no longer applies to institutional investors and to large-net-worth individuals.

The Securities and Exchange Commission's "full disclosure" rules have undoubtedly done much to protect the investor, though you can still find some who argue that they are more exacting than they have to be, and could deter some companies from trying to raise new money for expansion. These critics also fret that the ban on disseminating information about a company while its new issue is under prospectus regulation — intended to prohibit potentially deceptive promotion of the new issue — can deprive investors who own the company's existing securities of timely information.

Another argument is that individual investors don't really benefit as they should from the intended protection. Individuals who buy a new issue — and their number is small compared with those who buy securities already on the market — rarely examine the prospectus, or don't understand it if they do.

That's often true even in those cases where, at SEC insistence, the company states right up front such pertinent facts as that it has no product, no experienced management, no assurance of adequate financing, and so forth, and that it does face strong and experienced competition.

Sadly, buyers are all too apt to believe — despite the prominent disclaimer on the prospectus — that if the Securities and Exchange Commission cleared the issue for sale, the commission has endorsed it; and anything good enough for the SEC is good enough for them.

Nothing, of course, could be further from the truth. Full disclosure can protect against fraud. It can't guarantee a profit or protect against loss. *Caveat emptor* ("Let the buyer beware") is still the rule of the market. And it applies with particular force to new, unseasoned issues.

But if all too many investors ignore the material made available to them, the disclosure rules and SEC supervision still serve a vital purpose. By making pertinent facts public, they enable professional analysts and the increasingly watchful media to study companies in the public market, in turn providing more extensive and reliable information to the investing public. And the requirements for disclosure have undoubtedly made more companies conscious of their obligations.

Also, once a company has sold securities to the public, it has an ongoing obligation to file (with the commission and any exchange on which the securities are listed) annual and quarterly reports as well as prompt notice of any *material* developments that might affect the stock. Again, while these filings are publicly available, it's the financial press, statistical services, and securities analysts who carefully monitor these documents and spread the word to the investing public.

Filings are available for inspection at the Washington headquarters of the SEC and at its regional offices, as well as at the stock exchanges where the company's stock is listed. The SEC has been developing an Electronic Data Gathering, Analysis and Retrieval system, called EDGAR, under which companies can submit required data by computer. This will also permit securities analysts, the press, and the public to retrieve the material electronically as soon as it is filed. After some 10 years of incubation and a pilot stage with volunteer users, formal implementation of EDGAR began in 1993, with electronic filing mandated for around 1,700 major corporations. All companies are supposed to file through EDGAR by mid-1996.

The ebb and flow of offerings tend to follow business cycles. In times of general business uncertainty, there's a marked drop in new stock or bond offerings by companies that already have securities issues outstanding. And understandably, there's an even greater slack in the number of initial public offerings brought to market. In turn, when there's general prosperity, the optimism of the moment brings forth a disproportionate increase in the number of little companies with big plans and lots of stock to sell. And if the times are good enough, and the little companies' big plans sound appealing enough, demand for their offerings can be so great that it drives the stock's first official traded price up significantly from its initial offering price.

During the increasingly frequent outbreaks of "new issue fever" that have periodically afflicted the market throughout the postwar era, it has not been unusual for the initial stock offering of, say, a small computer company sold at $10 a share through the underwriting group to be resold on the first day of trading in the open market at $25 or $30 a share. Demand for such "hot" new issues has often been so heated, in fact, that broker participants in the offering were forced to parcel out their allocations of stock at 10% to 25% of the amount their customers requested. Some prospective buyers were unable to obtain any shares at all at the offering price; if they wanted stock anyway, they had to buy it in the aftermarket at the substantially higher prices resulting from the heavy buying pressure on the stock when it entered the open market.

During periods of intense speculation in new issues, it has become common for companies with no earnings, or even no product, to "go public" with an initial stock offering. Many of these companies never make a profit and are eventually forced into bankruptcy. Some are the products of unscrupulous promoters who knowingly peddle stocks that are not worth the paper they are printed on — sneaking past the regulators or through loopholes and often relying on the "small-issue" or Regulation A exemption so they wouldn't have to "tell all" in a full prospectus. But often it's just a case of would-be entrepreneurs unable to cope with the demands of the business.

During the late sixties, for example, scores of nursing home operators and fast-food franchisers sold their first batch of stock to a gullible public and were never heard from again, just as oil and uranium speculations soared and sizzled in the fifties. More recently, the process repeated itself with the initial stock offerings of marginal energy exploration and biotechnological companies. At the same time, scores of other companies in these and similarly promising areas were going public for the first time and rewarding their charter investors with significant profits on their purchase of stock at the offering price.

Consequently, there are both greater risks and greater potential rewards in buying new issues than in any other area of stock investing.

CHAPTER 7

What You Should Know
about Government Bonds

MORE people have *some* personal acquaintance with government bonds than with any other kind of security. Yet, paradoxically, government securities represent a huge market whose fine points are *fully* understood by fewer people than those of any other.

An estimated 85,000,000 Americans learned what it meant to lend their money to Uncle Sam during World War II when they bought the famous Series E War Bonds. Since the war, millions of other Americans have initiated their investment education by buying these bonds under the more peaceful name of Savings Bonds.

In recent years, as the budget and trade deficits and inflation trends wield a marked impact on everyday life, the day's doings in Treasury bills or the "long bond" often make the evening news. And a good many individuals have acquired stakes in such marketable government securities — directly or, more often, through money market and bond funds.

However, probably only the big institutional buyers plus the comparative handful of government bond dealers really understand the government bond market and know how it can be affected by subtle shifts in the credit and money policies of our own government or other governments half the world away. This is a market where $180 billion in securities changes hands each day. The average trade comes to around $25 million and profits are measured in small fractions of 1%.

There are scores of different government issues, with varying characteristics and terms. Some are issued for very short periods of time. These are *Treasury bills*, which the government sells every week with terms of 91 and 182 days; every four weeks, the Treasury offers bills with a life of 52 weeks. *Treasury notes* have maturities of two to 10 years. Long-term issues of *Treasury bonds*, often simply called *Treasuries*, have maturities ranging from 10 to 30 years, with the most recently issued 30-year bond usually referred to as "the *long bond.*"

In periods of high interest rates, already outstanding Treasuries will sell in the open market at a discount (just as we've seen in the case of corporate bonds) to give the buyer a return competitive with the yield on newly issued bonds.

Thus, in May 1982, the 30-year bond issued in 1977 and carrying a 7⅞% coupon could be bought at 60¹⁸⁄₃₂ (government bonds trade in intervals of ¹⁄₃₂ instead of the ⅛ customary for most securities). This means a $1,000 bond then had a market value of only $605.62, virtually 40% below par value. You'd be collecting interest of $78.75 a year, giving you a 12.85% current yield on that $605 investment, while the yield to maturity came to 13.34%. One word of caution: while you can be confident you'll get back the full $1,000 par value in 2007, realizing the full yield to maturity would depend on being able to reinvest each interest payment at that high rate. That's why, especially at a time of high rates, a good many investors with long time horizons are attracted to zero-coupons, which do give you that built-in interest reinvestment. In any case, you can always be sure of the total income you'll get, *if* you plan to hold the government bond till maturity.

By the same token, of course — and again, just as with corporate bonds — when general interest rates are low, already outstanding Treasuries carrying a higher coupon will sell at a premium — a price above par — and give the buyer a yield lower than their coupon rate. However, unlike most corporate and municipal bonds, Treasuries generally are either noncallable or can be called for redemption only in the last few years before their scheduled maturity. So (except if you buy a bond late in its life when its call date is close at hand) you don't have to worry much about having your high-coupon bond redeemed on you if interest rates fall; that assurance can help the bonds reach a higher price in the market.

For instance, the 30-year bond issued in November 1981 carries Uncle Sam's promise to keep paying you 14% for at least 25 years (the earliest call date) if not the full 30 years. Because of that long-term high-paying assurance, these bonds (listed in the newspaper tables as "14.00 Nov 06-11" to indicate both the call and regular maturity date) were trading around 155 in the spring of 1994.

Another, practical advantage of government securities is that, while fully subject to federal income tax, they are exempt from state and local income tax, and that can be particularly valuable in high-tax states. And with governments you don't have to worry about what analysts call *"event risk"* — the possibility that a corporation whose bond you happen to hold might find itself in a buyout or merger situation that results in its taking on new loads of debt; such a shift in capitalization, or some other unexpected corporate development, can result in a downgrading of originally high-rated corporate bonds.

Of course, you may have to pay for these built-in advantages of government bonds by having to accept a somewhat lower yield than for otherwise comparable corporates.

Treasury bonds trade at prices that usually change by only a few fractions from day to day. That's largely because of the immense size and unequaled liquidity of the Treasury market — the constant availability of large numbers of both buyers and sellers. By the same token, even tiny changes translate into millions of market value. And the Treasury markets are extremely sensitive to any news (or rumors) that might affect future interest rates.

Regularly traded by the same dealers and on much the same basis as government bonds are those bonds issued by various government *agencies*, such as the Federal Home Loans Banks, the Government National Mortgage Association (Ginnie Mae), the Federal National Mortgage Association (Fannie Mae), the Federal Farm Credit Banks, and the Student Loan Marketing Association (Sally Mae). These are government-sponsored but not government-*guaranteed*, though the underlying collateral such as mortgages or student loans may carry government insurance. Also, most agencies have been given by law the right to draw on a specified credit line with the Treasury. And there's widespread belief that if necessary Congress would step in with some kind of assistance, as it did to help the Farm Credit system in the late 1980s — not to mention the more recent and far more costly (and messy) S&L and banking bailouts. With variations depending on issuer and maturity, agency issues, which most experts consider very nearly as safe as direct government obligations, generally offer yields about 20 to 60 *basis points* over Treasuries (a basis point is ⅟₁₀₀ of a percentage point). If you live in a high-tax state, also check whether interest on the agency security is exempt from state income tax.

Treasury bills are, in effect, a short-term version of zero-coupons. The Treasury sells them at a discount from par and pays them off at par, so the difference between the discount purchase price and par represents the interest the buyer receives. The Treasury sells its bills at weekly auctions; dealers and other would-be buyers submit written bids and the Treasury accepts the best bids until it fills its sales quotas for that week. However, you can make sure you get bills at the *average price* for that auction by submitting a *noncompetitive bid* for bills as well as notes and bonds through any Federal Reserve Bank. The minimum purchase is $10,000 for bills, $5,000 for notes under four-year maturity and $1,000 for longer-term notes and bonds. You can also order them through your bank or broker; they will probably charge a handling fee.

Longer-term zero-coupon Treasury securities, which provide a "locked-in," secure yield till some specified future date (often tied to retirement, college entrance, etc.), have also become popular. These "zeroes" are actually instruments put together, or, more accurately, pulled apart, by dealers. In early 1982 Merrill Lynch introduced *TIGRs* (which stands for Treasury Investment Growth Receipts), soon followed by Salomon Inc.'s *CATS* (for Certificates of Accrual on Treasury Securities) and some other animal-inspired acronyms. The dealers took a large batch of bonds, *stripped* or separated out the semiannual interest coupons and the principal-payment portion of the bonds, then sold participations in each set. That makes it possible for you to select an instrument with a maturity date anywhere from half a year from now till 25 to 30 years in the future. For instance, $1 million (face value) of the 9% bonds maturing in November 2018 will pay $45,000 of interest every May and November until 2018, when the $1 million principal gets repaid. Through stripping, you'll be able to buy, say, $12,000 worth of the interest coupons that get paid in May 2007 (when your daughter is due to enter college) or $20,000 worth of the principal due in 2019. You won't get paid anything in the meantime (that's what makes them "zeroes") which is why in early 1994 you had to pay only about $370 to collect $1,000 in 2007 or $145 to get $1,000 in 2019.

In 1985, the Treasury began participating more directly by offering to do the stripping for the dealers, providing a more standardized product which it calls *STRIPS* (Separate Trading of Registered Interest and Principal of Securities). You can find "Stripped Treasuries" quoted daily on the Treasuries page of the *Wall Street Journal*.

Whatever marketable Treasury instruments you buy, don't look for a nice engraved certificate. Since 1979, all Treasury bills have been handled exclusively by computerized book-entry maintained for the Treasury by the Federal Reserve. In 1986, notes and bonds also were placed fully on the book-entry system, and holders of most older Treasury issues have also transferred them to the new system, so close to 99% of the marketable Treasury debt is now on the computer "books." The system makes it easier to trade, and virtually eliminates theft, loss, and counterfeiting problems.

For individuals, it's all handled by a program called *Treasury Direct*. An account is opened for you when you first apply to buy a marketable Treasury security. From then on, you'll not only get regular statements showing all your holdings, but Treasury Direct will electronically transfer interest and principal payments to your bank account.

Many individuals invest in government securities without ever taking direct ownership — they buy mutual funds (or perhaps unit investment trusts), which are available in great profusion. Major attractions for these investors include convenience, ease of access, and the relatively small amounts needed for transactions, along with the high degree of safety associated with the underlying government issues. As of early 1994, about $110 billion was invested in government bond funds.

Of course, virtually all money market and mutual funds, no matter what their type or specialization, hold some Treasury bills as the most liquid part of their portfolio. Indeed, Treasury bills, because there is always such a huge and ready market for them, are what the "cash" portion of the assets of mutual funds, institutions, and other large investors largely consists of. They must have "cash" on hand so they can meet demand for redemptions and other immediate needs for funds, but they want the kind of "cash" that earns its keep while waiting to be disbursed. Also, when money managers recommend that a certain percentage of an individual's portfolio be in cash for the time being, they mean it should be invested in bills or other readily redeemable short-term instruments.

There are other government bonds that are not traded in any market, bonds that can be bought only from the government and sold back to the government at set prices, bonds that never suffer any fluctuations in market price. Among them are the familiar *savings bonds* — now Series EE and HH, which replaced the earlier Series E and H. They can be bought at virtually any bank and often through payroll deductions. No commission is charged. They are handled free as a patriotic service.

When savings bonds were first introduced during World War II, you paid $18.50 for the smallest E bond; ten years later you could cash it in for $25, which worked out to an average annual return of 2.9%. You could cash it in earlier, but would receive a lower yield.

The 2.9% rate wasn't bad at the time, but as general interest rates mounted, the government was forced to liberalize the return on its savings bonds. It accomplished this by periodically shortening the maturity — the length of time you had to hold an E bond before you could cash it in at face value. By 1979 the maturity was down to five years for a yield of 6.5%.

In 1980 the Treasury switched to EE bonds, and in 1982 it initiated a market-based interest formula. The Treasury sets the interest rate twice a year at 85% of the going rate for marketable Treasuries due in five years. When you cash it in, you'll get the average of the floating rates throughout the time you held the bond. That's assuming this *average* is above the minimum rate guaranteed when you bought your bond — currently 4%. In any case, you must hold your bond for at least five years to get the full interest. The highest floating rate was 11.09% in November 1982; the rate set in May 1994 was down to 4.7%.

The other savings bonds — the H and now HH series — are offered at full face value and the buyer receives an interest payment every half year instead of having to wait to collect at redemption, as with the E and EE series. While terms for these bonds have also been liberalized over the years, the HH bonds (and still outstanding H bonds) do not get their rate adjusted every six months but get whatever the guaranteed rate is at the time they are issued — 4% as of March 1993. And HHs are no longer sold for cash; you can get them only in exchange for your E and EE bonds.

A unique advantage of the E and EE bonds is that you have the option of postponing taxes on the interest that accrues until the day you cash in the bond. And you can push back that day by simply holding on to the bond even after its stated maturity date. Interest, in line with the regular formula, will keep accumulating. For E bonds bought through November 1965, the maximum life is 40 years; for later E and EE purchases, it's 30 years from the time you bought. Then, you can still convert the EE bonds into HH bonds (which now have a maximum life of 20 years) and pay taxes only as you receive the semiannual HH interest.

Despite all the differences among various issues, government bonds have one common characteristic: they are regarded as the safest investments in the world.

What security lies behind them? The pledged word of the government of the United States. Just that. Nothing else. As long as that word is believed and accepted — as it must be by all Americans, since, in the last analysis, we are the government — government bonds, if held to maturity, offer the best protection you can find against the risk of losing any of your capital.

But because their prices do not rise with inflation, government bonds (like all fixed-income securities) offer poor protection against the risk that your dollars will lose something of their purchasing power if prices generally go up. That, as noted throughout this book, is where asset allocation should come into play for you. You'll want to balance inflation protection on one hand with a good return on low-risk securities on the other. The ratio allocated to each type of investment should depend on your particular needs and inclinations at a given time, along with your assessment of the current economic and market outlook.

CHAPTER 8

What You Should Know about Municipal Bonds

STATES, cities, and other units of local government, such as school districts and housing authorities, frequently need capital — to build schools, roads, hospitals, and sewers, and to carry on the many other public projects that are their responsibility. So they, too, issue bonds. These are called *municipal bonds*.

Unlike the federal government, which underwrites its own bonds, these local units of government go to investment bankers for their money, just as corporations do. Active underwriters include not just securities firms but also commercial banks. While the Depression-era Glass-Steagall Act (now largely eroded) long barred banks from underwriting public issues of corporations, they always retained the authority to underwrite most municipal issues.

The growth of municipal bond issues has been little short of fantastic since the end of World War II, when the total value of all outstanding municipal issues was about $20 billion. By the end of 1993, thanks to our expanding economy and public demand for all kinds of new municipal facilities, that figure had grown to more than $1.3 trillion.

With perhaps one million municipal bond issues on the market, the investor is confronted with a wide range of maturities, quality ratings, and yields. Interest rates on municipal bonds, which averaged between 2% and 4% in the fifties and between 5% and 7% in the seventies, surged along with general interest rates to all-time highs in 1980–

1981, and you could get returns of over 14%. In the early nineties, yields were generally back down to the 5.3% to 7.3% range.

What makes the rates especially attractive is that the interest collected on these municipal bonds is exempt from federal income tax. Indeed, while recent changes in the tax laws have tightened some exemption eligibility rules, they've actually enhanced the popularity of the municipals market. That's because considerably more drastic revisions in other parts of the law have made municipals one of the few remaining tax-advantaged investments available to many taxpayers.

Investors who earn $1,000 in interest and dividends from taxable investments are able to retain only $690 of their income if they are in the 31% tax bracket, or $604 if they're in the current top federal bracket of 39.6%. But if they receive $1,000 interest on a municipal bond, they can keep all of it, free of federal income tax.

Not only that, but in many states, on a municipal bond issued by that state or one of its cities, towns or other taxing authorities, the interest collected on that bond will also be exempt from state taxes. Thus, for instance, New York City residents with incomes in the $100,000 range might realize more "take home" income from 6% New York municipal bonds than they would get from an investment that yielded a taxable return of 9.9%; for a $250,000 New York earner, the taxable equivalent could top 11.3%.

Is it any wonder then that municipal bonds have proved attractive not only to investors in the upper income brackets but in even larger numbers to middle-income investors? In 1991, over 4 million individual taxpayers reported a total of $43 billion in tax-exempt interest. And nearly half of these owners of municipals had adjusted gross income of less than $50,000.

Of course, as in everything, you can't expect a free lunch, and investors in municipals "pay" for the tax advantage by accepting a lower coupon rate than for a taxable instrument of similar quality. The differential between these rates may vary widely; however, most of the time for upper-bracket — and quite often also for medium-bracket — investors, the effective after-tax yield is higher for municipals than for taxable alternatives. Always, however, it's important that you figure out just how the numbers apply to your particular circumstances when you're contemplating an investment.

And again, as with all bonds, if current interest rates shoot up, the price of outstanding issues will drop; while if rates slide, the price will rise. In the case of municipal bonds, price fluctuations involve an extra consideration: While interest is tax-exempt, the IRS will want its cut of any capital gains you may realize.

Although no one but an expert can hope to know all about the different characteristics, the different qualities, of municipal bonds, all investors should be familiar with the fundamentals. There are basically two types of municipal bonds. *General obligation bonds* normally are backed by the full faith, credit, and taxing power of the state or municipality that issues them. Both the principal and interest on such bonds are virtually guaranteed by the ability of the state or city to tap tax revenues as necessary to pay off its obligations.

Revenue bonds are issued to finance specific projects — toll roads, bridges, power projects, hospitals, various utilities, and the like. The principal and interest on such bonds are payable solely from the revenues collected on such projects. There are a few "double-barrel" bonds where the state promises backing in addition to the project revenues. But this is not usual.

Most municipals are quoted in terms of their yield. For instance, you might be told a certain issue, which, let's say, carries a 6.6% coupon rate and matures in 60 months, is currently being offered in the market at a 6.91% yield to maturity. This quotation system makes sense, since yield is the yardstick most bond investors use to judge the relative price of an issue. Your broker would have to check a table, or computer, to determine that at that yield "price" a $1,000 bond would cost you $987. However, some long-term municipals, including many revenue bonds, fall into a category called *dollar bonds* because (like most corporate and government bonds) they are quoted on a dollar price basis; in that case, of course, you know the price you must pay, but must compute the yield you'll receive. Another characteristic of municipals is that most issues mature serially — that is, a certain portion of the total issue falls due each year, and each annual maturity is priced and traded separately. By contrast, an entire dollar bond issue generally matures all on the same date.

The profusion of municipal financing for special purposes — for instance, attracting a job-creating factory by building the plant with tax-exempt money and counting on the corporate operator's lease payments to pay off the bonds — has led Congress to restrict the use of tax-exempt securities, most notably in the Tax Reform Act of 1986. Municipal offerings are now divided into *"governmental use"* and *"private-activity"* bonds.

Allowable private-activity projects include *publicly operated* airports, docks, public transit, electric, gas, and water supply, waste disposal, multifamily rental housing, and certain student loan bonds. But there is a state-by-state cap on the total amount of such issues that can qualify for tax exemption each year. And buyers of such private activity bonds issued after August 7, 1986, must consider their interest a tax preference for Alternate Minimum Tax purposes.

Most bonds for industrial parks, air- and water-pollution control, sports stadiums, and convention halls can no longer get tax exemption. However, state and local government units may still want to finance these projects because they feel the community benefits offset the higher financing costs they must assume. Such municipal issues may still have an advantage over corporate bonds, especially in high-tax states, because no state income tax is imposed. Thus, in 1993 a total of $12.3 billion taxable municipals was issued, representing 3.6% of total municipal financing.

Like corporate bonds, many municipal bond issues are rated by the major investment services like Moody's and Standard & Poor's. And, as in corporates, there are some low-rated "junk bonds" (especially those dependent on revenues from projects with uncertain prospects) whose high yields attract some people despite the correspondingly high risks. Particularly when buying municipal mutual funds, consider whether the fund's portfolio matches the safety or risk standards you are seeking.

In general, municipal bonds have a very good safety record. The general obligations are backed by taxing power. But shockwaves reverberated throughout the municipals world when in 1975 New York City could not pay off maturing obligations. A moratorium was declared and in time most holders of the affected securities grudgingly accepted conversion to issues of the Municipal Assistance Corporation (Big MAC) that the State of New York established as part of the rescue operation.

While a number of specialized revenue projects have had problems — particularly some that in effect used tax-free money to build a plant for a company that then defaulted on its rental payments — the great majority of revenue-backed projects have come off well. Among major issuers, the most dramatic exception was the $2.25 billion default by the Washington Public Power Supply System when two nuclear projects had to be abandoned and the courts freed members of the system from their obligations to pay for servicing these bonds.

These rare but dramatic crises led to development of bond insurance. To provide extra assurance — and obtain top ratings from Moody's and Standard & Poor's — roughly 35% of new issues today are insured by one of the handful of private bond insurers that have sprung up since the 1970s. Originally the premium for such insurance was reflected by as much as .25% to .5% lower interest yield than comparable uninsured issues; with active competition, the premium now amounts to only a few basis points.

In the past, most municipal bonds were bearer bonds. But since July 1983, all newly issued bonds must be in registered form, like stocks. In many cases, no bond certificate is issued at all; the bonds are issued and transferred by book entry on the computers of a financial industry agency called the Depository Trust Company.

Municipal bonds are bought by banks and fire and casualty insurance companies, but individuals constitute the single biggest market because of that all-important tax-exemption feature. Indeed, in 1992, what the government statisticians call "households" held 52% of all municipal issues, while mutual funds including money market funds held another 14%.

Zero coupon bonds have also found a welcome in the municipals

Table 8-1: The Value of Federal Tax Exemption

Based on 1994 Tax Rates

Joint Return With Net Taxable Income up to:	Single Return	Your Federal Tax Bracket:	TO MATCH A TAX-FREE RETURN OF: YOU WOULD HAVE TO EARN THIS MUCH:												
			2.00%	3.00%	4.00%	4.50%	5.00%	5.50%	6.00%	6.50%	7.00%	7.50%	8.00%	8.50%	9.00%
$38,000	$22,750	15%	2.3%	3.5%	4.7%	5.2%	5.8%	6.4%	7.0%	7.6%	8.2%	8.8%	9.4%	10.0%	10.5%
$89,150	$55,100	28%	2.7%	4.1%	5.5%	6.3%	6.9%	7.6%	8.3%	9.0%	9.7%	10.4%	11.1%	11.8%	12.5%
$140,000	$115,000	31%	2.9%	4.3%	5.8%	6.5%	7.2%	7.9%	8.7%	9.4%	10.1%	10.8%	11.5%	12.3%	13.0%
$250,000	$250,000	36%	3.1%	4.6%	6.2%	7.0%	7.8%	8.5%	9.3%	10.1%	10.9%	11.7%	12.5%	13.2%	14.0%
over $250,000	over $250,000	39.6%	3.3%	4.9%	6.6%	7.4%	8.2%	9.1%	9.9%	10.7%	11.5%	12.4%	13.2%	14.0%	14.9%

Calculations are before possible additional benefits from State and Local tax exemptions   Courtesy: Lebenthal & Co., Inc.

market. Since interest is tax-exempt, holders don't have to worry about the "phantom interest" that can be imposed on holders of zero corporate and government bonds. One popular use of zero municipals is to purchase them in the name of children, with maturity timed to coincide with college entrance.

The proliferation of municipal bond mutual funds (and unit investment trusts as well) has facilitated participation by investors wishing to place moderate amounts into municipals. Many accounts can be opened with $1,000, and they provide ready diversification and liquidity — it's easy for holders to sell when they want to get out.

There are also many municipal money market funds, invested in short-term municipals, for investors who want to have some of their cash reserves earn tax-exempt income.

The table on page 69 shows just what return an individual at various income levels would have to earn on stocks or other taxable investments in order to retain the same amount after federal income taxes that he or she could realize from tax-exempt municipal bonds. These figures are based on tax rates as they existed at the start of 1994.

While rates may continue to change, the table is intended to illustrate the basic principles of assessing yield differentials. You should be able to obtain an up-to-date table — and one that includes the impact of your state's taxes — from your broker or bank when you are ready to invest.

CHAPTER 9

What You Should Know about the New York Stock Exchange

THE stocks of the biggest and best-known corporations in America — and nowadays many corporate giants from around the world — are bought and sold on the *New York Stock Exchange*. In early 1994, the stocks of more than 2,400 companies, including 159 foreign companies, were *listed* on the NYSE, frequently called the *Big Board*. And if you hear anyone in the U.S. speak of "the Stock Exchange," you can bet the reference is to the New York exchange and not one of the smaller stock exchanges.

Trading volume has expanded spectacularly since 1947, when less than a million shares were traded on an average day. By the late sixties it regularly topped 10 million shares a day. The first 100-million-share day came in August 1982, and ever since 1985 the *average* daily volume has exceeded 100 million. The all-time high was 608 million shares on October 20, 1987, in the turmoil following the Dow Jones Industrial Average's 508-point plunge on October 19 — a 604-million-share day. These were by far the two most active days to date, but volume for all of 1987 averaged 188 million shares and, after averaging around 160 to 165 million shares daily in the quieter markets of 1988–1990, it soared again, reaching a record of 264 million per day in 1993, and 312 million for the first quarter of 1994. What's more, the stock exchange has geared up so it can handle billion-share days.

True, the explosive growth in trading volume largely reflects the big jump in institutional business. In 1993, this accounted for 44% of all

Big Board volume (it had been as high as 52% in 1988). Another 24% represented trading by NYSE members themselves, much of it as part of their *marketmaking* function (a vital role we'll discuss in chapter 11; essentially, it means that they stand ready to sell and buy stock in response to customers' buy and sell orders). But it bears remembering that this leaves 32% in so-called retail volume — which means that on a 260-million-share day, individual investors, small businesses, and the like typically place orders both to buy and to sell around 80 million shares — a figure far exceeding *total volume* anytime before the 1980s.

A 200-million-share day is likely to represent roughly $9 billion worth of stock. With so much money constantly at stake, the New York Stock Exchange stands as one of the most publicized institutions in the world, the very symbol of American capitalism.

Which doesn't mean that people really understand it. You might still call it "a business nobody knows — but everybody talks about." Back in 1939, when Wall Street still was shellshocked from the Depression, the exchange had famed pollster Elmo Roper conduct a public opinion survey — and one in eleven people actually thought the stock exchange dealt in cattle.

Such confusion with the Chicago Stockyards is probably gone now (as are most of the stockyards). But you still find people who think the stock exchange *sells* stock. It doesn't. It doesn't own any, sell any, buy any. If stocks sold on the exchange lose or gain a billion dollars in the aggregate on a given day, the exchange itself neither loses nor gains a nickel. It is simply a marketplace where thousands of people and institutions buy and sell stocks every day through their agents, the brokers.

Nor does the stock exchange set the price at which any of those stocks is bought or sold. The prices are arrived at in a two-way auction system. Each buyer competes with other buyers for the lowest price, and each seller competes with other sellers for the highest price. Hence, the stock exchange boasts that it's the freest free market in the world, the one with the least impediments to the free interplay of supply and demand.

Perhaps you've heard that the stock market is "rigged," that big operators drive prices up or hammer them down to suit themselves and make a profit at the little guy's expense. The history books tell us of the "robber baron" days after the Civil War when manipulators regularly tried to "corner" markets (snap up all the available supply of a stock) and defraud each other as well as the public. Then there were the wild excesses of the 1920s when big market operators resorted to "bear raids" (driving a stock's price down so they could pick it up at bargain prices) and many other questionable devices.

As anyone reading headlines knows, we haven't got rid of all the wheelers and dealers. You'll still find scandals on Wall Street, as you do in most areas of human endeavor.

But it's getting harder to get away with questionable practices that once stirred up only helpless rage. There are now laws, stringent laws, to prevent price manipulation, and also insider trading (which at one time was considered a routine "perk" for someone active in business or finance, and in some countries still is). And they are vigorously enforced by the Securities and Exchange Commission, as well as by U.S. Attorneys pursuing criminal charges. What's more, the fact that convicted offenders such as Ivan Boesky, Dennis Levine, and Michael Milken were not only required to pay heavy fines but sentenced to substantial jail time must serve as a strong deterrent.

The powers of the SEC, established in 1934, have been repeatedly broadened and strengthened by a series of additional securities laws passed since 1964. Thus the commission is in position to supervise the markets more closely and to enforce its rules and regulations more rigorously.

Actually, the commission leaves much of the regulatory work in the hands of the exchange, which, in turn, clamps down on its members and the firms they represent. When you see "Member New York Stock Exchange" on the door or letterhead of a securities firm, at least one partner or employee holds a membership on the exchange, and the firm itself is subject to the rules and discipline of the exchange. The NYSE rules are generally designed to prevent unfair trading practices and protect the individual investor. Like the securities laws, they have been repeatedly tightened since the 1930s. There is probably no business in the world that operates under more stringent regulation or with a stricter self-imposed code of ethics than the modern-day New York Stock Exchange.

For instance, the exchange has a computerized stock-watching service that keeps under constant surveillance the price and volume movements of all stocks traded on the exchange. The computer is programmed to flag automatically any unusual movements in a stock. These indications are followed up by investigators. Sometimes a rumor can make a stock "act up." Is there anything to it? If not, the exchange takes immediate steps to scotch the rumor. Sometimes it asks the company itself to clarify the facts in the situation and announce them to the public. And if the computer turns up evidence of illegal manipulation, the exchange turns those facts over to the SEC for action.

All the rules and policing efforts aim to assure a free and fair market — but that doesn't necessarily mean a quiet one. Stock prices can and do fluctuate sharply — they dropped 45% in 1973–1974 and 36% in three and a half months in 1987. What's undoubtedly most memorable about that 1987 slide is the 22% collapse on October 19 — by far the biggest single-day decline ever; in fact, nearly double the worst day of 1929. *Volatility*, as measured in sharp short-term movements up and down, has increased substantially as big institutions seek to eke out higher returns on the money entrusted to them. Over any longer term, however, price movements tend to reflect the prevailing optimism or pessimism of shareowners about what lies ahead for the economy in general as well as for specific companies.

Along with tighter rules for the markets, standards have also been raised over the years for companies that want to list their stock on the Big Board — a privilege for which, incidentally, they must pay an initial listing fee of $36,800, plus a per-share charge ranging from $14,750 per million for the first two million shares listed to $1,900 for each million shares above $300 million. Then they must pay annual charges of $1,650 for each of the first two million and $830 for each additional million shares. While the exchange "decides each [application] on its merits," the normal minimum qualifications in effect in 1993 included:

(1) 2,000 holders of *round lots* (that is, 100 shares or more). The round-lot requirement can be waived if *total* shareholders number at least 2,200 *and* trading in the stock over the previous six months averaged 100,000 shares a month.
(2) 1,100,000 common shares in public hands.
(3) $18 million market value for the publicly owned shares.
(4) Annual earnings of $2.5 million before taxes in the most recent year and $2 million in each of the two preceding years — however, if the latest year's earnings were at least $4.5 million, earnings in one of the two previous years can be lower so long as *total* earnings for the three years come to $6.5 million.
(5) Net tangible assets of $18 million.

Most listed companies exceed these minimums by a wide margin. Ever since the 1920s American Telephone & Telegraph (now AT&T Corp.) has been the most widely held U.S. company. It had approximately 2.4 million direct shareholders in 1993, plus an estimated half million more who held their stock in "street name." Exxon held the lead in total market value in early 1994; its common shares had an aggregate value of $114 billion, followed by General Electric with $92 billion, then AT&T and Coca-Cola ($63 billion each). In fifth spot was Wal-Mart Stores ($60 billion), whose 2.3 billion shares made it the company with the largest number of shares listed on the Big Board.

Not all companies prosper, of course. That's why the exchange has a set of minimum standards it expects companies to meet to keep their stock listed. A company may be *delisted* if the number of shares in public hands drops below 600,000 or their market value falls below $5 million; also there should be at least 1,200 round-lot shareholders.

These mathematical standards are not the only basis for delisting. In recent years, companies have been delisted because management refused to give equitable voting rights to holders of its common stock, or because of consistent failure to produce timely and meaningful financial reports. Indeed, the exchange may suspend or delist at any time a security whose continued trading it no longer considers advisable, even though that security still meets listing standards. However, the overwhelming majority of Big Board departures stem from mergers, acquisitions, or buyouts.

A listed company must agree not to issue any additional shares without exchange approval. It must have a qualified independent *registrar* to see that no more shares of stock are issued than a company has authority to sell. It must also have a *transfer agent* who keeps an exact record of all stockholders and the number of shares owned.

Listed companies must also agree to issue an annual report, and to publish promptly any important corporate news, including quarterly financial results and all dividend actions (or any decision to omit a dividend). Many requirements parallel filing requirements by the SEC — and copies of all reports to the SEC must also be filed at the stock exchange.

And what about the organization that plays host to the stocks of all these companies? How is the exchange itself set up?

The business of trading in stocks in New York goes way back to the early eighteenth century, when merchants and auctioneers used to congregate at the foot of Wall Street to buy and sell not only stocks but wheat, tobacco, and other commodities, including slaves.

Then, in 1792, two dozen merchants who met daily under a button-wood (sycamore) tree on Wall Street to trade various stocks agreed from then on to deal only with each other and to charge their customers a fixed commission. Thus began the New York Stock Exchange, although the name itself was not adopted until 1863.

Long organized as a "voluntary association," the exchange was incorporated in 1971 as a not-for-profit corporation. In good part the action was taken to relieve officers and directors of potential individual liability in the event of lawsuits against the exchange, and for other legal considerations. But the incorporation and a series of reorganizations over the years also reflect the steady, if not always voluntary, move from the old "private club" traditions to an organization more alert to the interests of its various constituencies — listed companies, investors, the nation as a whole — and not just the various categories of exchange members.

How do you become a member of the exchange? You buy one of the 1,366 *seats*, subject to approval by the exchange's board of directors. Since nobody but a mailman is on his feet more continuously than a floor broker, "seat" is a classic misnomer. It had its origin in the leisurely days of 1793 when the new association took up quarters in the Tontine Coffee House and the members were seated as they transacted business by auction, one security at a time.

What does a seat cost? That, like the price of a stock, is a matter of what a buyer is willing to pay and a holder is willing to accept. And that, in turn, depends on how good business is on the exchange at the time of the sale. In 1929, seats were sold for $625,000 each. Later, the number of seats was increased by 25%; adjustment for that "split" would make that price an even $500,000. It is hard to believe prices could ever fall again to the low they hit in 1942, when a seat was sold for $17,000 — less than the amount given today as a gift to the family of a deceased member out of the exchange's *gratuity fund*. In September 1987, a seat changed hands for $1,150,000, then dropped to an eight-year low of $250,000 in 1990, before starting to recover. In March 1994 a seat sold for $830,000.

While each membership seat must technically belong to the individual member, it is often financed by a member organization for one of its employees. Usually it's done through a so-called ABC agreement under which the new member agrees to relinquish the seat upon leaving the sponsor's employ. Incidentally, until 1953, all the member firms doing business on the exchange had to be partnerships. Now more than three-quarters are corporations, and the official term for both partnerships and corporations is *member organization*.

The Big Board members can perform a number of different functions — but, to avoid conflicts of interest, are not permitted to trade for their own account and at the same time deal with the public.

At last count, close to 500 members belonged to the 315 member firms that deal with the public — what you think of when someone speaks of a "brokerage firm." Most of these *commission brokers* handle the orders of their firm's customers on the exchange floor, and therefore are also often called the firm's *floor brokers*.

However, while at least one employee in the brokerage firm must hold a membership to give the firm direct access to trading on the exchange, this member need not actually work on the floor. Seat-holders may be senior executives of the firm, or hold a sales or adminis-trative job; because they're not on the floor, they are sometimes called *office members*. A member firm without its own active floor broker may arrange to have all its customers' orders executed through a larger firm. Or it may pass on its orders to one of the so-called $2 *brokers* (in recognition of what used to be their standard fee). There are about 500 $2 brokers (also formally called *floor brokers*), handling orders for other brokers — overflow business from firms whose own brokers are too busy, as well as the orders from firms lacking their own floor representatives.

Then there are about 400 *specialists* who, working as individuals or as part of specialist units, are assigned responsibility for maintaining markets in specific stocks. (We'll discuss their function in chapter 11.)

Finally there is a small group of about 12 *registered competitive market makers* as well as 4 *registered competitive traders,* who, to a limited extent, carry on the tradition of the old floor traders, buying and selling stocks wholly for themselves. Because, by virtue of their membership in the exchange, floor traders pay no commissions, they have been able to make money by moving in and out of the market, trying to make a quarter of a point here, an eighth of a point there, usually in the most active stocks. The SEC has long argued that such floor traders performed no useful economic function and should be phased out. The exchange has resisted this argument, but has come up with rules providing that these market makers and traders must direct their activities primarily toward helping stabilize or adding liquidity to the market. Rules also seek to make sure that these traders, who now account for under 1% of total volume, enjoy no advantage over the public.

Since 1977 it has been possible to get on the exchange without buying a seat outright. Members who are not using their seat themselves now have the right to lease it to others, but the renter must be approved by the Big Board directors just like a prospective new member. Leasing has become so popular that about 570 seats (two-fifth of the total) are currently leased under these arrangements, which can provide income for retired members, heirs, estates, or some who just hold the seat as an investment.

Also since 1977 the exchange has made available some *limited memberships*, which, in return for an annual fee, entitle you to *either* physical or electronic access to the exchange floor. In early 1994 there were 50 such members.

To provide widespread access to the Big Board market, the member organizations that deal with the public operate some 8,000 offices throughout the United States and a couple of hundred offices abroad. All sorts of modern communications devices keep all the offices of these brokerage firms in almost instantaneous touch with the exchange. As a result, the person who has an office next door to the exchange has no advantage in contacting his or her broker over someone who lives 3,000 miles away.

CHAPTER **10**

What It Costs to Buy Stocks

FROM the time the New York Stock Exchange was founded in 1792 until May 1, 1975, any broker in the business could have told you to the penny just how much commission you would have to pay on the purchase or sale of 100 shares or 1,000 shares of any listed stock. It was all very simple because those two dozen founding fathers of the New York Stock Exchange had agreed from the outset to charge the same commission on any security transaction. They had further agreed to deal only with each other — no outsiders admitted. For more than 180 years, the succeeding members of the New York Stock Exchange maintained that tight little monopoly. Technically, what was set were *minimum* commissions, so a few "white shoe" houses might charge more, but you could pretty much count on the minimum being the standard at just about any major brokerage house.

Then came *"Mayday"* 1975 when, by order of the Securities and Exchange Commission, fixed commissions became history.

So how much will it cost you to buy stocks today in this new era of competitive commissions?

There are several different answers to that.

The first is — a lot less than you probably think, especially if you are thinking in terms of the 6 percent and up commission you might pay on a real estate transaction, or the even higher up-front commissions often allocated to sellers of life insurance and many other products. Indeed, you'd be hard pressed to find any goods or services of comparable value that change hands at as low a commission cost as stocks. And that's held true, whether commissions were fixed or unfixed.

The second and more realistic answer is that the amount of commission you pay is going to vary with the total dollar value of your transaction. The number of round lots (100-share units) involved also plays a role; you can expect to pay more for 200 shares of a $25 stock than for 100 shares at $50, though both are $5,000 orders. Very roughly, if your transaction is a modest one — say, an investment of $2,000 or $3,000 — the commission is apt to be somewhere near 3% to 3.5% from a full-service broker. If your investment reaches $5,000, the commission may come down to around 2%. And by $20,000, it could be in the 1.5% range.

Despite the outlawing of fixed commissions, don't be surprised if you find three or four full-service firms all quoting you pretty much the same commission on moderate size transactions. It may well pay you to shop around, however, if you are talking big money — like $25,000 or $50,000. In general, what you want to look for is a firm that will best accommodate your *pattern of trading*. If, for instance, you trade several hundred shares maybe half a dozen to a dozen times a year, you should find a number of firms prepared to negotiate.

Besides charging you a commission, brokerage firms may also impose various service charges. Some may tack a postage and handling charge on to each order. Some may charge for keeping your stocks for you, especially if your account is "inactive," and a few even add a further charge for collecting dividends for you.

Of course, if you are a good customer, your broker might be willing to waive such service charges just as the firm might offer you a commission discount to hold your business. But remember, no firm wants to hold 100 shares of stock for you year after year, credit dividends to your account, and send you regular statements — all of which costs quite a bit of money — unless the firm gets some financial reward out of it.

Most full-service firms are quite liberal about supplying research services, though a few may charge for statistical reports you request on individual companies — especially if they pass on printed reports they themselves buy from one of the large research services. Some may also impose a fee if you want a detailed analysis of your holdings in a number of companies and how they fit your current objectives — though most firms would probably be delighted to get a look at your full portfolio and have the opportunity to recommend changes.

So, when you go shopping for a broker, don't just ask about commission rates. Ask about services available — and what each of them will cost.

Availability of different service levels at different costs is another fruit of the Mayday revolution. In the pre-1975 era, some defenders of the established system argued that fixed commissions made it possible to include a wide range of services that were important to investors. Such arguments failed to persuade proponents of change. They certainly didn't impress the SEC and the Justice Department, who felt strongly that no customers should be forced to pay for services they might not want, and called for *unbundling* — hanging specific price tags on all the services that a broker may render. Competitive commissions have, in effect, settled that argument. Brokers are free to offer service packages or charge separate fees, and customers can shop for the service and price they want.

One thing to remember is that some brokers may be willing to execute a small order for you, even if it costs them more than the commission you pay, in the hope that somewhere down the line you will become a more substantial customer, maybe even a big trader. But many brokers, probably most of them, aren't willing to take that gamble. They are interested in the big-ticket client — and their commission schedules reflect that preference. For people planning occasional, small-size orders, even firms seeking a broad customer base may suggest either a special type of account designed for them or investing in mutual funds.

What it all adds up to: Today you can get as much or as little as you want and are willing to pay for, so it pays to find your kind of broker. If you are an investor who makes up your own mind about what you want to buy or sell — a person who doesn't want any advice or help from a broker — you might as well take your order to one of the scores of discount, or "no frill," brokers who have sprung up all over the country. These brokers will buy or sell stock for you at savings that can be significant. But that is all many will do for you. They will not provide you with research reports on potential investments. They will not advise you on which stocks to buy and sell. They will not sit down with you for a long, friendly chat on your investment objectives. They will simply execute the buy or sell directives you give them.

On the other hand, you may want or need a good deal of help — maybe even a little psychological support. If you're that kind of person, then the old-line full-service brokers will happily give you everything you want — at a price.

Actually, by now there are also considerable variations among discount brokers — both in service levels and price. Be careful, though, when evaluating competitive commission charts, whether put out by discount or full-service houses. They are kindred in spirit to the rate charts you see in the now competitive long-distance phone business — the ones that show what different companies will charge for a sample call between a pair of cities at a particular time and duration. You can bet that the phone company putting out the chart will pick examples that put it in the best light. Similarly, some of the huge savings claimed may apply to the kind of trades you're not likely to make. In fact, for some small orders, one of the big full-service companies may have the lowest rate.

Another consideration that applies to both full-service and discount brokers is quality. It hardly pays to save a few commission dollars if your order is executed poorly or your account messed up. But admittedly, quality is hard to judge; what's more, quality and price are not necessarily related.

So while you're shopping around for a broker and collecting commission rate schedules, consider what each broker's service is going to cost you, including service charges, and how it fits your needs.

While you are looking for a broker, you may find yourself wondering what brought this revolution to Wall Street. For almost 200 years you had to pay the same minimum commission no matter what member firm you dealt with. So what finally brought competition, or, as one outspoken Wall Streeter put it, induced this bastion of capitalism to practice capitalism?

It all began in the 1950s, when big-money institutions — banks, insurance companies, foundations, trusts — began to realize that common stocks had proved historically good long-term investments, even if they can be volatile over the short term. When such a big institution goes into the market, it's apt to make quite a splash, because it buys and sells stocks in big blocks — by now, 10,000, 50,000, or 100,000-plus shares at a time.

Back in the 1950s and 1960s all commission charges on the New York Stock Exchange were based on 100 shares, a round lot. If somebody wanted to buy 5,000 shares of stock, he paid 50 times the fixed round-lot commission. For 10,000 shares, it was 100 times the round-lot commission.

That didn't make much sense to the institutions. They felt they deserved a commission break on their big-volume business. There were some ways to circumvent the full impact of the commission rule, in particular the *give-up* under which the firm executing the trade could share its commission with another *member* firm. The institutions quickly learned to use the give-up, *directing* their brokers to pass on designated portions of the commissions to firms that were supplying the institutions with research or other specialized services. Even statistical manuals, quotation machines, and other equipment managed to get paid for through give-ups. And mutual funds, in particular, used give-ups extensively to compensate retail brokerage firms for selling fund shares to their customers.

But while regulators and competitors fretted about abuses spawned by give-ups, the big institutions considered this system at best a cumbersome and insufficient palliative. They wanted a better way to trade blocks of stock — more directly, quickly, and cheaply. They found it — outside the New York Stock Exchange. They found that there were big securities dealers — firms like Weeden & Co. that were not members of the exchange, hence not bound by its commission rules — who were quite willing to trade big blocks of stock for reduced rates. These firms would buy, or *position*, a block of stock, thousands of shares at a crack, and then assume the risk of reselling the shares, hopefully at a profit, over an extended period of time.

In line with standard over-the-counter practice, such nonmember firms didn't bother with commissions. They bought the stock at a *net price*, a price a little lower than the price prevailing on the exchange but high enough to give the selling institution a better net return than if it had sold the stock on the exchange and paid the required commission.

Thus the *third market* was born. The *first* encompassed listed stocks on the Big Board and the other exchanges; the *second* was the traditional over-the-counter market for stocks that had no exchange listing, a market in which many major exchange members could and did participate. The third market was thus fashioned by taking listed stocks and finding a way to trade them over-the-counter, or, in a new-math equation: first market stocks + second market trading = third market.

Alarmed by the sensational growth of the third market and their loss of institutional business, some of the large member firms in 1966 asked the SEC to order the Big Board to relax the regulatory shackles. First, they asked for an amendment to *Rule 394*. That rule carried on the original 1792 requirement that members execute all orders for listed stocks on the floor of the exchange, effectively preventing any trading with nonmembers or splitting commissions with them. At SEC behest, Rule 394 was modified to permit members to buy or sell off the floor of the exchange — in short, to participate in the third market — *if* they could demonstrate that such a deal would result in a more advantageous trade to the customer.

That amendment helped, but more was needed. In 1969, rates were reduced on orders of 1,000 shares or more. But that still wasn't enough to satisfy the institutions, and some member firms began agitating for total abandonment of fixed commissions, a suggestion that shocked many of the more staid members of the exchange community. In November 1970 came a real bombshell. Robert W. Haack, then president of the New York Stock Exchange, spoke out in favor of letting the law of supply and demand, the rule of free competition, supplant the monopolistic schedule of fixed commissions.

This was heresy, indeed — and from a paid hand at that! And when Merrill Lynch, Pierce, Fenner & Smith, Inc., the world's largest brokerage firm, and Salomon Brothers, a member firm that played a dominant role in handling institutional business, endorsed the no-fixed-commission proposal, the fears of many smaller firms were scarcely allayed. Opposition was particularly strong among the "floor" part of the exchange — the specialists and other members who made their living on the exchange floor, as opposed to the "upstairs" members who represented firms doing business with the public — and they rallied in what they called the defense of the auction market.

But market forces — backed with increasing insistence by the SEC, the Justice Department, and Congress — inexorably dictated that if the Big Board wanted to compete it would have to become competitive. The SEC ruled that as of April 1971, rates on orders involving $500,000 or more should be set by bargaining between customer and broker. The next year the limit was lowered to $300,000.

Then in September 1973 the SEC decided the time had come to go all out; it ordered the abandonment of all fixed commissions on all exchanges, effective May 1, 1975. As an interim step it also ordered that by April 1974 rates on orders under $2,000 could no longer be fixed. While few member firms cared to take advantage of this small-investor exemption, Wall Street's largest firm, Merrill Lynch, provided momentum by promptly announcing reduced rates for its special ShareBuilder Plan.

Some three weeks after the 1975 Mayday, Congress passed major securities legislation that put its stamp of approval on competitive commissions. Further, it directed the SEC to push for a *national market system*. Such a system would provide competition among the various *markets* where a stock traded, thus assuring each buyer or seller, on each transaction, of the best price available anywhere, including over-the-counter. While the full-fledged national market envisaged by its advocates has not materialized, the *Intermarket Trading System*, started in 1978, does *expose* (Wall Street's legalistic term for having an order submitted to the public market) each order to price competition from the other markets.

The SEC heeded another call for increased competition — this time on the exchange floor itself. It decreed that as of May 1976 the commissions that brokers charge each other for handling transactions on the floor must also become negotiable rather than prescribed by a fixed-fee schedule. While these floor commissions are paid by the brokerage firms and not the customers, investors presumably stand to benefit since any transaction costs must, in the end, be borne by them.

Meantime, the 1975 securities act had also effectively settled the issue of whether institutional investors should be permitted to become members of the New York Stock Exchange. During the fight over commissions, some institutions wanted to buy seats on the exchange so they could buy and sell stocks directly on the floor (or at the low rates that members charged other members). Such membership by someone not primarily engaged in the stock and bond business was of course against the exchange rules, but the threat added to the pressure on the exchange. However, the new law barred exchange members from handling transactions for any affiliated company or institution — thus, even if an institution could gain membership, it wouldn't serve its purpose. But if institutions lost this battle, they had already won the war — after all, the demand for seats was only a ploy to win low commissions.

Where do the revolutionary changes on the exchange and the brave new world of free competition leave the brokerage firms? In many ways, their world has also been revolutionized. It was freely predicted that, while the big and *efficient* firms were likely to grow bigger and more prosperous, many others, without the protection of the fixed-rate schedule, would either be swallowed up by their big competitors or fall by the wayside. Indeed, in the years since Mayday, scores of firms have closed their doors and many others, big and small, have been taken over by stronger firms.

In line with these trends, you can find a good many Wall Street observers who expect that only a comparative handful of brokerage firms will be doing business by the end of the century. However, many others are confident that the future remains bright for efficient, well-managed small firms that find a specialized niche where they can deliver superior service.

At the same time, the big brokerage firms with their worldwide networks of offices have found little opportunity to just sit back and count the commission dollars rolling in. Competition has hit with a vengeance — not only from within the securities industry, but even more from increasingly aggressive banks and other financial institutions. Institutional commissions have been shaved to almost microscopic levels. Operating costs keep rising. And the stock brokerage business has always had feast-or-famine characteristics, with wide and unpredictable fluctuations in trading volume, which require maintaining facilities that are fully utilized only at peak times.

Many of the large firms sought to build a broader, more stable base and enhance their growth through active diversification. Starting in the mid-1970s, Merrill Lynch, often an industry innovator, ventured into insurance, real estate, merchant banking abroad, and investment counseling, and many major competitors undertook similar moves. But, as in many other industries, diversification seemed less attractive by the mid-1980s, and a number of companies, including Merrill Lynch, began to retreat from some of the new ventures.

In recent years most of the big players have focused on building up their prowess in what is known as the *capital markets*, generally on a global scale. This part of the financial services business encompasses the ability to trade big blocks of securities, to handle all aspects of investment banking, including mergers and acquisitions, and, increasingly, *merchant banking*. While traditional investment banking concentrates on raising capital for clients from outside investors, in merchant banking the investment firm is a direct participant in corporate deals, risking its own capital to help finance mergers, takeovers, restructurings, and the like. All these operations require immense amounts of capital, which explains why the securities firms in this game must be big (and often feel they must get bigger) and why, even then, they want to shed extraneous endeavors and concentrate their capital on the most profitable areas.

The all-pervasive demand for capital has also led to a number of prominent Wall Street firms being acquired by well-heeled corporations in other fields such as American Express, Prudential Insurance, Sears, and General Electric.

Where does all this leave the individual investor? Despite Wall Street's revolution, despite the ever-growing dominance of the big institutional customers in the stock market — a trend that is apt to continue — individual investors should still be able to count on doing business with their friendly broker (or, if they choose, a no-frills discounter) in almost any bigger-than-average town in the United States, and, through the ubiquitous "800" numbers, from any phone anywhere in the country. With the steady cost squeeze felt by securities firms, the prices paid by individual investors — for each given level of service — have, despite intense competition, more often sloped up than down. But that should enhance the likelihood that their full-service broker will get friendlier and friendlier as the new competition among member firms grows yet keener in the years ahead.

CHAPTER 11

How the Stock Exchange Works

TIME was when, say, a small-town lawyer in Georgia with a hankering for 100 shares of Coca-Cola would saunter down to his branch of a stock exchange firm (or a local firm that served as a *correspondent* for some big New York brokerage house). He'd watch a young boardmarker chalk stock prices onto the green-tinted board on the front wall of the *board room* as he discussed his plans with his broker, then commonly called a *customer's man*. The broker took the order to the branch's telegraph operator, whose fleet fingers Morse-coded the instructions to the New York office. Clerks there phoned the message to one of the firm's clerks on the exchange floor, who in turn passed it on to the firm's floor broker. The floor broker would then walk briskly — exchange rules forbid running — to the trading post designated for Coca-Cola transactions and buy 100 shares for the customer at the best price he could. Then a report would go back along this communications chain to the branch office and the customer.

Today, customers usually phone their broker (now a *registered representative* in the eyes of the SEC, and endowed with a title such as *account executive* or *financial consultant* by his or her firm). With a computer console at their desk, the brokers can quickly give the customers the latest stock prices or call up other pertinent information. Once an order is given, it will usually go by computer transmission from the branch office directly to the trading post where it is quickly executed at the best available price, with the report instantly flashed back to the office.

But with all the revolutionary changes in placing and executing an order, the basic principle remains intact. Each buy or sell order is exposed to the public auction process, designed to assure each buyer and seller that they received the best price available at the time.

True, the boardmarkers and Morse operators are long gone from brokerage offices, along with the once-familiar glass-domed tickers that clattered out stock exchange prices. But the traditional procedures for filling an order on the exchange floor still form the basis for today's transactions, even though the vast majority of individual orders now ride an electronic express called SuperDot that bypasses most of the old routine way stations.

To understand what happens to an order on the exchange floor, let's first consider the physical layout of the New York Stock Exchange, a large building at the corner of Wall and Broad streets in New York City, catercorner from Federal Hall where President Washington took the oath of office in 1789. The main trading room alone, under a 79-foot-high ceiling, could readily accommodate three full-size basketball courts, and there's additional stock trading space in two adjoining rooms, the "Garage" and the Blue Room. After a major expansion of the Blue Room, completed in early 1988, the total *trading floor* now covers 37,000 square feet.

Around the periphery of the trading areas are *telephone booths,* mostly just called *booths,* and now also jammed with teletype and other communications equipment. The "booths" are really narrow, partitioned workstations for clerks representing the various brokerage firms. They used to be the key communications link between brokerage office and trading floor, but, as we've already indicated, many routine orders bypass the booths entirely in this computerized era.

The unquestioned focal points of the trading rooms are the 17 *trading posts* — seven in the main room, four in the Garage, and six in the Blue Room. The trading posts now are made up of two facing, slightly bent-in semicircles. The new-style posts, fitted with a dazzling array of electronic equipment and occupying either 278 or 397 square feet, were phased in between 1979 and 1981. They replaced the smaller (about 100 square feet) but more numerous horseshoe-shaped posts that the exchange had used since 1929 and, on their retirement, donated to various museums across the country.

All buying and selling is done around the outside of the trading post. Between 100 and 150 different stocks are assigned to each post. They are further assigned to different sections around the perimeter — generally about 10 stocks per section, though some active issues like AT&T and IBM have a section all to themselves.

Thus, any broker with an order to buy or sell would head for the particular section where he knows he will find all the other brokers with orders for that stock. (Once a bastion of male chauvinism, the stock market community has, since the first edition of this book was published, become considerably more enlightened in offering career opportunities to women. Despite the fact that there are more and more women turning up in positions of responsibility on Wall Street every day, however, we are using the masculine pronoun here to keep descriptions simple.)

Most important, that's where the *specialist* for that stock would be. Specialists are exchange members who, according to one Big Board description, act as "dealers, agents, auctioneers, and catalysts" and thus "stand at the heart of the market." Each specialist confines his buying and selling activities to a particular stock or stocks. He is always at the post to accept orders for these stocks from other brokers and to assume responsibility for execution of these orders.

In addition, the specialist must be willing to buy and sell for his own account the stocks in which he specializes in order to fulfill his primary responsibility: to maintain a "fair and orderly market" in these stocks. He is also the key player in the workings of the new, automation-speeded order handling system (more on that in the next chapter).

The specialist system literally got its start by accident. An exchange member named James Boyd, while recuperating from a broken leg in 1875, decided to take a chair to the same spot on the floor each day and trade there only in Western Union, one of the most popular stocks of the day. Soon other brokers with orders that could not be filled right away left them with Boyd for execution, and the idea of a specialist for a particular stock took root.

As of 1994, approximately 430 members of the exchange operated as specialists, working in 40 separate specialist organizations, or *units*, that handle the stocks of all the companies listed on the exchange. Some big specialist units handle as many as 150 stocks; some only a few.

Now that we've met some of the key players on the exchange floor, let's take a look at the process by which customer orders are filled. We'll first trace the steps of the traditional process, before describing the shortcut route nearly all orders follow now.

Let's assume that with the passage of years Rod & Reel, Inc., has grown to the extent that its stock is listed on the Big Board and that your 100-share order has just arrived at the exchange floor booth of your brokerage firm. The clerk at the booth hands the order to his floor broker to execute. If the broker is not at the booth, the clerk can summon him by an electronic pager, or beeper. Formerly, the clerk pushed a button in the firm's booth and the broker's identification number flashed on the huge annunciator boards which dominated walls in each of the trading rooms. The boards, a familiar sight in many not-so-old pictures of the trading area, went dark in 1981.

With the order in hand, the floor broker would head promptly for Post 7 — the trading post to which, we'll say, Rod & Reel has been assigned . . . along with 103 other issues including Exxon and Bristol-Myers.

Let's further assume that your order is a *market order* to buy 100 shares of Rod & Reel. A market order means the broker is to execute it as soon as he can, at the best price he can get; the customer is willing to accept whatever that price proves to be.

Today the approaching broker can learn from the computer screen above the post not only that the last sale of Rod & Reel took place at 18¾, or $18.75 a share, but, more important, since the market can change instantly, that the present bid-ask for the stock is 18⅜–18¾. This means that 18⅜ is the best bid, the most anyone in the market is then willing to pay, and 18¾ is the best offer, the lowest anyone will sell for. Until a few years ago, the manually operated display boards at the post would only show the latest price, so the traditional opening query by a floor broker as he entered the *"crowd"* of brokers — two, three, or more may be at the trading position along with the specialist — would have been, "How's Reel?" That way he would give no hint whether he had an order to buy or sell Rod & Reel. In this example, the answer by one of the brokers, or perhaps the specialist, would be a brief "Three-eighths, three-quarters" (the $18 part of the quotation would be understood).

Today's broker might still use the "How's Reel?" opener to elicit a feel for the market, and perhaps draw a lower offer. After the bid-ask is restated, he may wait a few more seconds but then decide he must make a bid. He says, "One-half for a hundred," by which he means that he will pay $18.50 a share for 100 shares.

If he gets no response, he may raise his bid by ⅛ of a point, the minimum fluctuation in the price of most stocks. So he announces, "Five-eighths for one hundred." At this point the first broker, who was offering the stock at 18¾, might just decide he can't get that price. Or perhaps a later arrival in the crowd will decide to accept this bid of 18⅝. If either one of them decides to *"hit"* (accept) the bid, he says, "Sold," and the transaction is concluded, simply on the basis of that spoken word. Conversely, if a broker decides to accept an offering price announced in the course of an auction, he simply says, "Take it."

We've talked so far of a market order — to be executed as soon as possible after it reaches the floor, at the best price then obtainable. That's what most people use when buying or selling stock. However, you may want to buy or sell a stock only if it can be done at a certain price or better. Thus, you might want to buy 100 shares of Rod & Reel *if* you don't have to pay more than 18½. That kind of order is called a *limit order*, and you can specify whether it's good for a day, a week, a month, or "good till canceled." Unless clearly marked for a longer period of time, all limit orders are treated as day orders and canceled if they are not executed by the end of that day's trading.

Take, for example, a Rod & Reel limit order in which the stock will bc bought for you only if it can be purchased at 18½ or less. Perhaps when the order is executed, your broker will be able to get the stock at 18¼, nicely below your limit. On the other hand, the stock might drop to 18½, and your order still wouldn't be filled. That's because other orders to buy at 18½ were entered ahead of yours, and the supply of the stock offered at that price was exhausted before your order was reached. In that kind of situation, if you ask why your order wasn't executed, you'd hear that there was *"stock ahead."*

Limit orders can also be used in selling stock. Thus, if you owned Rod & Reel stock, you might be willing to sell it, but only if you could get $19 for it — or more. You could place a sell-limit order to that effect.

There's still another kind of suspended order: the *stop order*. Suppose you bought Rod & Reel at 12 or 13 and the stock rose to a level at which you had a nice profit — perhaps to 19 or 20. You might want to protect that profit in case the market dropped sharply. You could do so by instructing your broker to sell the stock if it declined to 18. This would be a stop order to sell. It would be executed if Rod & Reel ever fell as low as 18. If and when it hit that mark, your stop order would then become a market order, to be executed at the best price then possible. Again, because other people might have placed orders ahead of yours to sell at the 18 figure, the price might slip to 17¾ or even 17½ before your order could be executed.

Conversely, you might not want to buy Rod & Reel when it was selling at 18 because you felt it might fall further. But on the other hand, if there were a sharp rally, you wouldn't want to miss your opportunity to pick up the stock before its price went up too high. In that case you might place a stop order to buy by instructing your broker to buy Rod & Reel for you at, let's say, 19.

Obviously, when you place a limit or stop order, your brokerage firm's floor broker can't hang around the trading post waiting for the price of the stock to reach the level you specified. So he will leave your order with the specialist for the stock. This is another of the important market-maintaining functions of the specialist.

On each of the stocks in which he specializes, the specialist keeps a book. In this *specialist's book* are entered all the limit or stop orders given him for execution — orders that could not be executed because the specified price was "away from the market."

If a specialist gets two or more orders to buy a stock at the same price — or to sell it at the same price — he enters them in his book in the order in which he receives them. Those that are received first must be executed first, whenever the price auction permits, regardless of all other conditions or circumstances. Thus, if your order for Rod & Reel at, say, 18⅜ was the first one in the specialist's book, if and when any stock was offered at that price, your order would be filled first.

If a broker came to the post and there were no other brokers there with stock to trade, it would be up to the specialist to respond to his "How's Reel?" query by saying, "Three-eighths, three-quarters," if 18⅜ was the highest buy order and 18¾ the lowest sell order then in his book.

Since a specialist's primary responsibility is to try to prevent violent fluctuation in the price of any stock he handles, the specialist is expected to step in and offer to buy or sell stock when the *spread*, or gap between bid and asked prices, becomes too large. At the same time it's a fundamental rule that the specialist cannot buy stock for his own account until every order in his book (and any bid from the "crowd") at that price has been executed. Similarly, he can't sell for his own account until every order at the same price has been executed. In short, whether he buys or sells, he must provide the other party with a better price than any other bid or offer currently available.

With the exchange increasingly focusing on the quality of performance by specialists, the spreads are usually quite narrow. Normally, at any one time, the current bid and ask quotations on 50% of all listed stocks are only ⅛ of a point apart, and on 98% of all stocks the differential is ⅜ of a point or less. A number of the remaining 5% are high-priced and inactively traded issues.

Still another useful service the specialist performs is *stopping a stock* (something entirely different from a stop order). Suppose your broker came to the trading post with your market order for Rod & Reel when the best offering price in the specialist's book was 18⅝ and there were no better offers from anyone in the crowd. Anxious to get a lower price for you, yet not wanting to miss the market if it went up, your broker would ask the specialist to "stop" 100 shares for him at 18⅝. If another broker came up then and offered Rod & Reel at 18½, the specialist would buy it for your broker. On the other hand, if the stock was not offered at a lower price, but sold again the next time at 18⅝, the specialist would execute your buy order at that figure. If no other stock was around at that price, he would sell stock on his own behalf, since he had agreed that 18⅝ would be the maximum price at which your order would be filled. Similarly, a broker can ask the specialist to stop a sell order, guaranteeing a minimum price at which it will be executed.

How does a specialist earn his money? In part, from commissions known as floor brokerage, when he executes orders entrusted him by other brokers. (This commission is paid by the brokerage firm; their customer who placed the order doesn't pay anything extra for the specialist's services.) And in part, from his market-making activities, buying or selling for his own account the stocks in which he is the specialist. In the first instance, he acts as a *broker*, in the second, as a *dealer*. The practical and legal distinction is: A broker bargains *for* you, as your agent. A dealer bargains *with* you, as a principal in the transaction.

The specialist's book certainly gives him a "feel" for the market that no other broker or investor can match — an obvious advantage in making trades. But a specialist isn't free to buy his stock when he thinks it's going up, or sell when he senses it's headed down. After all, his prime obligation is to maintain an orderly market, and increasingly stringent exchange rules and surveillance procedures hold him to strict account.

Computerization now permits a continual record of specialist transactions, including every trade that specialists make for their own account — stating the time, the "tick" (whether up or down in price), and the number of shares involved. The exchange then computes their stabilizing percentage — to what extent they bought on down ticks and sold on up ticks, as they are expected to do most of the time. The exchange also evaluates their effectiveness as measured by each stock's continuity of price and spread in quotations.

Specialists trading for their own account represent close to 10% of total Big Board volume — but the percentage rose to 18% as they attempted to cope with the October 19, 1987, sell avalanche. Despite the frequent need to buy when others are selling, and vice versa (77% of specialists' trades in 1993 qualified as "stabilizing"), the constant fluctuations of the market and their well-developed "feel" for their stocks enable specialists to come out ahead on their trades more often than not. But it's a job that calls for strong nerves and lots of capital.

Minimum capital requirements have been raised repeatedly and steeply. A specialist unit now must have enough funds to buy at least 15,000 shares of each common stock for which the unit is the specialist, but in any case at least $1 million capital.

For the big specialist firms that handle dozens of stocks, this capital requirement comes to tens of millions of dollars. Some specialists rely principally on their own resources. But most supplement their own capital through private financing arrangements. The vast need for capital has also encouraged a few specialist firms to become subsidiaries of one of the giant securities firms, such as Merrill Lynch and Salomon Inc.

As the exchange sees it, these are means of strengthening the specialist system and assuring that it will remain a key component of the Big Board's market of the future.

CHAPTER 12

More about the Workings
of the Stock Exchange

THE rules of the New York Stock Exchange provide that all bids to buy and all offers to sell must be made by *open outcry*. No secret transactions are permitted on the floor of the exchange. Furthermore, a broker cannot conclude transactions between his own public customers without presenting on the floor their orders to buy or sell. For instance, a brokerage firm may have a market order to buy 100 shares of Rod & Reel and another market order to sell 100. It can't just *"cross"* these orders privately and effect a transfer of the stock between its two customers. It must send both orders to the floor, where the appropriate bids and offers must be made — in competition with all other orders then around. Even when, as we shall see in chapter 13, a member firm's trading desk assembles blocks of tens of thousands of shares to be bought and sold, when the order is sent to the floor to be crossed, it must automatically honor all higher bids or lower offers present at that time.

Over the past few decades, some critics in and outside the securities industry have argued that a "blackbox" market, in which all buy and sell orders would be fed into a computer that could automatically match and execute them, would be more efficient and serve investors better than the specialist-centered Big Board system. For its part, the exchange stoutly maintains that its auction system, with the human intervention of a specialist to facilitate the trading, works best. At the same time, the exchange leadership has realized the need for drastic adjustments in the way business is conducted if the Big Board is to maintain its preeminence.

This is particularly evident in the way most routine orders are now handled. In 1976 the exchange made a small, experimental start with *Designated Order Turnaround* or *DOT*, under which member firms who chose to participate could send market orders for up to 100 shares and limit orders up to 200 from their office directly to the specialist who would see that they were executed or entered into his book, and then also report back directly. Originally, all messages showed up via paper printer, not on a computer screen or electronic memory.

The system was gradually expanded and improved, and in 1984 was upgraded as *SuperDot*. Now the system accepts all securities traded on the NYSE. It's ready to transmit market orders up to 30,099 shares, while limit orders may be submitted up to 99,999 shares.

Brokerage firms can access the system in several ways. Most of the large member firms use their big mainframe computers to talk directly with the exchange's computer. Other firms may use the communications channels provided by service bureaus such as Automatic Data Processing. And some smaller firms may simply use personal computers to hook into the system.

But don't expect that before long, when you get the urge to invest in Rod & Reel, you will be able just to sit down at your home or office PC and tell the specialist's computer, "Go, fill my order." It's not a matter of technology, but of needed regulatory controls. So, while some brokerage firms may let you use your PC to send them your order, the firm itself must then transmit the order to the floor.

All the stock orders are channeled through a floor switch from which they can be routed either to the specialist or to the firm's booth on the floor. Each firm sets its own criteria for which orders go where. For instance, one firm may want any order over 4,000 shares to go to its booth and thereby the personal attention of its floor broker, while another may have its cutoff at 400 shares and yet another at 10,000.

If the order goes to the booth, the floor broker (or a $2 broker retained by the firm) will go to the trading post and handle the transaction in the traditional way within the crowd — only he's apt to deal in a much larger number of shares than the 100-share order we described earlier.

If a market order goes directly to the specialist at the post, he'll execute it promptly at the best price then available. He still observes "public outcry" — announcing the order to see if anyone in the crowd will better the price. The specialist also will accept a request to "stop" the order for you — guaranteeing you, on a buy order, the lowest offering price then on his book, but waiting to see whether a lower offer comes in before he executes the order.

Immediate execution also applies to *marketable* limit orders — those where the current market price is better than that stipulated in the order. For instance, if Rod & Reel is currently trading around 18½, you may be willing to buy at the market but fear that a sudden updraft might lift "Reel" beyond where you'd want to buy. To protect against that, you could place a limit order at, say, 19. Similarly, on a sale you could protect yourself against a sudden drop by specifying you won't sell below 18¼. If the market should indeed have moved against you in the brief time SuperDot takes to complete most trades (on more than 90% of orders, a report is on its electronic way back to your brokerage firm within one minute), your order would then be entered on the specialist's book like any other limit order.

And under a rule established in 1988, individual investors have an added protection against being swamped amid the avalanche of orders when the market turns hectic; market orders for up to 2,099 shares submitted on behalf of individuals (given a special "I" identifier by the brokerage firm) will receive priority delivery through SuperDot in what is called the *Individual Investor Express Delivery Service.*

Once the Dow Jones has moved 50 points up or down from the previous afternoon's closing level, the exchange starts imposing restrictions on certain orders used largely in connection with program trading. In *program trading*, large institutional investors or the trading desks of some major brokerage houses seek to profit from small price differences between index options or futures contracts (discussed in chapter 24) and the actual stocks that make up the indexes. It involves offsetting transactions in a "basket" of stocks and the corresponding index option or future. Computer programs are prepared that enable the program trader to submit orders for all the stocks in the basket with a single command; restrictions (such as when the "collar" is imposed after a 50-point move) make it more cumbersome, and thus less attractive, to execute program trades, but do not eliminate them.

The specialist's book, by the way — which used to be a long, narrow, leather-bound ledger with ruled sections for each price where he would enter limit orders as they came in — is now also electronic, and the orders arriving via SuperDot are entered automatically. (Since it's often possible for members of the "crowd" around the post to glance at the "book" screen, the depth of the market for a stock is now more widely known than when only the specialist could peek at the old-style "book.") As always, the first order entered into the "book" will be the first to be executed, once the "trigger" price is reached.

SuperDot now handles about 70% to 80% of the orders that reach the exchange on an average day. Since these include nearly all the smaller orders, they represent only 25% to 30% of the share volume — but, typically, that's still a hefty 50 to 90 million shares.

SuperDot is especially busy before trading opens each morning, with a service called *OARS* (for *Opening Automated Report Service*). About 5% of a day's orders come in by the time the opening bell rings at 9:30. Specialists used to have to sort manually through all the orders and then try to determine a fair opening price. Now the computers maintain a continuous tally, keeping the specialist abreast of the balance — or, more precisely, the *imbalance* — between the total buy and sell market orders as he prepares for the opening. Meantime, his "book" gives him an electronic tally, also continually updated, of all buy and sell limit orders that have been placed at each price level. He also sounds out buying and selling sentiment in the "crowd." Let's say, the OARS tally for Rod & Reel (which closed at 18¾ last night) shows buy market orders for 15,000 shares and sell orders for 20,000. The specialist's book holds buy orders for 3,000 shares at 18⅝, and there may be bids for another 1,000 shares at that price in the crowd. That would make up 4,000 of the 5,000-share sell-side imbalance. The specialist then may decide to buy 1,000 shares for his own account, and thus be able to open "Reel" at 18⅝.

When an opening price is set, all the pre-opening market orders are executed at that price, and so are all limit orders for which this is as good or better a price than the price limit stipulated by the customer.

Thus, in the exchange's eyes, SuperDot enables it to offer quick, efficient service within the framework of its traditional specialist-supervised auction system.

Also essential to an efficient securities market is that, as soon as a trade is completed, the news is disseminated to all the financial world. Suppose your order for Rod & Reel is executed at the stock exchange's Post 7 for, say, 18⅝. The sale is noted by one of the *floor reporters*, who are paid employees of the exchange. Standing outside each trading post, the reporters for unnumbered years used to write a report of the sale — the name of the stock, the number of shares involved, and the price — and hand it to a page who would take it to the pneumatic tubes that led from each post to the ticker room. There the sales report was typed into the telegraphic system carrying the news to the *tickers* found in every broker's office throughout the country. Many brokers' boardrooms, as well as the trading rooms of the exchange itself, feature enlarged electric or optical copies of the moving *ticker tape* that is spewed out by the tickers so everyone can keep an eye on market movements.

Once again, modern technology has come to the rescue of the beleaguered exchange, vastly speeding up the operation of getting reports to the ticker and its "tape." Now when a transaction is completed, all the reporter has to do is draw pencil lines through the appropriate coded boxes — stock symbol, number of shares, price — and insert the card into an electronic scanner. The scanner automatically "reads" the data and transfers the information to the computer that drives the ticker. The same exchange computer supplies the trade reports to more than 50 commercial quotation services, so all the transaction information is also available on the now all-pervasive computer screens of brokerage firms and other subscribers.

On the tape the name of every stock appears only as initials or a combination of letters, such as C for Chrysler Corporation, CP for Canadian Pacific, and CRR, which stood for Carrier Corporation until the air-conditioning manufacturer was acquired by United Technologies and now serves as the symbol for Conrail. Single-letter symbols used to be especially prized and identify some well-known corporations. Thus F stands for Ford and T for American Telephone & Telegraph. Perhaps the best known of all is X which stood for U.S. Steel. When "Steel" decided to change its name to mark its diversification, it took advantage of the symbol's fame by assuming the name USX Corp., whose ticker symbol remains X. But another famous symbol, J, for "Jersey" was abandoned when Standard Oil Company (New Jersey) changed its name to Exxon (symbol: XON).

Rod & Reel might have the symbol RAR, in which case the sale of 100 shares at 18⅝ would appear on the tape simply as:

RAR

18⅝

If 200 shares, instead of 100, had changed hands, the transaction would be noted this way:

RAR

2S 18⅝

If 1,000 shares were involved, it would appear on the tape this way:

RAR

10S 18⅝

However, if a block of 10,000 shares or more is traded, the full number is printed. Thus, an 11,000-share transaction would show as

RAR

11,000S 18⅝

Often, sales volume is so heavy that the ticker, which now can print 900 characters a minute, falls behind in reporting transactions. The ticker then goes into a *delete mode*. The first step is to print only the last digit, plus fraction, of the price. Thus, our sale at 18⅝ would appear as:

RAR

8⅝

It is assumed that people who are following the stock closely on the ticker will be able to supply the missing first digit. To avoid confusion, if the last digit is a zero, the full price is printed. Thus, if Rod & Reel were to go up over 20, the ticker in delete mode might read

RAR

20⅛

Along with the digit abbreviation, the volume of the sale is deleted, unless it involves a block exceeding a specified size.

If delays continue, *repeat prices* — transactions at the same price as the previous sale — are omitted.

Finally, the ticker can be set to report trades only if the price has changed by a specified minimum. By being able to adjust electronically both the price-change and volume-size criteria as high as needed, the exchange expects to be able to cope with any torrent of volume — with no serious delays once the daily openings (which are reported in full) are out of the way.

The new flexible-criteria system went on line in May 1989. It was developed after the October 1987 market upheaval saw the ticker at times fall as much as 190 minutes behind.

If the tape can't fully report the fast pace of trading, you may wonder why the exchange doesn't simply introduce a faster ticker. After all, the computer itself processes information as fast as the floor reporters can feed data to it. The answer is that anything above 900 characters a minute would be "blurred," almost impossible to read. In fact, this visible tape — though almost twice as fast as the system it replaced in the sixties — is called the *low-speed ticker*, in contrast to the *high-speed line* or electronic tape that goes to the quotation service *vendors*. Consequently, users can punch out quotations on their computer screens that are current even on the most hectic days.

In addition to keeping up with the fast pace of trading, the computer terminals can provide a much broader array of data on a particular stock. For instance, if you key in RAR, the display line on a plain-vanilla Quotron terminal might read

RAR N −18⅝−⅛ B 18½N.18¾N 7×12 v13,100 at 2:15

This tells you that Rod & Reel's last sale on the New York Stock

Exchange was at 18⅝, which was down ⅛ of a point from last night's closing price. The minus sign in front of the sales price shows that the 18⅝ transaction was at a *minus tick* — that is, down from the last *different* price; had it been higher than the previous *different* price, the *plus tick* would have been marked by a plus sign. Whether a stock is at a plus or minus tick (sometimes called upticks or downticks) is important because of the rules dealing with stabilizing transactions by specialists or floor traders as well as the regulations covering short sales.

The two figures after the "B" tell you the current bid-ask quotation, while the "7×12" indicates their *size*. In this case, the highest bid at the moment is 18½, with orders for 7 round lots (700 shares) on the specialist's book, while there are orders totaling 1,200 shares to sell at 18¾. Finally, the number after the "v" tells you the volume — 13,100 shares of RAR have traded today as of 2:15 P.M., when the latest trade took place. Depending on the terminal and system, you can also get an almost infinite range of other information.

You might wonder about the "N" markers next to the price quotations. They appear because a great many stocks are *dually listed* — they can trade not only on the Big Board but also on one or more of the regional exchanges. However, investors, and even most brokers and other professionals, had no ready way to keep abreast of the doings in the other markets. After long prodding by advocates of competitive marketplaces, the *consolidated tape* was introduced in 1975. It shows all the trades in NYSE-listed stocks, no matter on what U.S. exchange they take place. Trades in these stocks that take place in the over-the-counter Nasdaq system (in effect, the third market) are also reported. It's this consolidated tape that's used to prepare the stock market tables in the newspapers, and of course it's what shows up on the computer screens.

To let you know the source of a trade or a bid or ask quotation, the computer screens use, along with the N marker for the NYSE, B to identify the Boston Stock Exchange, C for Cincinnati, M for Chicago (formerly the Midwest), P for Pacific, and X for Philadelphia, as well as T for Third Market Nasdaq transactions. Thus, assuming Rod &

Reel was also listed on the Pacific Stock Exchange, you might have seen a display reading

RAR N −18 ⅝−⅛ B 18⅝P.18¾N

indicating that, while the last trade took place on the Big Board and that's also where the best current offering price of 18¾ is, the best bid price of 18⅝ at this point comes from the Pacific Stock Exchange.

In the early days of the consolidated tape, the Big Board's regular low-speed ticker tape also specifically identified trades taking place on another exchange — for instance

IBM & M

indicated the IBM trade took place on the Midwest Stock Exchange — but in the interest of speed and efficiency, this was soon dropped. Today the tape displays do not differentiate between trades that took place on the NYSE and those executed elsewhere.

While some 90% of Big Board-listed stocks are on the trading rosters of at least one other exchange, the NYSE continues to dominate the trading. The most active of the regionals, the Chicago, accounted for a little over 4% of 1993 volume, while another 7% went through Nasdaq.

The consolidated tape keeps watchers abreast of what's happening in all the markets, but to take advantage of this information — to enable stock buyers and sellers to get the best price currently available anywhere — required another system. As noted in chapter 10, persistent congressional and regulatory pressures led to establishment of the *Intermarket Trading System* (ITS) in 1978. Starting with a pilot program involving 11 stocks listed on both the New York and Philadelphia exchanges, ITS now encompasses over 2,000 dually listed stocks on the regional exchanges as well as Nasdaq. The intermarket quotes are displayed at each trading post and the system's electronic linkage permits any order to be quickly routed to the exchange where the best prices are available. ITS can also be used by floor traders and specialists, when trading for their own account, to "hit" the buy or sell offers posted by specialists at one of the other exchanges — adding to the overall liquidity of the markets.

One side effect of this broadened trading scope is that you will sometimes see major stocks quoted in sixteenths, thirty-seconds, or even sixty-fourths. On the Big Board, one-eighth (of a dollar) remains the minimum price differential, but sometimes narrower differentials are utilized for trades in other markets — usually by institutions dealing in large lots so even a few pennies a share represent sizable amounts.

Even with highly liquid markets, important news developments — such as a takeover offer, an unexpectedly bad or good earnings report, a major law suit, or even a changed recommendation by the securities analyst of a major brokerage house — can result in a sudden, one-sided torrent of orders on either the buy or sell side. Sometimes such a development will delay the opening of a stock for hours. Or, if it happens during trading hours, the exchange may order a temporary halt in trading. The specialist will consult with floor officials and perhaps one or two directors of the exchange. A *blue light* may be turned on over the trading post — a signal that more liquidity is wanted to assist in a "difficult trading situation," and also a formal request to the Registered Competitive Market-Makers to come to the post and buy and sell (against the imbalance, of course) at least one round lot.

As the specialist and officials go over the orders on hand and measure the interest in the "crowd," they may put out on the ticker a "range" within which they expect the stock to be priced when trading resumes. Giving potential investors such an *indication* may bring in additional orders; perhaps more important, it gives those who had placed a now-unrealistic order an opportunity to cancel. If the imbalance is great, a series of indications may have to be given out before the specialist and officials can arrive at an appropriate opening (or reopening) price, figuring in buying or selling by the specialist.

As just one example, before the opening on September 27, 1989, IBM announced its earnings would be well below expectations. The stock had closed at 117½ the night before. Soon after the exchange's 9:30 opening, an indication of 110–114 was placed on the tape at 9:33. Eight minutes later, the range was narrowed slightly with an indication of 110–113. Then, at 9:51, IBM opened at 111½, with 556,500 shares changing hands.

The exchange maintains an on-line price surveillance program based on trading data obtained from the computers that run the stock ticker. This program monitors all trades reported on the ticker throughout the market session. When the price movement of a stock exceeds preset standards, the computer calls attention to that fact. The surveillance section then retrieves from the computer's memory bank the chronological sequence of sales, before and after the suspicious transaction, and analyzes the record. If there is no apparent cause for the fluctuation, the surveillance section alerts a trading floor official, who will go to the specialist to find out just what happened — and why. Further investigation may sometimes lead to persons who had advance knowledge of some development — or thought they had.

The final step in the trading process consists of *settling* the transaction. Here, too, the advent of SuperDot has helped streamline the operation. When floor brokers in the "crowd" at the trading post accept another's buy or sell offer, no written memoranda are exchanged. Each broker simply makes his own note of whom he sold to or bought from, along with the details of the trade, including the time. The exchange is proud of the tradition that "a member's word is his bond," and there's no problem with brokers trying to renege on a trade that turned sour. But in the huge rush of trading, some clerical mistakes — wrong broker number, wrong price, wrong number of shares — inevitably creep in, and have to be laboriously tracked down and somehow adjusted in the after-hours comparisons. With SuperDot, the specialist's electronic mark of execution automatically "locks in" the trade and all pertinent facts — not only avoiding errors, but also speeding up the entire process of seeing that the buying customers get their stock and the selling customers their money.

As you can imagine, the brokerage firm handling your Rod & Reel purchase might in the course of the day have concluded many transactions with the firm representing the seller, while each firm also dealt with dozens of other brokers.

Thus, on a given day one firm might have sold 1,100 shares of Rod & Reel for its customers and bought only 1,000 shares for other customers. Internal bookkeeping within the firm can handle the transfer of 1,000 shares from its selling customers to its buying customers. But it would still owe some other broker 100 shares.

Time was when the broker who owed shares at the end of the day would deliver the actual certificates to the 1920-founded *Stock Clearing Corporation*, where other brokers to whom shares were due would pick them up. Later, member firms kept a supply of all stocks at the clearing corporation so shares could be transferred simply by debiting or crediting each broker's account. Dollar balances — the net amounts due them — were settled in the same fashion.

The "paper crunch" of the late 1960s, when the then-record volume swamped Wall Street's ability to process stock certificates, led to the Big Board's establishment of the *Central Certificate Service*. This was succeeded in 1973 by the *Depository Trust Company* (DTC), now owned by various members of the securities and banking industries, with the NYSE itself holding a 33% stake. DTC has eliminated nearly all that shuffling of certificates for some 600 participating broker-dealers, banks, and clearing agencies.

In the vaults of major banks and in the Depository Trust's own vault were stored in early 1993 some 130 billion shares of stocks for companies listed on the various exchanges or traded over-the-counter. Counting stocks, corporate bonds, and municipals, DTC holds over $6.3 trillion worth of over 900,000 securities.

When certificates are deposited with DTC, they are held in non-negotiable form until it is necessary to transfer them out in the name of a customer or a firm. The participants in a stock trade do not have to handle or even see the certificates until they are delivered upon request.

Computers make daily bookkeeping entries to reflect changes in the participants' position after the securities have been traded. All of this has obviously reduced the number of securities under a participating broker's care, thus freeing valuable space and personnel. And at the end of the business day, only one check need be delivered or received between each active participant and DTC.

Also helping immeasurably in the orderly processing of securities is the CUSIP numbering system, which assigns a specific identification number to more than 1.2 million securities — much as the familiar Universal Product Code (UPC) identifies each product on your grocer's shelf. The *CUSIP* name derives from the *Committee on Uniform Security Identification Procedures* (of the American Bankers Association), which developed the system in the 1960s for use in all segments of the financial services industry. The issue's CUSIP number is imprinted on all stock certificates and there's been talk of further simplifying handling by encoding all pertinent data so it will be computer readable. As far back as 1975, Congress directed the SEC to seek outright elimination of stock certificates as a means of settling securities transactions. This would lead to a system of computerized bookkeeping entry, presumably similar to what's now in use for government and municipal securities, as well as virtually all individual holdings of mutual funds.

If (and perhaps it's more a question of when) the system is extended to stocks, some investors might regret not having a colorful certificate they can finger (and possibly misplace or lose) — they'd just have their broker's statement, much as their bank statement is the only evidence of funds on deposit in their checking and savings accounts.

CHAPTER 13

How Large Blocks of Stock Are Handled

SUPPOSE you owned a considerable amount of stock in a company. Maybe you acquired the shares as part of your retirement benefits from that company. Maybe you inherited the stock. Or maybe you simply bought the block bit by bit over a long period of time. Now, you have decided you want to sell 5,000 shares, or 10,000 shares, or more. How would you go about selling that much stock?

It's true that, where once blocks were a source of excitement and widespread attention on the exchange floor, by now they're the basic components of the trading routine. So it's perfectly possible that your stock can get sold with virtually the same dispatch as an ordinary round-lot order, with barely a flicker on the ticker tape to mark the extra volume.

At the same time, you'd want to make sure that you're not dumping a lot of shares willy-nilly into a market that might not be prepared to absorb it. That could depress the price and you wouldn't get as much for the stock as you should. And you probably wouldn't want to drag the process out excessively by feeding a few hundred or even a thousand shares at a time into the market.

In considering how to handle your trade, the size of the block is a factor, but what counts more is the size in relation to the stock's *float* or potential market supply. As you might expect, it's much easier to execute a large order in an AT&T, IBM, or GE than in a smallish company that's traded less actively, especially if a sizable part of its shares are closely held by family, management, or some corporate part-owner. (In figuring the float, you deduct such closely held stock from the total number of shares outstanding.)

So, how best to proceed? To work out the best way to handle your particular stock at the particular time you want to sell, you'd be well advised to turn to your broker, one who is backed by the trading and information resources of a full-service firm.

Before looking at how block trading is handled, let's take a quick glance at how fast the practice has grown. What the Big Board calls "large blocks" (10,000 shares or more) averaged 9 trades a *day* in 1965. For the past few years, block trades have averaged 9 a *minute*, and in 1993 approached 15 a minute. What's more, the shares traded in these large blocks now account for about half of all Big Board volume, compared with just 3% in 1965.

Some blocks are not just "large" but gigantic; there's usually a bunch of trades each year that involves blocks of millions of shares. The record to date is 48.8 million shares of Navistar International on April 10, 1986, when a number of banks decided to dispose of large amounts of stock they had received a few years earlier in return for money owed them by Navistar's predecessor, International Harvester. Because the Navistar block sold at only $10.50 per share for a total of $504 million, the record for the largest block in dollar value belongs to Texaco; on June 1, 1989, a 42.3-million-share block of the big oil company sold at $49 per share for a total value of nearly $2.1 billion.

Amid the vast growth in the *number* of "large block" trades executed, the *average size* of these blocks has changed relatively little over the past quarter century; it's been running close to 25,000 shares per trade. Interestingly, however, the average size of non-block transactions (or, more accurately, trades below the 10,000-share "large-block" level) has gone up considerably, from around 200 shares in 1965 to over 1,000 shares per trade between 1987 and 1990, though it has receded some in the early 1990s. The long-term increase reflects an abundance of smaller blocks as well as the growing tendency for many ordinary trades to be for several hundred shares rather than just a single round lot.

The prevalence of blocks convincingly shows the heavy institutional presence in the stock market. But while the institutions predominate, it's by no means an absolute monopoly. A good many orders are placed by individuals, though admittedly more toward the lower end of the size scale.

Organization and procedures vary among brokerage houses, but, typically, orders for 5,000 shares or more go to the *block desk* or are given other special handling. (At some, the block criteria depend on how actively the stock trades.)

Block "desks" at big firms are usually vast rooms where dozens of quick-reacting traders sit in front of computer screens, telephone banks with almost constantly blinking lights, and assorted other advanced electronic equipment. Overhead and along the walls are ticker and news tapes as well as boards that list stocks that customers currently want to buy or sell and other pertinent data.

When you are ready with your order, you'll probably want your broker to check what price you can expect. The block experts may be able to come up with an almost instantaneous assessment for a relatively moderate quantity of an active stock; at other times they may have to go to some lengths to sound out the market. With a large block or inactive stock or poor market, you might have to be willing to let your stock go for less than you hoped for when you last looked up the price — *if* you want to go ahead.

It's possible to specify your order as "all or none." That means you're willing to go through with the trade only if your entire block can be sold for at least the minimum ("limit") price you set; if that can't be accomplished, you'll just keep your stock.

Sometimes, after working on your order for a time, the block desk may come back and suggest that you accept a lower price to get your deal completed. It's still, of course, your decision whether to go along and finish the sale quickly, or ask them to keep trying at the higher price, or settle for whatever part of the block has been sold and hold on to the rest.

When they get your order, the block traders will try to "find the other side of the market," to uncover a buying interest in the stock that would match your desire to sell. They will check such potential buying sources as the firm's institutional client base, foreign buyers, and large individual investors. Especially for stocks not actively traded, the company might be contacted to see if it is interested in buying back its own stock, as many large companies often are.

The block desk is in constant touch with the firm's floor brokers on the stock exchange, who'll check on interest in your stock at the trading post where it's handled. They look for "other side" interest both in the "crowd" and on the specialist's book. And the specialist, in his role as market-maker, often helps brokers dispose of sizable blocks.

Frequently when a big order comes in, the brokerage firm, with its block desk working feverishly, will find buyers or sellers for the whole block among its own customers, thus handling both sides of the transaction. Member firms will still have to *cross* — that is, execute the offsetting buy and sell orders — on an exchange floor. In a Big Board cross, as we've noted earlier, all outstanding orders on the specialist's book at a higher "buy" or lower "sell" price must be executed as part of the cross.

If the brokerage firm in such an "in-house" transaction can't find enough buy orders among its customers to equal the sell order, it may buy the balance of the shares for its own account (as part of the crossed trade) and assume the risk of selling the stock later. That's called *positioning* — the firm assumes a position in the stock. In fact, to seal a deal with a major institutional customer quickly, a brokerage firm may buy the entire block outright from the selling institution, and then work on reselling it.

Sometimes, larger blocks are handled as a *secondary distribution*. The brokerage house purchases the block at a negotiated price and then brings it to market at a set price, much like the offering of a new security. A *spot secondary*, which can be organized and executed quickly, is usually offered right after the close of Big Board trading, at a price closely related to the final trade on the exchange. The offering broker's sales force is alerted to contact potential customers for the security. As an inducement to buy, customers are offered the stock on a commission-free basis. In effect, the seller pays all the costs; the price at which the firm acquired the block was calculated to allow room for all the expected expenses.

In the past, such secondaries often involved a number of underwriters to share the risk; they then organized selling syndicates bringing in still more brokers. But now most spot secondaries are done in-house by a single firm. Among the reasons are the greater financial size of the major brokerages, the large number of institutions who can buy big chunks of an offering, an emphasis on speed, and the heightened competition and shaved profit margins that make the brokerages more reluctant to bring in others.

In case any of the shares or bonds offered have not been previously registered — as, for instance, happened when Rod & Reel issued stock to the owners of some of the companies it acquired — a registration statement must be filed with the SEC before these securities can be sold. The offering procedures for such *registered secondaries* are then just about the same as apply in the underwriting of new issues.

Some of the biggest stock offerings in history have technically been secondaries. That includes the initial public offerings of Ford Motor in 1956 and Reader's Digest Association in 1990. Both the two-thirds of a billion dollars' worth of Ford stock and half billion dollars' worth of Reader's Digest shares were sold not by the companies but by foundations set up by the founding families.

There are also restrictions on executive officers, major stockholders, directors, and others considered in a *control* position when they want to sell stock in their corporation. The stock may have to be registered, although there are provisions for casual sale of relatively small amounts of stock at well-spaced intervals. Since it's often difficult to determine whether and to what extent a person is subject to the complex rules, most brokers play it safe and insist on legal clearance before undertaking to sell a block of stock for company executives or members of controlling families.

With big institutions the mainstay of everyday block trading, efforts have been made to let them trade directly with each other. Most prominent is *Instinet* (originally the Institutional Network), a computerized network on which subscribers can enter their interest in block purchases or sales. No institution has to tip its hand, since only the computer knows who's on the "other side." Once a bid and offer coincide, the touch of a key can confirm the transaction, which is then reported, like trades in Big Board–listed stocks on all U.S. markets, on the consolidated ticker tape. However, Instinet (now owned by global information giant Reuters Holdings) has in recent years accounted for less than ⅕ of 1% of total "consolidated tape" volume of NYSE-listed stocks.

An entirely new market segment is developing, based on Rule 144A, which the SEC adopted in April 1990 and further expanded in 1994. It exempts from ordinary registration rules stocks and bonds issued to and trading exclusively among large institutions and investment banks. This is an important expansion of private-placement rules, which all along permitted the offering of a securities issue (usu-ally bonds or preferred stock) to a very small group of investors without having to go through all the registration requirements of a public issue. The new rule permits not just issuance but also active trading (albeit still within a relatively limited circle) of these registration-exempt securities. The theory is that the eligible traders should be sufficiently sophisticated and powerful not to need most investor safeguards, and that this will make the American markets more competitive in large-scale global financial dealings.

The major exchanges and Nasdaq have obtained permission to try after-hours (or pre-dawn) sessions with special rules geared for institutional and overseas traders. So far, the impact has been minuscule, but proponents are convinced that these are early steps toward a truly global 24-hour market.

CHAPTER 14

How Small Stock Orders Are Handled

ALL stocks bought and sold on the stock exchange are traded by brokers on the exchange in round lots, units of 100 shares, with the exception of a few relatively inactive stocks that are sold in 10-share units.

But what if you want to buy or sell just 20 shares of our hypothetical Rod & Reel Company on the exchange? The answer is that you can buy or sell an *odd lot* — anything from one to 99 shares — of any stock listed on the New York Stock Exchange.

Your cost of buying or selling it, figured as a percentage of the total value of your order, is likely to be slightly higher than it would be on a round-lot trade. As we've noted, most commission schedules are structured to charge proportionately more for smaller orders (smaller both in transaction value and in the number of shares).

Historically, the odd-lot customer also was obliged to pay a kind of service fee, over and above the regular commission. However, that charge, known as the *odd-lot differential*, which used to be mandatory under the rules of the New York Stock Exchange, has now been scrapped, though a few minor wrinkles still differentiate an odd-lot from a regular round-lot transaction.

Nowadays, your broker sends your odd-lot market order via Super-Dot to the exchange specialist's post where it is immediately executed, based on the current bid-asked quotation. That is, if you are buying, you get the asked price — the lowest at which any round-lot owner is then willing to sell, not just on the Big Board but on all the other U.S.

stock markets tied into the Intermarket Trading System. If you are selling, you get the bid price — the highest any round-lot buyer is then willing to pay.

Compared to this automatic price formula for odd lots, a round-lot order gets "exposed" to the auction process and you may conceivably get a better price than the posted bid-asked. If, for instance, the bid-asked "spread" for Rod & Reel is 37½–37¾, it's possible that your 100-share buy order gets filled at 37⅝ or (though rare) even at 37½, while the 20-share odd-lot order would be executed at the automatic 37¾. But unless the spread between bid and asked is unusually wide, the prospect of a meaningfully better price on a 100-share order is more potential than real.

If you place an odd-lot limit order — setting the maximum price at which you're willing to buy or the minimum price at which you'll sell — it is executed whenever (round-lot) trading reaches your desired price. And any "overnight" market orders entered after trading closes one day and before it reopens the next will be executed at the opening price in that stock.

It all seems simple and logical now, but it took quite some doing to get to the present system. Until 1976, the Big Board relegated the handling of odd lots to specialized member firms called *odd-lot brokers*. A 1969 merger left just one such firm, Carlisle, DeCoppet & Company. An odd-lot firm never dealt directly with the customer, only the customer's broker. If you bought 20 shares of Rod & Reel, Carlisle, DeCoppet would supply your broker with the 20 shares from its own inventory. If you sold 20 shares, it would buy the odd lot from your broker and put it in its inventory. And to adjust this inventory, it would, as needed, buy and sell round lots of the stocks on the floor of the exchange.

The odd-lot broker was *obligated* to fill your market order for any stock at whatever price prevailed on the *next* round-lot transaction after your order reached the trading post. For this service it collected an odd-lot differential of ⅛ of a point, or 12.5 cents a share, on every share of stock bought or sold. If you bought an odd lot, you paid ⅛ point above the price at which the next round lot traded; if you sold, you got ⅛ point less.

In January 1976, over the objections of the stock exchange — but with the obvious blessing of the SEC — Merrill Lynch challenged the time-honored system. It announced that it would begin buying and selling odd lots out of its own inventory. Most important, if you placed an odd-lot market order and were willing to wait until your stock opened on the exchange the following morning, your odd-lot order would be filled at the same price as the first round-lot transaction — with no odd-lot differential. Or you could place an odd-lot market order for immediate execution, to be filled at the current bid or asked price — without differential.

This move obviously was a serious blow to Carlisle, DeCoppet since Merrill Lynch, which accounted for about a quarter of all odd-lot business on the exchange, was by all odds its biggest customer. The exchange promptly announced that it would buy out Carlisle, DeCoppet and use its computer facilities to go into the odd-lot business itself. It would rely on the specialists in each stock to supply the required odd lots from their inventories — as specialists on the American Stock Exchange (where there were no separate odd-lot brokers) had done all along. The Big Board promptly extended one of the benefits of the Merrill Lynch plan to all odd-lot investors, arranging to have odd-lot orders at the market opening executed without charging a differential.

Some years later, with SuperDot up and running, the exchange also provided for odd-lot market orders entered into the system during the day to be executed at the current bid or asked quotation, with no differential. And in the early 1990s, the system was further extended to handle limit orders without imposing the differential surcharge. Thus, the major surcharge levied on the odd-lot customer became history.

However, when you find the bid-asked spread is wide (especially half a point or more), it makes sense to discuss the situation with your broker. You may then want to place a limit order; in that case, you know you'll get your price or better — but you take the chance that your order may not be executed.

You may wonder what happens if you have a round lot plus some extra shares, say, 115 shares. The exchange would call this a *PRL* or *partial round lot* and it would be executed all at one price.

How important are odd-lotters in the overall brokerage picture? In the aggregate, their number has grown significantly in the postwar era as part of the tremendous total expansion of the shareowner population. Yet, odd lotters as a group have accounted for a steadily decreasing percentage of the volume of total shares traded.

In the era that culminated in the bull market of 1929, the small-scale buyer represented almost 20% of stock exchange volume. Twenty years later, odd-lot trading was still accounting for about 15% or 16%. But from then on it headed pretty steadily downward to a level of less than 10% in 1968 and below 5% in 1974. Since 1985 it has been less than 1%.

There are several ready explanations for this trend. The explosive growth in institutional volume has of course sharply lowered the proportion of all individual trading.

And many of those who in former days would have been drawn to odd lots now invest in mutual funds rather than directly in shares on the exchanges.

There's still another factor. While total value of stocks outstanding has skyrocketed, the continuous stream of stock splits and other distributions, as well as the issuance of new stock in both old and new companies, has kept the price of the average Big Board stock around 30 — which is, indeed, somewhat lower than in many earlier years. And it's obvious that $3,000 for a typical round lot today no longer looms as big and hard to afford as $3,000 did in the 1920s, or even the 1950s and 1970s.

CHAPTER *15*

Buying Stock through Accumulation Plans

A new way to buy stocks in small amounts was born in January 1954. That's when the New York Stock Exchange inaugurated its *Monthly Investment Plan* — commonly known as *MIP* — under which investors could purchase a stake in any regularly listed stock for as little as $40 a month — or even $40 per quarter.

MIP itself was dropped by the Big Board in 1976, but the stock-buying mechanism it pioneered remains very much alive, and forms the basis of many so-called *accumulation plans*. They offer a convenient way to acquire stocks, and certain other investments, in readily affordable amounts. They also permit automatic reinvestment of the dividends you receive, even if they come to only a few pennies.

Until MIP came along, the smallest amount of stock anyone could buy was one share. Sure, you might on occasion end up with a *fractional share*. For instance, a 4-for-3 stock split (or its equivalent, a 33⅓% stock dividend) would entitle each 100-share owner to an additional 33⅓ shares. Or a merger or restructuring might call for you to receive, say, 1.105 new shares for every old share you held. When that happens, the company will often simply pay you cash for your fraction of a share. In other cases, a credit for that odd amount of stock stays tucked away on the corporate books.

But under the system ushered in with MIP, fractional shares are not an unavoidable aberration — they're the very heart of the program. That's because you're not buying by the share, but *by the dollar*. Just as you might pull up to a gas station and ask for $10 or $15 worth of premium unleaded, here you ask for $40 or $140 or some other dollar-amount worth of stock. You get whatever number of shares your dollars buy, figured out to the fourth decimal place. It works the same, whether you buy roughly 3⅓ shares of a $12 stock, or ³⁄₁₀ of a share of a $125 stock.

The basic plan wasn't formulated, of course, because someone thought it a neat idea to buy less than one share of stock. Rather, MIP was designed as an easy way for people to invest regularly and, through such systematic investing, to build up a worthwhile interest in a stock.

MIP was sometimes called "buying stock on the installment plan" — but that is inaccurate. It could help you accumulate stock, a little at a time, with regularly budgeted purchases; you didn't have to wait to become an investor until you had set aside enough money to buy the shares you wanted. But, unlike buying a car or a refrigerator "on time," where you get possession of something you haven't paid for yet, you never bought any of the stock on credit — you just bought the shares literally a fraction at a time.

Even though MIP is gone, it's helpful to examine its workings, because they set the basic pattern for the plans around today. Suppose you wanted to buy shares in Rod & Reel at the rate of $50 a month. Let's assume the commission charged was 6 percent. That would leave $47.17 (after a commission of $2.83 or 6 percent of $47.17) with which to buy shares of Rod & Reel at whatever price would prevail at the opening of the market the day after each payment is received. If that price turned out to be, say, 37⅜, you'd be credited with exactly 1.2621 shares (47.17/37.125 = 1.2621).

You're entitled to dividends on all shares, including fractions, from the moment the shares are bought. Usually, unless you order otherwise, the dividend proceeds are automatically used to buy additional shares at the prevailing market price, further building up your holdings.

You also have full voting rights and all the other privileges of a stockholder, including getting annual and other stockholder reports and proxy statements.

When you wanted to close out an MIP program, you'd get a stock certificate for the full shares you had accumulated, plus the cash value of whatever fractional share remained. Or you could ask for your position (including the fraction) to be sold. Like purchases, sales were made at the opening price the morning after the order was received.

At its 1954 inaugural, MIP fitted right in with the NYSE's ongoing "Own Your Share of American Business" campaign and won considerable support among the Street's retail houses. Easily the plan's most enthusiastic promoter was Merrill Lynch, whose ubiquitous efforts to attract small investors had made its name a household word at the time. And as interest by other houses slackened over the years, the Merrill share of MIP business rose to over 90%. When the exchange lifted the requirement for fixed commissions on small orders in April 1974 (a year before the Mayday 1975 abolition of all fixed commissions), Merrill Lynch renamed its MIP accounts *Sharebuilder*, broadened the plan's scope, and introduced a commission schedule with rates lower than those it charged on regular transactions of the same size.

You never had any obligation under MIP to actually buy stock every month, though you could be dropped from the program if you skipped too many scheduled purchases. Sharebuilder (which underwent another name change to *Blueprint* in 1987) didn't establish even a nominal requirement for repeat buying in individual accounts. You're free to place an order whenever you choose, or you can just sit with a position. And Blueprint lets you buy not only Big Board but also over-the-counter or American Stock Exchange stocks, as well as mutual funds (including a money market fund) and also positions in gold or other precious metals. In line with the original MIP formula, all purchases are by the dollar. When you sell, however, that's done by the share — no fractions, unless you want to sell your entire position in that security. You'll get a check for the sales proceeds — or you can ask for the money to be left in the account (or put in the money fund), so it'll be there the next time you place a buy order. You can ask to have stock certificates delivered to you for your holdings (there's usually a charge for that). And Merrill Lynch now imposes a small annual maintenance charge for individual Blueprint accounts ($30 as of 1994).

While it's always up to you when or whether to buy, establishing regular habits of thrift through systematic investment has much to commend it, and the plans carrying on the MIP principle make the task easy for the small buyer. Consistent buying of a stock, kept up whether that stock rises or declines in price, provides the advantages of "dollar cost averaging." This technique of regularly investing a set amount of dollars in a stock regardless of price or market fluctuations (discussed in detail in chapter 32) has proven to be one of the most successful methods of buying stocks over the years, whether done within the format established by MIP or by an investor acting on his or her own. It eliminates reliance on luck in trying to guess periodic market swings. Instead, you gradually accumulate positions at prices averaged over a long period of time. This tends to reward the patient investor in quality stocks to a much greater extent than random trading patterns.

While it's still possible to open an individual account such as Blueprint, the vast majority of accounts today are opened within group plans set up for corporate employees or a company's stockholders or members of "affinity groups" such as associations, labor organizations, and credit unions. Brokers and other plan administrators like group plans because they provide a large batch of subscribers and a steady stream of investment funds from payroll deductions, dividend receipts, and the like.

A particularly important sector is *employee stock purchase plans*. Some major companies encouraged employee stock ownership long before MIP was devised, but the new system simplified procedures and relieved companies of most of the administrative burdens. Also, some companies a bit shy about promoting their stock to their employees were happy to shift this solicitation task to the brokers. Meantime, the growing realization in recent years that Social Security and regular corporate pension payments would need supplementing for comfortable retirement has pushed up employee interest in investment plans.

All this has led to a mushrooming of employer-sponsored accumulation plans. Typically, employees sign up for payroll deductions for a year at a time (they are free to drop out but not re-enter during that year). Shares are bought and allocated to the participants once a quarter. Usually, the company picks up the commission tab for the entire purchase, and in some plans also provides a discount of up to 15% from the stock's fair market value.

Especially in employee plans intended as a retirement supplement, the scope of permissible investments has often been extended beyond the employer's own stock. Participants may be able also to select other stocks, mutual funds, or CDs.

Another highly popular type of accumulation program, generally called *automatic dividend reinvestment* — now often given the acronym DRIP for Dividend Reinvestment Plan — is directed at a corporation's shareholders. If you sign up, the dividend payments on your stock will be channeled into the purchase of additional shares. Most sponsoring companies absorb the commission cost and may even offer discounts up to 5% on the price of the stock bought. One minor catch is that the IRS considers the absorbed commission as well as any discount from the actual market price as an additional (and taxable) dividend payment to you. Also, in most company-sponsored programs, only stock you hold in your own name is eligible for reinvestment; the companies figure it would get too involved to check with the various brokerage houses on which of their constantly changing list of customers who own the stock in "Street name" would like to participate. Nonetheless, some companies do offer commission-free reinvestment to brokerage account holders.

An important extra offered by many companies to dividend-reinvestment participants is the right to buy still more stock by sending in a check before the quarterly reinvestment date. You won't get a discount and will have to pay brokerage commission (but since the stock is bought at a large-transaction institutional rate, your proportion of the bill will be small). Such a dividend-reinvestment-plus-additional-purchase program can help you accumulate a "dollar-averaging" investment position in a quality stock. A small number of companies with such plans even permit you to join before you own any of their stock — you just send them (or, rather, the plan's trustee) a check for your initial purchase.

In all accumulation plans, participants regularly get individual statements, showing all transactions (including dividend reinvestment) and present holdings. Except for limits that may be imposed on an employee's stock paid for in whole or part by employer contributions, plan participants are normally free to sell their investment at any time, paying regular commissions. However, there may be tax penalties on sales in retirement-type accounts, or on early sale of stock acquired at discount.

Since both employee-purchase and dividend-reinvestment plans concentrate a heavy amount of buy orders on the quarterly purchase dates, the buying procedure is modified. Rather than having the order filled automatically at the next morning's opening price, plan administrators may space out the purchases over several days so as not to distort the market. All the purchases are combined to calculate an average price — which is then applied to each of the participating accounts.

At times, a company may use stock it holds in its treasury rather than buying shares in the market. The *fair market value* of such treasury shares is then determined by averaging the high and low prices for the stock in stock exchange trading on the designated purchase date.

Certain banks have also initiated accumulation plans. Customers agree to have a specified sum withdrawn from their bank account each month and applied toward a stock purchase. The bank combines the funds collected for each stock in the plan, makes bulk purchases, and then allocates the shares to the individual accounts.

Fractional shares are also standard in mutual funds, where investors buy by the dollar and in most cases choose to reinvest their dividends.

As their very name implies, accumulation plans and their offshoots are not intended for the in-and-out trader. But the plans, with their fractional-share concept, offer a practical — and generally very effective — way for persons who can invest only limited amounts at a time to build a long-range nest egg.

CHAPTER 16

Nasdaq Brings the Over-the-Counter Market into the Big Time

WHAT is by now easily the second biggest stock market in the United States (and currently lays claim to being number two in the world) is not a stock exchange housed in an imposing building with a noisy trading floor, but an electronic network spanning the entire country, with expanding links to the global market. Its trading is conducted under the auspices of the *National Association of Securities Dealers* (*NASD*). It's called *Nasdaq*. The name is derived from National Association of Securities Dealers Automated Quotations system, but the NASD no longer considers it an acronym but a proper name in its own right and so has dropped the original all-capital-letters spelling. In 1993, Nasdaq handled over $1.3 trillion worth of transactions.

Nasdaq computer terminals instantly show the best currently available bid and offer prices for any stock traded on the system and in many cases permit automatic execution of a trade at that price. The NASD proudly hails Nasdaq as "the stock market for the next 100 years." That, of course, differs from the view of the Big Board, which stoutly maintains the superior virtues of the auction system and the skillful participation of the specialist. Both sides can put forth good arguments, and, in the best American tradition, the competition should induce both sides to come up with superior service.

Beyond argument, however, is that Nasdaq has revolutionized the over-the-counter market and propelled it from a backwater to the mainstream of securities trading. Actually, Nasdaq officials now feel theirs is no longer just the state-of-the-art showpiece of *over-the-counter* (often just called *OTC*), but a full-fledged independent market. However, since Nasdaq's roots are in OTC and it's the fundamental OTC trading principle that sets it apart from stock exchange trading, the general discussion of OTC on the following pages includes Nasdaq as well.

At this stage you may well wonder: Just what is this over-the-counter market? Actually, it's best defined in terms of what it's *not*. Over-the-counter traditionally encompasses all trading that takes place away from a securities exchange. That's why it's also referred to as the *off-board* or *unlisted* market.

The term itself goes back to early American financial history when you might go up to the counter of a banking establishment to buy or sell certain securities. Also, some factories used to raise capital by selling their own stock over their front-office counter.

Today, there are more than 50,000 unlisted equity issues outstanding in the United States. However, a great many of the companies with unlisted stock are small, unknown financially outside their immediate home area, and have little stock held by anyone but the owning families, management, and sometimes employees. Perhaps 16,000 trade with some regularity, but even in many of these stocks activity is modest. Thus, trading is overwhelmingly concentrated in the few thousand issues that form the core of the Nasdaq market.

OTC trading is not restricted to stocks. It's the forum where the vast majority of all bond trading takes place. Virtually all trading in U.S. Treasury bonds is conducted in multimillion (and up) batches through the trading rooms of the major government bond dealers. (That had long held true even while the Big Board formally maintained listing of Treasury issues; nowadays the American Stock Exchange offers some listed trading, intended for "odd lots" up to $99,000, in about 700 government and agency issues.) Most corporate bond trading is also handled off-board, and for most municipal securities OTC is the only market.

As far as you're concerned, you place your OTC order with the same individual broker at the same brokerage firm you use for Big

Board stocks. What's more, nowadays it really shouldn't make much difference to you whether the stock you're interested in is traded on a major exchange or on Nasdaq — it's the stock itself you should concentrate on.

What is different: Whereas in exchange trading the firm acts strictly as your agent, in OTC it normally performs as a *dealer* or principal, holding ownership of the stock it sells you or buys from you. Your firm may maintain its own inventory in the stock, or it may buy it from another dealer for resale to you.

Technically, while on an exchange the price is determined by a two-way auction, in OTC it's arrived at by negotiation — negotiation between the securities dealers on both sides of the transaction, and negotiation between your dealer and you, the customer. As electronic progress brings automatic order execution ever closer in both types of market, you may find the distinctions increasingly blurred from a practical viewpoint. That said, you still should be aware that the procedural pillars on which the two markets are built make for very different market structures.

Over-the-counter trades are most commonly transacted on a *net price* basis. (That, again, is because your "broker" acts as a dealer or principal, not an agent.) You do not pay a commission; instead the securities dealer builds a profit margin or *markup* into the price you're asked to pay. Similarly, when you sell, the dealer buys from you at a price that subtracts a *markdown* from the market's current wholesale or *inside price*.

OTC trades may, however, be executed on an *agency basis*. When your broker does not deal in the stock, it operates as an agent, seeking to obtain the best possible wholesale price for you from a market-making dealer. It then charges you a commission, just as when the broker buys or sells a stock for you on a stock exchange. The commission will probably be about the same as you'd pay for an equivalent Big Board order. As a matter of fact, on most routine OTC trades today, the markup or markdown imposed by most retail brokers is likely to approximate the commission charge on a listed stock — so the market in which a stock trades isn't apt to make much difference in your transaction costs when you deal with a reputable broker.

The dealers operating actively in the over-the-counter market are members of the NASD. This association sprang up in response to early New Deal legislation and particularly the Maloney Act of 1938, which called for a *self-regulatory organization* to oversee and police the market. Its some 5,200 member firms throughout the U.S. range from little one-person shops to all the major securities houses that do business with the public (and which, of course, are also members of the New York Stock Exchange). The NASD requires members to abide by its Rules of Fair Practice and a Uniform Practice Code; it has the right to hear complaints and discipline members and their employees, subject to SEC supervision.

Some 475 of the NASD member firms act as market-makers — a few in a mere handful of stocks, but many of the major brokerage and investment banking firms make markets in many hundreds and about 10 deal in over a thousand stocks. A market-maker is responsible for doing just what the name says — to make a market in the stock. It must be prepared, on a continuing basis, to buy from or sell to other dealers and customers for its own account, and regularly announces the prices at which it will buy and sell. Like a stock exchange specialist, the market-maker usually keeps close tabs on developments in the companies whose stock it trades. The research department of the market-making firm is also likely to publish periodic reports on these companies.

Before Nasdaq, when you wanted to buy or sell a stock in which your securities firm didn't make a market, its OTC department traders had to rely on an extensive telephone network to find current quotations for the stock (they were expected to contact at least three market-making dealers). But even the most diligent traders could never be sure they reached the dealer with the best price at that moment — nor that, after they "shopped" the market, this "best" price would still be available.

The basic daily reference bible for the OTC professionals in those days were the *pink sheets,* compiled and printed on pink paper by a company called National Quotation Bureau (since 1963, a subsidiary of Commerce Clearing House). The sheets would list for each stock whatever bid and/or asked quotations a market-making dealer submitted, along with the dealer's phone number. The pink sheets (still issued in somewhat curtailed form today) represent a momentous job, compiled late each day and distributed overnight. While they were for a long time the broadest and best available portrait of the OTC market, numerous entries depended on unreliable submissions by small dealers, and even under the best circumstances the highly perishable information was often obsolete by the time it reached subscribers.

Market information for investors was even more sketchy. Newspapers published at most a very limited list of OTC stocks, and the quotations made available to them were in the form of a broad (and, according to critics, a rather misleading) range that made ample allowance for dealers to tuck in their markup.

In its extensive, Congress-ordered study of the securities markets in the early 1960s, the SEC found even more shortcomings in OTC — a market it described as "relatively obscure and even mysterious for most investors, and ... comparatively unregulated" — than in the listed markets. Concerns included the lack of adequate price and transaction information, which also made it hard to tell when some dealers imposed excessive markups or markdowns. There was opportunity to abuse the pink sheets — dealers failing to stand behind the prices they listed, and, worse, some manipulators using the sheets to create a false impression of value or market activity. And then there was the general lack of requirements for accurate and timely information from OTC-traded companies that inhibited informed trading and, again, could lend itself to market manipulation by some fast operators.

The resulting securities legislation in 1964 (plus various follow-up laws) significantly added to SEC powers in the OTC area, including stronger policing and ability to suspend trading in OTC issues (previously the commission could ban trading only on exchanges). The larger OTC-traded companies were required to file regular reports similar to those of listed companies. Also, the NASD was enabled to assert a stronger supervisory role. Rules now provide for regular inspection of all dealer organizations by the NASD, which was given authority to compel compliance with all rules and regulations. Sales personnel must take tougher examinations, and controls have been established to enforce honesty in advertising and sales literature. Market surveillance was increased by both the NASD and the SEC. They keep a close eye on price fluctuations and unusual activity in any stock. All in all, most of the regulations that had long been imposed on stock exchanges and their member firms were gradually extended to the over-the-counter market.

And, ironically, it was the evident dissatisfaction by the SEC and Congress with the traditional OTC market structure that led to the most important consequence — it spurred the NASD to leapfrog ahead in the electronic trading race. The NASD contracted with Bunker Ramo Corporation to develop a computerized system, and by February 1971 Nasdaq was ready to go on stream. It has since steadily expanded the number of stocks covered and especially the scope of available services.

In essence, Nasdaq permits market-making dealers to enter their up-to-the-second bid and asked quotations into the system, while brokers and their customers can find the equally up-to-the-second best available price. In a major upgrading move in 1982, the more active stocks became eligible for the *Nasdaq National Market* (originally the *Nasdaq/NMS* or National Market System), with each trade reported as it occurs — just as on the exchanges. For other Nasdaq stocks, current bid and ask prices were displayed, but dealers reported only the total shares traded at the end of each day. However, since another major service upgrade in 1992, immediate reporting of each trade was also extended to this "regular Nasdaq" sector, which is now called The *Nasdaq SmallCap Market*.

Access to the data is provided on three levels.

Level 1 is what you find on the regular quote machines now ubiquitous at brokerages and many corporate offices. You punch out the code for the stock and the computer (having sorted all the quotations submitted by the market-makers) flashes the current best "bid" and current best "asked" (or "offered") price on the screen, along with the latest reported sale, the price change from yesterday's close, the volume so far today, and the day's high and low — just about the same information as you'd get for a stock listed on a stock exchange.

Level 2 service, intended primarily for (non-market-making) traders and investment professionals at institutions, lists not just the best available price, but all the prices submitted by the various market-makers, any special indications (as, for instance, that a bid is firm for 10,000 shares), and also the name of the market-maker — so traders would know whom to contact.

Level 3 provides the same detailed data, and — being designed for use by a dealer who makes markets — has the important extra capability of letting the dealer enter bids and offers into the system, and change them any time.

An incidental consequence of the computerized trading system was the need to assign ticker-type symbols to each security so that users could access the information. Leaving symbols of one, two, and three letters to the major exchanges, Nasdaq basically uses four, such as AAPL for Apple Computer, MCIC for MCI Communications, and INTC for Intel, to cite three of Nasdaq's most popular stocks. A fifth letter may be added to distinguish among different classes of securities by the same company, or to mark a special situation, such as F for a foreign security (but Y if it's an American Depositary Receipt, as, for instance, RTRSY for Reuters ADRs) or E if the company is currently delinquent in its SEC filings.

The system is designed to let all the dealers and their traders get faster and more thorough market information, with everyone knowing what is the best market at the moment and who is making it. Consequently, quotations tend to be more competitive, the spread between bid and asked prices narrower, and the total market more liquid.

In standard Nasdaq operations, the computer display simply points traders toward the dealer they want to contact. The actual trade may still be concluded by a quick phone call between traders, though by now about 60% of all trades are executed by some type of automated system.

To expedite orders for individual investors, NASD in 1984 introduced *SOES* (it rhymes with "shows" and stands for Small Order Execution System). Your brokerage firm can place your market order to buy or sell and it will be automatically executed at the best price then in the system. In that respect, it's similar to the execution service investors get from the Big Board's SuperDot. Since 1990, you can also have a limit order entered into SOES through its Limit Order File.

To facilitate trading among broker/dealers, SelectNet was launched in 1990. From their trading room terminals, dealers can approach other dealers with their bid or offer; the other dealer has the option to accept, reject, or make a counteroffer. If a trade is agreed to, the computer will "lock it in," update the price and volume statistics, and attend to all the other electronic "paperwork."

Another automated helpmeet, brought on line in 1990, is the Automated Confirmation Transaction (ACT) service. It enables market-makers to verify trades within minutes, instead of having "mismatches" in the clearing process show up the next day or later. (A *mismatch* occurs when one dealer thinks it made a sale to another dealer but that dealer's records don't show the same trade size, purchase price, or — at times — any transaction at all.) While such technical improvements may not interest the average investor, they provide everyone with better markets. They cut down the time the dealer's capital is tied up and quickly clear up clerical mistakes. The future will no doubt bring massive further progress in automating the trading *processes*, letting humans concentrate on the judgments that lead to trading *decisions*.

Nasdaq expanded its frontiers in 1992 with the opening of Nasdaq International, which permits trading in London of Nasdaq securities during much of the London trading day.

Just as in getting stocks listed on a stock exchange, companies must apply for listing on Nasdaq and its National Market component. To be considered for listing, the companies must meet the same SEC registration requirements as exchange-listed stocks — including initial filings, regular issuance of earnings reports, proxy statements, and the like.

Current minimum listing requirements for the Nasdaq SmallCap Stock Market are $4 million in assets, $2 million in stockholders' equity, at least 100,000 shares with $1 million market value in public hands, a minimum bid price of $3 a share, and two dealers willing to make a market in the stock. These standards, representing some significant stiffening, were approved in 1991. Aside from adjusting for inflation and otherwise updating the standards, the revisions were designed, as the NASD delicately put it, "to head off attempts by highly speculative companies to circumvent" the SEC's tough new penny-stock regulations by anchoring in the "safe harbor" that a Nasdaq listing would provide.

To qualify for the more elite National Market, a company also must have earned $400,000 after and $750,000 before taxes in the last fiscal year (or in both of the preceding two years), have at least 500,000 shares with $3 million market value in public hands, and a minimum bid price of $5. Under an alternative standard, companies in the "development" stage that are not yet making a profit can qualify for National Market listing if they meet stiffer requirements in other respects, such as a three-year operating history, $12 million in tangible assets, and at least 1 million shares worth $15 million in public hands.

As of March 1994, nearly 3,400 companies had stock listed in the National Market, with another 1,300-plus in the SmallCap. The National Market group accounted for 87% of all Nasdaq shares traded and more than 97% of trading in terms of dollar volume. In fact, measured in dollars, the top 100 stocks alone were responsible for some 53% of all Nasdaq trading.

Aside from the prestige and strong market coverage, an advantage of National Market listing is that the Federal Reserve now grants these issues automatic margin (credit extension) eligibility, just as it does exchange-listed stocks. Other Nasdaq stocks may also become eligible for margin — but they must establish their qualifications on an individual basis. Also, National Market stocks are exempt from the state "Blue Sky" requirements that ordinary OTC securities must observe.

And what about the companies that haven't made it into Nasdaq? They are traded pretty much in the traditional OTC ways, with pink sheet quotations the basic reference, and dealers phoning the advertised market-makers to determine the current market. Of course, the entire market's operation has been upgraded, with higher standards and stricter surveillance, especially in such areas as markups and the posting of bona fide prices.

And the NASD is moving to extend some level of electronic service to the relatively more active of these "pink sheet" companies. In 1990 it introduced an electronic Bulletin Board (OTCBB). Essentially, it's just an electronic version of the pink sheets, covering nearly 4,500 stocks, but it enables the approximately 390 firms that make markets in these stocks to continually update their latest bids and offers. Unlike Nasdaq, which requires market-makers always to have a "firm" price on both the bid and asked side in the system, the Bulletin Board (like the printed pink sheets) lets dealers display quotations on only one side if they wish. Or they can simply note an interest in a stock by entering a "bid wanted" or "offer wanted" solicitation.

Market-makers are the linchpin on all levels of OTC operation, and, in today's markets, are probably the feature that most clearly sets apart Nasdaq from Big Board trading. Whereas only the designated specialist can make a market in a stock on the exchange floor, any NASD member can register to make a market in any stock, provided the dealer meets a minimum capital requirement. Consequently, the NASD reports an average of 12 market-makers per Nasdaq security; in some of the most active stocks there may be more than 40 market-makers. Aside from having to display firm prices for at least 1,000 shares for National Market (or 500 for SmallCap) issues, they can't just walk in and out, moving into the market for a stock when interest is hot, and quickly switching their capital to other stocks when interest in the first stock lags. In case of unauthorized withdrawal, they are barred from again making a market in that stock for 20 business days. Surveillance computers will also quickly note if a dealer enters a quote "away from the market" and, as on the Big Board, can check the time sequence of transactions if there is questionable activity or a suspicion of trading on inside information.

Proponents maintain the multiple market-makers competing with each other make for narrower price spreads and greater market depth, while those rallying around exchange trading posts see superior merit in the concentration of order flow and the specialist's obligation to maintain an orderly market. Both systems generally work well, though both can leave investors shaken on days of market collapse. In fact, some snide observer commented after the October 1987 crash: "The specialists [on the NYSE] seemed powerless to stem the tide, but at least you knew where to find them, while many [Nasdaq] market makers just stopped answering their phones." NASD defenders responded vehemently that this was a gross distortion spread by Big Board adherents; they maintain that most dealers were continuously on the phone (and dealing) and the problem was mostly overloaded phone lines. In any event, both markets have since instituted measures that, they hope, will ameliorate the problems in future crises.

All in all, Nasdaq has clearly become a creditable marketplace, with prominent listing in the daily newspapers and regular coverage on the airwaves, and remains the chosen home of many companies that easily qualify for Big Board admission. But against these gains, it has had to accept the erosion of various market segments that used to be major OTC constituencies and have been successfully wooed by the Big Board during the past quarter century. At one time, banks and insurance companies were almost exclusively traded over-the-counter; now nearly all the larger members of these industries are listed on the NYSE. The Big Board has also attracted many larger ADRs (the American Depositary Receipts of foreign companies), though Nasdaq has maintained the lead in both the number of ADR listings and shares traded. And whereas in older times, even major companies, when first going public, spent at least some time getting "seasoned" in the OTC market, now it's possible for Initial Public Offerings involving substantial companies to start their trading right on the Big Board.

Despite such competition, Nasdaq has done well. In the number of shares traded, it pulled just about even with the Big Board in 1993, and on quite a number of days its share volume is actually larger. Of course, in dollar terms, the Big Board's lead is still substantial — though in 1993 Nasdaq moved up to 59% of the total dollar value of NYSE trades.

To reiterate, Nasdaq is a solid Number Two (its volume is well over 10 times that of the American Stock Exchange) and an important market for the average investor.

CHAPTER 17

Other Exchanges — and a Look Abroad

WHENEVER you hear anyone mention the "stock exchange," you can take it for granted they're talking about the New York Stock Exchange, the Big Board. The NYSE certainly dominates stock trading in the U.S.; but it's equally evident that it has no monopoly on stock exchange activity. The American Stock Exchange provides a bustling market, and so do a number of regional exchanges. Furthermore, our increasingly global economy has made American investors conscious of stock markets abroad.

While the various exchanges in the United States differ somewhat in their rules, regulations, and operating mechanics, fundamentally they function pretty much the same way as the NYSE — providing a setting for buyers and sellers of securities to meet via a continuous, open auction system. Exchanges active in interstate commerce must be registered with the SEC and are subject to the commission's supervision. That includes approval of all exchange rules and seeing that the exchanges hold members and their employees to proper standards.

Most prominent is the *American Stock Exchange* (known as the *Amex* for short). Before 1953, it was called the New York Curb Exchange, a name derived from its start as an outdoor market, along the curbs (and into the middle of the streets) of downtown Manhattan. By the 1840s, the brokers gathered regularly at Wall and Hanover streets, and later on Broad Street within sight of the snugly housed NYSE. While the rugged traders began to get more formally organized as the

New York Curb Agency in 1908, they continued to brave the New York weather until 1921, when they moved into their own building (repeatedly expanded but still in use) behind Trinity Church.

The trek indoors deprived the city of one of its literally most colorful spectacles. Clerks perched on the windowsills of their offices in adjoining buildings used to relay orders to their brokers — often clad in exotic and brightly colored garments so they could be readily spotted — who conducted the actual trading right in the street. Most of the trading was done by hand signals. That practice was long retained indoors, and one such hand signal is featured in the Amex portion of the film clip that introduces the *Wall Street Week* TV show each week. However, today's floor brokers and clerks rarely use such signals; besides, as on the Big Board, the bulk of orders now flows to the specialist electronically.

The Amex was traditionally regarded as a kind of prep school for the New York Stock Exchange. General Motors, Quaker Oats, and various oil giants are among the many Big Board stalwarts who got their seasoning on the "Little Board," as the "junior" exchange was sometimes called. But this role has diminished as, on the one hand, the NYSE became increasingly aggressive in wooing companies early in their trading career, while, on the other, the success of Nasdaq made companies less anxious to achieve exchange-listed status (at least, not until they could jump to the Big Board).

The Amex still lists such well-known American companies as computer-maker Amdahl, New York Times, Turner Broadcasting, and toymaker Hasbro. But by far the biggest Amex resident is B.A.T. Industries, the British conglomerate once known as British-American Tobacco. Other big Amex stocks include UK-based chemist Courtaulds, and major Canadian companies such as Imperial Oil, Brascan, and Ford Canada. The Amex also lists many smaller Canadian oil, gas, and mining companies, as well as many U.S. natural resources businesses. While best known for this resource sector, the Amex roster of over 800 companies actually represents a wide range of industries, from food to construction to entertainment to all types of retailers to financial services. Also housed on the Amex are preferred stocks, warrants, and bonds of a number of companies whose common stocks are listed on the NYSE.

Catering generally to smaller companies than the Big Board, the Amex tends to have more speculative stocks — often they are developing companies that hold great promise, but entail correspondingly high risk of failure. Consequently, the Amex market is proportionately strongest (both in volume and price trends) during periods of speculative enthusiasm and investor interest in smaller companies. Amex institutional activity has run at about 30% of total public volume in recent years, but it's still an exchange heavily impacted by individual investor moods.

Stock trading on the Amex grew briskly from about 1.1 million shares a day in 1960 to a record 18.1 million shares in 1993. However, it hasn't kept pace with the explosive growth on the Big Board. In the 1960s, Amex share volume was about one-third of the NYSE's; at the peak of the "hot issues" boom in 1968 the ratio climbed to 47%. In recent years, however, it's been well below 10%. And since the average Amex stock trades at a considerably lower per-share price than the typical NYSE listee, the disparity in dollar terms is much bigger. The dollar value of trading on the Amex now runs under 3% of the Big Board total; 30 years ago it was over 12%. As one offset to its reduced market share in stock trading, the Amex has become a leader in the trading of listed stock options (see chapter 24) and certain other specialized products, especially instruments related to international finance.

In March 1992, the SEC permitted the Amex to open an *Emerging Company Marketplace* for "start-up" or "incubator" companies. These companies are subject to substantially lower listing requirements and are also exempt from a number of disclosure and corporate governance standards such as outside directors and audit committees. These companies — which may have great promise but are clearly quite speculative — are listed separately in newspaper tables and their ticker symbols carry an EC suffix, but brokers may not always warn clients about the companies' special status.

Despite its junior status, the Amex takes pride in its modern trading facilities; indeed, it outpaced its big crosstown rival in some automation developments such as computerized stock surveillance. Its AUTOPER system (counterpart to the Big Board's SuperDot automated order handling system; the PER stands for Post Execution Reporting) was the first to utilize touch-screen techniques to expedite order execution.

Proposals to merge the NYSE and Amex (pushed by leading securities firms, whose business, of course, requires them to own memberships on both exchanges, and who therefore hoped joint operations might cut expenses) led to a feasibility study in 1970. Neither exchange expressed any great enthusiasm for the idea of a complete merger, but they did form the jointly owned Securities Industry Automation Corporation (SIAC) in 1972 to consolidate their technical facilities. They agreed to look further into the idea of a full combination. However, in July 1975, the Amex board of directors voted unanimously against a merger. Various subsequent merger suggestions involving the NYSE or Amex with various regional exchanges or with each other have surfaced from time to time, but so far have not led to any action.

Mergers have left their mark on the regional exchanges. The largest came into being in 1949, when the Chicago Stock Exchange effected a consolidation of its activities with the exchanges in Cleveland, St. Louis, and Minneapolis–St. Paul, and assumed the name of *Midwest Stock Exchange*. The now-defunct Detroit and Pittsburgh exchanges turned down the 1949 merger invitation, but in 1960 the small New Orleans Stock Exchange agreed to be absorbed by the Midwest. Chicago represented most of the action throughout, and in late 1993 the Midwest reverted to the *Chicago Stock Exchange* title. Meantime, the San Francisco and Los Angeles exchanges combined in 1959 to form the *Pacific Stock Exchange*, with interconnected trading floors in the two California cities (however, stock trading became concentrated in Los Angeles, options trading in San Francisco).

Similarly, the Philadelphia exchange — the proud senior among all U.S. exchanges, having been founded in 1790, two years before the "buttonwood agreement" that launched the Big Board — combined with two Midatlantic neighbors to form the Philadelphia-Baltimore-Washington (PBW) Stock Exchange. However, it has since reassumed the plain *Philadelphia Stock Exchange* name. Among the active regionals, only the *Boston Stock Exchange* has steered clear of the merger movement.

Regional exchanges were originally organized to provide a marketplace for the stocks of local companies. But as these companies grew and acquired national reputations, they usually wanted their securities listed in New York. Consequently, trading on the regionals languished.

However, the regional exchanges have managed, in effect, to turn the tables on the Big Board. Nowadays, most of their trading (at times, over 95%) consists of stocks listed on the NYSE. That's possible because by now nearly all actively traded Big Board stocks are *dually listed* and eligible to be traded on one or more of the regionals.

Some decades ago, the regionals served as a place where Big Board member firms could "meet" nonmembers for trades not possible on the Big Board floor. Specifically, since members were not permitted to split their Big Board commission with nonmembers of the NYSE, they had no way to pay a nonmember for contributing to a Big Board trade. So, if a securities dealer that did not belong to the Big Board had a sizable block of some Big Board stock to buy or sell, it might arrange to have the order executed on a regional exchange by a firm that had memberships both on the NYSE and the regional. The NYSE member was then free to develop the other side of the order — finding a purchaser to match the dealer's sell order or a seller to match its buy order. In that way, the nonmember and the member firm could split the commission.

Under congressional and SEC mandate, the restrictive rules have disappeared. Since 1976, there have been no restraints on a member firm's ability to execute a customer's order for a Big Board stock wherever it thought best — in the over-the-counter market, on a regional exchange, or on the New York Stock Exchange. And the introduction of the consolidated tape and the Intermarket Trading System facilitate finding the best market for a stock at any particular time and directing orders there. Specialists at the regionals are encouraged to make competitive markets, which has increased their order flow. At the same time, the trading desks of brokerage firms often find it convenient to "cross" trades of large blocks on a regional exchange, which can bypass an accumulation of orders on the Big Board specialist's books.

The Pacific Stock Exchange enjoys a unique distinction. It stays open half an hour after the Big Board closes, which currently means trades can be executed until 4:30 P.M. Eastern or 1:30 Pacific time. When some unusual corporate event or cataclysmic general news "breaks" right after the New York closing hour, there may be a flurry of excited trading out West. But no need for you to get too excited by it; assuming you heard the news in time to place an order, there'd be no time to get all the pertinent facts, much less analyze them. And more often than not, the quick Pacific response has proved to be an overreaction compared with the early Big Board trading the next morning.

The wave of dual-listed trading has largely bypassed the Amex. For a long time, the rule was that a stock could not be traded on more than one exchange in the same city. In 1980, the SEC rescinded this requirement and the NYSE took on some stocks while they were still trading on the Amex (normally, Amex trading stops when a stock "moves up" to the Big Board), but the impact was minimal. There has been no such dual New York trading since 1983. And while the regionals eagerly pursue business in NYSE stocks, they rarely bother to compete for trading in any Amex-listed stock. However, as with Big Board stocks, trades for Amex-listed securities may be executed over-the-counter through Nasdaq facilities. Any such trades are duly reported on the Amex Consolidated Tape, the junior exchange's counterpart to the NYSE's Consolidated Tape.

One special case among the regionals is the *Cincinnati Stock Exchange*. It had declined an invitation to join the Midwest Exchange and carried on very limited trading until the late 1970s. Then it began to offer a computer-based automatic trading system managed by Control Data Corporation. The system provides for the computer to match and execute orders without the intervention of specialists or other market-makers. However, the exchange never attracted many orders and the rapid development of other electronically aided systems on the exchanges and over-the-counter seem to have bypassed the Cincinnati experiment.

For the individual investor, the key point about multiple listings is that, through more competitive marketplaces, they should make it easier for you to get the best available price, whether buying or selling. It doesn't require extra study; the prices from all markets are already factored in when you look at a newspaper or a quotation terminal.

It's also worthwhile to have a nodding acquaintance with foreign markets — though, as we'll explain, you'll probably want to make any actual international investments through convenient U.S. facilities.

Close both geographically and in financial organization is Canada. By far the biggest stock market there is the *Toronto Stock Exchange*. There are also major exchanges in Montreal and in Vancouver (particularly active in mining stocks).

Canada does not have a national agency like our SEC to regulate its securities business. Instead, each province has its own commission. The *Ontario Securities Commission,* by virtue of its supervision of Canada's financial capital, Toronto, and the nation's industrial heartland, is the most influential. While in earlier days, securities regulation was considerably less rigorous north of the border where a good deal more let-the-buyer-beware sentiment prevailed, standards have since been stiffened substantially, particularly so in Ontario.

Among the worst abusers were boiler shops with a crew of telephone salespeople peddling the stocks of questionable if not fictitious oil and mining companies to potential victims throughout North America. Over the past quarter century, stiffer laws, regulation, and international cooperation have sharply curtailed such ventures, though, of course, we'll probably never be able to wipe out all such confidence schemes — in Canada, the U.S., or anywhere in this world.

Meantime, the legitimate markets in Canada are very much part of the worldwide trend toward more efficient trading. For instance, the Toronto Stock Exchange calls itself the "world leader in automated exchange trade execution." Its "Market-by-Price" service is designed to give the investor a current look at the specialist's book, showing not only the best bids and offers at the moment, but also all tradable orders at the next few levels up (for offers) or down (for bids) — in short, letting traders know how much stock is available at different prices.

Across the Atlantic, the preeminent market is the London Stock Exchange. You won't find an active trading floor at the exchange's headquarters; it was closed down in early 1992. For several years before that, the modern-looking trading posts you could view from the visitor's gallery were virtually deserted. The few people on the floor were clustered at the post devoted to options trading — and now the options exchange has moved to new quarters. Don't get the wrong idea — the stock exchange is very much in business. However, the trading is now more patterned after Nasdaq, and it's the unseen computers that do the work, responding to orders that traders give, receive, and instruct to be executed at their office desks.

London has been able to maintain its position as the leading securities market center in Europe, actively trading many securities of Continental countries as well as those of America and the Far East. As Europe heads toward more economic integration, London will have to fend off competition not only from Germany (the strongest European economy) but also from France, where the Paris Bourse has put in automatic transfer and transaction systems in an effort to become a major international securities player, and possibly from some other would-be competitors on the Continent.

In the Pacific area, the Tokyo Stock Exchange has a strong lead, though stock markets in Singapore, Australia, Hong Kong (at least for now), and elsewhere also attract considerable attention. Since 1987, Tokyo and the NYSE have been alternating as the world's number-one exchange, depending on the fluctuations in the relative strength of their markets, with London a steady number three. (Of course, if you consider *markets* rather than just *exchanges*, Nasdaq, as noted in the preceding chapter, pushed into the number-two spot starting 1992.)

The Big Three exchanges, with many major stocks traded on all three, have become the accepted weather vanes of daily stock movements, and in tandem provide round-the-clock trading. As Americans arise, the business news reports tell them what happened during Tokyo's day and how London fared in early trading (of course, West Coast residents can also hear how the Big Board opened as they sip their morning coffee). By late morning, New Yorkers know how London closed. And not long after the NYSE shuts down, Tokyo traders are prepared to start the next day. Some exchanges and Nasdaq have added special "off-hours" trading sessions, with relatively modest impact so far. But more moves are contemplated that proponents hope will provide a far more comprehensive 24-hour pattern.

Such increasingly close coordination of the global markets has obvious advantages for the world economy and those who play major roles in it — and indirectly for all of us who benefit from a more efficient economy and market. But that doesn't mean you have to follow, much less participate in, a 24-hour marketplace. As Gordon Maclin, former chairman of the NASD, warns, the off-hour markets have "too much volatility, too little liquidity for most small investors." If you get the urge to trade in the middle of the night, he suggests, "take two aspirins and call your broker in the morning."

In fact, although — with U.S. stocks now representing only around one-third of total world capitalization as against two-thirds two decades ago — it makes sense to at least *consider* putting some money into foreign securities, that doesn't mean you must venture *directly* into foreign markets at any time of the day.

Aside from timing and communications problems, you'd have to deal with different currencies, possible exchange restrictions, different trading rules and requirements, the need to arrange for certificate delivery and dividend collection, and sundry other headaches. Even more important, information on foreign companies is much harder to come by, both because of distance and because of far more limited disclosure rules. Accounting procedures also may vary significantly from U.S. customs; moreover, securities regulation and market surveillance tend to be far more lax.

Fortunately, there are easier ways to add a foreign touch to your portfolio. You can invest in mutual funds that specialize in foreign securities or you can acquire a stake in foreign companies that have securities traded in the U.S. market.

Particularly for your first venture abroad, you may want to choose a mutual fund (see chapter 18), which will provide both diversification and professional guidance. There are two major categories of funds that concentrate on foreign stocks. *Global* funds invest in a worldwide portfolio that includes the U.S. as well as a broad array of foreign countries. The proportion of fund assets invested in each country and region will vary from time to time, depending on the fund managers' view of the relative opportunities and risks in each sector.

International funds concentrate on securities of non-U.S. companies. Some may roam the world, others focus primarily on a specific region such as Europe or the Far East or even a specific country such as Japan, Germany, or Mexico. Some funds in these narrow-focus groups are among those with the best long-term track records. But, of course, narrow-based funds are also the most vulnerable to sudden turns in a specific stock market. In particular, there's often a rush by fund sponsors to create new funds covering a suddenly "hot" area or country. With several groups bidding for a limited supply of securities, this can exaggerate a quick run-up, followed by a period of painful readjustment. In short, while mutual funds can be a good vehicle for international investing, it's still important for individual buyers to consider the prospects and risks when they invest.

Another specialized category is *world income* funds. These invest primarily in bonds or other fixed-income securities from around the world, normally including the U.S. Such funds seek to enhance their income and also guard against possible adverse interest trends in the U.S. or other specific groups of countries by having their eggs in a goodly number of baskets — but varying the number of eggs in each as they foresee changes in the outlook of each region.

One major factor that all fund managers (and, for that matter, all individual investors) must constantly consider in international investments is *currency risk*. There'd be no profit investing in country X if the stock doubles in the local market but the country's currency now is worth only half as many dollars as when that stock was bought. On the other hand, when the dollar goes down against a currency, even a flat local stock market or relatively low interest rate on bonds may translate into satisfying dollar gains.

Remember that you don't avoid the impact of such exchange-rate variations when you buy a foreign stock in the U.S. Indeed, currency fluctuations also affect the performance of many U.S. companies that do a lot of their business abroad. When the dollar is down, the profits that their foreign operations earn (in foreign currencies) contribute a much greater dollar amount to the company's consolidated earnings; conversely, a strong dollar means these operations add fewer dollars to the parent's earnings report.

Now, what if you've decided you want to buy some foreign securities directly? You'll have a wide choice right here in the U.S. through *American Depositary Receipts* or *ADRs*. The system is simple. Regularly issued shares of the foreign company are placed with a trustee or depositary, such as the London branch of a U.S. bank, which issues receipts against them. These ADRs can then be traded — in dollars — on the NYSE, Amex, or Nasdaq in exactly the same manner as American stocks. If you hold an ADR, you're entitled to all the ownership privileges of the underlying shares, including dividends and stock dividends. If the company offers stockholder rights to, say, purchase an additional issue of stock, it probably won't want to bother to register the new or additional stock with the SEC, and thus it can't be issued to U.S. holders; consequently, the depositary will usually sell the rights abroad and pass on the proceeds to you.

In some cases, each ADR represents one share of the foreign stock. However, since many foreign markets prefer to have their stocks trade at much lower per-share levels than is customary in the U.S., one ADR may instead cover five, 10, or more of the underlying shares. It's all a matter of bookkeeping, and when you get a financial report it should spell out what the earnings, dividends, and other per-share data are in terms of your ADR. And companies which have ADRs outstanding are usually covered in the stock manuals and by brokerage reports, so it's relatively easy to gather information on them.

ADRs were first developed in 1927 to ease the bother and delay of shipping certificates across the Atlantic by steamer, but they've grown far more popular in the age of jets and electronic transmission. There are now some 980 ADR issues (more than six times the 1961 level). There are well over 100 issues each from Australia, Britain, and Japan; if you're country-hopping, you can find an ADR for companies from Austria to Zimbabwe.

Not on the ADR list is Canada, because there the system is even simpler. Most major and a great many smaller Canadian issues can be traded directly in the U.S. markets. One caution: You have to keep in mind that Canadian companies usually report in Canadian dollars, which in recent years have been much lower than the U.S. dollar (there have also been a couple of periods since World War II when the Canadian dollar was at a premium). Even more important, when you see a quotation on the stock from the Toronto Stock Exchange and on the same stock from the Big Board, the figures will differ considerably because they are in different dollars.

One aspect to remember with all foreign investments — direct, in ADRs, or through mutual funds — is that dividend payments will likely be subject to foreign tax withholdings. The maximum amount of withholding varies by country and is often covered by tax treaties with the U.S. In case of mutual funds, you can expect an annual statement spelling out just how much was withheld on your holdings in each country; on ADRs, you should get a statement from the depositary or your broker. Usually, you'll be entitled to offset much or all of these withholdings against your U.S. tax. Admittedly, this doesn't help much if your investment is in an IRA or 401(k) plan not subject to current taxation, and the tax factor should be one consideration when you compute your total return from such investments. Still, it will usually be very worth your while to have some foreign diversification.

Besides, you might ask, which is really the foreign investment — Coca-Cola, which gets around 75 percent of its income from abroad; or Honda, which gets about 60 percent of its earnings from the U.S.?

CHAPTER 18

Mutual Funds — a "Packaged" Way to Invest

TODAY, many investors find that the most practical entry into the world of securities is through mutual funds or other forms of *packaged investments*. In essence, by buying a single security you acquire a stake in a whole group of investments. The main allure is that you obtain 1) considerable diversification, even if your investment is small, thus spreading your risk, and 2) professional investment management, usually at a moderate cost.

You can find specific funds to meet most any investment objective from "aggressive growth" to "preservation of capital" to "income" to specialization in one industry or country. You can also find funds that combine objectives such as "growth and income." And close to 15% of American households have entrusted well over half a trillion dollars of their "cash" holdings to money market funds, a special type of mutual fund whose distinctive characteristics will be discussed in the next chapter.

Mutual funds are the most popular category of what's known as an *investment trust,* or, in line with the basic federal regulatory law enacted in 1940, an *investment company*. The concept on which they operate is simple. Suppose you and some of your friends — say, 20 of you — each have $1,000 to spare. Instead of investing the money individually, you might decide to pool it. You turn the whole sum over to one individual, or manager, to invest for you.

In that situation, the 20 of you would constitute an investment company, in miniature.

Now let's assume you're lucky and that at the end of the first year your manager is able to report that he (or, as is the case in a number of major funds, she) has made money for you. The value of the stocks that the fund owns has risen from $20,000 to $22,000. Each share in it is now worth $1,100 ($22,000 divided by 20).

You've been so successful, as a matter of fact, that some of your other friends would like to join your little fund. The 20 of you must now make one of two decisions.

You may decide that you're going to restrict the fund to just the original members and their original capital, thereby creating a *closed-end* fund. Newcomers can become shareholders in your company only if and when one of the original 20 wants to sell his or her share to somebody else for whatever he or she can get for it, the typical right enjoyed by the shareholders of any company.

The alternative plan would involve a decision to expand your fund and take in new members. Since your own shares are now worth $1,100 apiece, you decide to allow others to buy in on that basis — $1,100 a share. That $1,100 would represent the *net asset value* per share at that time — a figure determined by taking the current market value of all the investments the fund holds and dividing it by the number of fund shares outstanding. Net asset value per share is a constantly changing figure for two reasons: (1) the total value of your fund's holdings fluctuates as the prices of the securities that it owns change in the market; (2) the number of shares outstanding changes, too, as additional shares are sold (either to new buyers or to present fund participants who want more shares) while the fund also continually redeems shares for those owners who want to sell.

If you decide that your fund should be operated in this manner, you will have transformed your company into an *open-end* fund. That's the type generally known as a mutual fund.

As you may have noted in our thumbnail description above, prices of mutual fund shares are determined in a different manner from those of stocks. In contrast to stocks (including those of closed-end funds) and bonds, whose price at any time depends directly on what a buyer is then willing to pay and a seller willing to accept, open-end mutual funds are always bought and sold on the basis of their exact net asset value (often simply shown by the abbreviation *NAV*). The funds, which must be ready to sell or redeem shares on demand every business day, consequently compute their net asset value daily. This NAV is the price you pay if you buy, or receive if you sell (or, more precisely, redeem) shares — plus a possible sales charge, or, less often, minus a redemption charge.

These days most mutual funds are sponsored by large organizations that operate whole groups or "families" of funds. Many are independent companies that concentrate on the mutual fund business. Also active are several major brokerage houses, which have set up specialized fund subsidiaries; their funds are primarily designed for sale through the firm's own brokerage offices but may also be available from others. Others in the field include insurance companies; some own units that sell funds to the general public, and many life insurance companies offer stock and bond funds in connection with their variable annuity policies.

The sponsors normally act as *distributors* (the legal term for the organization that makes the shares available to investors) or principal underwriters and, depending on the fund, you may buy (and sell) them by giving orders to your regular securities broker, some other authorized investment professionals, or the fund's own "800" number. Most funds that do direct marketing make sure their phone number is prominently displayed in commercials or the print ads that pepper investment publications.

Most funds have a minimum initial purchase requirement that may run from a few hundred to many thousands of dollars — often with a lower minimum if you open an IRA or other special type of account. You generally buy "by the dollar" — you send in a check and the fund administrator figures out how many shares (down to three or four decimal places) your payment will cover, based on the NAV determined at the end of the day your order is received.

To pay for the sales effort (including compensation for the individual broker or other salesperson), many funds impose a sales charge or *load* when you buy. The maximum permitted load is 8.5%, though in today's competitive age most funds charge less. Whatever the load percentage, it is figured on the *total* amount you pay. Thus, if you put $100 into a fund with the maximum 8.5% load, only $91.50 ($100 − $8.50) would be used to buy fund shares. Consequently, if you think of the sales charge as the mutual fund equivalent of a commission, you'd be paying 9.3% ($8.50 charge on $91.50 invested = 9.3%) in this case. On the other hand, you normally don't pay any charge when you sell these fund shares, whereas on a stock investment you pay one commission when you buy and another when you sell.

In the newspaper quotation listings for mutual funds, you usually find the first price column headed "NAV"; it gives the actual net asset value at which you can normally redeem the shares. The next column, usually labeled "buy" or "offer price," is what a share costs when you pay that fund's full load.

Often, funds have sliding schedules with lower loads for larger purchases — say, a basic 6.5% load which is reduced to 6% if you invest at least $10,000, 5% for $25,000, and perhaps as little as 0.75% for a million-dollar investor (most likely an institution, of course). If you're not prepared to invest the minimum needed for a lower load but think you'll want to put more money into the fund later, certain funds let you file a *Letter of Intent* that makes you eligible for the lower load when your total purchases reach the required minimum. But, unless you're definite about your future plans, make sure it only gives you the *right* and not the *obligation* to buy additional shares.

In fact, such obligations — imbedded in long-term commitments to keep buying — were once the source of major abuse and, though far less frequently used today, can still cause problems for unwary investors. During the first explosive growth of mutual funds in the 1950s, one segment of the industry relied heavily on moonlighting salespeople who themselves were little acquainted with securities and had little supervision. This aggressive sales force pushed so-called *contractual* plans under which customers agreed to fixed monthly purchases, often for as long as 10 to 15 years. While the total load on purchases throughout the plan's life might be only 5% to 6%, most of this sales commission was collected right up front. Typically, if the customer signed up for a $50-a-month plan, of the $600 paid in the first year, $300 would go to the sellers and only $300 would actually be invested in the fund. If the buyers wanted to cancel their contract and redeem what shares they had, it would usually be several years, even in good markets and with successful funds, before they'd get back as much as they'd invested.

In a 1966 report, the SEC found that 20% of all those who bought such contractual plans were forced to sell at a loss because they couldn't keep up the payments. And most of those were the investors, sometimes signing up for just $10 or $20 a month, who could least afford such a loss. In the *Investment Company Amendments Act of 1970*, Congress enacted some protective provisions. For instance, you can cancel your contract within the first 45 days and get the commission fully refunded. Within 18 months, you can cancel, with 85% of the commission returned. Also, sales forces are under stronger supervision.

Most promoters lost interest in contractual plans after the 1970 restrictions were enacted, but a few are still around. While there are good arguments for disciplined, steady investing, be careful of straitjacketing yourself.

Some funds do not charge a sales fee and are known as *no-load* funds. Since that makes the "NAV" and "buy" prices identical, newspaper tables usually show "NL" in the "buy" column for these funds. Most no-loads are sponsored by direct-marketing organizations that advertise heavily but wait for you to contact them by phone or mail; thus, they have no sales agents to compensate. Some brokerage houses (especially discounters) have agreements with certain no-load funds that permit them to execute orders for them, but the brokerage firm may charge a small commission for its service.

Another category, which has gained some popularity in recent years, is the *rear-load* fund. Like the no-loads, these funds sell their shares at net asset value with no initial (or "front-load") sales charge, but do impose a "contingent deferred sales charge." Under such a charge, you may have to pay, say, 6% for shares you redeem within a year, 5% for redemptions in the second year, and so on, until after six years you can redeem shares without fee. Other funds start with 4% the first year, and let you redeem without penalty after four years. The idea is to give you the benefit (as in no-loads) of having all the money you invest put to work for you right away; but, if you're a short-term holder or frequent switcher, the rear-load fee makes you pay for some of the costs of opening and handling your account. There are also some funds (including some no-loads) that charge small redemption fees, or per-check fees if they permit you to make withdrawals by writing checks on your fund account.

One other, much debated charge is the *12b-1 fee*, named after the SEC rule that authorizes it, which funds may impose, in place of or (mostly) in addition to load charges. Unlike the front or rear loads, which you pay at the time you buy or sell fund shares and which are charged directly to you, 12b-1 fees are recurring charges that are assessed on the fund as a whole, based on its total assets (the fee's official name is *asset-based sales charge*). Thus, you "pay" in the form of an increase in the fund's total expenses, which translates into a deduction from each share's net asset value. The rationale for the 12b-1 fee is that it permits fund assets to be employed to attract new shareholders, which is supposed to be beneficial for present holders because a bigger fund is expected to be able to operate more efficiently.

While 12b-1 practices among funds vary widely, a majority of front-load funds haven't imposed 12b-1 fees; the rest have generally kept them at the low end, in the 0.25%-to-0.50% range. By contrast, 12b-1 fees are imposed by a substantial majority of rear-load funds, and have often been in the 1%-to-1.25% range. The whole 12b-1 issue has been very controversial. It's noted, for instance, that annual imposition of a 12b-1 fee can negate the advantage for long-term holders of rear-load funds. In such a fund you may avoid paying any load by becoming a long-term holder, but if there's also a 12b-1 fee, over the years it may cost you more than if you had invested in a similar fund with the load up front and no recurring 12b-1 charge.

In 1992, the SEC finally approved a new NASD rule (the NASD

gets into the act because its members do most of the fund selling) that put specific ceilings on 12b-1 fees effective July 1993. The maximum permitted annual charge was set at 0.75%, but up to an additional 0.25% can be imposed as a "service fee," which the fund can then pay to brokers for "providing ongoing information and assistance" to their fund-owning customers. Incidentally, the rule bars no-load funds from charging regular 12b-1 fees; however, they may assess the up-to-0.25% "service fee" to help defray advertising and other sales promotion activities.

Another part of the new rule sets a cap on the total sales charges that may be levied over the years by any fund that charges a 12b-1 fee. In essence, whenever the fund sells $100 in new shares, it earns the authority to levy a total of $6.25 (6.25%) in sales charges, immediately or (as will be true in most cases) over a period of time. These charges may be in the form of front or rear loads, 12b-1 fees, or any combination. And to the extent these charges are not collected right away, the fund is entitled to interest at the prime-rate-plus-1% on the as-yet-unassessed portion. Furthermore, the 6.25% cap does not include the 0.25% "service fees," which may be assessed year after year indefinitely. But if a fund forgoes collecting any service fee, its 12b-1 lifetime cap is raised from 6.25% to 7.25%.

The new rule does cut the permitted annual 12b-1 rate below the level that a number of funds had been imposing. It also puts some limit on fees piling up "forever," though it will take more than eight years for the 0.75% annual fee to reach the 6.25% cap. And, remember, 12b-1 fees are assessed on the assets of the fund as a whole, not on the individual holder. So even if you hold your shares for 10 or 15 years, the new rule won't free you from 12b-1 assessments. What it should mean is that, if there are a lot of longtime holders, after a while only a portion of fund assets can be used to calculate the annual fee; as a result, the maximum permitted charge on *everyone* (old or new) in the fund will work out to be less than 0.75%.

For a number of years, a good many fund sponsors have offered funds split into two categories. One class (frequently called "A") carries a front load; the other (often "B") instead has a rear load and usually a 12b-1 fee. Except for the fee structure, the funds are identical. The complex new rules will no doubt lead to further modifications and probably some additional share classes. As one example, some fund groups propose to overcome the problem of longtime holders being permanently saddled with 12b-1 fees by automatically converting their holdings, after a certain time, into an "A" or other no-further-fee version of the fund.

In any case, the fund's 12b-1 practices as well as all other fees must be clearly spelled out in the prospectus required to be furnished every fund buyer (and updated at least annually). The SEC now requires each prospectus to include a table that shows how much a $1,000 investment would entail in fees and operating expenses over one, three, five, and 10 years. The table must follow standardized rules to make one fund's fees and expenses easier to compare with those of other funds. In the uniform expense tables you'll find a note that the calculations "assume a 5% annual return." This has nothing to do with any estimate of *investment* returns; it's just that, since many of the management fees are based on a percentage of total assets, an asset figure is needed for each year so you can compute the expenses. And the SEC told everyone to use 5% growth a year, strictly as an example, to put figures for all the funds on an equal basis. Presumably, you hope the fees on your investment will be higher than shown in the prospectus example — which would happen if the fund achieved a higher investment return and, hence, a larger growth in assets.

The standard table first shows *Shareholder Transaction Expenses* — the sales and redemption charges that are imposed on individual holders when (and only when) they decide to buy or sell. By contrast, the 12b-1 fees are part of the *Annual Fund Operating Expenses,* and, like the fees for managing the fund's investments and the other costs of operating the fund, are paid out of the assets of the fund and thus borne by all the fundholders.

While the sponsoring organization or its affiliates generally furnish administrative and investment management services, each fund must have its own board of directors (or trustees), voted for by the shareholders in that fund, with a majority of the directors not affiliated with the management company. These independent directors — and, at stated times, the shareholders — must approve the agreement that spells out the fees received by the investment managers. These fees vary considerably, depending in part on the size and type of funds (for instance, an international fund requiring expert advice around the globe tends to be on the high end; relatively low fees are charged by bond funds, which require comparatively few investment analysts). Similarly, other operating expenses, such as custodian and auditing fees and shareholder servicing, also vary considerably. Again, when evaluating a fund, you should compare the entire fees and expenses with those of other funds of the same type.

According to respected scorekeeper Lipper Analytical, total annual expenses (management, fund operating, and 12b-1 expenses, but not any front- or rear-load charges) have recently averaged about 1.4% of assets for most standard types of domestic stock funds, 1.9% for global stock funds, 1.8% for specialized sector funds, just under 1% for bond funds, and 0.75% for municipals — but with considerable individual variations within each category.

A fund's expense level certainly bears watching. It obviously affects how much investment income filters through to the fund's shareholders, and, what's more, the impact is compounded — the more it takes out of one year's earnings, the less investment funds are working for you the next year. Just the same, the most significant factor for any fund is how successful it is in its investments. After all, just as one company may be in the business of manufacturing widgets, and another in the selling of groceries, a mutual fund is in the business of making investments.

But its financial reports are usually presented in a form somewhat different from those of other businesses. The key tabulation to look for shows operating results and changes in net asset value on a per-share basis. The table will show *net investment income;* that, however, only reflects the dividends and interest the fund has earned on its securities portfolio, less the fund's expenses. You have to add to that figure the *realized gains (or losses),* which means the money the fund made or lost on the securities it sold during the period covered by the report, and also the *unrealized gains (or losses)*, which is the gain or loss in the market value of the securities the fund still holds in its portfolio. It's the sum of those figures that represents what really matters most — the *total return* the fund has earned for you during the period.

One happy way in which mutual funds and most other investment companies differ from ordinary corporations is that they pay no income taxes — provided they pass substantially all their dividend, interest, and capital gains receipts on to the fund's holders. That's only fair — *double taxation*, when a corporation pays taxes and then you in turn have to pay taxes on the dividends paid out of those already-taxed earnings, is bad enough; but it would be *triple taxation* if first the corporation, then the share-owning mutual fund, and finally you the fundholder would all have to write a check to the IRS.

So what happens is that the fund will pay out the equivalent of its net investment income in dividends — often monthly, quarterly, or semiannually — and pay out separate capital gains distributions, usually near the end of the year. You must enter these sums on your tax return, on either the dividend or capital gains lines — unless of course you have an IRA or other tax-deferred account. As in the case of savings bank interest, you are liable for the tax whether you actually receive the dividends in cash, or, as many fund investors do, instead have dividends automatically reinvested in more shares of the fund. *Automatic reinvestment* is a pretty painless way to have your investment grow. And, with rare exceptions, even funds that impose a load charge on new purchases will not charge a fee on dividend reinvestments.

Let's assume that the XYZ Fund starts the year with an NAV of exactly $12. During the year, it earns dividends and interest of 68¢, and incurs expenses of 15¢, leaving it a net investment income of 53¢ per fund share. In addition, the fund realizes $1.05 from capital gains, but the investments it kept in its portfolio lost 11¢ in market value during the year (that's the "unrealized loss"). As far as you're concerned, that means the fund earned for you a total of $1.47 per share (0.53 + 1.05 − 0.11 = 1.47). That would have built up the NAV from $12 to $13.47. However, since the fund paid out 53¢ in dividends and $1.05 in capital gains distributions, the NAV actually ended the year at

$11.89 (13.47 − 0.53 − 1.05). Thus, in this quite realistic example, while your fund provided you with a substantial 12.25 percent total return ($1.47 on the start-of-year NAV of $12), if you just looked at the NAV, you'd feel you were down for the year.

So, while looking at the NAV quotations in the newspaper gives you an idea how your fund's investment portfolio is faring from day to day, it bears repeating: In mutual funds, keep your eye on the total return. It's really far more significant than the yield, which is often prominently featured in ads and reports, especially (but far from exclusively) for bond funds. Yield is normally figured as the annualized percentage of the NAV that's paid out as investment-income dividends (even if a fund mostly collects *interest* on the securities it holds, what it pays out is *dividends*). For instance, some funds holding lower-rated bonds may be paying out high current dividends, but in the meantime the value of the portfolio is plunging. That could leave you with a fat (and taxable) reported yield but a decidedly negative total return.

Taxable distributions also raise a timely point on investment timing. Since, to meet tax law requirements, many funds distribute the bulk of their capital gains for the year sometime in December, it can be worthwhile to postpone a planned investment till after the distribution is made. Otherwise you may quickly find yourself with what in effect is a large refund (and corresponding lowering of the NAV). That "refund" would be based on capital gains the fund realized long before you bought into it — but you'll be taxed on them nonetheless.

Total return is almost always expressed as a percent of net asset value. But be sure to check just what the specific return you're looking at represents. For instance, we're accustomed to seeing interest rates or dividend yields quoted as annual percentages. In total returns, however, the figure you see most often in fund reports or financial press tabulations is the *cumulative return* for the specified period — whether that's for four weeks, 12 months, 10 years, or the entire life of the fund. For instance, if during one quarter the NAV has risen from $10 to $10.18 (and there have been no dividend distributions), the total return will be reported as 1.8% (which works out to a compounded annual rate of about 7.4%). And when looking at long-term performance, remember that, say, a 10-year return of 104% doesn't mean the fund averaged better than 10% a year. It tells you a $1,000 investment 10 years ago (with all dividends reinvested) is now worth $2,040 — but the compounded return works out to only 7.4% annually.

Some results for multiyear periods, however, are presented on an annualized basis. Another difference to watch for is whether load charges (and, in some cases, *any* expenses) are figured in. All the different presentations may be perfectly reasonable — but you want to be sure you know which yardstick is being used.

Also, in volatile markets, returns may vary sharply from month to month — and range from positive to negative and back. A negative return occurs when the value of the portfolio has fallen by more than the amount of any dividend and capital gains distribution. You must expect that to happen every now and then, just as fluctuations are inevitable in any single stock you own; the idea is to keep your eye on the longer term.

If you've decided that mutual funds are a good idea for you, a first step might well be to decide what type or types of fund are most suitable in your situation. There are no official definitions, and individual analysts may differ somewhat in the categories they set up for pigeonholing funds. One convenient set of performance tabulations (prepared by Lipper Analytical Services) is found on the second-from-last page of the *Wall Street Journal*; it features a different fund category each day. But remember: Within each category different funds still vary considerably in their policies and strategies.

One major group consists of *equity funds*. As the name implies, these funds invest mostly in stocks, though they may also hold some bonds, along with varying amounts of "cash" (i.e., money market securities). All funds keep some cash-type securities on hand, so they'll be able to meet share redemption requests and other short-term operating needs; also, when there's a big influx of share buyers, it may take some time before the fund manager finds suitable stocks into which to put the new cash. And fund managers may want to build up a higher than usual cash position at times when they think the safe income from Treasury bills or commercial paper makes a better investment than more stocks or long-term bonds.

Among major categories in the equity group:

Growth (sometimes called "Capital Growth") funds concentrate on stocks they expect to increase in value, and give no consideration to current income; they usually have moderate turnover — that is, they prefer to stick with the stocks they pick.

Small-Company Growth funds seek out smaller companies that they feel have good growth prospects. Because small companies that succeed may do so spectacularly, offsetting the loss of the many that don't make it, small companies as a whole have often outperformed the stock market over the long run, but they are far more volatile, and hence risky.

Capital Appreciation (sometimes called "aggressive growth") tries to have its portfolio value grow over the years through active trading ("high turnover"). Such funds may move heavily into cash when they don't see favorable market opportunities. Some may be authorized to leverage their operations through margin trading, options dealing, and the like.

Equity Income funds seek mainly to provide a high current return. They invest in stocks with good yields (such as utilities) and may supplement their holdings with some bonds.

Growth and Income funds try to blend two popular objectives. They look for stocks that should go up in value but also pay good (and, hopefully, increasing) dividends.

Tapping world markets are *International* funds that invest primarily in foreign stocks and *Global* funds, which seek a mix of U.S. and foreign securities.

Then there are more specialized equity funds, such as those that concentrate on *Natural Resources*, or *Gold*, or so-called *Sector* funds that limit themselves to a specific industry such as biotechnology or chemicals or communications.

Yet another type of equity fund that has become increasingly popular is the *Index Fund*. It seeks to mirror the performance of the general market, by investing in the same stocks (and in the same proportion) as a broad-based market index, especially the Standard & Poor's 500-stock index (S&P 500). The concept first took hold among pension-fund managers in the 1970s; they felt that, if investment managers often had difficulty outperforming the averages, why not (at least in part) simply invest in the averages? Then in 1976 Vanguard introduced the first index fund directed at individuals. After all, over the long term, the market as a whole has been an excellent performer. And since stock selection in an index fund is a largely mechanical process, you can save considerably on investment management and stock trading costs; index funds, accordingly, tend to have low expense ratios. While the S&P 500 is the most common criterion, index funds have been patterned after other indexes, including those representing some specialized market segments (such as an index representing the universe of small-capitalization stocks and, more recently, also some devoted to mid-capitalization stocks to fill the gap between large and small), global securities, and various bond indexes.

The advent of index funds — and, to an even greater extent, the proliferation of index options and futures contracts, which we'll discuss in chapter 24 — uprooted one of the oldest Wall Street adages. It long was a truism that "you can't buy the market," i.e., you can only buy specific stocks, which might follow quite different trends than the market as a whole. Now you can indeed "buy the market" — in fact, several versions of the market.

Another fundamental grouping are *bond funds*, which in recent times have often outstripped equity funds in popularity. One reason no doubt is that many investors were shaken by high stock market volatility, while bonds for most of the past decade have offered relatively high yields. Another factor may be that it's pretty easy for people to buy a specific stock, while bond markets are not geared toward the small-scale investor, so there's a greater tendency to do your bond investing through funds.

Different types of bond funds are available by issuer — such as corporate, government, tax-exempt municipals, global — and in most of these groups also by maturity — long-term, intermediate-term (usually in bonds maturing in three to 10 years), and short-term (one to five years). Generally, the shorter the maturity, the less volatility.

Government securities (including "Agency" bonds carrying Uncle Sam's backing) are of course tops in protection against *credit risk,* though you can't avoid *interest rate risk;* if rates rise, the price of bonds goes down, and so does the value of a fund's portfolio. To some extent, bond funds can moderate the rate risk by selectively holding bonds of different maturities.

A specialized category are *Ginnie Mae* funds, which invest in debt certificates backed by government-insured mortgages. They usually offer a somewhat higher yield than regular government funds. Again, you needn't worry about credit risk, but you must accept some *prepayment risk.* If interest rates fall, many homeowners will rush to refinance and pay off the mortgages that underlie the Ginnie Mae certificates. These prepayments are passed on to the certificate holders, who will probably have to settle for lower interest rates when they reinvest these returns-of-capital. And if rates rise, the Ginnie Mae fund's market price (just like other bond funds — and bonds) tends to go down. In short, there's risk if rates either go up or down substantially. Is it a born loser, then? No. Since you're getting somewhat higher interest than equivalent straight government bonds, you'll do well in a period of relative interest stability.

Among corporate bond funds there's a major distinction between *high-quality* funds that hold investment-grade bonds (some seek to keep most investments rated A or better, others will include BBB-rated securities) and the *high-yield bond* funds, more commonly called *junk bonds* (of course, as many found out, the high yields can be realized only as long as the companies issuing the bonds can keep up interest payments). Even among high-yield funds, there are differences between funds that restrict themselves to the top-level of the "non-investment-grade" area, and those willing to take on highly speculative securities.

Straddling the barrier between stock and bond funds are *balanced funds,* which usually try to be at least 25% in bonds and 25% in stocks, and apportion the other 50% as seems attractive at the time.

Another specialized group is the *convertible* fund, which invests in convertible bonds and preferred stocks that provide a current income stream, while the fund hopes for capital gains through an increase in the price of the underlying stock that would make the conversion privilege more valuable.

These general classifications may give you some guidance as to which type (or, quite likely, types) of funds may best suit your objectives and temperament. But remember, once again, that the funds broadly grouped within each area may still differ considerably in their specific objectives and how they pursue them. You should ask for and look at the prospectus — preferably, for a couple of funds. In the prospectus, each fund must spell out what its objectives are, what investments and trading practices it may use — and, just as important, what it won't do (for instance, whether or not the fund may supplement its strategies by using options or futures contracts).

Identifying funds that match your objectives is of course only the first step; your big concern is how likely a given fund is to succeed in meeting them. As you are endlessly told, "past performance is no indication of future results." Just the same, it pays to study a fund's record. What has been its long-term achievement? If possible, check how the fund has performed in both bull and bear markets. Does it still have the investment manager who achieved those results? There's a lot of argument about how important a "star" manager is, but you want at least to be aware of any shifts. How high is the annual portfolio turnover? You may want your fund run by an "aggressive" manager who does a lot of trading, or you may want more conservative efforts with an eye on long-term potential.

Along with reviewing the prospectus, you can get some answers and guidance from the periodic mutual fund reviews found in many financial magazines and newspapers, from some specialized publications prepared by agencies such as Standard & Poor's, Moody's, Value Line, and the two widely quoted firms that specialize in tracking mutual fund performance, Lipper Analytical and Morningstar Inc. And, of course, by chatting with your broker.

It may make sense to divide your investment among several types of funds — say, a high-quality bond fund for sustained income, a growth fund for long-term appreciation, and perhaps some money in a more speculative aggressive growth fund if you can afford the risk. If your funds are all part of one sponsor's "family," you can probably switch part or all of your investments from one fund to another without having to pay another load or other transaction fee. And this can often be done by telephone.

However, any such switch is still a "taxable event" to the IRS, and (unless it's in a tax-deferred retirement or similar account) you'll have to report a capital gain or loss on your holdings in the fund you switched out of. Also, while the fund-sponsoring companies like to provide the service to help customers whose objectives change — because of changes in their personal situation, or a reassessment of the market and economic outlook — they increasingly frown on "market timers" who want constantly to get in and out of funds, trying to catch market swings. They feel this interferes with sound management of the fund and incurs costs that must be borne by all fundholders; consequently, many funds have imposed restrictions on how frequently you can exercise the switching privilege.

Mutual funds are basically designed to be a longer-term investment, so don't try to react to every zig or zag of the market, or think of switching every month the fund's performance figures lag those of its fellows. Of course, if you become dissatisfied with the performance of a fund — just as when you no longer like a stock — it may be best to get out and look for an alternate investment.

But what about when the investment goal you've built toward is finally at hand? Say, you're starting retirement. Many mutual fund groups have *automatic withdrawal* plans. You can arrange to have a regular monthly or quarterly check sent to you, while the rest of your fund stays intact and, you hope, keeps earning for you.

A number of funds also permit you simply to write checks on your fund account — which gives you full flexibility, whatever you decide to use the money for. The amount is taken out of your account only when the check clears.

All the convenient services offered both for building up your investment and in arranging withdrawals and exchanges have no doubt contributed to the attraction of mutual funds, which in recent decades have dramatically increased their share of the individual investor's dollar. The investment trust concept goes back at least to eighteenth-century Scotland, while the first American-style open-end mutual fund was started in Massachusetts in 1924. But by 1941, U.S. mutual fund assets totaled barely half a billion. Forty years later, they had climbed to $250 billion. In the unprecedented boom that followed, fund assets more than quintupled. By early 1994, an estimated 38 million-plus Americans had $2.1 trillion invested in mutual funds. That record total included close to $600 billion in taxable and municipal money funds, a little over three-quarters trillion in equity funds, and almost as much in bond and income funds.

CHAPTER *19*

More about Packaged Investments

MUTUAL funds are by far the biggest and most solidly entrenched example of investment packaging. But, as we've indicated, today's investor also has a choice of many other types of packages, and eager investment houses are constantly at work trying to develop yet other forms. They aim to give the individual retail-level access to all sorts of fancy investment instruments that are normally available only in wholesale lots — and, of course, to earn some money for the investment house.

This chapter discusses some of the more important such packages available today.

Money Market Funds

No doubt the most significant innovation in this field is the specialized variety of mutual fund known as a *money market fund*. During the past two decades, it has developed into one of the most popular investment vehicles in financial history. Indeed, in a number of recent years, total assets in money funds were larger than assets in either equity or bond mutual funds. To millions of Americans, the "money funds" are literally ready "money," as accessible as their checkbook or telephone.

Money funds follow the general concepts of mutual fund organization, but they invest exclusively in short-term instruments — by definition, obligations that come due in less than one year. However, the SEC now requires the *average maturity* of each fund's portfolio to be under 90 days (lowered from 120 in 1991). Usually it's much shorter than that; in spring 1994, the industry average was under 50 days.

Typical holdings include U.S. Treasury bills, short-term issues of government-backed agencies, CDs or other forms of bank time deposits (money placed with a bank at specified rate for specified period), bankers' acceptances (bank-guaranteed instruments used to finance international trade), commercial paper (short-term IOUs issued by major corporations), and some other corporate obligations. Funds may even hold some bonds that have become "short-term" because they will mature within one year.

Some funds will invest only in U.S. government and agency instruments for highest safety but somewhat lower yields than the general funds that will go after higher-paying bank and corporate paper — though they, too, may have a substantial amount invested in government-backed issues. A separate set are tax-exempt money funds that invest in short-term municipal securities. And more recently some money funds have been organized that can invest in short-term instruments abroad — trying to take advantage of possible higher foreign yields but in return taking higher risks from currency fluctuations as well as additional credit uncertainties.

A quickly noticed difference from ordinary mutual funds, whose net asset value (and, hence, price) moves up and down along with market fluctuations, is that money funds work to keep their NAV at a steady $1. How can they do it? Since funds are required to invest in high-quality instruments due to be paid off in a short time, they do not have to "mark to market" — that is, adjust their portfolio for daily market changes. Such changes are usually quite small anyhow, and mainly reflect slight movements in interest rates. Only if an issuer runs into serious trouble and its ability to pay on schedule is cast in doubt will a fund have to write down the value of those holdings. Basically, because all the fund's holdings accrue steady interest, the fund shows earnings every day, and, to keep a steady $1 NAV, it simply declares a daily dividend to match these earnings.

Say, you put $1,000 into the PQR Money Fund, which has $100 million in assets, divided into 100 million shares with $1 NAV each. So you're initially credited with 1,000 shares. The next day the fund accrues interest earnings of $15,000 or $.00015 per share (for simplicity, we assume share purchases and redemptions for the day canceled each other out, leaving the total shares at 100 million). Instead of increasing the value of each share you hold, the fund declares the $.00015 per share as a dividend. Since it's taken for granted that your dividend is automatically reinvested, you now hold 1,000.1500 shares, at $1 each, bringing the value of your fund holdings to $1,000.15. Naturally, the size of the daily dividend (and thus the amount of added shares to which you're entitled) varies with each day's investment results. Incidentally, while you *earn* dividends every day, they are usually *credited* to your account only once a month. However, should you close out your account in the middle of the month, you'd get full payments for these accrued but not yet paid dividends.

Money funds won their first big following in the 1970s, giving people who had been limited to the low, regulated interest then paid on bank and savings accounts a chance to participate in the higher-yielding instruments previously available only to institutions or wealthy investors. But soon investors also began to appreciate the convenience and flexibility of the funds. Many funds permit withdrawals by writing checks on the account. Funds sponsored by brokerage houses enable you to have any cash in your securities account invested in the interest-earning money fund; dividends on your stocks and proceeds from securities sales are automatically "swept" into your account. And when you decide to buy some stocks, the money is simply transferred out of your fund account.

Merrill Lynch carried the concept further with the 1977 introduction of its Cash Management Account or CMA. Aside from keeping all your spare cash in the brokerage account constantly invested, it lets you write checks not only on your money fund holdings but also on the borrowing power (margin value — see chapter 22) of your securities holdings. In addition, you receive a Visa debit card, with purchases charged against your money fund or margin balance. Once the CMA's success was clearly established by the early 1980s, other major brokers, including discounters, opened their own versions of these *central asset accounts,* which usually carry an annual fee.

In a money fund the key consideration is the yield you receive. The regularly reported *seven-day yield* is the net income generated during the preceding seven-day period, expressed as an annual percentage rate. Many newspapers publish these yields on a weekly basis, often accompanied by the *effective yield,* which is a slightly higher version of the same figure since it assumes continuous compounding of the income. Returns for longer periods may also be reported, on a cumulative return or an annualized basis.

Essentially, the yields of all funds reflect the interest trends of the money markets. When managers think rates are headed down, they may seek to improve performance by lengthening the average maturity of their portfolio (thus latching on to current high yields for a while longer); conversely, if they expect higher rates, they'll shorten maturities so funds will be available more quickly for reinvestment at higher rates. (Of course, their expectations of rate trends might be wrong.)

More important differences are in the various funds' investment policies. Some may "stretch" for some extra yield by going after somewhat riskier investments; that's true even in the government area where some funds may have a heavier proportion of repurchase agreements (repo's). Repo's are essentially very short-term (often overnight) loans between financial institutions, secured by government securities. Nonetheless, they carry some risk in case the firm on the other side of the trade suddenly runs into trouble, and gets closed down by regulators, making the collateral at least temporarily unavailable. As for corporate investments, there's always the chance of sudden deterioration in a company's status. Considering the short period most of these securities are outstanding, the wide diversification of the funds, and the limitation of even the greater risk-takers to relatively high-quality paper, the degree of safety is pretty good — but you should check the fund's investment policies, as outlined in the prospectus, and the list of its actual holdings to see whether you like the particular risk-reward relation.

It's also worthwhile to check out the fund's expense ratio and policies. Some fund sponsors have agreed to absorb certain expenses temporarily, which enables the fund to show a higher yield — but if and when the sponsor stops the practice, the comparative yield will presumably drop. Money funds generally impose no load charges, so every dollar you put in goes to work earning interest. Some funds may levy service charges on check writing or frequent withdrawals.

As for security of principal, some funds *have* been caught with commercial paper of companies that suddenly entered bankruptcy. In each case so far, the fund's sponsoring company took over the defaulted paper and the fund's net asset value stayed happily at $1 a share. At worst, such a default could have caused a drop of a couple of pennies a share for a while. But that does show the funds are not totally risk-free (and, of course, the investments are not government insured). In fact, in early 1991 the SEC voted to tighten regulations to increase safety further. Funds now may have no more than 5% of their assets in less-than-top-grade commercial paper.

Even with this caveat, money market funds offer an attractive spot for your short-term "money" to earn more money — normally at rates better than money market or similar accounts at banks.

When you seek out a money fund, first give thought to what type (or types) of fund best suit your needs — general, government, tax-exempt. Whatever categories you select, you won't lack for choice. Just about every mutual fund organization sponsors at least one, and generally several, to meet different customer objectives. Other considerations being equal, it can be helpful to be with a group or brokerage firm where you have other accounts, because of the ease of transferring funds.

Closed-end Funds

Though it boasts the older pedigree, the *closed-end* branch of the investment trust family has during the last generation been far outstripped by its vibrant younger brother, the open-end mutual fund. The Big Board still lists some broad-based investment funds founded before the Great Depression, like Lehman Corp. (under its new identity of Salomon Brothers Fund) and Tri-Continental Corp. But the majority of closed-ends created over the past decade concentrate on special investment areas, such as the Germany Fund, Duff & Phelps Utilities Income, or a great number of bond funds.

As noted earlier, stocks of closed-end funds trade just like those of other corporations, such as General Electric or Exxon. That, as you must never forget, means the shares trade at whatever price some buyer is willing to pay and some current holder willing to sell. At times, a fund's stock may trade at a *premium*, a price greater than its net asset value per share. At other times it will trade at a *discount*, a price below the NAV. Premiums were frequent in the 1960s. And enthusiasm generated by special events, like the opening up of Eastern Europe, may lift the price of funds concentrating on potential beneficiaries. But generally in recent decades, closed-ends (especially the funds investing in stocks) have sold at discounts, sometimes steep ones.

While discounts can be disconcerting to shareholders — especially if they bought at higher prices — once the discount exists, some investors are enticed by the idea of being able in effect to buy the fund's portfolio at a "bargain" price. One caution: The stocks in the portfolio could, of course, fare poorly, thus shrinking the fund's net asset value. Besides, there's no guarantee the discount won't grow even steeper.

However, as long as the discount exists, there's always the possibility of liquidating the portfolio, so that shareholders would realize the prevailing value of the underlying stocks. Or the fund could be turned into an open-end company, in which case its own shares become redeemable at net asset value. Such a conversion has, in fact, been undertaken by some funds, and major shareholders are urging it on some others. And, recognizing the potential future problem, some closed-ends in recent years have been issued with provisions that could turn them into regular mutual funds if they sell at discounts a few years hence.

Open- and closed-end funds do much the same type of business. But the difference in their setup makes for some difference in operation. Open-end managers must always be ready to redeem shares on demand, but if they're successful they can usually count on a net influx of funds that will enable them to make more investments. A closed-end fund cannot increase its original capital at will; it would have to register and sell a new issue of stock. However, many funds make stock available for dividend reinvestment. Some closed-end funds also have preferred stock or debt outstanding that adds leverage to their operation. As we explained in chapter 5, since the bond and preferred holders are entitled to a fixed amount of interest or dividends regardless of how much the fund earns, there'll be bigger earnings for common stockholders in good years, but less (or a deficit) when results are down.

One reason organizers of new funds planning to invest in overseas securities or other specialized areas may opt for the closed-end version: They're going after investments that lack the liquidity of most domestic securities and that also may take considerable time to realize their potential. Therefore the managers want the fixed pool of capital made available by a closed-end fund; they want to avoid being subject to early redemption demands from impatient fundholders.

Whether open- or closed-end, the funds will distribute to you whatever net investment income and capital gains they realized during the year, since the income is taxable not to the fund but to you. And if you're a long-term investor, it's probably to your advantage to have these distributions automatically reinvested, thus reaping the benefits of compounding.

Unit Investment Trusts

A specialized spinoff of the investment trust concept — offering diversification and low administrative expenses in return for limited flexibility — is the *unit investment trust* or UIT. As in an investment trust, you acquire a proportionate stake (in this case called a unit) of a professionally assembled set of securities. However, there is no further active investment management; no changes are planned in the investment portfolio for the life of the trust. And while the sponsors (generally, major brokerage firms) undertake to maintain a secondary market for the units — which should enable you to get out of your trust units if you want to — UITs are designed for holding, not active trading.

UITs were first devised in the late 1960s by assembling a number of different municipal bonds and then dividing this portfolio into $1,000 units. This gave small investors a practical way to enter the municipals market. What's more, their $1,000 investment gave them diversification and, though the bonds themselves commonly pay interest twice a year, the trust arranged to distribute income on an evened-out monthly basis.

Soon, UITs were introduced for corporate bonds and also for government issues, especially Ginnie Maes. Aided by the rise of interest rates in the 1970s and early 1980s, UIT popularity spread and was extended to a wide variety of securities packages. Most are income-oriented. Bonds (with many variations as to particular type, maturity, and other characteristics) continue to represent the bulk of the UIT market. But there are also some equity trusts, often concentrating on strong-dividend stocks like utilities but also some offering wider perspectives such as a trust based on the Standard & Poor's 500-stock index. Others cover investments denominated in foreign currencies, and participation in floating-rate notes so income will change as market rates move up or down.

Some of the bond UITs are insured by a private insurance company, which is pledged to make good on any default in interest or principal repayment. The cost of such insurance may lower the UIT's annual yield by perhaps a quarter of one percentage point or a bit less, which many UIT investors appear eager to pay for the extra protection.

UITs generally may carry a sales load of around 4.5% — less for Ginnie Maes and short-term issues. But, with only minimal administrative functions required, the ongoing operating expenses tend to be low — around 0.20% to 0.25% of assets a year (the insurance charge, if any, would be extra).

While the makeup of the portfolio is designed to stay fixed, some of the issues in it may be called or otherwise redeemed. In that case, each UIT unit usually gets its proportionate share of the principal repayment. And, of course, with less principal remaining invested, the amount of future interest payments will be lower. Even before the last bonds in the portfolio mature, the trustee can terminate the UIT (and pay off the holders) when, due to maturities and prepayments, the portfolio gets too small to justify maintaining it. Equity trusts may have a planned life span (announced when the UIT is offered) of anywhere from one to 25 years. The UIT's trustee also has the right, if he sees clear danger in one of the holdings, to sell that issue. In some cases, a replacement issue may be bought; in others, the trust will distribute to its unit holders whatever it realized on the sale. Such emergency actions have been very rare.

While the structure of the UIT normally doesn't lend itself to automatic reinvestment in the UIT itself (the number of units is fixed, and, besides, there are no fractional units issued), many UIT organizations will arrange for you to reinvest the monthly distributions — usually in a separate bond fund — at no fee, or, at most, a reduced load charge. Whether you cash your check or arrange for reinvestment, any tax liability for income — just as in investment companies — is passed through directly to you, the holder.

Real Estate Investment Trusts

First given legal recognition in the early 1960s, real estate investment trusts (REITs) operate very much like specialized closed-end funds, except that, instead of stocks and bonds, their portfolio consists primarily of direct investments in real estate, as lender or owner or both. Many REITs have been sponsored by leading builders, others by banks.

The idea, of course, has been to open a way for eager investors with limited funds to participate in the real estate market, which was booming for the greater part of the post–World War II era. The REIT offers managers experienced in the business, a reasonable amount of diversification, a liquid investment in a business where it's otherwise often difficult and expensive to get out of an investment, and relatively limited risk. At worst (which, unfortunately, has happened at times), you'd be out most of or all the money you put up, but, unless you bought on margin, you couldn't be plunged into debt.

A good many REITs have come through in good shape. However, many others were upended, especially during a severe shakeout in the mid-1970s, the Texas real estate calamity in the 1980s, and, more recently, the real estate collapse in the Atlantic states.

REITs vary greatly not only in quality of portfolio and management (which admittedly is hard to judge), but also in financial structure and operating policies. Many are heavily leveraged, with bonds (and occasionally preferred stock), commercial paper, and bank borrowings enabling them to assume larger investments — multiplying the stockholder's earnings if things go well but carrying the threat of wiping them out when some investments sour while the REIT's own lenders must still be paid.

Then there's the type of investments in which the REIT engages — which should be spelled out in its prospectus and annual report. Riskiest (if potentially lucrative) are construction loans, which depend on a contractor's ability successfully to complete construction and then find paying occupants. (Defaulted construction loans, of course, have also been a major source of problems for the banking and thrift industries.) Other REITs concentrate on property ownership, which may be a conservative investment if in a well-managed project already operating satisfactorily, but speculative if development is in early stages. Sometimes, a share of the equity comes as a "kicker" enhancing a construction loan, or possibly a refinancing agreement. Safest, by and large, are REITs that concentrate on mortgages in solid, operating properties.

As in other investment trusts, a REIT's realized income (and the tax liability related to it) is passed through to the shareholders. And like a closed-end fund, the price at which a REIT share sells may be higher or lower than the per-share value of the net assets. But because there's no ready market price for most of the assets, there's no net asset value that can be readily computed. In fact, quarterly financial statements (like those of corporations in other businesses) are based primarily on cost and depreciation, plus possible adjustments (such as write-downs for a loan in default).

In short, a carefully selected REIT can be a suitable vehicle if you want to have some funds invested in real estate, but it's a considerably more complex investment than a mutual fund or UIT.

Limited Partnerships

Some investment packages are structured in the form of a limited partnership, largely for legal, tax, or technical reasons. Partnerships are, of course, one of the most ancient forms of business organization, but the concept attained new glamour in the second half of this century as an investment vehicle — a means for outsiders to participate in oil and gas, real estate, entertainment, and many other booming fields, while reaping large tax advantages in the process.

Participating in such partnerships can indeed be a worthwhile strategy. But many of the ventures were sold far more on the opportunity to get tax breaks than on the economic worthiness of the projects in which they invested. In particular, most projects were expected to incur large operating losses in their early years — losses that the partners could then write off against their ordinary income. The tax-shelter fever soon spread from the wealthy to the merely well-to-do, and enticed even some people in the more moderate tax brackets to jump in, with results that were often — to put it mildly — disappointing. There were also many abuses and cases of outright fraud.

Atop all these reasons for caution, the 1986 tax act and other legislation have sharply cut down, when they did not entirely eliminate, the tax benefits any "passive" partner — that is, one not active in the business — can claim. In fact, under various circumstances, partners can be left with adverse tax consequences. So, even more than before, if you contemplate buying into a partnership (as with any other investment) your first rule should be: If it doesn't make economic sense, it doesn't make investment sense.

Essentially, *limited partnerships* (LPs) have a general partner who is experienced in the industry; he manages the project in return for a percentage of the partnership and often also a fee for his services. Participations or shares are sold to limited partners — usually, in units of at least $25,000 to $50,000 and often more, but still a good deal less money than it would take to get into such a venture on your own. The limited partners divide up proportionately their share of the profit, if any. In case of losses, the liability of limited partners is limited to the amount of their investment — in other words, they can't lose more than what they've agreed to commit. But in some cases, partners were asked to make only partial payments at the beginning, leaving them liable for substantial further contributions if needed in the future.

While you can't buy or sell your LP interests as if they were shares of stock, the typical investment partnership usually has some arrangements under which the managing partner may buy back an interest or a sponsoring organization seeks to maintain a secondary market. But such a market is rather illiquid, and, especially if things haven't been going well, it may be difficult to get out without taking a fair-sized markdown.

A more liquid market is provided by *Master Limited Partnerships* or MLPs. They divide the limited partnerships into much smaller units so they are the equivalent of a share of stock in a corporation, and can be transferred freely from one holder to another. They may be listed on the stock exchanges or traded actively over-the-counter. Some MLPs are, except for the legal structure, the virtual equivalent of corporations. Basketball fans, for instance, can buy a partnership share of the Boston Celtics on the Big Board (most sports leagues insist on their teams being organized as partnerships, with a general partner who is responsible for team operations). Others have been organized to operate in traditional limited partnership fields like natural resources or real estate, but with a widely distributed ownership.

Another group of MLPs, however, has been created by general partners and sponsors with numerous outstanding limited partnerships that have suffered losses and erosion of assets. They are trying to persuade their limited partners, who have found it difficult to get out of the old partnerships, that by molding them together into a larger master limited partnership (a so-called *rollup*), they will have a more liquid and viable operation — albeit often at a substantially lower market value than before.

In MLPs, as in all limited partnerships, the IRS considers you a full participant in the operation. The partnership must furnish you with a Form K-1 showing your share of the partnership's income and expenses, which you must include on your tax return (even if you can't claim all the losses).

Because of the special structure of a partnership, the obligations you assume, and the more limited amount of operating information you get, you should be even more careful than in other investments. Study the prospectus and other available documents, see how it fits into your personal investment situation, and, if you plan any substantial commitment, go over it with your tax and investment advisers.

To repeat: It can be a sound investment, but it requires extra care.

CHAPTER 20

Getting Started — Doing Business with a Broker

SUPPOSE you decide that the time has come for you to put some of your extra savings into securities. What do you do next? How do you go about buying stocks, bonds, or other investments?

If — like most people new to the investment area, and a great many experienced investors as well — you're eager to get personalized advice and service, you'll probably want to seek out a full-service brokerage firm. It can buy or sell for you securities listed on any exchange or traded over-the-counter and also offer you a wide variety of mutual funds. Most firms also provide many other investment services, from central asset accounts to retirement programs to commodities trading and limited partnerships, not to mention savings instruments like bank certificates of deposit, often on more favorable and convenient terms than you might find directly at your local bank. But what's probably most important for you is that they offer the services of trained professionals who can discuss with you what stocks to buy and, more generally, how to develop an investment program that best suits your individual needs and preferences. Through your broker, you have access to the firm's research department with its reports and opinions on specific stocks as well as the overall market.

For those who feel they can reach buying and selling decisions on their own and are only looking for a firm to execute their transactions — as we discussed in chapter 10, a discount broker may well meet their needs at lower cost. The major discount houses also can handle orders for virtually any stock or bond; most offer mutual funds; and many may be able to provide you with additional, special-ized products. They may also supply you with brochures containing generalized investment advice. But, when you call, you'll be dealing with an "order taker," not an adviser.

If you are strictly interested in mutual funds, there are a number of fund sponsors that deal directly with the public and that can be reached by mail or "800" numbers. These firms generally offer a "fam-ily" of funds — different funds to meet the different objectives and preferences of customers — but, of course, they market only their own funds. They'll be glad to send you brochures explaining the var-ious investment choices their funds provide, as well as newsletters on the economic and market outlook — along with the legally required prospectuses. A number of major fund sponsors — among them Fi-delity, Vanguard, and T. Rowe Price — also offer discount brokerage service to customers who want to buy specific stocks. In addition, nu-merous banks now offer you access to mutual funds and discount bro-kerage. But again, there are no individual advisers on what funds or stocks may be best for you.

When looking for a broker (especially the full-service variety), a good way to get started is to seek recommendations from friends, asso-ciates, or professional contacts such as your lawyer or accountant. Ask them for brokers they've been satisfied with. Or check the advertise-ments by brokerage firms, both in print and over the air. While it's worth remembering that any advertising is carefully designed to put a firm's best foot forward, regulatory requirements, as spelled out by stock exchange and NASD rules, set high standards for advertising by securities firms. Often, some firms will offer investment forums in your area, which may not only give you worthwhile information but will enable you to develop some sort of feel for the firm and its local representatives — and whether you think they'd be right for you.

If you're not familiar with the brokerage firm, you'll certainly want to check out its reputation, reliability, and strength. You'd do that when you sign with a contractor to put new siding on your home; you should be at least as careful with commitments for your financial house. Your Better Business Bureau, federal and state regulatory agencies, as well as other local contacts can help here. The safest approach is to confine your search to firms with long pedigrees — including well-regarded local firms.

Some people shun brokers because, frankly, they distrust them. They're afraid of being sold a bill of goods, a block of stock in some worthless company. Maybe it happened to someone you know.

Can it happen today? Yes, it can. Because no law or regulation has ever been devised that can guarantee that some dishonesty will not exist in the marketplace. Occasionally — very occasionally — you may encounter a con artist one jump ahead of pursuing regulators who's intent on having you buy some stock as he runs up the price while preparing to unload his own holdings. Policing efforts can never stamp out all the *boiler rooms* — stashed away in low-rent locations with a bunch of phones staffed by quickly assembled salespeople who make cold calls all over the country peddling questionable investments, often low-priced penny stocks. So the best advice is: Stick with quality in selecting investment advisers as well as investments.

And there is always some chance that you will come across a broker who is more interested in the level of activity in your account than in the quality of these transactions. He wants to keep you constantly buying or selling something, so his commission dollars keep piling up. Such *churning* is usually easy to spot, as when a broker frequently calls customers to recommend the sale of a stock whose purchase he had advocated only a short time ago. Particularly vulnerable to churning are *discretionary accounts,* where individual investors have given over complete trading authority to the broker — a type of account not recommended for most investors.

One other word of caution: If any broker or securities dealer tries to dissuade you from buying stock in some well-established company, and instead switch you into Wildcat common or Pipe Dream preferred, you should probably look for another brokerage house.

None of these abuses occurs often. Few businesses are as competitive and at the same time as closely regulated as the American securities business. But certainly, no business is without its share of predators. And a business that involves the handling of large sums of money is particularly vulnerable, despite all efforts to exorcise the demons.

Over the years, the securities industry has done quite a good job of policing itself, of trying to rid itself of unprincipled elements. And it keeps on stepping up its efforts — in part, no doubt, prodded by the steadily increasing pressures from regulators and lawmakers on the state as well as federal levels.

The SEC has made it unmistakably clear that it intends to hold to strict standards every brokerage firm and each of its individual brokers in every office. Furthermore, the commission made it clear that unless the New York Stock Exchange, which had been accused of treating disciplinary matters too tenderly, did a more thorough policing job, it would hold the exchange and its member firms responsible.

Unquestionably, the exchange has increased the efficiency of its own police force, which schedules surprise calls on branch offices of member firms all across the country, checking customer trading records and the character and performance of their salespeople. Member firms have followed suit — indeed, some were well ahead of this enforcement parade and long ago initiated regular policing of their own offices. In addition to upholding business ethics, it's a good way to forestall SEC crackdowns and customer lawsuits.

What are these *compliance officers,* as they are called, looking for? They are looking for any violation of regulations, or, more broadly, for any abuses of the public's right to fair dealing or failure by brokers to observe *suitability* standards — making sure that recommended investments are suitable for that particular customer. So they can determine what *is* suitable, securities laws and stock exchange rules impose on brokers a *know-your-customer* obligation. They must inquire not only into their customers' financial status, but their investment background and objectives, the extent of their market knowledge and sophistication, the degree of risk they are able and willing to assume.

In particular, compliance officers are looking for evidence of churning or other high-pressure sales tactics, such as a barrage of "act right now" phone calls, undue persuasion of widows, attempts to prey on the unsophisticated and the unsuspecting.

They are looking for misrepresentation: "The stock is bound to go up . . . you can't miss."

They are looking for abuses of any discretionary authority that a customer may give a broker to manage an account, to buy or sell whatever and whenever he thinks best.

They are looking for margin trading or active participation in options and futures strategies by customers who plainly lack the resources or sophistication to undertake the risks involved.

They are looking for the flagrant incompetence or the willful malfeasance that could result in the recommendation of a clearly unsuitable investment — say, a highly speculative stock for a retired couple to whom safety of capital and steady income is paramount.

They are looking for situations in which securities firms — or individual officers or employees — seek to further their own undisclosed interest in a stock by promoting its sale in order to enhance the value of their own holdings.

In sum, they are looking for any abuse of the implied guarantee that as a broker you will deal fairly and honestly with your customers.

The SEC holds the home-office executives of member firms wholly responsible for supervising their branch offices. This was brought home to doubters as early as the mid-1960s, with actions instituted against several leading firms that resulted not only in the expulsion of employees committing the actual violations, but in fines and suspensions levied against the firms' top officials for alleged failures to properly supervise. Such enforcement actions and penalties have become progressively tougher.

We've also seen brought into the open in recent years some of history's biggest cases of abuse by Wall Street insiders — abuses that led not only to SEC sanctions but to criminal convictions. Unfortunately, we'll probably always be stuck with a flock of sharp operators utterly lacking in moral scruples, including some in very high places. Which doesn't mean that they — or top management lax in supervising them — should be tolerated.

At the same time, the public furor stirred up by the big headline cases tends to be disproportionate to the problem involved. As we've noted, the vast majority of securities salespeople are honest, scrupulous, and concerned with the welfare of their customers — if only because they know that the way for them to be successful is to make money for their customers.

And to guard against the abusive minority, to help protect investors against the high-pressure, "fast-buck" peddlers of dubious stocks, the SEC quite some time ago — with the cooperation of industry trade groups and the Better Business Bureau — published an investor's guide. Its ten recommendations have surely stood the test of time:

(1) Think before buying.

(2) Deal only with a securities firm you know.

(3) Be skeptical of securities offered over the telephone by any firm or salesman you do not know.

(4) Guard against all high-pressure sales.

(5) Beware of promises of quick, spectacular price rises.

(6) Be sure you understand the risk of loss as well as the prospect of gain. [To which we might add: Also make sure you understand all the expenses — from commissions to possible ongoing fees to the costs you'll incur when you want to get out of the investment.]

(7) Get the facts. Do not buy on tips or rumors.

(8) Request the person offering securities over the phone to mail you written information about the corporation, its operations, net profit, management, financial position, and future prospects.

(9) If you do not understand the written information, consult a person who does.

(10) Give at least as much thought when purchasing securities as you would when acquiring any valuable property.

With these golden rules in mind, you now head bravely for a brokerage firm. But, you worry, will they be interested in me if I have only a modest amount to invest?

Frankly, some brokers won't be. But there are a number of "retail" houses that have invested heavily in promoting service to smaller investors and remain committed to helping them invest their money wisely.

You may be assigned to representatives who specialize in smaller accounts. Especially if you plan initially to invest less than $5,000 or so, you may well be advised that your best choice is some type of mutual fund, or perhaps a CD or specialized account offered by the firm. The representative should discuss your specific goals as well as your resources, and suggest just what funds or other investments might serve you best.

Before you or any customer can either buy or sell securities through a brokerage firm, you must formally open an account with that firm. Procedures are quite simple. The firm will want to establish your credit reliability so that it can be sure you can pay for whatever securities you order. And it will want to know about your investment background in line with the know-your-customer rule.

The broker has to be sure of your credit responsibility because a stock transaction does not *settle* — that is, the seller gets paid and the buyer gets the stock — until five business days after the trade takes place. (The SEC has proposed a rule shortening the settlement period to three days, effective no later than 1996.) So you have five business days (Saturdays, Sundays, and holidays don't count) to come up with the payment. If special circumstances warrant, the brokerage firm can extend the payment deadline an additional two days. But if payment is not received by then, a further extension can be granted only by the exchange. This is because by your delay you will have violated the Federal Reserve Board's Regulation T, which governs all matters of credit on stock transactions. If there's no valid extension, the transaction must be canceled and enough of your account liquidated to satisfy all costs.

In the case of mutual funds or most stock accumulation plans, credit is not a factor, because the purchase is made only when payment is received.

If your first transaction with a brokerage firm involves the sale of some stock that you already own instead of a purchase, you will still be required to open an account. The brokerage firm must still comply with the know-your-customer rule. As a start, the routine of opening an account provides the broker with some assurance of your true identity and that the securities you offer for sale are really yours.

If you want to open a *margin account* instead of, or in addition to, a regular cash account, so that you can buy securities by paying only a portion of their cost at the time of purchase, the broker will want to be especially sure of your financial solvency. After all, when you pay only part of the cost, the balance of the money needed to pay the seller is lent you by the broker — even if the debt is secured by the stock (which the brokerage firm will hold in its name).

Many husbands and wives prefer to open *joint accounts* with a broker, just as they have joint checking accounts. If one of them dies, the other can generally sell the securities without waiting for the courts to go through the sometimes slow-moving or complicated legal procedures involved in settling an estate. But because of tax considerations and variations in state law, a married couple may want to consult an attorney before opening a joint account.

Thanks to the *Uniform Gift to Minors Acts,* which all 50 states enacted between 1955 and 1960, it's simple to open accounts for your children or the children of relatives or friends. These laws permit an adult to designate him- or herself as a custodian — with no need for court appointment or other formalities — in order to handle investments for a child. Such a custodian can buy stocks as a gift for a minor, collect any dividends in the child's name, and eventually sell the investment for the benefit of the minor.

The Gift to Minors Acts solved a once thorny problem. If brokers sold stock that was registered in the name of a minor — who, in the eyes of the law, could not be responsible for his or her acts — that minor could, on coming of age, repudiate the transaction, and the broker would have no redress. So until the new laws were passed, the only legally safe way to handle stock for children was to set up a court-authorized trust fund — an expensive and cumbersome procedure.

Whatever the nature of your account, the person servicing it is officially known as a *registered representative*. The title means that he or she — after passing a searching examination about the operations of the securities business administered by the Big Board or NASD — is duly registered in line with federal and state securities regulations.

Today's registered representatives — called account executives or financial consultants by some firms — tend to be broadly educated and highly trained in the investment area. A good many have graduate degrees. And many major Wall Street firms put them through rigorous training courses where they plug away at lessons in accounting, economics, security analysis, all the details of securities laws and regulations, investment account management — and, of course, salesmanship. It costs a sponsoring firm thousands of dollars to train each representative, so they look for persons with a serious commitment to succeed. These modern-age securities salespeople bear little resemblance to the "customer's men" of the 1920's whose market wisdom depended largely on tips and rumors and who concentrated on selling stocks and bonds to old college chums or clubhouse cronies.

It's also worth noting that today's registered representatives are an increasingly diverse lot. Some are young. Some are old. Some are Democrats. Some are Republicans. Some are men. Some are women. Some have been in the business for years. Some are comparative newcomers. They also come from all kinds of ethnic and racial backgrounds.

The registered representative is "your broker" in the sense that he or she is the person you deal with when you do business with a brokerage firm. If at any time you find the service less than satisfactory, all you have to do is ask the manager to assign you to another. Incidentally, a good many (but far from all) women investors have indicated they would feel more at home with a woman broker. If that fits your case, just ask the manager of the brokerage office to assign you to one.

And if you don't like the brokerage firm itself, try another where you may feel more comfortable.

Probably far more important in deciding who is the proper broker for you is selecting one who generally agrees with your philosophy. Any major full-service firm you contact is bound to have many brokers with many different investment attitudes. It is important for you to find one who understands your particular approach. Are you someone who wants to take wild risks with a portion of your money, or are you one who wants to invest for the long term? Make sure that you tell your broker what your goals are, and ask for his or her philosophy in return. Most brokers will be glad to spend some time discussing their views, and, as we've emphasized, they are legally required to understand your needs.

You can talk to your registered representative with complete candor, because whatever you disclose about your affairs will be held in strict confidence. A broker doesn't reveal who his customers are, much less anything about their circumstances.

The more you tell your registered representative about your finances — your income, your expenses, your savings, your insurance, and whatever other obligations, like mortgage or tuition payments, you may have — the better he or she will be able to help you map out an investment program suited to your particular needs. If you also have accounts elsewhere, it may still be to your advantage to let the broker know the extent of your holdings, so you can get more informed advice.

It is a part of your broker's job to see that you get information or counsel whenever you need it. Don't be embarrassed about asking simple questions — about a company, about some financial term, or about the way your orders are handled.

In turn, you should observe certain obligations toward your broker. Some are routine and obvious. Pay promptly for any securities you buy. Promptly inform the firm of any change in address. And remember, your broker won't be able to carry on long phone conversations during trading hours. Like all salespeople, registered "reps" make their living on the phone.

If you give your broker an order to buy or sell, be sure there is no misunderstanding about what you want to be done. Your broker may seem overly meticulous — but it's not only to give you prompt and efficient service, but also because the cost of correcting errors has gone up like everything else. Moreover, the firm very likely penalizes its brokers for any error, an error that might very well be attributable to you.

If you are sure your instructions have not been carried out, you are entitled to have the error rectified. And, to repeat, if you feel your broker is pushing you to trade more often or more aggressively than you want, by all means switch brokers.

If you have a major complaint that you can't resolve with your broker and the local office manager, take it to the firm's headquarters. If you still can't get satisfaction (and are convinced you have a good case), you can file a complaint with the stock exchange or the NASD and you can have your case arbitrated. You can also call or write the SEC if you feel convinced there have been regulatory or legal violations.

But customers also must play fair. Just as a few brokers may try to churn accounts, some customers will happily pocket speculative profits when things go right, but quickly claim they were misled if a trade produces a loss.

Keep in mind that brokers know that the way to hold on to accounts is to help customers succeed. When your broker sells you on the idea of buying a particular stock, it's likely because he himself believes in it and thinks it fits your investment strategy. Some investment products may yield the broker greater "production credits" (the key to broker compensation) than others, and at times there may be special credits for selling certain stocks — say, when an underwriting is involved (but that may also save you commission costs). It's fair enough, when you get a recommendation, to ask whether there's a special sales incentive. If so, you should weigh that fact and perhaps require a bit of extra convincing — but remember, it may still be a perfectly sound investment for you.

More important, remember that even the best advisers are not infallible. There are times when well-researched recommendations can prove disastrous, sometimes because of hidden shenanigans in the recommended company, but more often because its management was unable to cope with conditions that turned unexpectedly adverse.

Just as you must make sure when you purchase stocks that you pay your broker within five business days — when you sell stock, you must see to it that the stock is delivered to the broker and properly endorsed in the same timely fashion. Most securities owners today find it more convenient to leave their stock certificates with their brokers. Keeping securities in *street name* (so called because they are registered in the name of a Wall Street firm) is almost certainly safer than trying to take care of them yourself. The broker handles all the safekeeping, storage, and insurance problems. You can be sure the securities can't be lost or misplaced, and are right on hand when you need them, whether to sell, respond to a tender offer, or exercise some right within a limited time span.

Street name securities are carried in the customer's account just as cash might be. The customer gets periodic statements showing exactly what securities and what funds are in the account. The broker will collect the dividends and interest, and credit them as cash to the customer's account. Many central-asset and some other accounts have linkage provisions under which all cash received is promptly invested in a money fund. The broker is also responsible for mailing to the customer all annual reports, proxies, and other notices received from companies whose stocks are held in the account.

Even when they're in street name, the brokerage firm cannot borrow money on securities in your cash account (though it can on those in a margin account) nor can it sell or lend them except with your express authorization. Those securities belong to you. The surprise audits that are sprung on all member firms at different intervals by the New York Stock Exchange further help to ensure that brokers are faithful to their trust. Every single share of stock held in street name — whether in the broker's own vaults or on the books of the Depository Trust Company — as well as every dollar in each customer's account must be accounted for.

And don't worry if you decide to change brokers. Your new firm can have your entire account transferred with little fuss. You don't even have to have any dealings with your old broker. However, in spite of regulations mandating prompt action, some brokers losing accounts may try to drag the process out, so some patience as well as persistence may be required.

To ensure financial solvency, the exchange insists that member firms have substantial capital reserves. Thus, a brokerage firm's liabilities, the amount it owes, may never be greater than 15 times the firm's capital. As a precautionary step, the exchange may require a member firm to reduce its business once its net capital ratio reaches 12 to 1. Even earlier, at just 10 to 1, it may prohibit a member firm from trying to expand its business.

In 1970, the SEC put the full weight of its authority behind these capital requirement rules and undertook to see that the 15-to-1 ratio also applied to nonmember firms, which had previously operated on a 20-to-1 standard.

But what if a broker goes under, despite all the regulations of the stock exchange and the SEC?

For years, an adequate answer to that was that brokers simply didn't go broke. Despite the debacle of 1929, member firms of the New York Stock Exchange boasted a 99% solvency record over a 50-year period — better than the banks.

But in 1963, the respected house of Ira Haupt & Company went under, victim of a commodities swindler who had secured his obligations with phony salad-oil warehouse receipts. To make sure customers received the securities and cash left in their accounts with Haupt — and to preserve investor confidence in general — the stock exchange quickly devised a plan that obligated all members to help foot the shortfall on Haupt's books.

Then came the crisis that began with the "paper crunch" of the late 1960s. The "back office" operations of many firms were swamped by the then-record volume, setting off a chain reaction of misplaced, undelivered, and often untraceable securities records throughout Wall Street.

All told, nearly 200 brokerage houses ran into trouble — many fatally; others were pushed into "shotgun" mergers with stronger firms. While emergency assessments of the exchange community (to supplement the quickly exhausted special trust fund set up after the Haupt disaster) were used to replace customers' securities lost at the sinking firms, it was clear that more reliable machinery was needed — such as a government-backed insurance system for investors comparable to that provided by the Federal Deposit Insurance Corporation for bank depositors.

Congress responded by voting in late 1970 to establish the *Securities Investor Protection Corporation*, or *SIPC* (pronounced "Sipic"). It will now advance up to $500,000 per account (including up to $100,000 in cash deposits) in case of the liquidation of any SIPC member, which includes member firms of all the securities exchanges and the NASD, except those who do only a mutual fund business. Just like the FDIC identification used by banks, SIPC membership is routinely cited in brokerage house commercials and literature. You should make sure that membership is carried by any broker you deal with.

While SIPC is empowered to draw on up to $1 billion of federal funds as a backup, its own fund is built up primarily from assessments on the securities business of SIPC members. In 1979, a uniform member assessment of $25 per year went into effect.

Not long after SIPC started, one securities firm arranged with a private insurance company for supplemental coverage. Soon many other firms followed. Today such private supplemental coverage is widespread and may run up to $10 million per account.

Keep in mind that, of course, neither SIPC nor any other insurance can protect you against market fluctuations, or against the risk that an investment goes down in price or could even become worthless. What the insurance does offer is protection against your brokerage firm's being unable to come up with the securities and cash you entrusted to it. In other words, the risk of investing is properly yours, but you shouldn't have to concern yourself about the physical safekeeping of your investment instruments — and that's a pretty comforting step of progress.

CHAPTER 21

What It Means to Speculate

SPECULATING is an inevitable part of the business of buying securities. But then, speculating is an inevitable part of just living.

Whenever you are confronted with an unavoidable risk — as indeed you are in many circumstances every day — you must speculate. You must meet the risk; you must take your chances. Often you are presented with a choice of risks. When you make up your mind which one you will take, weighing the good and the bad features of each, you arrive at a speculative decision.

An executive with a "must" meeting in another city may trust that his scheduled morning flight will get him to his destination on time despite a forecast of severe weather, or he may decide to fly up the evening before, cutting short some equally vital tasks at his home base. In making his choice, he must inevitably speculate.

The manufacturer who must pick Jones or Smith for a key job must speculate on who will be the better performer.

The farmer's whole operation is one vast speculation. When he puts the seed in the ground, he is speculating on his ability to grow a crop and sell it at a profit despite bad weather, pests, blight, and changing market prices. But when, while buying seed in town, he stops off to buy a $1 state lottery ticket, he's gambling.

When, in these examples, people take risks they cannot avoid, they are speculating. But when they take a risk that they don't have to take, they gamble.

That is one distinction between speculation and gambling. There is another. Speculation involves an exercise of reason, while gambling involves nothing but chance. The person who speculates can make an intelligent forecast of the hazards on the course. The gambler stands or falls on the flip of a coin or the draw of a card.

In the purchase of any stock or bond, even a government bond, there is an element of speculation. You can't avoid the possibility — the risk — that it might decline in value. For that matter, as we pointed out at the very beginning of this book, you take a risk when you simply hold money — the risk that it won't buy as much in the future as it will today.

When people buy securities, however, they don't have to operate exclusively on luck or happenstance. They can make a fairly intelligent estimate of how much risk they are assuming on the basis of the record. And there's a wide range of risk to choose from — all the way from a government bond to the penny stocks of companies whose assets are made up principally of hope.

There is obviously a wide gap in the amount of risk between the rank speculation of such penny stocks and the solid investment that a government bond represents. However, the distinction between investing and speculating can get hazy as you move away from either of these extremes. There are certainly many different levels of investment stature, but the slope is gradual, with no precise boundaries and considerable overlap. And a great many securities have both investment and speculative characteristics, in varying degrees. It's been well said that what is one person's speculation is very often another's investment. To a large extent, the difference between investing and speculating is not so much a matter of a particular security's merit as it is of the motive for which that security is bought.

A good traditional definition of an investor is a person who puts money in a company in the expectation of earning a solid and regular return on it over the long run, through dividends and price appreciation. Perhaps even more descriptive of today's sophisticated investor is: a person who *buys value* and has the *patience* to let the market reflect it, a policy that can yield very substantial returns.

Speculators usually take a short-term view. They are interested in making a quick profit on their money (especially as part of it is usually borrowed and saddles them with interest expenses) and then selling. They also tend to sell quickly if a stock's market action disappoints them. They are prepared to take big risks, but if they hit it right, they stand to make a lot of money.

Never forget that investment fashions change over time. In part, it's a matter of passing fads, accentuated at times by well-publicized gurus. But often the new fashions reflect fundamental shifts in the economy — shifts that sooner or later find their way into the accepted wisdom.

Time was when ultraconservative buyers of securities for a bank, insurance company, or personal trust thought that only government bonds, some municipals, and first-quality corporate bonds deserved the title "investment." Gradually, nearly everyone learned that some stocks have proved safer than many corporate bonds over the long term, even apart from their superior inflation resistance. Especially after World War II, professional managers turned increasingly to equities to fill their portfolios.

Attitudes toward individual groups of securities also keep changing. A hundred years or so ago, railroad securities were the investment of choice by prudent guardians of widows or minors; they looked askance at the upstart industrials, many of which evolved into the giants that stoked Smokestack America into world economic leadership and in turn became the standard blue-chip investments. Much later, some of these giants saw their foundations, anchored in what became known as "the Rustbelt," gravely weakened, though more recently many of the heavy-capital-goods producers appear to have acquired new vigor.

Meantime, other groups advanced in investment quality recognition — and later often lost at least some of their shine when it was discovered that they, too, had not located the fountain of eternal, troublefree growth.

This happened even in the relatively sedate area of utilities. In the 1950s and 1960s, utilities acquired a reputation as an outstanding investment for conservative income seekers, with high current dividends and virtually "guaranteed" growth that should lead to rising future dividends (along with rising stock prices) to combat future inflation. Then numerous power companies were faced with nuclear-plant and environmental problems, escalating construction and fuel costs, and an emphasis on conservation over consumption. Some companies foundered, others had to cut back or suspend dividends. However, many utilities still (or again) provide good current income along with fair (though not exuberant) growth prospects.

More colorful was the cult of the "Nifty Fifty" that reached its peak of popularity in the late 1960s and early 1970s. These half-hundred or so stocks represented solidly established leaders in the most promising growth fields. Money managers talked of "one-decision" stocks; the idea was you could buy them and never worry about there coming a time to sell. And for that high-quality growth, a stock price of 30 to 50 times earnings didn't seem too high.

Here, too, reality proved harsher. Some of the "Nifty" companies saw their industry or their own position erode, but even those with continued good performance could not live up to the exaggerated expectations of the marketplace, and their stocks had to take a breather.

Other illustrations abound. But the lesson they teach is not that people should shy away from participation in an inescapably risky market. Rather, the greatest risk of all may well be seeking to shun all risk and sit on the sidelines; that's the surest way to have the value of your money erode.

The lesson drives home that true investment can't be passive; that there are no "one-way" stocks. It's always important to assess the kind of risk you can afford and the securities that meet your particular investment profile, to have a reasonable amount of diversification, and then to keep atop your investment situation. That doesn't have to mean daily price checks, but follow your securities enough (and look not just for stock quotations but for company news, industry developments, et cetera) so that you have an idea of what to expect and can react appropriately. You'll probably want to seek periodic appraisals from your broker or financial adviser. And most public libraries subscribe to some advisory services where you can check up on your investment on your own.

Also keep in mind that even the highest-quality stock may be a poor investment at a time when its price has soared too far. The reverse is only partly true. At a low-enough price, some stocks with uncertain outlook may become a reasonable speculation — but for others the prospects may be so poor that the stock would not be a bargain at any price.

One aspect that has long affected many investment decisions is tax treatment. The federal income tax, through most of its history, imposed substantially lower rates on long-term capital gains than on ordinary income. *Capital gains* are the profits you realize on the purchase and sale of securities, or almost any kind of property. If you held the property for at least a specified minimum period to qualify as *long term* (mostly the minimum was set at either one year or six months), you paid tax at no more than half your regular rate, with an absolute top rate of 25 percent. And as part of a liberalizing trend, the effective rate was lowered still further by the 1981 tax law to 40 percent of your regular rate or an overall maximum of 20 percent of your profit. *Short-term* gains were taxed at the same rate as your regular income.

Then came the big tax revision act of 1986, which drastically lowered most regular tax rates but provided that all capital gains would be taxed at the same rate as your other income. When a new top regular tax bracket of 31% was added in 1990, however, the maximum for capital gains was left at 28% (which was the top regular rate set by the 1986 tax except for those middle-class earners caught in the 33% "notch"). Further, the 28% capital gains cap was retained in the 1993 revisions, which raised the top bracket to 39.6%. Unfortunately for many investors, this cap benefits only top-bracket earners; all those in the 28% bracket (or below) continue to pay full tax on capital gains. By contrast, before 1986, a middle-class family might be in the 35% bracket but their capital gains were taxed at only 14% (40% of 35%).

What's the fuss about? Well, in the first place, *risk capital* has been very important in building the economy of this country and is vital now to make us more competitive and to provide more jobs. And people are more willing to put up money for a risky but promising venture when they know that, if the venture succeeds, Uncle Sam won't grab so big a share of their gains.

There's also the argument of fairness. Capital gains aren't like other income; they represent growth in the value of an asset, a good part of which may be due to inflation. And the tax depletes capital that otherwise could be reinvested. Thus, it penalizes prudent long-term investors who would like to change the makeup of their portfolio. Suppose that over the years you built up a portfolio of growth stocks that have gained nicely. Now, with retirement approaching, you'd like to put greater emphasis on more stable securities that will also provide a higher current yield. But when you cash in your growth stocks (or your growth mutual fund), you have to pay tax on all the accumulated gains, and so are left with less capital to reinvest in the new portfolio. You might even feel that this is as if, when you enter a new job, you'd be expected to pay a tax on the experience and growth you acquired in your previous position because that was the "capital" you used to qualify for the new one.

Whatever the arguments, everyone must live by the currently prevailing order. However, even when there was no difference at all in the tax rate, capital gains had to be reported separately. One reason is that, while the government insists you share your gains, it's much less eager to share any losses. You can write off a maximum of only $3,000 in *capital losses* a year. The unused part of the loss, however, can be carried forward and taken in future years. And the $3,000 is a *net* figure. So if, for instance, you have an $18,000 loss and a $14,000 gain one year, your net loss would be $4,000. You could then deduct $3,000 that year, leaving you with only $1,000 to carry over.

When capital gains were taxed favorably, investors with little need for immediate cash often preferred companies that reinvested heavily for future growth rather than paid out high dividends, since, they hoped, that would result in more long-term capital gains, and less currently taxed income. The 1993 act, by again creating a substantial rate differential for high-income taxpayers, has revived considerable interest in capital-gains-oriented investments.

The higher taxability of capital gains is heightening the appeal of IRA, Keogh, 401(k), and other tax-deferred retirement plans where you can let all types of investment income accumulate, and pay taxes only when it comes time to withdraw funds.

Making such investments is certainly a wise move. But overall, it's perhaps too easy to let tax considerations dominate investment decisions. For instance, when capital gains preference was available, far too many investors were tempted to hold on to stocks in which they had gains, and then saw these gains evaporate while waiting for them to qualify as long-term. Similarly, you may risk more than it's worth if you decide to change your timing in the hope of new legislation.

Interestingly enough, professional speculators generally show much less concern about the tax impact of their trading. After all, they normally operate on a much shorter time horizon. And they're apt to concentrate not on obscure stocks that might prove long-term winners but speculate predominantly in the 50 or 60 active stocks — many of them topflight investment issues — that dominate Big Board trading and provide the liquidity and movement a speculator savors.

What's behind a speculator's decisions? Remember that, at any given time, the price of a stock, or the price of all stocks, represents the combined judgments of all the people who are buying and selling. Well, most times, speculators stake their judgment against the public's. Serious speculators may study the stock of a company in minute detail, and on that basis feel that they know better than the public what that stock is really worth — or, rather, *what the public will sooner or later determine is its real worth*. Similarly, they may think that they have a better feel for where the market as a whole is going. And since, in acting on their judgment, time is of the essence, they tend to favor the market-leader stocks that they can both get into and out of quickly.

On the assumption their judgment is right, the speculators seek to augment their profits — or protect them once they are made — by using various specialized techniques of trading, techniques more fully discussed in chapters 22 to 24.

They may buy on margin — financing part of the purchase on credit so as to multiply their investment leverage.

They may pyramid profits — plowing any realized gains back into the market. Normally used in conjunction with margin credit so that, as long as the price of the stocks goes up, a relatively small cash investment can pile up large "paper profits."

They may sell short — selling borrowed stock they don't own, hoping they can later buy the stock (and close out the loan) at a lower price.

They may buy or sell puts or calls, which give the buyer the *option* (the right but not the obligation) to sell (put) or buy (call) a stock at a predetermined price during a specified period.

They may buy or sell financial futures — contracts that reflect the moves of various stock averages, stock groups, or other financial instruments.

As any news-watcher knows, periodically some sharp operators make headlines with their questionable activities or outright manipulations that often *utilize* some of these speculative techniques. Keep in mind, however, that none of these techniques in themselves constitutes unfair or dishonest manipulation of the market. On the contrary, all are legitimate procedures that make for greater trading activity and a more liquid market. Often, in fact, the average investor would find it difficult to sell stock if the speculators were not willing to assume the risk the investor wants to escape. The techniques can be abused, as can any activity in life. But the obvious answer is to crack down on the abuses (and abusers), not on the activity. After all, the answer to drunk driving is not to ban all motor vehicles.

There's also periodic public clamor about all market speculators and their "ill-gotten" gains. People are apt to say that "there ought to be a law" to curb them. In 1905, the renowned United States Supreme Court Justice Oliver Wendell Holmes delivered a definitive reply to all such critics. "Speculation," he wrote, "is the self-adjustment of society to the probable. Its value is well known, as a means of avoiding or mitigating catastrophes, equalizing prices and providing for periods of want. It is true that the success of the strong induces imitation by the weak, and that incompetent persons bring themselves to ruin by undertaking to speculate in their turn. But legislatures and courts generally have recognized that the natural evolutions of a complex society are to be touched only with a very cautious hand. . . ."

CHAPTER **22**

How You Buy Stocks on Margin

ONCE a security buyer has assured a broker of adequate financial responsibility, he or she can open a *margin account* (instead of or in addition to a cash account) and buy stocks — any of the stocks listed on a United States securities exchange or the Nasdaq National Market System plus specified other over-the-counter stocks approved for margin transactions by the Federal Reserve Board — by making merely a partial payment on them.

It's easy to think of the cash a margin buyer puts up as a *down payment*. After all, just as when you buy a car or appliance on credit, part of the total price is paid up front, the rest is borrowed. However, there are no regular installment payments to be met in margin buying. In fact, few if any margin purchasers contemplate eventually owning the stock free and clear by paying off their loan balance. They want to utilize the extra leverage they get from investing with borrowed funds and expect to keep the loan till they close out their margin position by selling the stock.

Such leveraging can multiply profits but also greatly increases risks. It is a perfectly legitimate practice for those who know and can afford these risks. But no one should trade on margin unless he or she has both the temperament and the resources to accept losses with reasonable equanimity. You can't be a margin trader — nor should you be — if you have only a widow's mite. It's also no game for investment novices. You should be very wary of brokers or advisers who outline an ambitious margin trading program when you've had little investment experience.

But even if it's not for you, it's wise to be familiar with the rudiments of margin trading, and the impact it can have on the general market. Besides, the day may come when modest use of margin facilities makes sense for you.

Also, the popular central-asset accounts are structured in the form of a margin account. That's because the check-writing and debit-card features that come with the account permit you to draw on the borrowing power of your securities. Actually, a majority of account holders never use this borrowing power — but it's there.

So what are the key rules governing margin buying?

First, the New York Stock Exchange says that no one can *open* a margin account at any of its member firms without depositing into it at least $2,000, in cash or an equivalent in securities.

The exchange also has the right, when concerned about undue speculation in a particular stock, to demand higher margin deposits, or even to forbid margin trading entirely in that stock. But, for many years now, this authority has been invoked infrequently.

In addition, individual brokers may impose stiffer margin requirements than the *minimum* standards set by exchanges or regulators. Some firms, for instance, will not permit a customer to buy any stock on margin unless that stock sells above $5 a share. Other brokers require larger down payments.

Finally, and *most important*, there's the Federal Reserve Board. In 1934, Congress ordered the Fed to regulate stock market credit. Accordingly, its *Regulation T* sets the minimum percentage of the payment you must make when you buy stock on margin. The Fed has changed the percentage from time to time, depending on the availability of credit, the amount of margin trading, and on how worried the board was about inflation. The Fed tended to raise the percentage when it wanted to cool speculative fever in bull markets; conversely, when volume dried up in bear markets, the Fed was more willing to provide some stimulus by reducing the minimum margin requirements.

In the first 40 years of margin control, the Fed changed the minimum percentage 22 times. It ranged from a low of 40%, in effect from 1937 to 1945, to 100%. While the 100% rate prevailed, from January 1946 to February 1947, nobody could buy on margin.

However, since January 1974, the Regulation T requirement has remained unchanged at 50%. Of course, the very fact the percentage has been kept the same for so long means that if and when the Fed does make a change, it will pack a tremendous psychological punch.

For a simple explanation of how margin works, suppose that, with the Fed margin requirement at 50%, you buy $10,000 worth of some marginable stock. You put up $5,000 and your brokerage firm lends you the other $5,000. Naturally, when it does that, it charges you interest on the money it lends. How much depends in large part on how much interest the firm itself has to pay its bankers for the $5,000 it borrows from them to lend to you. Your broker is normally charged the so-called *brokers' loan rate*, which banks tend to change more frequently (both up and down) than their *prime rate*. Your broker will generally charge you the prevailing interest rate (either the brokers' loan or the prime) plus at least 0.5% to 1%, and in many cases more. This surcharge, which the broker retains to help pay for its operations, tends to vary with the size of your loan (the bigger your borrowing, the less the charge) and perhaps the amount of business you do.

The same Regulation T minimum margin requirements apply if you borrow directly from a bank or other lending institution for the purpose of financing stock purchases (though the bank is permitted to give you as much credit as it sees fit when you borrow for other purposes — say, education or medical bills — and put up stocks you own as collateral).

You may be able to borrow a greater proportion of the purchase price, perhaps as much as 90%, from unregulated lenders, though the interest cost as well as risk will probably be high. Any broker or registered representative who helped you arrange such a loan would run afoul of the SEC. So could you, if you falsely specify in a loan application that you are borrowing for a non-securities purpose.

When a broker borrows money from a bank and lends it to you so that you can buy stocks on margin, it has to give the bank some security on the loan. That loan security, in effect, is the very stock you buy on margin. Hence, when you open a margin account, you must agree to leave your margined stocks with the broker and to let the firm *hypothecate*, or pledge, them as security for whatever bank loan it may need in order to carry margin accounts.

When you buy $10,000 worth of stock on margin, you pay commissions on the full $10,000 worth of stock, but you are also entitled to the dividends on all the shares. This income may offset some of your margin loan-carrying costs. However, what virtually all who buy on margin are after is speculative profit.

Suppose someone with $6,000 to invest has picked out a stock selling at $60 a share which he thinks will go up. Under a 50% margin rule, his $6,000 will buy 200 rather than just 100 shares of that stock. If the stock goes up six points, this speculator makes $1,200 instead of $600, a 20% profit instead of 10%.

But suppose the stock goes down in price? There's the rub.

It's not just that a drop of six points would cost you $1,200 instead of $600; more dangerous to your peace of mind and financial health is that your equity (ownership value) will have shrunk by $1,200, to $4,800, while your margin debt is still $6,000. Should the stock continue to fall and erode your equity, you'd end up receiving a *margin call* from your broker. That's a demand to put up more margin — additional cash to restore your equity to a more acceptable level. If you can't put up more money (or deposit other securities you own), the broker has the right to sell your stock — or as much of it as may be necessary — to raise the required cash. Also keep in mind that the payment you make to satisfy a margin call is to *restore the value of your collateral*, you are *not paying down your debt*.

Part of your risk is in the timing. You may be perfectly right in judging that a stock is way undervalued and is bound to rise. But if in the meantime it sinks further, a margin call may force you to bail out, and you'll be on the sidelines when the stock finally lives up to your expectations.

How much more margin money will be required? The answer is

governed by the *margin maintenance* rules of the New York Stock Exchange and by those of the individual broker. The Fed was charged by Congress in the 1934 securities legislation with regulating the flow of credit *into* the stock market, so it isn't in the picture at all after the original purchase. Even should the Fed later raise its margin requirement for initial purposes — say, from 50% to 75% — that will apply only to new purchases, not to stock already in the account.

But maintenance is a definite concern of the stock exchange, under whose rules a broker must ask customers for more margin whenever their equity in the margined stocks falls below 25% of the current market value. Many brokers have margin maintenance requirements that are higher than the minimums set by the New York Stock Exchange.

To illustrate: The 200 shares our margin customer bought at $60 a share had a market value of $12,000; since he borrowed $6,000, his equity was $6,000 or 50%. Now suppose the stock dropped to $40 a share. The 200 shares would then be worth $8,000 and the customer's equity ($8,000 market value, less the $6,000 loan) would be $2,000 or exactly 25% of the market value. Any further drop would mandate a margin call, to restore at least the 25% ratio. Actually, the broker would probably ask for somewhat more than the minimum amount, to assure that another margin call wouldn't be needed right away if the stock continued to decline.

Our example was based on the customer buying only a single stock on margin. Actually, most margin customers have positions in a number of stocks in their accounts. And margin requirements are figured on the customer's overall position — the total value of the securities and the total debt for the account. Thus, a sharp drop in one stock won't necessarily trigger a margin call, provided other stocks in the account hold up well.

Thanks to modern data-processing equipment, which wasn't available during the 1929 crash and was still quite limited in the 1960s and 1970s, brokers can instantly compute the exact position of an active margin account. Nowadays, margin accounts are generally "marked to market" daily, so brokers can tell just where they stand.

As we've noted, investors don't have to pony up cash to meet a margin call if they own acceptable securities in another account or in their safe deposit box that they can put into the margin account as additional collateral. Margin customers are also permitted to substitute one stock for another in their margin account. This is usually the result of trades made by the customer. But if the stock bought is higher in value than the one that's sold, 50% (or whatever the Fed's current initial margin requirement is) of that value difference must be placed in the account.

Conversely, if, in a substitution, proceeds from the stock sold exceed the cost of the new purchase, the customer can withdraw from the account the amount above the Fed's current initial margin requirement, provided that the account is fully margined (unrestricted). If the account is restricted (because the current value is below the Fed requirement for initial margin), the customer can withdraw at least 40 percent of the difference between the purchase cost and the sale proceeds.

One other restriction on margin trading should be noted. The exchange has put a brake on the heavy margin traders who may move in and out of a given stock several times during one day's trading. Brokers are now required to see that such *day traders* operating on margin, as most of them do, have enough capital in their accounts to cover the initial margin requirement each time they trade during the day — not just on their position at the end of the day.

The strict margin regulations were born of the bitter experience of 1929. Back in the 1920s, you could buy securities with the barest of down payments. Typically it was 20%. Often it was less. And an occasional customer even "bought" securities 100% on credit — without putting up a dime. That's how a few people made a fortune on a shoestring. But it's also how more of them brought disaster on themselves and thousands of others.

With such lenient margins, it was easy for speculators in a rising market to *pyramid* their *paper profits*. Suppose someone bought 200 shares of a $50 stock by putting up $2,000 of the $10,000 cost. If the stock advanced to $75 a share, he could pay off the $8,000 margin loan and still pocket $7,000. But, more likely, in the euphoric environment, he'd keep the stock and the loan, and use the increased equity to buy more stock — on a 20% margin basis, he could now build his holdings up to $35,000 worth of stocks. If his luck and the market upswing continued, he'd buy more and more stock. He never had to put up any cash beyond his original $2,000 payment. Meantime, his equity was mounting (at least on paper) — but so was his margin debt.

That was a common story in the 1920s. Then prices started to decline in the fall of 1929, and speculators who had bought stock on zero to 20% margin faced margin calls. Many couldn't raise even a few thousand dollars cash except by selling securities. That very act of selling, of course, depressed prices further, resulting in more margin calls and more forced selling.

As for the brokerage houses, the low margins had left them in a precarious position, as lenders on rapidly deteriorating assets. If, for example, the brokerage firm had lent a customer $16 to buy a $20 stock and that stock had plunged to $14 by the time a margin call could be issued, not only had the customer's entire $4 equity in the stock been wiped out, but the broker now had a $2 loss on its loan. With the customers frequently lacking the cash or unwilling to "throw good money after bad," all the brokers could do was to sell the customer out, dumping the stock into a declining market, and further fueling the vicious circle.

There's nothing wrong with reinvesting stock market profits to buy more securities, or with repeating that process again and again. In fact, that's the basis for a sound long-term investment plan. And for the speculatively inclined who can afford the risk, using *some* borrowed funds to get more leverage can be a sound practice, too. The danger is in going out on a limb and counting on a rising market to bail you out. That, as we've seen time after time, can not only wipe out the unlucky speculator but have rippling effects throughout the securities market and the general economy.

That's why the stricter margin rules were instituted. In particular, the stock exchange rules insisting on margin calls before a customer's equity sinks too low is intended to make sure the brokerage house can get its loan repaid, thus safeguarding not only the firm but its other customers.

The regulations have certainly helped in limiting (though not eliminating) excessive speculation and the impact of margin debt on the markets. At times of severe market drops, heavy flurries of margin calls have still been set off, and the required selling in the accounts has temporarily exacerbated the market decline, but on a much smaller scale than in earlier eras. And the computerized tracking of margin accounts has led to far more effective controls.

CHAPTER 23

What It Means to Sell Short

WHEN investors open a margin account, they are asked to sign an agreement giving their broker authority to lend their marginable stocks to others. It is this lending or *hypothecation* agreement that makes it possible for other customers to sell stocks short.

Short selling normally accounts for only 6% to 9% of all the transactions on the New York Stock Exchange — and much of it represents transactions by Big Board specialists as part of their market making. Yet probably no other market technique excites so much public interest — or is so widely misunderstood.

A short sale is nothing but the reverse of the usual market transaction. Instead of buying a stock and then selling it, short traders first sell a stock they have borrowed, then *cover*, or buy it back, at what they hope will be a lower price.

If it is legitimate to buy a stock because you think it's going to go up, why isn't it just as legitimate to sell it because you think it's going to go down? Why shouldn't you be able to try to make a profit in either direction? It can be fairly argued that the right of a bear to sell, or *go short*, is just as vital to a completely free market as the right of a bull to buy stocks, or *go long*.

Regardless of the logic of the situation, many people think it just isn't morally right to sell something you don't have.

But what about the magazine publisher who sells you a three-year advance subscription?

What about the farmer who sells his whole crop to a grain elevator when the seed hasn't even sprouted yet?

Both of them sell something they haven't got, just on the strength of a promise to deliver. That's all a short seller does.

Furthermore, it isn't really true that short sellers sell something they don't have. They have to borrow the stock that they sell, and sooner or later they have to give it back. They just hope to be able to do this with stock they can buy for less than the price at which they sold the borrowed stock.

Where do they borrow the stock? From their broker.

Where does a brokerage firm get the stock to lend? Usually from its other margin customers, who signed the lending agreement when they opened their accounts. If the broker can't supply a particular stock from holdings in its margin accounts, it will borrow it from another broker, or from some individual stockowner who makes a business of lending stock. But the broker *cannot* borrow stock from the account of any of its regular cash customers without specific authorization.

Why should one broker lend stock to another? Because the lending broker gets paid for it by the borrowing firm. (Since short selling is a margin transaction in which the sellers owe stock, it's their broker, not the short sellers themselves, who holds the proceeds received from whoever buys the stock, and will hold them until the short sale is closed out by an offsetting purchase.) Sometimes, if the stock is in heavy demand and is difficult to borrow, the broker will even pay a premium to borrow it. Any such premium payment is, of course, charged to the short seller. If the price of a stock on loan increases significantly, the lending broker will demand more money for lending it. If the price drops, the borrowing broker will demand a proportionate refund of the money it has paid.

Sometimes a lending broker will demand return of the shares. If the borrowing broker can't find someone else willing to lend the stock, it is forced to buy the stock in the market and thus close out the short position whether the customer likes it or not. Consequently, a short seller always faces some risk of being forced to close out at an unfavorable moment.

In other respects, a short seller operates under essentially the same rules as a margin buyer. Assuming the Federal Reserve has a 50% margin rule in effect, the short seller must put up cash equal to 50% of the market value of the stock that's borrowed. Under stock exchange rules, the minimum margin cannot be less than $2,000.

Suppose someone wants to go short 100 shares of a stock selling at 60. At 50% margin, she would have to put up $3,000 cash. If the stock dropped to 50, she could buy it back, cover her short position by returning the stock, and make a profit of $10 a share, or $1,000, less taxes and commissions.

Perhaps, when the stock hit 50, she thought it would go still lower. That would mean additional profit, but she wouldn't want to risk losing the profit she already had. To protect herself against a rising market, she might place a stop order to buy at 52. If the stock does go up to 52, the stop order becomes a market order to buy at once. Then she would still have a profit of $800, exclusive of commissions, taxes, and other expenses. Among her costs, she is also liable for whatever dividends might have accrued on the stock, because lenders remain entitled to all dividends while their stock is on loan.

There is one important difference in the amount of maintenance margin required for margin buyers and for short sellers. The minimum requirement of the New York Stock Exchange for maintenance of margin is 25% for the long position. But when a customer uses margin — as he must — for going short, the minimum is increased to 30%, or $5 a share, whichever is greater, and — as with all margin accounts — a brokerage firm is free to impose higher requirements. (If the stock itself is selling below $5 a share, the NYSE minimum requirement is 100% of the market value, or $2.50 a share, whichever is greater.)

Under the 30% maintenance-of-margin requirement, the broker will call for more money whenever the amount of the margin that the short seller would have left if he bought the stock back and covered his short position is only 30% of its current market price. Let's suppose someone sells short 100 shares of a stock at 60. If the initial margin requirement was 50%, he would have to put up $3,000. Now, instead of declining to 50, suppose the price of the stock goes up to 70. If he were to cover at that point, he would owe $7,000, or $1,000 more than he sold the stock for originally. That means he would have only $2,000 margin left in his account (the $3,000 put up originally minus the $1,000 market movement), or a little less than 30% of the current value of the stock ($7,000 × .30 = $2,100). By that point, unless he decided to take his loss and close out the transaction, he would receive a maintenance call to deposit at least $100 additional margin.

In some cases, short sales are made for defensive purposes as in *selling against the box*. That's when you sell short a stock, while holding on to the identical security, safely stashed in your or your broker's vault or "box." This procedure was used mainly by investors who wanted to nail down a profit, but postpone actual selling of their stock till a short-term gain could grow into a long-term one. Under a few other circumstances investors may use a short sale to close out a position while they are temporarily unable or unwilling to produce a stock certificate — for example, if they are waiting for an estate to settle or some special restrictions to expire.

Nowadays, puts and calls have become far more convenient and flexible tools than short sales for most defensive and hedging strategies. And certainly, for the main short-selling contingent, the bearish speculators, the rapid development of the options and financial futures markets in the past two decades has made these new tools (discussed in the next chapter) the instrument of choice when they wish to bet on a price decline in a stock or in the market generally.

While there is a legitimate place for short selling in a free and orderly securities market, it cannot be denied that short selling has often been used for illegitimate purposes. Such abuses have frequently led to demands that short selling be outlawed. Short selling contributed some particularly gaudy chapters to the history of the New York Stock Exchange in the nineteenth century, when it was a favorite tool of such famous market manipulators as Commodore Vanderbilt, Daniel Drew, Jay Gould, and Jim Fisk. These men frequently tried to catch each other in market corners. A market *corner* is created when one man or group succeeds in getting such complete control of a particular stock that others who may have sold it short cannot cover their purchases by buying the stock back, as they eventually have to do, except on terms dictated by the controlling group.

One of the classic corners is the one that involved the old Harlem Railroad. Vanderbilt got control of the Harlem and then proceeded to extend the road down Manhattan Island. Drew, who was also a stockholder in the road and had realized a handsome profit as the stock advanced in price, now saw an opportunity to make a much larger profit. He induced the New York City Council to repeal the franchise that had been granted for the extension of the road, on the assumption that this bad news would depress the price of the stock. Simultaneously, he sold the stock short.

His maneuver succeeded in driving the price of the stock down, but as Drew sold, the Commodore bought. In the end, Drew and some of the members of the City Council who were associated with him in this notorious exploit found that they had sold short more stock than actually existed. They could not cover their short positions except on terms dictated by Vanderbilt — and the terms were ruinous. That is perhaps when the famous couplet, credited to Drew, came into our literature: *"He who sells what isn't his'n/Must buy it back or go to pris'n."*

Though not on such titanic scale, short selling often proved an effective manipulative device for *pool* operators, who would join forces to bid the price of a stock up and then drive it back down again with short selling to make a big speculative profit. Often such pool operators risked very little of their own capital in these *bear raids*. They would stimulate public interest in a particular stock by adroit publicity and creation of considerable activity in the market for that stock. That activity was usually more apparent than real, because it would be generated by *wash sales*. A wash sale, now outlawed by the SEC, simply involved the simultaneous purchase and sale of large blocks of stock. Such big volume would attract the public, which inevitably seems to buy whenever there is a lot of activity in a stock. As the public bought and forced the price up, pool operators would wait for the strategic moment when they thought the stock was about as high as it could get, then begin selling it short, hammering the price down to a level where they could buy it back at a hefty profit.

Even now, with strict rules against manipulation, short selling is fraught with danger. It's a truism that you may be perfectly right that your target company is way overpriced. But even if it's fated for bankruptcy, if in the meantime other people with misplaced optimism drive the stock up, *you* may be in bankruptcy court before the company gets there. That's the reverse of margin buyers being sold out before their stock rises — only the risk on the short side is far greater. When you buy on margin, all you can lose, in the worst case, is your equity plus the full amount of the loan. That's bad enough. But if you're wrong on a short sale, there's no theoretical limit to your loss at all — the stock you're obligated to buy back can soar an infinite amount.

And in addition to price risk, you face the risk that you may be unable to keep borrowing the stock. Since the owner of the stock your broker borrowed for you may demand it back at any time, there's always the danger of a *short squeeze*. Ironically, that's especially true when more and more people decide a stock is way overpriced and consequently "short" it. The supply of lendable stock may soon dry up. Then the shorts may have to hunt desperately for stock they can borrow to maintain their short position, and many may be forced to bail out at a loss.

One of the important reforms introduced by the Securities and Exchange Commission was a regulation aimed at preventing abuse of the right to sell short. In February 1938, it decreed that a stock can be sold short only in a rising market, however temporary that rise may be.

The rule, generally referred to as the *uptick rule*, works this way: If a customer places an order to sell short, that order, as it goes to the floor, must be clearly marked as a short sale. The floor broker is forbidden to execute that order except at what is, in effect, a higher price. Thus, if a stock were last sold at 50, the broker could not sell that stock short except at a price of 50⅛ or higher — in other words, on an uptick. However, the broker could sell the stock at 50, the same price as the last sale, in those cases where the *last previous change* in the price had been upward. Thus, one or two or six transactions might have taken place at 50, but a short sale would still be permissible at that price, provided the last *different* price had been 49⅞ or lower. This is called selling on a *zero uptick*.

The *short interest*, or number of shares held short in each stock, is reported monthly by the New York Stock Exchange, the American Stock Exchange, and, since 1986, the NASD for its National Market System. Paradoxical as it may seem, a big short interest — both for specific stocks and the market as a whole — is generally regarded as bullish. This is because, as the short interest grows, so does the potential volume of future buying orders. As we know, ultimately every one of those short sellers must buy back the stock that's been sold short in order to make delivery of the shares.

After the markets have gone down sharply, shorts are apt to "take profits" — that is, start to cash in on their gains by closing out their positions. And once the market starts up, other shorts may rush in, trying to salvage what gains they have left from the preceding downturn, or, if it's too late for that, to limit their losses. That's how the short interest offers a cushion for the market.

It's probably inherent in human nature — the public always wants the market to go up and generally believes that it will. Most investors act accordingly. In the light of such perpetual bullishness, who could deny an old bear the right to sell short on the assumption that the public is wrong again?

CHAPTER 24

Options and Futures Grow Fast
in the Present

NEW tools that have quickly become favorites in the speculator's arsenal are stock and index options and financial futures. But while their speculative applications get most of the publicity, the same tools are also available for conservative income and hedging strategies.

Be aware, however, that most brokers assume that anyone ready to engage in options or futures is of a speculative bent. So if that's not your game, it's wise to emphasize and re-emphasize your more conservative objectives. Also, remember that no strategy is riskless. And certainly no one should engage in options or futures trading until they've acquired a fair amount of experience in stock market fundamentals.

There's an important distinction between options and futures. An option gives you the *right* but not the *obligation* to buy or sell something at a specified price within a specified time. It might be 100 shares of General Motors stock, a three-bedroom house, or, if you're a movie producer, the right to some script that struck your fancy. If, for any reason, or none at all, you decide you don't want to go through with the deal, you can just walk away from it, and the most it could cost you is whatever price you paid to get the option.

By contrast, a futures contract is a binding agreement to deliver or receive something of value at some predetermined time in the future — whether a carload of soybeans, a 50-acre estate, or, in an earlier culture, your hand in marriage. You're committed, unless you can buy your way out of the contract or can arrange for someone else to take over your obligation.

Financial options are often thought of as a fairly low-risk bet on whether a stock, or the market in general, will move up or down. But keep in mind that it's "low risk" only in the sense that it takes a relatively small amount of money to buy or sell an option. However, it's very easy to lose most or all of that stake very quickly if the stock doesn't move your way. By the same token, it's possible to make proportionately big profits if the stock performs as you hope within the limited lifetime of your option.

So, let's make it clear at the start: There are many legitimate reasons, including speculation, for going into options — but be sure you know what you are doing, and why. Be especially wary of any broker who urges you into a program of rapid options trading, promising big returns and claiming there's little risk.

Financial options come in two basic types: *Calls* give you the right to buy; *puts* the right to sell. The venerable names derive from the concept that you can call on the other party to deliver the stock or other instrument to you, or, conversely, put the stock to that party (make it accept). The "other party," incidentally, the one that sells the option, is known as the *writer* of the call or put. The price the buyer pays (and the writer collects) for the option privilege is called the *premium*.

For a simplified look at the mechanics, suppose you think our old friend Rod & Reel (RAR) is likely to increase in price over the next few months. Let's further suppose it's now October, with RAR stock trading at $50 a share and a "January 50" call option at $4. That means, if you now pay $400 (the $4 premium times 100 shares), you get the right to buy 100 shares of RAR at $50 a share — known as the *strike price* (or sometimes, *striking price*) or, in the formal nomenclature of the exchanges, the *exercise price* — at any time until the contract expires in January. (One standard stock option covers a put or call on a 100-share round-lot of stock; there is no such thing as an odd-lot option. Our examples of how options work will be based on per-share prices for both the stock and the option.) If you exercise this RAR option, your effective cost would be $54: the $50 strike price plus the $4 per share you paid for the option. So RAR would have to rise to at least 54 (actually somewhat more, to allow for commissions) for you to break even. But suppose RAR shoots up to 60 by January. That would make your option worth $10 (since you or anyone to whom you sell the option could buy a $60 stock for $50) and you'd have a six-point gain, for a 150% return on your $4-per-share investment. If you had bought the stock outright in October, you'd have a 10-point gain, but that's only 20% on the $50-per-share purchase price.

Suppose instead that RAR dallied in the low fifties. In that case, you'd have lost most of the money you paid for the call (at 52, your $50 option would still be worth $2, but that's only half your purchase price), while holders of the stock itself enjoyed a small gain. If the stock failed to rise at all above 50, your option would end up without any value. On the other hand, even if RAR plunged to 40, all you'd be out is the $4 a share, or $400, you paid for the option, while the owner of 100 RAR shares would have lost $1,000.

Conversely, if you expected RAR to go down, you might have bought a put. Assume a "January 50" put was also available at a $4 premium; the stock would have to drop to 46 for you to break even. If the stock dropped to, say, 42 by January, you'd be well ahead; your put option would then be worth $8 (since you could sell a $42 stock for $50) or double what you paid for the option. And if, instead, RAR stock shot up way beyond $50, no matter how high it rose, your loss would be limited to the $400 you paid for the option.

In our example we used options that were precisely *at-the-money* when the put or call was bought — the $50 strike price matched the $50 at which the stock itself happened to be selling at the time. If the market price of the stock rose to, say, $52, the $50 call option would then be *in-the-money* (it would pay for the holder to exercise it), whereas if the market price fell to $48, the call option would be *out-of-the-money*. The situation is, of course, reversed for puts. A $50 put is in-the-money as long as the stock trades below $50, out-of-the-money when it rises above $50. Note that being in-the-money doesn't necessarily mean the buyer made a profit. If you paid $4 for a January 50 call and the stock goes to $52, you're still a couple of dollars below break-even.

The stock options concept is generations old. So-called "put and call brokers" offered to write options in various popular stocks. But each was a distinct contract, with its own specific terms. The buyer normally expected to hold on to the option until he exercised it or it expired worthless.

Then the whole concept was revolutionized in April 1973 when the *Chicago Board Options Exchange* (known as the CBOE or, in many newspaper listings, the Chicago Board) initiated an organized market for trading in calls. In 1975, the American Stock Exchange joined in. The Philadelphia and Pacific stock exchanges followed, and so eventually did the New York Stock Exchange. Originally, trading in these *listed options* (a term differentiating them from the individualized, and technically over-the-counter, contracts written by the old-line put and call brokers) was restricted to calls; exchange trading in puts was first authorized in 1977. In the early 1980s, options began to be offered on U.S. Treasury securities as well as stocks.

By creating standardized contracts, the exchanges made it possible to trade freely in the listed options in much the same way as you trade in stocks, on SEC-regulated markets. While there must be a buyer and seller (writer) in every options trade, technically the contract they buy or sell is not with each other but with the *Options Clearing Corporation* (OCC). This organization was initially set up by the CBOE and is now owned jointly by all the U.S. exchanges offering options. It is the organizational middleman that makes it possible for you to *close out* (buy back) your contract at any time, regardless of what the other party in your original trade does with its contract. It also makes sure that if and when you choose to exercise your option, someone who has written such an option is assigned to make the required stock delivery (or to buy the stock you are putting). After holders, through their broker, notify the OCC they want to exercise their option, the OCC uses an "established random selection procedure" to pick the brokerage houses that must honor these options;

the brokers, in turn, can use either random selection or a "first-in, first-out" system to determine which of the writers among their customers will be *assigned* (the brokers must tell their options customers which system they use and how it works). Thus, once an option you have written is in-the-money, you always face the "luck of the draw" risk that it will be exercised against you, even if you had planned to close it out by buying an offsetting put or call.

Under the listed options system, you can buy and sell options any time during their life. That lifetime normally runs up to eight months. However, on some of the more popular stocks, the exchanges have added special long-term versions called *LEAPS* (for Long-term Equity AnticiPation Securities), which can run up to three years. Stock options normally expire on the Saturday following the third Friday of the month, making that Friday the last trading day.

The system determining what monthly contracts are available for each stock option is somewhat complicated. Originally, all listed options were set to expire in January, April, July, and October. Only the nearest three of these months were offered at any one time. Thus, in December, you could trade in January, April, and July options; once the "Januaries" expired, they were replaced by "Octobers." As options began to be offered on more and more stocks, it was decided to spread out the expirations, and February-May-August-November and then March-June-September-December cycles were instituted for newer options. However, since most of the big and actively traded stocks were among the first on which options were issued, the "January cycle" is not only the biggest of the three cycles, but also contains the largest number of prominent companies.

The system has undergone several modifications. At this writing, four expiration months are offered at a time: the two nearest calendar months, plus, beyond that, the next two months in the particular stock's basic cycle.

Also standardized are the strike prices at which options are offered — usually in five-dollar intervals. For example, if Rod & Reel common is selling at 50 at the time the new July options series starts trading, both call and put contracts would initially be offered with strike prices at 55, 50, and 45. Should the RAR stock subsequently climb to 55, contracts with a 60 strike price will be added — not just for July, but for any other maturity currently trading. Similarly, should RAR drop to 45, 40 options will start trading, and if the stock touches 40, they'll add a 35 option.

The previously established strike-price options also remain listed (e.g., the 55 option even after RAR common drops to, say, 38), but most of the trading is concentrated on the strike-price contracts (or *series*, the official term for each specific strike price and expiration month combination) close to the present market price for the underlying stock. After all, few people are interested in buying or selling a contract at 65 or 35 for a stock currently selling at 50, because the stock is less likely to move so far in a limited time.

With the profusion of contracts, newspapers, if they print options quotations at all, will list only the relatively most active. The comprehensive daily report in the *Wall Street Journal* nowadays offers a unified alphabetical listing covering all the exchanges and showing the 1,400 most active options series, plus a separate list of the 100 most active LEAPS contracts. However, quotations for any expiration month and strike price of any listed option can be readily obtained from your broker or any standard quote machine.

Incidentally, the $5 price interval is standard for strike prices between $25 and $200. Strike prices are set at $2.50 intervals below $25, and 10 points apart above $200. Adjustments are made for stock splits and other special events. For instance, if there's a 3-for-2 split, an option for 100 shares at $45 will turn into one for 150 shares at $30. (However, if this were a 2-for-1 or similar "whole-share" split, the exchanges find it simpler to give you two options contracts for 100 shares each — rather than one contract for 200 shares — at the adjusted exercise price of $22.50.) And suppose there's an acquisition under which stockholders of PQR Corp. get $13 plus half a share of STU, Inc. per PQR share. Normally, it'll be arranged that a call on 100 PQR shares will now be entitled to 50 shares of STU stock plus $1,300 cash — exactly what each existing holder of 100 PQR shares receives.

Just as in trading stocks or bonds, the current price of any put or call option depends on the price a buyer is willing to pay and a seller or writer willing to accept in the open market at that time. Analytically, the option price or premium can be broken down into two parts. First is the *intrinsic value*, what an in-the-money option is worth were it exercised right away. For instance, with RAR stock at 54, a 50 call would have an intrinsic value of $4, a 45 call of $9, a 55 put an intrinsic value of $1. If the underlying stock is at or out-of-the-money, the intrinsic value is zero (you don't go into negative numbers). The other part of the premium is called the *time value* — it's what the buyer is willing to pay for the possibility that during the remaining life of the option, the stock price will move in the desired direction. Thus, while your $50 call on a $54 stock already has an intrinsic value of $4, if the option still has two months to run, someone might think that by then RAR could rise a good deal further, and so be willing to pay, say, $7 for the $50 call. That would be $4 intrinsic and $3 time value, and the stock would have to rise to at least $57 for this buyer to break even (again, before counting commissions). For the $45 call, buyers might be willing to pay only $1.50 for the time value, bringing the total premium for the call to $10.50 (because of the higher total price for the call, the potential leverage is less than for the $50 call, and thus of less interest to the buyer). As for the $55 call, the stock would have to rise by $1-plus before the call gets any intrinsic value, but the high leverage — the potential for big percentage gains on a relatively small investment should RAR stock really take off — might cause the call to sell for $4, with the entire amount representing time value.

While the intrinsic-value part of an option price is mathematically determined and changes in absolute relation to the movement of the underlying stock, the time-value portion reflects many different factors. First, of course, is time itself — other considerations being equal, the longer the remaining life of the option, the more time for the underlying stock to move in the desired direction, and thus the more attractive (and higher-priced) the option privilege. Also, as we observed, when the option's strike price is fairly close to the stock's current market price, there's a better chance of attaining (or increasing) intrinsic value before the option expires, and this typically helps fatten the time value. Also, a volatile stock — one that tends to have big up- and down-swings — is more likely to hit either call or put strike prices than a stock that usually moves in a narrow range; hence, it usually commands a higher time-value premium.

And then there are the psychological factors; in a bull market atmosphere, calls in general are apt to have bigger time-value premiums than puts, and the reverse is true in bear markets. Of course, the attitude toward specific stocks can play an even bigger role; if there's widespread belief RAR stock is headed higher, option buyers will bid up the premium on its calls; when there's pessimism about the stock's outlook, it's the put premiums that are apt to rise. In addition, option premium prices are influenced by such factors as the prevailing level of interest rates and the expected return available on alternative investments.

The interaction of the many factors is reflected across the pricing matrix of expiration months and strike prices for the puts and calls on each company's options. Many out-of-the-money series (especially if expiration is near) will sell for a fraction of a dollar — and, of course, low prices are what attracts many traders to the options market. At the same time, contracts that are "deep" in-the-money may fetch $20, $30, or more, with virtually all of that amount representing intrinsic value.

As we've already mentioned, standard newspaper tables show only the nearest three of the four expiration months; you'll also find the tables strewn with the standard notation "r" to indicate that particular option series did not trade that day, and "s," which means there is no contract in that month at that strike price. In any case, you'll want to use newspaper tables as only a rough guideline; option prices can move so rapidly, it's vital to get the current bid and asked prices when you're contemplating an order. These prices are right on tap at a broker's quote machine. While the differential (spread) between the bid and ask quotation may be proportionately large compared with actively traded stocks, quotations are normally available on every contract variation that's authorized for trading (even if there have been few if any actual transactions), and the specialists or floor traders on the exchanges are expected to fill an order for up to 10 contracts (i.e., for options covering up to 1,000 shares) at the ask price if you want to buy, or the bid price if you want to sell. On actively traded options, you may be able to get a price somewhere between the bid and asked.

In explaining the mechanics of options trading, we have used for our examples buyers who bought calls on stocks they expected to rise or puts on stocks they expected to fall; speculative purchases, but with limited risk because the buyers could, but did not have to, exercise their option.

You may wonder who'd be on the other side — who would care to write the calls or puts that made them dependent on someone else's choice — that would *require* them to go through with the deal when and only when it would be to their disadvantage? One answer is the options professionals on the floor of the exchanges who are confident that the premiums they collect on the many options that expire worthless generally more than offset their cost on those that are exercised against them. And remember, they determine the premiums at which they are willing to trade; consequently, these premiums reflect the risks they see in that particular option. This is an admittedly simplified explanation; these professionals, constantly alert to moves in the markets, are prepared to act fast to *close out* (buy back) contracts that move against them, and they undertake a great many hedging strategies that minimize their risks. Also, as exchange members or authorized traders, their transaction costs are minimal.

Another major source is *covered call* writing, especially by institutions who own large blocks of stock. A call is covered when the option writer owns the underlying stock. Even if the stock shoots up way beyond the strike price, since you already own the stock you're called on to deliver, all that can happen is that you kick yourself for having to forgo the profit that would have been yours if you could have kept the stock. By contrast, the writer of a *naked call*, who doesn't own the stock, can face sky's-the-limit losses. Some sudden event such as a takeover bid could easily lift the stock's price by 20 or 30 points, and a call that was trading at $2 might hit $28 or more before the stunned writer could dismount.

Because the risks, however unlikely you may consider them, could be so catastrophic, even individuals willing to speculate aggressively should shun writing naked calls. Actually, before permitting you to engage in naked-call writing, reputable brokerage houses would not only try to make sure you understood all the risks, but would require you to have a substantial net worth in your portfolio (probably over $100,000), and to maintain an ample good-faith margin to make sure you can meet your commitment. Even if you qualify, beware any brokers who minimize the riskiness and ask you to authorize a series of transactions.

By contrast, covered calls are considered a relatively riskless way of earning some extra income on an investment — though the opportunity is better for big-volume institutions than for individuals, who must factor in higher commission costs. The attractions for the covered writers include: (1) they are well rewarded for the risks they assume by the premiums they receive; (2) they get immediate use of this money on which to earn income (and the money is theirs to keep, whether or not the option is exercised); (3) they keep collecting dividends on the underlying stock until and unless it is called from them. It's all but certain that an option will be exercised if the stock is even one-eighth above the strike price at the time the option expires. But, assuming you wrote an out-of-the-money option (say, an RAR 55 call when the stock was at 51) the very fact that the call is exercised means that, in addition to the premium you collected on writing the call, you are realizing a gain in the stock itself since the day you wrote the option — in this example, $4 a share (55 − 51).

Some investors look for favorable opportunities to write options on stocks they already hold in their portfolio, figuring that, on balance, the extra income from premiums will compensate them for possibly having to give up ownership of the stock; in addition, the premium would somewhat cushion their loss if the stock goes down. In our RAR example above, when the stock was at 51, you collected $2 a share for writing a 55 call option; after the stock moved up sufficiently for the call to be exercised, you in effect (and also for tax purposes) sold at $57 ($55 strike + $2 previously received premium). That's a six-point gain since the time you wrote the option. On the other hand, had RAR dipped to $47, your true loss would have been only two points (the four-point actual drop less the two-point premium you collected). However, whether or not you sold the stock at that stage, you'd have a taxable $2 gain on the option that expired worthless (in IRS eyes, it's "Sales Price $2 . . . Cost $0").

Investors may also buy stocks with the express purpose of writing calls on them. Some major brokerage houses have elaborate computer programs that enable brokers to see on their screens the potential results of writing (or, for that matter, buying) options on various stocks at different strike prices and expirations. It will show what the profits or losses would be (after all commissions) at different prices reached by the underlying stock. It might show, for instance, that, at the moment you're inquiring, buying 500 shares of RAR common at 52 and simultaneously writing 5 "January 55" calls at 2¾ would give you a 20.9% (annualized) return if the call ends up being exercised, lesser amounts if RAR fails to reach 55, but that you'd be "protected" down to 49; i.e., you could get out of your position without a loss as long as RAR didn't fall below $49.

While the computers will give potential results for just about any stock, the brokerage houses also have specialists looking for those stocks that seem to offer the most attractive opportunities, based on a specific stock's outlook, volatility pattern, and the level of premiums.

A different kind of stock and option combination is the *married put* — simultaneous purchase of stock and a put on it. This is for investors who think a stock is going up, but are willing to pay for protection (for a limited time) against it turning down instead. For instance, you may buy RAR at $50, along with a $50 put for a $2 premium. That of course means the stock would have to rise to $52 before you can break even (not counting the commission costs). However, if your expectations for the stock are realized, and it shoots up to $55, $60, or beyond, you make a substantial gain, even though your put will expire worthless. If, on the other hand, RAR starts sinking, your put enables you to get out at $50 — all you'll have lost is the $200 ($2 × 100 shares) option premium plus the commissions, relatively cheap insurance under the circumstances.

Other investors buy puts as a hedge on downturns in stocks they already own. Sometimes, it's insurance tied to a very specific requirement. Say you plan to cash in your 200 shares of RAR to pay your daughter's $10,000 tuition bill due in six months. So you couldn't afford any sharp decline in RAR's current $50 price, but you'd also hate to miss out on any rise in RAR stock over the next half year. If you can buy two $50 six-month puts at $3, you'll be paying $600 in insurance, but you know you'll get the $10,000 you need from your RAR stock — and you'll fully share in any run-up of the stock in the meantime.

Others will buy such puts simply as a hedge against a possible downturn in some of the stocks in their portfolio, especially if they already have goodly gains and want to hold the stock because they think its long-term outlook is bright. Actually, these people should root for their puts to expire worthless — much as you're happy when you've "wasted" your airplane trip insurance. And in this case, the cost of your "insurance" — i.e., what you paid for the now worthless option — is deductible as a capital loss. But it's worth having in case of a crash. When you've bought an RAR $50 put and the stock sinks to $40, you have a chance to reassess the investment value of the stock and either: (1) decide RAR no longer seems attractive, exercise the put, and get out of the stock at $50; or (2) feel the stock is still a worthwhile long-term holding, sell the put for $10 (plus any possible remaining time value), and hold on to the stock at what is in effect a $10 lower cost basis — before adjusting for the cost of your options premium and the commissions involved. As for the tax impact, when you don't exercise the option, you must pay a capital gain on the profit from your put, but can keep your cost basis for the underlying stock unchanged.

Do keep in mind that options are not suited for hedging an entire portfolio on a long-term basis. The cost of the premiums and the recurring commissions, since you'd constantly have to roll over expiring options into later maturity months, would mount rapidly; the insurance would probably end up costing more than the protection it offers. Besides, if you accept the basic rationale for long-term investing in stocks — that, while you must allow for lots of fluctuations and for severe disappointments in some of the stocks, a well-chosen equity portfolio has over time proven the most dependable vehicle for investment growth — then there's no economic sense in such a search for constant and complete "insurance." But put protection can come in handy on select occasions. Suppose some of your stocks (and, likely, much of the market) have had a vigorous run-up and, in the technicians' phrase, are "extended"; suppose further that you feel the "momentum" could well carry them higher and that you wouldn't want to miss out on that rise, but at the same time you fear a substantial "correction" could come any time — then buying a put on a couple of your holdings can be sensible insurance and surely help you sleep better.

Another factor to consider in all types of options transactions is which series (specific strike price and expiration) you want to deal in. Professional traders generally pay most attention to nearby maturities with strike prices near the current market; that's where options prices tend to be lowest and the leverage and arbitrage opportunities highest. But for the investor placing orders for one or a couple of contracts at a time, the proportionately high retail commissions cut deeply into the leverage and make short-term, low-price trades far less attractive. It's a good idea to get the quotations for several strike prices and expiration months and (after adding in commission costs) consider which might best serve your objectives. There's no mathematical formula, since you must assess your initial costs in terms of where the price of the underlying stock may be moving. However, while this may not be the accepted options wisdom, the most advantageous procedure for the small-scale participant may be to buy or write contracts with five to eight months of life remaining, thus avoiding rapid turnover and repeated commissions.

Another potential option use is locking in the price of a stock when you're unable or unwilling to buy it right now. Suppose you think RAR is a good investment at the current price of $50 but you don't have any spare investment cash handy. A bonus check is due in four months, but by then, you fear, RAR might already be a lot higher. Under these circumstances, you might buy a $50 call, assuring your right to purchase RAR at that price no matter what happens to the stock in the meantime. And if, by the time you're ready to buy, RAR instead has sunk to $45, you'll have lost the premium you shelled out; however, you'll be able to buy RAR stock directly in the market for less than you had been willing to pay earlier — if you still want it.

Or suppose you think RAR at the current $50 is a bit too pricey but that it would be a great buy if you could get it at $40. Then you just might consider writing a $40 put on RAR, collecting an immediate premium in return for agreeing to accept RAR stock if it reaches a price you've already decided is attractive. Even so, any naked put carries considerable risk and at the very least you had better keep close watch. If the market, and especially RAR, starts dropping rapidly, you may feel that $40 wasn't such a bargain after all; in that case, you might prefer to quickly close out your put, buying it back at a loss but eliminating your obligation to buy the stock.

Aside from simply buying or writing an option, there are many more complex strategies. Most of them are best left to the professionals or experienced, well-capitalized traders; however, some may be of broader interest. A particularly straightforward example is the *90/10 strategy*, which some of the exchanges and brokerage houses promoting options suggest as a comparatively modest-risk play for the investor. Simply put, out of the funds you set aside for participating in this strategy, you risk 10% in calls on a stock you expect to move up over the next few months, but place the other 90% in a safe money market instrument like Treasury bills or a money fund. Thus, even should the underlying stock disappoint and your option expire worthless, you'll still have 90% of your original principal, and the interest earned on it can offset a part of your option loss. And if you're right and the stock does advance briskly, the option leverage will provide a bigger overall return than if you had invested the full funds in the stock itself. However, remember that, while your potential loss is limited, the profit part of the strategy works out only if the stock rises sufficiently during the limited life of your option.

Among the more sophisticated option strategies are straddles and spreads and various combinations based on them. In a simple *straddle*, the trader buys a put and a call on the same stock at the same strike price. This may be used in a volatile stock that the trader feels will probably move sharply in one direction or another (depending on news and market psychology) but he doesn't know in which direction. While one of the two legs in the straddle will presumably turn into a total loss, the trader counts on a big enough move in some direction to more than offset the combined premium cost. You can get detailed descriptions of this and other options strategies, as well as examples showing the mathematics involved, in brochures available from the OCC, exchanges, and brokers.

A variation of the straddle, called a *strangle*, consists of buying out-of-the-money calls above and puts below the current price of the underlying security, and is particularly popular in options on Treasury securities. Being out-of-the-money makes the cost of the options relatively cheap, but it requires more movement in the underlying stock or bond before one of the strangle legs has some value.

Spreads consist of the simultaneous buying and selling of a call (or put) on the same stock at different strike prices or sometimes (in a *calendar spread*) different expiration months. Spreads are most often used for stocks expected to move relatively little during the option life. The spread trader expects the premium on the call he buys will rise more quickly (or drop more slowly) than on the call he sells. The size of the potential gain is relatively limited, but so is the potential loss. This also means that commission costs can loom large in the trader's profit or loss calculations — one more reason why such trading is mostly left to the professionals, whose transaction costs are low.

You can guarantee holding on to most of a gain you've attained in a stock with a *hedge wrapper*, buying a put below the stock's current price and offsetting at least part of the cost of that option by writing a call above it. For example, if your RAR stock, which you bought back when it was $30, has risen to $54, you might be able to buy a $50 put at $3 while selling a $60 call at $2. Even if RAR sags, you're assured at least $49 a share (the $50 put strike less the $1 net cost of the options); on the other hand, the call you wrote means the most you can get for the stock is $59 ($60 strike less $1 option).

Incidentally, in all options contracts, if you as a buyer decide to exercise them, or as a writer are assigned to deliver or accept stock, your broker will normally charge you the same commission as if you bought or sold the stock on an exchange. That's why investors in options often find it more attractive to close out an option contract by selling or buying an offsetting contract.

The strong and growing popularity of the listed stock option market led to the development of more complex option products, many of which now overshadow stock options in activity and attention. Particularly prominent are *index options*, based on the movement of a stock index rather than of an individual stock. Sometimes well-established yardsticks like the Standard & Poor's (S&P) 500-stock index, the New York Stock Exchange composite, or the Value Line index are used. But, increasingly, a new index is specially created to serve as the base for an option, as for instance the S&P MidCap, which is comprised of 400 "mid-size capitalization" stocks. As of spring 1994, the MidCap stocks had an average market value of $1.2 billion, compared with $6.4 billion for the S&P 500 companies.

Trading and procedures in index options are in many ways the same as for stock options. You can buy or write either puts or calls at various established strike prices and designated expiration months, and throughout the life of any contract you can always close it out by buying or selling an offsetting contract in the market.

But there are also some marked differences. Probably most important is that there is no "index" or actual basket of underlying stocks to deliver if an option is exercised. Instead, the writer pays and the call holder receives the cash difference between the strike price and the value of the index on the settlement day. Thus if, when the July options expire, the S&P 500 index stands at 393, the owner of a 385 call would receive $800 ($8 for the 393−385 difference times 100, the standard multiplier for these options, or, you might say, the index equivalent of 100 shares). Any outstanding July calls with strike prices of 395 or higher, or puts at 390 or below, would expire worthless.

Incidentally, because of the often wild trading in the stock markets on option expiration days as big-time traders try to adjust offsetting positions in the index options and in the major stocks that made up the index, the final settlement price of most index options is now computed from the *opening* rather than the closing prices of the underlying stocks on that expiration Friday. The monthly expiration days have been dubbed *witching hours;* and the third month of each quarter brings a *triple witching hour,* because not only (1) stock options and (2) index options, but also (3) index futures (discussed later in this chapter) all expire on the same day.

Early index options (just like the original listed stock options) were offered with expirations three, six, and nine months away. But because most participants are interested in hedging or speculating within a limited timespan, most index options are now offered with contracts expiring in each of the next three months, plus often a later month or two.

Another major difference between index and stock options deals with how they may be exercised. The options on stocks are traded *American style,* which means holders of puts and calls can exercise them at any time during the option's life. As a result, if you have written a call and the underlying stock shoots up beyond the strike price, you could suddenly find yourself called on to deliver the stock weeks or months before the option expires. However, a number of index options are traded *European style,* with exercise permitted only on the last trading day. This can make the contracts more attractive to active writers who know that a contract can't be exercised on them if it moves into-the-money early on (and perhaps for only a brief period before falling out-of-the-money again), thus disrupting their hedging and other options strategies. Of course, if you own an in-the-money call or put, you can cash in on it at any time by simply selling the contract — which, as we noted, is how the vast majority of options positions are closed out, anyway.

Long the most popular of the index options is the Chicago Board Options Exchange's *S&P 100* index, mostly referred to by its ticker symbol *OEX*. Introduced as the first index option in March 1983, the OEX was originally put together by the CBOE and named the CBOE 100; later, the exchange arranged for sponsorship by Standard & Poor's, and thus the more prestigious S&P name. It consists of 100 of the biggest stocks, weighted by their market capitalization (stock price multiplied by shares outstanding), so that the largest companies within the index exert the largest impact on it. The CBOE now also trades the *S&P 500* index option (SPX), which is based on Standard & Poor's long-established 500-stock index, the broad yardstick against which many investment managers measure themselves. The OEX S&P 100 is traded American style (exercisable at any time), the S&P 500 options European style (exercisable only on the closing day).

In April 1983, the American Stock Exchange also moved into the index field with the *Major Market Index* or *XMI*, which in 1988 switched to European style. Of the 20 blue-chip stocks in this index, 17 are also in the 30-stock Dow Jones Industrial Average. The XMI uses the same arcane computation method as the "Dow" and prides itself on achieving a 97 percent correlation with the Dow's movements. Why then, you ask, don't they just use the Dow Jones average directly? Well, it's not for lack of trying by the Amex or the CBOE (which had wanted a Dow index before setting up its OEX). But Dow Jones & Co., the compilers of the average and publishers of the *Wall Street Journal*, have tenaciously defended their average against any such usage. They not only refused any official association, but launched a stern legal defense against any unauthorized use of their name or average. So the options exchanges had to work out a bypass.

While the great majority of options traders operate with short time horizons, for those interested in stock trends more than a few months away, both the CBOE and Amex have come out with longer-maturity versions of their pacesetting contracts. LEAPS contracts for the S&P 100 and 500 indexes on the CBOE and the Major Market on the Amex all have December expirations for up to three years hence. Also, their valuation levels are set at one-tenth that of the standard index; i.e., when the S&P 100 index is at 355, for LEAPS-100 purposes it is figured as 35.5. (For both the short and long terms, you then multiply by $100 to get the actual dollar value on which the contract is based, equivalent to a stock option based on 100 shares of stock.)

There are numerous other index options on the various exchanges, and more are being developed. The Amex won the right to options trading of S&P's new MidCap index, starting in 1992. Among other Amex index options are the Institutional Index, based on the 75 stocks most widely held by large institutions, and the Japan Index, based on 210 Tokyo stocks, with the index traded in dollars but computed so as to reflect the stocks' yen price changes.

More specialized index options include those based on stocks in specific industry groups, such as the Pharmaceutical, Biotech, and Computer indexes on the Amex, and the Utilities and Gold & Silver indexes on the Philadelphia Stock Exchange. The Philadelphia also offers options on the Value Line Composite and National Over-The-Counter indexes, while the Pacific Stock Exchange is host to options on the Wilshire Index. The Big Board offers options trading on its own New York Stock Exchange Composite index.

The options indexes have been fashioned to appeal to large institutional investors, which may buy or sell 500, 1,000, or more contracts at a time to hedge against broad market moves that could adversely affect their portfolio. Some applications meet quite specific needs. As just one example, say, with the S&P 100 Index at 380, a money manager thinks the market is likely to have a sizable correction, so he wants to hold back on investing the $5 million in extra cash reserves he has on hand. But he doesn't want to get caught, should the market take off. He could buy 1,000 OEX 385 calls (with expiration two months off) at around 6 for a total cost of $600,000, with the rest of his reserve continuing to earn interest in short-term instruments. Should, against his expectations, the market now jump 10% (to around 420 on the OEX), the 385 options should be worth at least $3,500,000 (plus possible remaining time value). Thus, while the prices of stocks he wants would now be higher, he'd have more cash to pay for them — and, in any case, the options profit will have enabled him to show a respectable growth in his fund's asset value.

As we've indicated, index options are mainly for use by institutions and professionals who trade many contracts at a time, can keep an eye on fast-moving markets, and have large resources. They are not designed for hedging by individual investors (your portfolio isn't likely to match or mirror any index). Even if you want to speculate, great care is required. Some options authorities do suggest applying the "90/10 strategy" to index options; they say that, as a "conservative to mildly aggressive" speculation, you could place 90% of the money you allocate to this strategy (which certainly should be only a portion of your total investment funds) into safe Treasuries, and 10% into index calls if you're bullish or index puts if you're bearish on the market. As a minimum precaution in any index speculation you may want to risk, you would be well advised to stay strictly on the buy side of any call or put, where your risk is limited to the money you've put up.

Another specialized category is *currency options*, a field dominated by the Philadelphia exchange. At this writing, it offers contracts pitting the dollar against the currencies of seven major countries (Australia, Britain, Canada, France, Germany, Japan, Switzerland) as well as against the European Community's currency "basket," the European Currency Unit or ECU. The exchange has also added "crossrate" options contracts of the yen against the mark (with the dollar uninvolved) as well as the mark against the pound. Most of the Philadelphia currency options are offered in both American and European style.

Because foreign currency units are usually valued in cents and fractions of cents, you'll find strike prices and premiums are quoted in pennies or less, in contrast to the dollars used in stock and most other option prices. Thus, when Germany's Deutsche Mark (DM) is worth about 60¢, the tables may show strike prices ranging from perhaps "54" to "66" [cents], and the quotation for a three-month 60 at-the-money call may be shown as "0.98," which would mean just under 1¢ for each of the 62,500 DM that make up one contract. The cost of the option would then be $612.50 (62,500 × $0.0098), while the value of

the currency covered by the contract would be $37,500 (62,500 ×
$.60). For Japanese yen, the quotation you see *before* the decimal
point is for ¹⁄₁₀₀ of a cent but there are 6,250,000 yen per contract, so
the currency value of a contract with a strike price of "90" would be
$56,250.

As might be expected, currency options are utilized mainly by
financial institutions and businesses engaged in foreign trade. You're
not likely to find an option handy for hedging the costs of an overseas
trip you're planning for later this year, though it might be used by
some individuals to hedge sizable commitments in other currencies.
But most of such individual participation as exists in currency options
is speculative — which, we can only stress once more, is a legitimate
objective, but involves high risk.

Most index, currency, and other specialty options are now matched
with futures contracts covering essentially the same risks and traded
on commodity exchanges. Futures, as we noted at the start of this
chapter, differ from options in that they impose a definite obligation
on both buyer and seller. That obligation must either be canceled
(closed out by buying or selling an offsetting contract) or settled at
expiration time. Organized futures markets began well over a century
ago to facilitate the handling of agricultural commodities. For instance, on the venerable Chicago Board of Trade, a farmer who
expects to harvest 50,000 bushels of wheat in late spring might decide
in early March to sell 10 5,000-bushel "July" contracts at $2.70 a
bushel. In this way, he has locked in what he considers a satisfactory
price for his crop, which he is obligated to deliver in July. Meantime,
a flour miller may have been on the buy side of this and many other
futures transactions (with maturities ranging from, say, May through
next March), assuring itself of an orderly inflow of raw material at
agreed-upon prices, regardless of which way the market may move
between now and the designated delivery dates.

In most cases, the farmer doesn't actually expect to deliver the
wheat in his contract, nor the processor to buy it. Both will probably
sell and buy in more convenient "actual" or cash transactions. But

they count on the price trends in the futures market to roughly track those they'll find in the actual market, so their net cost or revenue will be close to what they counted on when they bought or sold the futures. In financial futures, there isn't even the question of delivering a carload of Standard & Poor's indexes or of Deutsche Marks; assuming the contract isn't closed out earlier, it'll be settled by payment based on the cash value of the particular financial instruments.

Actually, the way financial futures contracts work, what matters is the *change* in the value of the contract while you hold it — a change that is computed and adjusted for *daily*. Say, for instance, you decide to buy a December S&P 500 Index future on the Chicago Mercantile Exchange at 415. This makes the current value of the contract $207,500 (each index point is multiplied by $500, which, as you may note, is five times the customary $100 multiplier used in index options; thus, each futures contract involves a substantially larger amount than one options contract). However, all you're required to put up for this contract is an initial margin of $10,000 (minimum margins may vary among exchanges and brokerage houses, and are subject to change). Furthermore, unlike stock market margin — which is a form of down payment and obliges you to pay interest on the unpaid balance — futures margin is considered a good-faith performance pledge which you must maintain in your account; it can be in the form of Treasury securities or other high-grade securities on which you can keep *earning* interest.

Your account is marked-to-market every day. If the next day's closing price on the contract is 414.20, your original $10,000 margin balance is reduced by $400 (the .80 decline × $500) to $9,600. The following day, the contract recovers a bit to 414.30 (+.10), so your margin balance goes up $50 to $9,650. Should the price of this futures contract decline enough to leave you with a margin balance under $5,000 (the minimum *maintenance margin* on the "Merc"), your broker will have to issue a margin call, requiring you to deposit enough to restore your balance to the *initial margin* requirement of $10,000.

When the contract expires in December, the futures price (which may at various times have been a bit above or below the actual S&P 500 level, depending on traders' optimism or pessimism) becomes automatically equal to the actual index. Suppose by then it has risen to 425. You'll have a net gain of $5,000 (425 − 415 purchase price × $500), though most of it will already have been credited to you through the daily mark-to-market. Similarly, if the index has fallen to 402, you will, in effect, already have paid for most of the $6,500 loss through decline of your margin balance and additional margin deposit.

If you're bearish on the market and want to sell a futures contract on the S&P 500, the same $10,000 minimum margin and daily mark-to-market apply; only your margin balance goes up when the index goes down, and vice versa.

When your brokerage house credits or debits your margin balance each day in line with market fluctuations, that doesn't mean its own accounts grow correspondingly fatter or leaner. It is in turn debited or credited by the exchange's clearinghouse, balancing the overall market accounts. Since there must always be both a buyer and a seller on every trade, there must always be the same number of long and short positions in each contract, and the daily gains by one side will be matched by losses on the other.

Futures on financial instruments began to arrive in the 1970s. The initial emphasis was in the interest-rate area, as, for instance, a contract based on the yield of Treasury securities. Some foreign-exchange instruments were also introduced. Stock index futures arrived in 1982, with the relatively small Kansas City Board of Trade leading the move with futures on the Value Line index, closely followed by the Chicago Mercantile Exchange for the S&P 500 and the New York Stock Exchange (through its newly established New York Futures Exchange subsidiary) with futures on the NYSE Composite. All this the year before the CBOE and Amex were able to launch their index options.

Nowadays financial futures are available on a great variety of U.S. and some foreign stock indexes, as well as currencies, interest rates, and Treasury and municipal bonds. In fact, financial futures now supply the major portion of business for most commodity exchanges. Plans are afoot for futures on several other types of financial instruments, such as health and auto insurance and even pollution rights (what some utilities will need to keep operating certain power plants).

In addition, there are quite a number of *futures options*. These are also traded on commodity exchanges; they represent calls or puts not directly on an index or currency package, etc., but rather the right to buy or sell a futures contract on these instruments. Since, as we've seen, the standard index future is for five times the amount covered by an index option (with a multiplier of $500 instead of $100), one futures option also usually covers five times the amount of the equivalent index option. Large institutions often find the larger size more convenient.

The proliferation of all these *derivatives* (i.e., securities based in some way on the value of other financial instruments, interest rates, and so on), coupled with ready availability of sophisticated computers, has led to the phenomenon of *program trading*, especially by big institutional investors and some major investment banks. Program traders try to take advantage of small price discrepancies between stock index futures, futures options, or index options and the prices of the underlying stocks through computer-driven simultaneous trades. Traditionally, arbitrage operations (buying and selling securities or commodities in different markets at different prices) have been considered an effective way to smooth out such price discrepancies and increase the liquidity of the markets. However, the impact of program trading (which is often driven by the moment's price movements in the sensitive futures markets) seems frequently to add volatility to the stock market, with wide short-term price swings not just day-to-day but sometimes in a matter of minutes.

The differences between stock and option markets and the futures market also extend to regulation, where there is a major turf war between the SEC and the *Commodities Futures Trading Commission* or CFTC. Adherents of the SEC feel that the impact of futures and futures options trading on the regular stock, bond and options markets is sufficiently pronounced so they, too, should come under the

SEC umbrella. So far, however, the commodity exchanges and traders have been able to beat back most every challenge to CFTC jurisdiction, though some measures, including some requirements for stricter and more extensive CFTC supervision, may be enacted.

One big factor is that the low margins on futures contracts can make it far cheaper to operate in the futures markets. At the same time, keep in mind that the margins required on a specific contract are continually adjusted as its market value rises and falls; if the market moves against you, you will quickly be required to put up additional margin. Above all, remember that when you have a long position in a stock or an option (whether call or put), the price set when you purchased is the maximum you can lose. That can be sad enough. But in a futures contract, whether you're long or short, you may repeatedly be forced to put up more money.

Still another way to acquire a financial stake in the fluctuations of foreign financial markets is the international stock index *warrant*, introduced on the American Stock Exchange in 1990. The warrant provides either a put or a call on a stock index that can be exercised during a specified period, usually two to five years, so in a way it's similar to a long-term index option. But each warrant comes with only one strike price and expiration date, though there may be several different warrant issues, with different expirations and strike prices, covering the same index. As in the case of traditional warrants that give you the right to buy a stock at a certain price (see chapter 3), these warrants are traded in the same way as shares of stock.

The pioneering issue was a put warrant (now expired) on the Japanese Nikkei index that showed up on the Amex under the unlikely name of Denmark (Kingdom of). How come? Technically, a warrant is a security issued by an organization that has registered it with the SEC and is responsible for seeing that you get paid if you choose to exercise that warrant (in options, the issuer and guarantor is the OCC). While most subsequent warrants have come out under the direct sponsorship and name of financial organizations — among them Salomon and PaineWebber as well as some foreign institutions like Norway's Eksportfinans — for the original Nikkei warrant

Denmark had been enlisted (for a fee) to lend its credit and prestige because sponsors thought such an independent entity would be helpful in launching the warrant concept. One successor to the Danish tradition is Austria (Republic of) under whose sovereign imprimatur the Big Board lists Stock Index Growth Notes (SIGNs) tied to the S&P 500. Recent Amex additions include warrants on the Hong Kong market (for which Amex now also offers index options) and on the Financial Times Eurotrack 200 index.

Following the ground-breaking Denmark yen warrant, both the Amex and Big Board have listed a number of warrants and other types of derivative securities. There are, for example, issues related to the Financial Times-Stock Exchange 100 Share index (the FT-SE or "Footsie 100," the standard British stock index) and the French CAC index, as well as to currency and interest rates.

Among other fanciful issues are Merrill Lynch S&P 500 Market Index Target-Term Securities (MITTS), traded as Big Board stocks though they're in the form of a zero-coupon senior debt obligation; at maturity, you're guaranteed repayment of principal but any "interest" equivalent you receive would depend on the gain in the S&P during the life of the MITTS. Separately, the Amex in early 1993 launched Standard & Poor's Depositary Receipts (the initials SPDR are pronounced *Spider*), a unit investment trust (that is, a fixed portfolio — see chapter 19) intended to track the performance of the S&P 500 index.

Another derivative issue is PaineWebber Long Bond Yield Decrease Warrants (listed on the NYSE), which depends, as the name implies, on the interest rate trend for the Treasury's 30-year bonds. This is just a sampling, and many more such issues will no doubt be offered on various exchanges.

Yet another recent extension of the options concept are *Contingent Value Rights* or CVRs. They result from some mergers where the acquiring company issued stock, and promised the recipients that this stock would have a specified minimum value by a certain date. This guarantee was met by issuing the CVRs, which trade separately from the underlying stock. If the stock is below the target price at the specified date, the CVR will make good the shortfall (up to a certain limit). The CVRs are exercisable only at expiration, so, in effect, they are a European-style put. Contingent rights may also be issued if an acquiring company promises potential additional payments based on the acquired unit's earnings over the next few years.

You may have noted that a great many of the index options, financial futures, and related instruments have an international scope. While the global marketplace is steadily advancing in stocks and bonds, cross-border (and cross-ocean) activity is particularly pronounced in these super-modern, sophisticated instruments, which can be specially crafted to meet the requirements of a particular industry. More and more contracts enjoy a global marketplace as U.S. and foreign exchanges trade the same or closely equivalent instruments.

One ambitious venture launched in mid-1992 is *Globex*, put together by the Chicago Board of Trade (which is considering withdrawing and pursuing alternative strategies) and Chicago Mercantile Exchange in conjunction with a unit of the Reuters financial information conglomerate. It offers electronic trading in certain contracts during the 18 hours each day that the Chicago exchanges are closed, initially with computer workstations located in Paris, London, New York and Chicago. Links with several other U.S. commodity exchanges and the major French exchange are scheduled, and the Globex sponsors expect to arrange further worldwide expansion. While Globex appears to be off to a slow start, some other exchanges hope to launch their own international electronic programs. Thus, even if somewhat hesitantly, the age of round-the-clock, round-the-globe trading may truly be taking shape.

CHAPTER 25

How to Follow Your Stock

ONCE you've started on the investment road, you'll want to know how the securities you are interested in are doing in the marketplace.

Where do you look? Many big metropolitan dailies carry a list of most if not all New York Stock Exchange stocks and a number of issues traded in other major markets, especially if the companies are active in the paper's circulation area. The widely available *USA Today* lists the 1,500 most active NYSE stocks, along with many Nasdaq and American Stock Exchange issues. For the most comprehensive listings, you can turn to the *Wall Street Journal* or, on a weekly basis, to *Barron's* or the Sunday edition of the *New York Times* — all of which are distributed throughout the U.S.

At first glance, the stock tables may seem intimidating, but with a little patience and experience you can easily tap the mass of data they offer. Some papers provide more complete information than others in their tables, but the basic format is quite uniform.

What's made available for use in these standard tables has been expanded significantly over the past couple of decades. You can now get the yield and price/earnings ratio of each stock and a 52-week price range that's adjusted for stock splits. Also, a number of newspapers use boldface, underlining, or special markings to highlight stocks that had a big move up or down, were unusually active (that is, trading volume was well above the average daily level for *that* stock), or made new yearly highs or lows during that trading session. And, of course, the newspapers — just like the ticker — use the consolidated tape; that is, their New York Stock Exchange table includes trades made in those stocks on the regional exchanges and over-the-counter as well as on the Big Board itself.

When you look at a stock table, your biggest problem may well be locating your stock in the long alphabetical list. That's because, to save space, company names are heavily abbreviated, and often hard to pick out from similar names in the fine print. (The *Wall Street Journal*, which uses wider columns, often spells out a bit more of the name and also helpfully lists the ticker symbol.) In the standard tables, the condensation gives you, for instance,

FBosIF	for	First Boston Income Fund,
FBosSt	for	First Boston Strategic Income Fund,
FtBrnd	for	First Brands,
FFB	for	First Fidelity Bancorp,
FstUC	for	First Union Corp, and
FUnRI	for	First Union Real Estate.

So it may take a little detective effort. Keep in mind that the order of listing is strictly alphabetical. And knowing the approximate price range of your stock can be a helpful clue in spotting it.

Our Rod & Reel might show up as "RodRI," and the entry for yesterday's trading might look like this:

52-week				Yld	P/E	Sales				
High	Low	Stock	Div	%	Ratio	100s	High	Low	Last	Chg
42½	33¾	RodRI	2.00	4.9	9	17	40¾	40⅛	40¾	+¾

The column headings make much of the information self-explanatory. To the left of the stock name, the *52-week range* shows that Rod & Reel has had a considerable price move over the past year — presumably largely upward, since it now trades far closer to the high of the range than the low. As noted, the price range is adjusted for any stock dividend or stock split. Incidentally, the range covers the last 52 weeks *plus* the current week, *except* for the latest trading day. That is, the long-term range is always one day behind the rest of the table. Had Rod & Reel sold for 43 yesterday, the 52-week high would still be shown as 42½. The "43" in the *daily* high column would show by how much the old high was bettered; in most papers the "43" would be preceded by a "u" to indicate that a new yearly high had been made, while a new yearly low would be marked by a "d" (for down) in front of the *daily* low (some papers, like the *Wall Street Journal*, have readily visible up and down arrows in the left margin). In addition, some papers print a separate list of each day's new highs and lows.

The *dividend* figure immediately following the name of the stock notes that Rod & Reel currently has an annual dividend rate of $2, which, as the next column shows, represents a *yield* of 4.9%, based on last night's closing price of 40¾. The dividend figure is often followed by a small letter, referring you to a standard footnote. These footnotes can be very important, because they may indicate that the dividend shown includes (or excludes) extra dividends, or that this was the dividend paid last year, or that it represents only the total paid so far this year for a stock not on a regular dividend basis, or a number of other dividend payout variations.

The P/E ratio — *price/earnings ratio* — of the stock is computed by dividing the market price by the company's earnings per share. P/Es can be computed on last year's earnings, or on an analyst's expectations of earnings this year, next year, or even longer into the future — all of which may be important for analyzing the potential value of the stock. But for purposes of the stock tables, the P/E is based on the earnings reported for the latest four quarters — usually excluding any extraordinary items. Thus, if Rod & Reel sells at 40¾ and earned $4.45 per share over the past four quarters, its price/earnings ratio would be 9.2 ($40.75 divided by $4.45). This would be rounded to 9 in the stock table.

The *sales* figure shows the number of 100-share round lots traded in the stock that day. The *high*, *low*, and *last* (often called *"close"*) figures give you a bird's-eye picture of how Rod & Reel moved during the trading day.

The *net change* figure (+¾) shows the difference between the closing price that day (40¾) and the closing price the preceding day (which, a little arithmetic will tell you, must have been 40).

Occasionally you may notice that the price of a stock is lower than the day before, but the net change figure doesn't show a corresponding drop. That's because the stock is being sold *ex-dividend.*

Suppose Rod & Reel pays its quarterly dividend of 50 cents to stockholders who are on its books as of the close of business on Thursday, September 15. Since currently it takes five business days after you buy a stock before the seller has to deliver it, you must buy it by Thursday, September 8, in order to be on the company's books on the *record date,* the 15th. Put another way, anyone who buys the stock starting Friday, September 9, won't get possession in time to be eligible for the dividend. On the *payment date* (say, October 6) the dividend check will belong to whoever owned the stock September 8, even if that person sold it first thing September 9.

This also means that (other things being equal) each share of Rod & Reel the morning of the ninth is worth 50¢ less than it was the night before. Consequently, the net change reported on the ninth (the ex-dividend day) is not calculated from the previous day's actual close (say, 41) but from the close *minus* the value of the dividend (that is, 40½). Therefore, if Rod & Reel sells at 40⅞, the change would be reported as +⅜, at 40¼ as −¼, at 40½ as no change.

Since stock prices change in intervals of 12.5¢ or ⅛ of a dollar, how do you adjust if the dividend is, say, 30¢? The rule is that you simply adjust by the next higher multiple of ⅛. So, for 30¢, the ex-dividend markdown would be ⅜; if the stock closed yesterday at 38 and opens ex-dividend at 37⅞, it would be reported as +¼.

And to make everyone aware that a stock is trading ex-dividend that day, it is marked with an "x" in the stock tables, and also on the computer screens throughout the day.

The same broad array of daily trading information is made available for the American Stock Exchange and Nasdaq's National Market. However, even many papers that carry full data on Big Board stocks may limit themselves to just "closing price and net change" reports for stocks in these markets.

Another table you'll find in many newspapers these days covers mutual funds. They are listed alphabetically under the name of the fund sponsor. The standard table shows the *NAV* or *net asset value* computed for each fund that day; the *Buy* or *Offer Price*, which is the NAV plus the fund's maximum sales charge (the price per share you'd actually pay when buying a small amount of the fund); and the *Change* in the net asset value from the day before. There's also a uniform set of footnotes that tell the type of load charged by the fund and give other important information.

Prices reported in the newspapers for bonds have their own special characteristics. Although bonds are usually sold in thousand-dollar units, their prices are quoted in percent-of-par, which makes it appear as though they have a hundred-dollar denomination. Thus, a quotation of 98 indicates a price of $980. One of 98¾ would indicate $987.50.

Since government bonds are traded not in eighths but in thirty-seconds, a special price reporting formula has been developed for them. For example, a printed quotation of 99-16 actually means $99^{16}/_{32}\%$ of par or a price of $995. For many years, the price would have been reported as 99.16, but to avoid confusion with a decimal point, most papers now use the hyphen (99-16) or a colon (99:16). Actually, active Treasuries are often sold on a price change of just ¹⁄₆₄ rather than ¹⁄₃₂, with the more precise quotations displayed on the traders' computer screens during the day.

With the help of these tables, you can monitor regularly the current value of your investments, and also follow securities you're thinking of buying. But don't fall into the trap of worrying about each day's trading pattern. You should be looking primarily at longer-term trends in your search for sound longer-term values.

Of course, along with the stock movement, you'll want to keep posted on what's happening to the company itself. Once you own the stock, you should be receiving regular quarterly and annual reports, but there's quite a time lag involved. Unless your company is a super-giant or else very prominent locally, your hometown paper isn't likely to have news on it. The *Wall Street Journal*'s daily earnings and dividend tabulations cover just about every actively traded company; the *New York Times* has more limited but still fairly comprehensive coverage. And both these major journals now carry a daily index of all the companies mentioned in that day's paper.

Another good data source for you could be your public library. Many libraries carry either Standard & Poor's (S&P) Corporation Records or Moody's Investment Manuals. These two basic reference sets are arranged differently — Moody's (owned by Dun & Bradstreet) has separate manuals for industrial companies, bank & finance, utilities, transportation, etc. S&P (a McGraw-Hill unit) divides its volumes not by type of industry but by alphabet (A-B, C-E, etc.). However, both services provide the same general information — a capsule description of a company's operations and history, details on each class of stock and bonds, and key financial statistics for a number of years. Also, both have separate loose-leaf volumes (updated daily or semi-weekly) that carry reports of latest earnings, dividend changes, and other major corporate developments — a convenient place to check up on your companies every now and then.

In addition, many libraries subscribe to various business periodicals and investment services, such as Standard & Poor's *Outlook* and Value Line. The weekly *Outlook* provides analysis and investment advice on individual stocks and mutual funds as well as on overall strategy. The Value Line service features an analytical writeup along with a unique mathematical rating system for each stock. Without necessarily accepting the service's specific evaluations, you may find study of its rating techniques a good learning experience while getting a quick reading on a given stock.

CHAPTER 26

How to Follow the Market

ANYONE interested in investments will almost certainly want to know not just how specific stocks but how the general market is doing.

And almost every daily newspaper and TV or radio news roundup will make at least brief mention of the average movement of New York Stock Exchange prices. Easily the best-known yardstick to take the measure of the market is the Dow Jones average, or, more precisely, the *Dow Jones Industrial Average* (DJIA).

There are actually four Dow Jones averages. The Industrial Average is based on the stocks of 30 leading manufacturers, distributors, and service companies. The *Transportation Average* (in earlier days, the Railroad Average) is now made up of 20 railroads, airlines, and trucking companies. The *Utility Average* consists of 15 electric and gas utilities (as of this writing, no telephone company has been included among the Dow Jones Utilities — but, somewhat incongruously, American Telephone & Telegraph has been one of the "industrials" since before World War II). Finally, the *Dow Jones Composite* includes all 65 stocks that make up the other three averages.

However, most of the time, when people speak of the "Dow Jones Average" or simply "the Dow," they're talking of the DJIA. If they meant one of the other Dow Jones averages, they would specify Utilities or Transportation or Composite. What's more, if you hear someone say, "The market's up three point twenty-five," you can safely assume it means the Dow Jones Industrials are up three and a quarter points.

What makes the Dow so widely followed? There's its long history; the Dow was started (as a 12-stock index) in 1897. And, of course, its originator and compiler, Dow Jones & Company, not only publishes the *Wall Street Journal* but also operates the *Dow Jones News Service*, whose *"broad tape"* newswire has long been the principal during-the-day news source in every major brokerage office as well as at most other financial institutions and corporate headquarters.

Nowadays the Dow Jones averages and rival indexes are computed continuously and are instantly available on desktop quotation machines. But for many decades, when the averages were put together by pencil (and perhaps an adding machine), the four Dow Jones averages which appeared hourly on the Dow Jones broad tape were the only published indicators of general trading trends while the market was open.

With all its preeminence, the Dow does not lack for critics. Statisticians shudder at the way the average is put together. It was quite simple at the start. Just add up the prices of the 30 stocks, divide by 30 — and there's your average. But then came stock splits and stock dividends (which, of course, meant a lower price per share, while each investor got more shares), special distributions and spinoffs, and some companies disappeared through mergers or business mishaps — all of which required adjustments to keep the average meaningful.

The solution fashioned by the average's custodians: figure out an artificial *divisor* that will get you the same result with the new stock lineup that you had with the old. Let's assume there was a day when the sum total of the 30 stock prices was 1200, which would make the *average* $\frac{1}{30}$ of that, or 40. But one of the stocks was being split 4-for-1, bringing its price down from 80 to 20, and, consequently, the 30-stock total from 1200 to 1140. Since there was no change in the true value of the stocks, the Dow system would now call for lowering the divisor from 30 to 28.5, the figure that's needed so that your "average" still comes out to 40 (1140 divided by 28.5 = 40).

As over the years the splits (and other happenings requiring adjustments) kept piling up, the divisor was forced lower and lower. In spring 1994 the divisor for the Dow Jones Industrials was .4203 (more splits will almost surely lower it further) — which means a single point change in just one stock (with the other 29 stocks unchanged) will drive the "average" up or down by more than 2¼ points.

The same system is used to calculate the other Dow Jones averages, though, because they didn't experience quite as many splits as the Industrials, their divisors have been lowered a bit less drastically. The following table lists the divisors as of February 1994. It also shows how much a one-point move in a single stock affects each average. The final column shows how much the average would move if *each* of the stocks in it moved exactly one point (in the same direction).

Table 26–1: Impact of the Dow Jones Divisors

Dow Jones Average	Divisor	If 1 Stock Moves $1	If Every Stock Moves $1
30 Industrials	0.4203	2.3795	71.39
20 Transportations	0.5664	1.7656	35.31
15 Utilities	1.8965	0.5273	7.91
65 Composite	2.1777	0.4592	29.85

Thus, even when the headlines scream that "the Dow [Industrials]" have "soared" or "collapsed" 30 points or more, the actual movement of the 30 component stocks averages out to but a fraction of a dollar per stock.

You may also see "daily highs and lows" listed for the various Dow Jones averages. Usually, these are not the highest and lowest level reached by the *average*. Rather — a vestige of the pre-computer days — they're *theoretical* figures arrived at by putting together all the highs (and, correspondingly, all the lows) reached by each of the stocks any time during the day. Some stocks could have made their highs early in the morning and then sold off sharply, while others peaked at the end of the day. Thus, you usually end up with much higher "highs" and lower "lows" than the average itself actually attained during the day. That's one reason why, for most reckonings of market trends, analysts ignore these intra-day figures and concentrate on each day's *closing* average — that is, the average based on each stock's closing price.

Among other criticisms often leveled at Dow Jones is that the computation method gives excess weight to higher-priced stocks: a 5% swing in a stock selling at $120 will have three times the impact of a 5% move in a $40 stock — though the latter might well have many more shares outstanding and represent a bigger company. In particular, this system diminishes the relative impact of companies that have repeatedly split their stock — which are apt to be the most successful companies in the group.

Some also argue that the Dow Jones stocks (especially the Industrials) are not representative of the general market, since they are mostly "blue chips." That, of course, is the design of the Dow Jones — to be a selection of the *leading* companies in each area. In fact, the Dow has also come under fire for *not* meeting that objective — for sticking too long with a preponderance of "smokestack America" stocks; only in relatively recent years has it extended recognition to such current lifestyle representatives as Coca-Cola, McDonald's and American Express.

Finally, one inescapable consequence of having comparatively few stocks in the average is that if anything unusual happens to one of the "Dow stocks," it can rock the whole average. For instance, on September 24, 1985, merger reports caused General Foods (then one of the "30") to shoot up 16⅝ points. That, in turn, lifted the Dow Industrials nearly five points. Without General Foods, the Dow would have been down nine points. And, indeed, other major market yardsticks — which included General Foods but gave it less weight in their computation — were down for the day.

Volatility can be far more severe in the Dow Jones Transportation Average, since there are only a few major stocks available to represent the airline segment. In early October 1989, UAL (the parent of United Airlines) accounted for an overawing 27% of the total price of the average, and AMR (which owns American Airlines) another 10%. When a proposed buyout of UAL at $300 a share collapsed on Friday, October 13, the repercussions set off an avalanche of selling in the general market, with a 190-point drop in the Dow Industrials. But this broader market weakness was largely contained by Monday, while the transports were in for an even bigger beating. In less than four trading days, UAL stock collapsed 33%. What's more, the UAL upheaval also forced withdrawal of a hostile takeover bid then being mounted against AMR, which quickly tumbled by 25%. In the process, the Dow Jones Transportation Average suffered a 295-point or 16% loss in four days, while the drop in the Dow Jones Industrials for the same period was held to 4%. However, volatility works both ways. Between the Fourth of July and Labor Day that year, UAL had doubled in price, leading the Dow Jones Transportation Average up some 360 points or 31%, while the Industrials gained a more modest 12%. So, even after the October debacle, both UAL and the Dow Jones Transportations were still at what would have been record levels anytime before mid-1989.

Those dissatisfied with the Dow (or merely eager for additional yardsticks) now have considerable choice. The most prominent competitor is the *Standard & Poor's 500-stock composite index (S&P 500)*. It's made up of approximately 380 industrials, 45 utilities, 55 financial, and 15 transportation stocks. In contrast to the Dow Jones, where it's the 30 Industrials, not the 65-stock Composite that gets the attention, S&P followers concentrate primarily on the "500."

Most analysts agree the S&P 500 is more scientifically constructed than the Dow, and certainly more comprehensive. It is computed by multiplying the price of each stock by the number of shares outstanding. Thus it measures the *market value* of each stock — how much the company would be worth if someone would purchase all its common stock at today's market price. Stock splits and stock dividends take care of themselves automatically since the lower per-share price is offset by the larger number of shares created by the split.

This *market-weighted* system means the bigger a company's total stock value, the bigger its influence on the index — which many analysts feel gives a more accurate market picture than the share-price-is-all-that-counts Dow Jones method.

The 500 stocks that make up the S&P index represent more than 75% of the total value of Big Board stocks, while the 30 Dow Jones

Industrials represent somewhat under 20%. But the very fact that the S&P index is weighted by market value means that a relatively small number of big blue-chip stocks also dominate the "500." So, in practice, the Dow and S&P run fairly close together on a day-to-day basis. However, the S&P 500 is less likely to be swayed by a dramatic event in a single stock. For instance, the day in 1985 that the General Foods 16-point run-up lifted the Dow five points, the S&P (more representative of the overall market) was down nearly two points.

The three major stock markets each have their own index, all based on the market value of their stocks. The New York Stock Exchange composite includes all Big Board common stocks; since, as we've noted, the S&P 500 represent approximately three-quarters of the Exchange's total market value, the NYSE index, not surprisingly, matches the S&P fairly closely — though it's far from a mirror image.

The American Stock Exchange Index is also based on total market value. But unlike other indexes, it also makes allowance for dividends paid on the stocks, thus measuring *total return* — the combination of share price fluctuation and investment income received. Total return is of course what investors are after, and how mutual funds and portfolio managers measure their performance. When comparing their performance with the indexes, fund managers and analysts must make allowance for the income received in addition to the change in the index number — on the Amex that's already figured in. Since the Amex is host to smaller, generally more speculative stocks, it tends to be more volatile than the blue chip–dominated indexes. It particularly reflects the fortunes of the smaller companies in the energy sector, including Canadian oil and gas stocks.

The Nasdaq index encompasses some 4,100 stocks. Since it is based on market value, the bigger over-the-counter stocks carry the heaviest influence. Even so, this index largely reflects corporate life below the blue-chip level, since the total market value of the Nasdaq-indexed stock comes to only about 15% of the total value of Big Board stocks.

For analysts seeking to follow overall market patterns, the *Wilshire 5000*, which, as its name implies, is composed of roughly 5,000 stocks, offers by far the widest coverage. But since it, too, is based on the total market value of each company, the larger stocks exercise a major influence on its movements. This brings the Wilshire stock swings closer to those of the major yardsticks than you might expect from an index that measures so many small companies.

By contrast, the *Value Line geometric* index of 1,700 stocks ignores market valuation. It uses a geometric formula that measures the daily percentage change in the price of each stock. In effect, each day you have an *equal amount of dollars* invested in each and every stock, no matter how big or small the company. Consequently, it's dominated by "second-tier" stocks, and it's Value Line rather than the more inclusive Wilshire to which analysts turn to see how the unweighted stock population is doing. (Value Line also puts out an *arithmetic* index, on which the Kansas City Board of Trade index futures are based.)

Numerous other indexes — often, as we noted in chapter 24, designed to serve as the base for index options or futures — have developed followers in the financial community. Incidentally, you may have observed that, while the Dow Jones yardsticks are called averages, nearly all the others are referred to as indexes. To the statistician, an average consists of adding the value of all the components and then dividing by the number of components used, whether you measure the Dow stocks or the number of children in an American household. In an index, you add up the figures and then relate to a base figure (say, 1987 = 100) as when you measure the rise in consumer prices. The base doesn't have to be 100. S&P opted for 1943 = 10, so its index value in the 1960s (when it developed the current 500-stock index) would be at about the level of the typical stock's dollar price. That's the theory. By now, with all the adjustments in the Dow divisor and steep rise in the stock indexes, the figures have taken on a life of their own. The average is strictly artificial and nobody bothers about the base year of the indexes — everyone just looks at the current numbers.

Today's stratospheric numbers have also laid to rest a "solution" once put forth by some market followers: "split" the Dow Jones, perhaps 10-to-1 or more, to get its quote down nearer the price of the average stock. That might have made sense 15 or 30 years ago. Now the "average" is so high everyone recognizes it as just an arbitrary number, and even the indexes like the S&P, despite their original intent to be near the level of actual stock prices, have shot way up. Not to mention the Nikkei or Japanese Dow Jones, which, even after its more than 60% collapse, was just above 14 *thousand* when it bottomed in 1992.

While most of the indexes — like the majority of stocks — tend to move in the *same direction* much of the time, there is often significant difference in the *rate* or *amount* of the movement. But what's especially important to remember is that this *relative* performance also keeps on changing.

Thus, it's often said the Dow Jones Industrials are stodgy performers compared with the more "aggressive" stocks represented in other indexes. This has indeed been true more often than not over long time spans. But there are always many cross currents, as the table on page 262 illustrates. It shows how some of the widely followed indexes fared from January 1973 — the Dow Jones market peak that proved to be "the last hurrah" of the long post–World War II bull market — till January 1994, when all the major indexes reached new highs, with the Dow at 3978 (some have since climbed still higher peaks). To keep our example simple, we only show two intermediate points: August 1982, just before the big mid-1980s bull market started; and August 1987, the high before the October 1987 crash.

Over this 21-year period, the roughly 275% advance in the Dow Industrials was topped by most of the others, largely because the Dow lagged badly during the dismal 1973–1982 period. (One reason for *that:* By the time the Dow peaked in early 1973, the starting point for our table, much of the rest of the market had already been in decline for some years.) In the huge 1982–1987 upsurge, the Dow led all the others by a substantial margin. The relative performance of the indexes points up that, in general, secondary stocks starred from the mid-1970s to early 1980s; then the limelight shifted back to the big capitalization stocks. Some analysts think the pendulum may have begun to swing the other way again in the early 1990s, with the Nasdaq the clear market leader. However, the Dow has also moved up briskly, especially in the 12 months through January 1994.

The S&P 500 and NYSE Composite — the two indexes which, after

Table 26–2: How Various Indexes Fared in Past Two Decades

	Index as of				Total Period 1973–1994	Percentage Gain Achieved in		
	01/11/73	08/16/82	08/25/87	01/31/94		1973–82	1982–87	1987–94
Dow Jones 30 Industrials	1051.70	792.43	2722.42	3978.36	278%	−25%	244%	46%
Standard & Poor's "500"	120.24	104.09	336.77	481.61	301%	−13%	224%	43%
New York Stock Exchange Composite	65.48	59.75	187.99	267.10	308%	−9%	215%	42%
American Stock Exchange	65.23	238.27	362.18	485.68	645%	265%	52%	34%
Nasdaq Composite	136.84	159.68	455.26	800.47	485%	17%	185%	76%
Wilshire 5000	1090.31	1066.15	3299.44	4798.07	340%	−2%	209%	45%
Value Line (geometric)	115.54	113.83	289.02	304.59	164%	−1%	154%	5%

the Dow, are most heavily weighted toward the blue chips — ended in nearly a dead heat for the full 21-year period. Both outperformed the Dow, while trailing the Amex and Nasdaq. But it's worth noting that the NYSE index, which by virtue of encompassing all the Big Board stocks is a bit broader than the S&P 500, was the better performer of the two over the first decade, while the S&P caught up in the second.

Especially dramatic was the Amex index, which nearly tripled between 1973 and 1982, while most everyone else was in the minus column during this energy-troubled period. Thanks to that big head start, the Amex easily topped the group for the entire 21-year period, even though its advances since 1982 were decidedly modest compared with the other major indexes.

The Value Line index, which, as we've noted, is structured to give the greatest recognition to the small companies, had a 30% gain between 1973 and 1980, but gave it all back in the next two years. It shared only modestly in the mid-1980s upswing, and by early 1994 had barely recovered the ground it lost in 1987–1990.

In our look at relative performance, we have, as noted, purposely simplified our example. Behavior in the real-life market is a good deal more complex, with many big and little fluctuations, waves, and cycles along the way, as well as constant variations both among and within the different stock groups. That just emphasizes the point — you won't find uniformity in the market, or in the averages and indexes.

While some indexes may be better constructed than others to measure what they're intended to, don't get trapped into thinking that the "best" index is the one showing the best gains. That's confusing the messenger with the message. An index's job is to tell you what the market, or a part of it, is doing. That's why analysts follow a number of indexes, keeping an eye not only on overall trends but on the divergences within the market.

In the later stages of a maturing bull market, the blue-chip stocks often continue to make new highs, but lethargy prevails among the lesser, "secondary" stocks. That tends to show up not only in weaker performance by such indexes as the Amex, Nasdaq, and Value Line, but also in fewer new daily highs on the Big Board, failure of volume to expand as the market moves up, and weakness in a variety of other "technical" measures closely watched by market analysts. On the other hand, smaller-capitalization stocks are often the first to raise their heads as an economic recession bottoms out, and then to do better in the early stages of a recovery.

The stock market as a whole is one of the *Leading Indicators* — an index issued monthly by the U.S. Department of Commerce that currently includes eleven economic measurements that have been found generally to move up or down ahead of the national economy. The index has turned into an increasingly murky forecaster in recent years, and many economists feel that another revision of its components and structure is in order.

But the stock market is expected to remain in any revised index. Indeed, it's been considered one of the best indicators — though perhaps an excessively nervous one. Some years back an economist wise-cracked that the stock market had forecast "seven of the last five recessions" — meaning that a market setback had duly preceded each recession; however, the market had also headed down a couple of times when the economy refused to follow. That has since also proven true after the cataclysmic October 1987 stock market plunge; despite fears of imminent recession, the long economic expansion continued at a moderate pace. Then the 20% stock decline in 1990 signaled the recession which plagued the start of the decade.

One other point to remember: While the different stock indexes measuring different aspects of the stock market have moved at different speeds, and sometimes in different directions, over the long term virtually all of them have recorded substantial gains. Which simply reflects the fact that common stocks have provided the highest average return of investment over the period during which detailed statistics have been gathered.

CHAPTER 27

How to Follow the Financial News

AS an investor, you'll want to keep apprised of the financial news that affects the economy in general as well as your specific investments. Here's a listing of some business/investment publications and television programs that you may find helpful.

Dailies

The *Wall Street Journal:* truly the Bible of the investment community, "the *Journal,*" with its satellite-linked printing plants, is available almost everywhere every business morning. Now normally in three sections for more convenient topical arrangement, it offers a tremendous array of market tables, helpful charts, company news (including extensive daily tables of earnings and dividend reports), indications of industry and economic trends, and analysis of current market conditions and future market directions. It is also justly renowned for the scope and quality of its general reportage. Many journalists consider the *Journal* not only an indispensable tool for all investors, and for business people generally, but also one of the best daily newspapers of any kind in America.

The *New York Times:* probably the most prestigious general newspaper in the land, the *Times* over the past few decades has sought to upgrade both the depth and liveliness of its financial coverage. In the late 1970s the *Times* began devoting a separate section, called Business Day, to business news Monday through Friday. It presents a quite comprehensive array of market quotes and economic news, plus some interesting columns on market and business developments. The *Times* is seeking to broaden its reach with a national edition in which Business Day is a major attraction. Both the *Times* Business Day and the *Wall Street Journal* now carry each day an index of all corporations mentioned in their paper that day — a valuable resource. Special mention should be made of the widely distributed Sunday edition of the *Times;* its thick business section carries an outstanding series of articles and columns, along with financial tables summarizing the week's action.

USA Today: its daily "Money" section has much the same characteristics as other parts of the self-styled "nation's newspaper." There's a light once-over of major news events, a handful of longer stories, a few nuggets of miscellaneous information, and a couple of paragraphs of "Street" gossip, plus New York Stock Exchange, Nasdaq, mutual fund, and a few other market quotations. It doesn't pretend to be either a thorough or a balanced diet, but it's a convenient way to keep in touch, wherever you are.

Many local papers, especially metropolitan dailies, have expanded the space devoted to business, often with fairly extensive market quotations and news stories on market action but relatively little on corporate developments outside their immediate area. Most do run some nationally syndicated columns, which range from excellent to mediocre.

Two other dailies deserve mention, even if they are by and large too specialized for the average investor:

Investor's Business Daily: started in the mid-1980s as *Investor's Daily*, this Los Angeles–based national paper is crammed with nononsense corporate and financial news reports. Its extensive market tables list such special stock characteristics as relative price strength (how the stock's price has changed over the past 12 months compared to stocks generally), trading volume, and earnings growth. There are also graphs charting the movements of various stocks.

Financial Times: The U.S. edition of this London daily, printed on distinctive peach paper, has excellent coverage of business, economic, and political developments around the world, along with substantial coverage of the U.S. markets.

Weeklies

Barron's National Business & Financial Weekly: Put out by Dow Jones & Company, the publisher of the *Wall Street Journal, Barron's* is a weekly tabloid that contains an encyclopedically comprehensive history of the week's transactions in a wide variety of financial markets. It includes a range of minute details even the *Journal* does not bother to record. *Barron's* also contains numerous feature articles, the iconoclastic commentary of Alan Abelson in his front-page "Up and Down Wall Street" column, weekly chronicles of the various doings in the real estate, commodities, and options markets, hard-hitting profiles of specific companies, and probably the largest collection of advertising by concerns offering assorted investment expertise.

Business Week: This flagship of the McGraw-Hill armada of business magazines has a look and style similar to *Time* and *Newsweek;* it delivers its weekly amalgam of economic news features and investment analysis in much the same slick, pithy fashion. *BW* has historically been aimed primarily at business managers rather than investors per se, although it does have a valuable weekly-performance financial section. Its chief strengths are its extensive (if at times dogmatic) coverage of trends in the worlds of finance, industry, and economics.

Biweeklies

Forbes: Perhaps the most comprehensive and surely the most sprightly of the general magazines for the moderately sophisticated investor, *Forbes* covers all the markets and the people who make them. Its specialty is the short, punchy profile of changing companies and the dispassionate look at new investment gimmicks. Another *Forbes* hallmark is its large and varied stable of columnists — among them financial journalists Ben Weberman and Mark Hulbert and active Wall

Street stalwarts Robert Salomon, Gary Shilling, Laszlo Birinyi, Kenneth Fisher, David Dreman, and Frederick Rowe.

Fortune: Famous as the chronicler of bigness in American commerce, this Time Warner magazine has seen "Fortune 500" become an everyday term in the business dictionary. Its annual comprehensive rankings of the largest companies in the country and the world remain the accepted standard, whose success has inspired rivals like *Forbes* and *Business Week* to come up with their own versions of bigness listings. In its regular issues, *Fortune* tends to concentrate more on in-depth looks at significant economic issues and business developments, including mini-case studies of specific corporations, than on background for personal investment decisions.

Financial World: Sometimes described as a smaller, less comprehensive version of *Forbes,* FW often treats its subjects in greater depth, complete with detailed explanations of their implications for the slightly less sophisticated investor. It also includes independent appraisals of a large number of companies.

Monthlies

Money: Another Time Warner publication, *Money* is the financial journalism success story of the past decade. Its editorial design is tailored toward coverage of the complete financial/investment needs of the average middle-class American family, from stock selection advice to tax shelter, vacation home buying, and franchised business investing tips. *Money* stands out by concentrating as much on the changing needs of the individual who makes the investments as it does on the specific characteristics of the vehicle in which he or she is investing.

Kiplinger's Personal Finance Magazine: Long published by the Kiplinger Washington Newsletter organization as *Changing Times,* the magazine now devotes itself primarily to discussing the pros and cons of various investment opportunities (especially in mutual funds) and also regularly advises middle-class Americans on other aspects of managing their money in such areas as car repair, health care and fitness, and home improvement.

Television

Nowhere is the increasing hunger of Middle America for a broad range of investment information more apparent than in the growing presence of investment-oriented shows on the nation's television screens. The ready availability of cable (both network and local) has accelerated the trend. The following list includes some of the major shows, with airtime in the eastern U.S. as of spring 1994; as you're undoubtedly aware, schedules are often shifted and many stations offer delayed or repeat programs, so inquire of your local broadcasters.

Wall Street Week (PBS, Friday, 8:30 P.M.): This is the granddaddy of all televised investment roundups. Host Louis Rukeyser, a master showman given to outrageous puns, summarizes the week's general economic news and specific investment happenings, grills his assorted panelists on their interpretation of the current scene, and interviews a guest expert on his or her assessment of stocks, bonds, or other investment vehicles. The show also serves to give viewers a quick introduction to how investment professionals approach their work.

Adam Smith's Money World (PBS, Thursday, 8:00 P.M. in New York; many other stations run it over the weekend): Economist and author "Adam Smith" (George Jerome Waldo Goodman) cleverly covers a single topic each week through both interviews with experts and various reports exploring different aspects of the chosen topic.

The Nightly Business Report (PBS, daily, 6:30 P.M.): This Miami-based broadcast looks like other networks' evening news, except that it concentrates exclusively on business and investment topics. It delivers a nightly roundup of the day's financial activities and market results, along with brief interpretations, suited for veteran and beginning investors alike.

Another full-fledged financial program, covering the day's markets, major business news, and special features, is *Money Line* with Lou Dobbs (CNN, weekdays, 7:00 P.M.). Its weekend cousin, *Money Week* (CNN, Sunday, 2:00 P.M.), is, as the name implies, a weekly summary. Dobbs also offers short, punchy business updates during the day on weekdays. Another good-quality weekend roundup is *The Wall Street*

Journal Report (CBS, Sunday, 7:30 A.M.) with Consuelo Mack. And during the week, the early riser can get started on CNN's worthwhile pre-breakfast twins, *Business Morning* and *Business Day*.

CNBC (which stands for Cable News & Business Channel, an awkward acronym coined to show affinity with part-owner NBC) bought out the bankrupt Financial News Network (FNN) and features continuous coverage of the business scene. While the stock market is open, its "Money Wheel" reportage, commentaries, and live interviews are supplemented by a running ticker tape at the bottom of the screen.

Investment programs are also found on many local channels. For instance, Los Angeles has a local investment channel, KWHY, with an informal but informative style, and more such stations or dedicated channels are springing up around the country.

Radio

Sound Money (NPR, Saturday, 11:00 A.M.): Produced by Minnesota Public Broadcasting, this hour-long show hosted by Bob Potter covers all aspects of personal investing without either talking down to or assuming too much expertise on the part of its listeners. It usually features Chris Farrell, a *Business Week* editor in New York on general investment trends; Erica Whitlinger, a Minneapolis investment adviser, on investment fundamentals; and a guest expert in some area of investing. Listeners can ask questions through both live and tape-recorded call-ins.

Market Place (NPR, weekdays, 7:30 P.M.): Prepared at the University of Southern California, this program provides a summary of major business events and several features, interviews, and commentaries on financial and economic matters.

These publications and shows can be useful resources, providing you with essential facts and stimulating ideas — the raw materials for becoming a more skilled investor. But, remember, they can't deal with your precise needs and goals and they can't make the decisions for you. In the final analysis, it's up to you to work out your own investment destiny.

CHAPTER 28

How Your Broker Can Help You

ALL in all, the best answer individual investors can find to the question of what stocks or other investments to buy is likely to be what they work out for themselves through study and investigation.

So where, you ask, can Mr. or Ms. Investor, even when willing to do his or her own investigating, turn for the necessary information? As we pointed out in the last chapter, you can get much help from the press and over the air. What about more specific guidance, addressed to your personal interests and needs? One good answer: Seek out a broker, preferably a member firm of the New York Stock Exchange.

Here are some of the most important ways in which a full-service broker can help you:

- Assist you in your investment education — through seminars, courses, brochures sponsored by the firm, as well as direct explanations from your individual broker
- Help you define your investment objectives
- Make recommendations on specific investments as well as appropriate allocation of your assets among different investment categories
- Make recommendations on the timing of your purchases and sales
- Or, if you choose, provide money management through in-house investment counseling service, outside managers arranged for by your broker, or a discretionary account entrusted to the broker (some of these services may entail special fees, as discussed in the next chapter)

As we noted in chapter 20, the overwhelming majority of today's registered representatives or retail brokers consists of hardworking professionals — honest, scrupulous, eager to help customers succeed. But even if the reliability of your broker can be taken for granted, what about his or her ability? How competent is your particular broker likely to be when it comes to giving you sound advice about your money and how to invest it?

Obviously, that's a question to which there is no absolute answer. Nobody could possibly contend that each of the thousands of brokers in the securities business is preeminently well qualified to give investment help. Some are and some aren't. But the standards of professional ability have been steadily raised, thanks to training programs that many leading brokerage firms have been operating for years — not just for new brokers, but increasingly also ongoing training for experienced hands.

Certainly, as a general rule, brokers are highly qualified to advise you about your investments. After all, registered representatives work at the job of investing at least eight hours a day, five days a week. And most have been doing it for years. They have facts, figures, and information at their fingertips that nobody else can easily lay hold of. They have ready access to basic reference works such as Standard & Poor's Corporation Records or Moody's Manuals as well as immense amounts of research material and computerized data made available by their firm. They should be able to get key facts on almost any publicly owned company in the United States.

Many investors rely almost entirely on their broker's recommendations, and the results are often very satisfactory — especially if you and the broker have carefully discussed your investment objectives, resources, and needs, and if you then discuss how each recommendation fits into your plan.

But whatever your relation with your broker, it's wise to do some homework of your own. "Investigate before you invest" is still one of the soundest pieces of advice anyone can give you. Personal observation, news reports, or other mentions you come across may whet your interest in some companies. You might then start your investigating by looking these companies up in the investment manuals at your broker's or at the public library, or at least check out the basic statistics in compact monthly summaries like the Standard & Poor's Stock Guide that provides a one-line tabulation of stock price, price range, dividend record, and per-share earnings for the past five years.

If your preliminary investigation leads you to develop an interest in a few specific stocks, brokers can often supply you — within reason, of course — with reports on these companies. They buy these reports from accepted research services or they are prepared by their own research departments and often made available to customers without charge.

Research (which we'll discuss in more detail later in this chapter) has become vitally important in the brokerage business. Its quality is one factor that can give a firm a genuine competitive advantage. Not all firms can give you the same well-qualified advice about how good a particular stock may be for you in your particular circumstances and with your particular investment objectives.

This, plus variable commission rates and service charges, can make a decision about which brokerage firm to use almost as important as deciding which stock to buy. How can you form an opinion about which broker might best be able to help you? Well, you might visit three or four different firms and ask them about the same stock. That would give you some idea of how well informed each one was, what kind of research service each one provided, and the cost, if any.

Based on the responses you get — especially if cross-checked against some preliminary research of your own — you should be able to make a reasonably informed judgment about the quality of their research — provided, of course, that you have leveled with them about how much money you have to invest, what your financial situation is, and what you want most out of your investments: safety of capital, dividend income, near-term price appreciation, or long-term growth. The more complete the information you provide about your circumstances, the more pertinent the broker's recommendations are apt to be.

You need not feel that you are imposing on a broker when you ask for advice or use the company's research services. After all, that's part of the job for which brokers and their "full service" firm get paid — by you. Many brokerage houses advertise their willingness to set up a program for the new investor, or to review the holdings of present shareowners, making suggestions about what to buy or what to sell — and why.

Incidentally, a good many people have been introduced to a broker and learned the ropes of the investment business on a team basis through the medium of an investment club. Typically, an investment club will be composed of a dozen or more neighbors, business associates, fellow commuters, or members of a social organization. They meet once a month, put perhaps $20 or even $50 apiece into a common pool, and spend an hour or two discussing the best possible investment for their money. These are serious sessions in which the pros and cons of various stocks are ardently debated.

A number of brokers are willing to provide the clubs with company reports and meet with them to answer questions and guide the discussions. The commission return for the time and work involved is negligible. But they value the opportunity for missionary work, for educating club members in the techniques of investing, and, frankly, for eventually developing worthwhile individual brokerage accounts.

In view of the rise in commission expense on small transactions, investment clubs now often start by investing in a company with a dividend-reinvestment program. Typically these programs permit stockholders not only to reinvest their dividends but also to purchase limited additional amounts of stock directly through the company plan at little or no commission cost. Thus, club members make one initial purchase in the open market, and then build up value through reinvestment in that company until they have a big enough nest egg to consider making other investments.

If you are interested in starting an investment club, helpful information is available from the National Association of Investors Corporation, 1515 East Eleven Mile Road, Royal Oak, MI 48067. Telephone: (313) 543-0612.

Through active participation, investment club members get a good grounding in the investment facts of life. They learn, as every investor must, that difference of opinion is what makes the market. And if you as an investor can arrive at buying or selling decisions that are better grounded in fact than those of others, you are likely to be right more often than they are.

Taking a different approach to choosing a broker, if you are the type of investor who does all your own research and never wants a broker to offer any advice but just to act as an order-taker, you might well, as we've noted earlier, consider one of the well-established discount brokers.

Most full-service firms pride themselves on their research departments. These departments are staffed with analysts who spend all their time following developments in certain assigned industries and companies. Quite a few analysts acquired firsthand experience working in the industry they now cover; all are expected to become experts on it, and to be familiar with technical as well as economic developments for the industry and the companies in it. They must read countless business and industrial publications and also the output of competing brokerage houses. And most important, analysts must establish and maintain contact with key officials in all the major companies they cover. They keep in touch through regular visits and frequent phone calls. This is one way they seek to assess the quality of a company's management — the key factor, after all is said and done, in determining a company's success. Shrewd analysts also find such contacts an invaluable source for news and perspective about the company's competitors, suppliers, and customers.

Over the years, officials in companies covered by such research have generally come to respect qualified securities analysts and developed good working relationships. However, they must guard carefully against revealing anything that can be construed as inside information. That's something the SEC gets very tough about.

Publicly owned companies are obligated to reveal promptly to the public any information that may influence the price of their stock — what the SEC calls "material" information. The news may be favorable or unfavorable. It still must be disseminated. But it definitely should not be disseminated through a private comment to a securities analyst. If someone is given such news, the company is required to make it public quickly for everyone, while any "tippee" acting on the inside news can be penalized.

Oh, by the way, that "tippee" designation could apply to you, if you buy or sell based on what you knew, or should have known, was non-public information. When suspicions are aroused about market action that occurred prior to some unexpected news, investigators with their computers tend to look at every trade that has taken place in the stock, and especially in any options where the opportunity for massive profits on a quick move is much greater.

For most market dabblers, however, the main problem is not acting on inside information (which they rarely if ever obtain) but hungering for tips that are at best questionable and quite often outright frauds. Not that the person from whom you got the tip is dishonest; more likely, some manipulator planted a false rumor and counted on gossips to spread it like dandelion seeds in the wind. Stories abound about the tips people picked up in the wild 1920s from shoeshiners and elevator starters. In the technocratic 1990s, a major source is computer "bulletin boards" on which subscribers to various services can pick up information and join in an electronic gabfest. You can indeed obtain helpful information and advice from these modern marvels; remember, however, it's possible that the parties at the other end are well-intentioned but unskilled amateurs. What's more, according to some regulators, market manipulators are increasingly turning to bulletin boards to plant rumors and tout their stocks. So make sure you always check out information carefully — a rule that, of course, should apply to all your investment activities.

As for those who truly have privileged information — the officers and directors of a company who had better know more about that firm and its prospects than anybody else could possibly know — they have long been under special trading restrictions. Officers, directors, and holders of more than 5% of a company's stock are required to report to the SEC every purchase or sale they make in their company's securities. A list of such transactions is published monthly. An insider is never permitted to sell his own company's stock short. Further, if an insider realizes any profit from buying and selling his company's stock within a six-month period, that profit is recoverable by the company, whether or not inside information was used. And that's just as true if the transaction is made in the name of a spouse, other relative, or friend.

While repeated, high-profile cases show that the battle against insider information is never over, the controls are considered generally effective. Certainly, U.S. business practice has moved far from the pre-1929 situation when many company officials considered the privilege of trading in their company's stock on the basis of inside information simply part of their compensation — a philosophy that is still very much alive in many other countries.

Similarly, an inside pipeline to company officials who could provide advance news of earnings reports, dividend action, or merger doings once was the stock in trade of a number of analysts. Not only has that been outlawed; today most analysts go about their business in a far more analytical manner. Armed with an intimate knowledge of a company's past record, its financial statements, and the performance of its stock, an analyst can come pretty close to making a reliable earnings estimate by piecing together the myriad parts of a corporate mosaic — size of inventories, labor conditions, plant cost, capacity, new product development, order backlog, quality of management, and other related data, for each of the company's major units or product lines.

Yet the analyst at any given time may still lack one vital piece of information — perhaps the status of a labor contract or facts about inventory — that would complete the elaborate portrait being pieced together. In such circumstances, analysts would have no qualms about calling their contact at the corporation — and normally both analyst and corporate official would feel confident they are not dealing in inside information.

And, as we've already indicated, analysts can often pick up valuable information to complete their mosaic by checking a company's principal competitors. The competitor may even have some earnings estimates that the analysts can compare with their own. Finally, in most cases, it's considered perfectly proper for analysts to get back to the original company and check out the company's reactions to their conclusions.

Analysts are responsible for keeping their firm's registered representatives informed about all important developments affecting the companies they follow. Periodically, they prepare reports on these companies for distribution to the firm's customers and the public. Usually, they also prepare much longer and more detailed reports for their institutional clients. So that readers may allow for possible bias, many research reports disclose any special interest the firm or its executives might have in the stock, as a result of their own holdings, representation on the company's board of directors, or a long-standing underwriting relationship. (In response to a series of major cases brought by the SEC over the past three decades, securities firms are obligated to maintain a "Chinese wall," so that confidential information the firm's investment bankers learn when discussing underwritings or mergers doesn't get disseminated to the firm's sales and trading arms.)

The computer revolution has been particularly helpful to securities analysts in their complicated studies. They can access the elaborate databases of statistical service agencies as well as of their own firms, and many analysts have constructed special programs of their own to cover their industries and companies. Analysts save themselves not only endless hours of drone work, digging figures out of old corporate reports and manuals, but they can undertake much more complex studies in far shorter time.

The computer systems at most large firms permit the registered representatives in the branch office to retrieve instantly the latest opinion of the firm's research department on individual stocks, with updated earnings and dividend projections. Their computers are also programmed to provide investment suggestions that fit various objectives, with estimated rates of return and other pertinent data.

An almost unlimited number of securities can be reviewed by the computer to find those that will match some predetermined set of standards — for instance, stocks that have shown consistent growth of earnings over some specified period, or stocks whose price performance has exceeded some established yardstick, or stocks that match some particular standard for dividend payout in relation to earnings. Such computerized screening or filtering (chapter 37 presents some specific examples) can help analysts in their search for stocks that may be undervalued or overvalued in relation to the market as a whole or to any specified segment of it.

These techniques are carried further in dealing with portfolio management. That's an infinitely more complicated job because the computer must deal with a much wider range of criteria. Stocks must be chosen not only to satisfy the individual client's circumstances — cash available for investment, income requirements, tax considerations, and the like — but also to fit the degree of risk the investor is prepared to assume, and evaluate each stock in relation to the others in the portfolio, so that they form a combination that can best further the investor's objectives. Computers can apply new analytical methods to differentiate between that element of risk in a given portfolio attributable to general market action and that portion inherent in the specific securities included in the portfolio. In tailoring a portfolio to a specific investor's needs, the computer is used to review speedily a vast number of alternative investments — a far greater number than an individual analyst could review in months or years.

Such computerized analysis, on a highly sophisticated plane, is most frequently applied in the management of institutional portfolios. And to help pension fund trustees evaluate the performance of their fund managers, major brokerage firms have created highly sophisticated techniques to diagnose fund performance. These programs not only calculate the rates of return earned on the assets under management; they also determine the amount of risk taken, the degree of diversification, and the impact of the fund manager's attempts at stock selection and timing. Each pension fund being evaluated is also compared with hundreds of other professionally managed portfolios, gauging the relative performance of the fund manager.

For the technical market analyst who is interested in trying to predict long- or short-term swings in the market on the basis of such factors as the ratio of put-to-call volume on the options exchanges and of bullish-to-bearish sentiment of the advisory services, cyclical and random variations in price movements, and other esoteric data, the computer can answer an infinite range of mathematical problems. In addition, computer graphics can offer analysts an instant picture of trend lines, moving averages, volume data, high-low-close figures, and other aids to predictions for the market as a whole or for individual stocks.

Most firms also develop (in-house or through purchased services) detailed statistical models of what the economy is apt to look like, and securities analysts have their computers work these economic projections into their corporate forecasts.

How much you lean on your broker for help is up to you. Your broker is ready to provide you with the facts and figures you need to make specific investment decisions and to help you to interpret them, but the actual buy or sell decisions are up to you — unless you deliberately make another decision; namely, to turn the decision-making over to a paid agent.

Most brokers like the idea of having the customer call the shots. Not only will you be less inclined to blame them for whatever might go wrong if you determine your own investment course; more important in the long run, you will be a better and more successful investor if you make your own decisions.

CHAPTER 29

Financial Advice — at a Price

DO you want more specific help with your investment problems: information, advice, recommendations — more than you feel your broker can give you?

You can get it — at a price. Whether the price is worth it to you is something else again.

Maybe you want something more than advice. Maybe you don't want to worry about your investment problems at all. If that's the case — and if you have at least $100,000 to invest, preferably a great deal more — you can turn your entire investment problem over to an *investment adviser*, also sometimes called an *investment counselor*, or — especially when handling institutional accounts — a *money manager*. There are hundreds of counseling firms available all around the country, in the business of guiding the investment destiny of their clients — for a goodly, if normally tax-deductible, fee. They make all the buying and selling decisions for you, and see that the orders are properly executed by a brokerage firm.

In the main, these investment advisers do a sound job for their clients, which include many institutions. But their services are obviously beyond the reach of the average investor.

Recently, various brokerage firms have introduced programs under which they arrange for customers to have their accounts managed by selected investment advisers. Still, the usual minimum is an account value of $100,000, sometimes more. In a typical arrangement, customers fill out extensive questionnaires and discuss their situation, objectives, and willingness to assume risks with their broker. Based on the resultant profile, broker and customer then decide on a suitable investment manager from the firm's approved list. The manager makes the investment decisions; the broker monitors performance of the account and keeps the investor informed and advised.

The most popular version of these plans are called *wrap* accounts, because all management and service charges as well as all trading commissions are "wrapped" into a single annual fee — commonly 3% of the portfolio value; less for very large accounts. The wrap fee lets you know just how much the program will cost you and avoids worries about possible churning by the investment manager. Some plans, however, use *directed commissions,* under which the customer pays a fee directly to the manager and is billed separately for transaction costs.

The managers may be willing to accept smaller accounts (and at proportionately lower fees) when working through brokerage firms than they do for direct customers, in return for the higher volume and lower marketing costs of this business. And since the firms carefully review relative performance, the managers have a strong incentive to perform well to stay on the list. From the customers' standpoint, the program can give them access to top-performing investment managers whom they could not retain otherwise, along with the extra clout that can be exerted by a major brokerage house with mega-millions' worth of accounts to award. At the same time, it leaves the customers with their own personal broker for advice and handholding.

Many banks will also be glad to take your investment problems off your hands. But again, it's at a price that average investors may consider beyond their range.

Then there are *financial planners* who seek to assess your overall financial situation and advise you on how best to meet your goals. This broad approach, which may include advice on managing your expenses so as to allow room for your investment and savings objectives, contrasts with that of investment advisers who make specific securities and other investment decisions for you. In practice, however, the terms "financial planner" and "investment adviser" or "counselor" are often used loosely and almost interchangeably, especially since there are no formal boundary lines and most of the practitioners perform overlapping functions.

Planners, too, vary widely in background, qualifications, and integrity — ranging from superb professionals to fly-by-night artists. As when seeking out other professionals, it's best to get recommendations from business associates or friends. It's also wise to look for membership in one of the recognized professional associations such as the Institute of Certified Financial Planners, the International Association for Financial Planning, or the National Association of Personal Financial Advisors. Some planners work on direct fees only. Others get commissions on the investment products they sell you; there's nothing necessarily improper in that (obviously, all professional advisers must get paid for their services in some way), but it raises the possibility of conflicts of interest. So it's wise, and perfectly appropriate, to ask about such compensation, and factor it into your decision.

Where else might the average investor turn for help?

There are dozens and dozens of investment advisory services, all of them only too willing to help, regardless of how competent they are. Once again, as you no doubt suspect, the range of competence is from superb to abysmal. They offer the investor a bewildering array of publications and services, at costs that typically range between $100 and $500 a year, and sometimes quite a bit more. Some are simply compilations of statistical information. Some review business conditions as they affect the investment outlook. Many undertake to give advice about the general market, usually in a weekly letter sold on a subscription basis. Some provide recommendations about hundreds of different securities — what to buy, what to sell, what to hold. They may offer subscribers an elaborate stock-rating service and maintain supervised lists of those investments that they consider particularly attractive.

Some services are perennially bearish, but the majority are usually bullish. By and large, virtually all are more concerned with the short-term outlook — what the market is likely to do in the next couple of months — than they are with the problem of long-term investment.

And regardless of their different approaches to the investment problem, they generally share one common characteristic: They will tell you how successful they've been in calling the turns in past markets and in recommending good buys and good sells at just the strategic moment. There is, of course, the standard disclaimer that past results are no guarantee of future performance — a disclaimer that probably gets the same degree of attention as the Surgeon General's warning on cigarettes.

The *Investment Advisers Act of 1940* is intended "to protect the public and investors against malpractices by persons paid for advising others about securities." It requires all investment advisers who receive compensation in any form for their service to register with the SEC. They must state the name and form of the organization, names and addresses of the principal officers, their education and business affiliations for the past 10 years, the exact nature of the business, the form of compensation for their services, and so on.

In addition, the services must maintain data on their accounts, correspondence, memorandums, papers, books, and other records, and furnish copies of them to their clients or to the SEC at any time upon request. Banks, lawyers, accountants, engineers, teachers, newspapers, and magazines are exempt from this registration — an exemption which some view as overly broad.

Also exempt are brokers, as their advisory service is presumed to be incidental to their execution of orders on a commission basis. However, this exemption does not apply to brokers if they perform an advisory service for which clients pay specifically.

Significantly, the SEC has no responsibility — indeed, it has no right — to judge the competence of any adviser or the quality of his or her service. (This is similar to its role in the registration of security offerings; as noted, the SEC is not allowed to pass judgment on the quality of the stocks and bonds that are registered with it, as long as all pertinent facts are revealed.) Thus, a schoolboy grinding out investment letters on his mother's kitchen table, a three-time bankrupt, or just about anyone else is free to peddle his wares as long as the required background facts are filed with the commission.

Of course, securities law does prohibit "any person" from distributing information that is false or misleading, and the SEC as well as the attorneys general of many states do try to crack down on abusers. But it's not easy to prove a case — and some court decisions have made the task more difficult.

The SEC also seeks to guard against conflicts of interest in the service that investment advisers offer the public. In other words, an adviser cannot offer advice about a stock if he has a stake in your acting on that particular advice (say, he has an interest in a company that is trying to get rid of a block of the stock he wants you to buy) unless he reveals that this is the case.

Again, how good is the advice that investment services provide? There's no real answer to that, because there is no way to accurately compute and compare all their batting averages. Some make straight-out recommendations. Others hedge their suggestions with all kinds of qualifications. And, of course, those who had great success during one market cycle may be near the bottom next time — and vice versa. One respected source on advisory services' track records is the *Hulbert Financial Digest,* published by Hulbert Financial Services of Alexandria, Virginia; it specializes in analyzing performance of financial advisory services and newsletters. (Editor Mark Hulbert is also a regular *Forbes* magazine columnist.)

But one other note of caution: Investment letters that focus on near-term market trends and recommendations of specific stock purchases and sales for quick moves are not likely to be of much use for the average investor. By the time the letter reaches you and you can act on the advice, a fair part of the move (assuming the author was right in the first place) may already be history. True, some "letters" offer, at premium cost, overnight delivery or even fax or telephone alerts — but you are still likely to lag behind the professionals with their "real time" monitoring and instant market access. A more fundamental, and far more important, consideration — *moving quickly in and out of stocks is apt to cost you more in commissions than you can gain from price appreciation.*

Consequently, the interest of most investors may be better served by concentration on longer-term, good-value recommendations. If you want to go beyond ideas suggested by your broker and brokerage firm (or if you don't use a full-service broker), your best sources might be (as we discussed in chapters 26 and 27) the major services that provide ratings and analysis of most of the actively traded stocks and the advisory columns of the leading financial magazines — preferably checking one against the other. Much of this advice you may be able to get at your library. And if you feel it's worth your while to pay for additional specific advice, try to make sure that it's cost-effective for *your particular needs.*

CHAPTER 30

How Good Are Common Stocks?

PROBABLY the most convincing evidence of the value of investing in common stocks is the data supplied by several studies measuring the rate of return on New York Stock Exchange stocks — dividends plus price appreciation. These studies have been conducted by the *Center for Research in Security Prices* at the Graduate School of Business of the University of Chicago. The center, whose initials, CRSP, lead to the proud pronunciation "Crisp," developed the most definitive measurement of the stock market that has ever been made.

Basically, the questions to which the center addressed itself were these: Just how good are common stocks as investments? What average rate of return might investors expect to realize if they simply selected stocks at random from among all those listed on the New York Stock Exchange — without any professional guidance or research information? And what would be their average risk of loss?

Obviously, such questions could be answered only in terms of the historical record. And this CRSP set about compiling. It took five years to put the initial set of data on computer tape because of the high standards of accuracy that were established by Professors James H. Lorie, director of the center for its first 15 years, and Lawrence Fisher, who supervised the original data compilation.

First, CRSP insisted on going back to January 1926, so that it could not be accused of ignoring the 1929 bull market or the consequent crash. It also insisted on covering all the stocks that had been listed on the exchange at any time since 1926 — not just a cross section or sample, but all the stocks — good, bad, and indifferent — including those of companies that went broke or were delisted for other reasons. For the many stocks that came and went during the past 66 years, the data compilers, in effect, "bought" each stock the first time it appeared on the Big Board roster and "sold" it the last time it was quoted.

CRSP recorded the price at each month's end for each stock. Since those prices had to be comparable throughout the whole period, it meant they had to be adjusted to account for every stock dividend, stock split, spinoff, merger, or other change in a company's financial structure. In addition, they had to record every dividend paid by every listed stock throughout the period.

The center's file of price and dividend data is unquestionably the most authoritative record that exists.

The initial study was published in 1963, telling the story of the market and the rates of return you could earn through 1960. CRSP, which has continued compiling the basic data, has generously prepared for this edition the detailed analyses shown in the table on pages 290 to 295, covering investment results through 1991.

The table shows the investment return that would have been realized over any given period if someone had bought one share of each Big Board stock and had reinvested all the dividends received.

While the table may seem forbidding, it is really not difficult to read. Obviously, you don't want to read it line by line, any more than you would the phone book. But you can quickly look up how a hypothetical investor would have made out during any given pair of years within that 66-year span. To give one example, to check out the period from the last trading day of 1959 to the end of 1982, find your starting or "Bought" year at the top of the page, then go down the "1959" column until it intersects the line marked "1982." There you see "12.00." That means investors would have realized an annual total rate of return of exactly 12% had they bought all the stocks on the Big Board at the beginning date and reinvested all their dividends till the end of our example. Total return — which measures both dividend receipts and changes in a stock's market price — means each dollar invested would have grown at a compounded annual rate of 12% during the 23 years of our example.

Since our hypothetical investment covers all the listed stocks, the rates of return for each period can be taken to represent an average of all the possible returns that were realized on individual stocks. Of course, on some stocks, the rate of return would have been tremendously higher, while on others there would have been a 100% loss.

It can be instructive to look up some random dates — perhaps to find the typical return the stock market has offered in the years since you left school, or since your child was born. However, the real point of the table is to show the impressive statistical evidence of strong overall stock market results.

Take the "12.80" figure at the bottom of the first column. It means that an investment in every Big Board stock on December 31, 1925, would, with the reinvestment of dividends, have yielded a compounded return equal to almost 13% a year for the 66-year period to December 31, 1991. And that means you would have stayed almost 10 percentage points a year ahead of inflation, which rose at an average compounded annual rate of 3.1% over those 66 years.

Other significant findings:

(1) In all the 2211 year-to-year combinations possible between year-end 1925 and December 1991, there are only 72 with negative rates of return — in other words, losses, where declines in the market price more than offset the value of the additional shares that had been bought with the income from dividends. And most of these loss periods were for relatively short time spans. For investments held at least seven years, there were only five occasions that resulted in losses; you would have realized at least some profit in every investment period lasting 10 years or longer.

(2) Results for individual periods are widely scattered, ranging from −45.8% (the single year 1937) to +140% (in 1933, on the snapback from the market's depression bottom the year before). However, these ranges narrow quickly. There are only 20 periods with compounded returns worse than −15%; likewise 20 periods where the

Table 30-1: Rates of Return on Investment in All Common Stocks Listed on the New York Stock Exchange with Reinvestment of Dividends (Before Commissions and Taxes)
Percent per Annum Compounded Annually

Bought as of Year End

TO YEAR END	1925	1926	1927	1928	1929	1930	1931	1932	1933	1934	1935
1926	0.21										
1927	14.64	31.14									
1928	23.37	36.88	42.88								
1929	6.04	8.06	-1.91	-32.66							
1930	-4.64	-5.81	-15.65	-35.19	-37.63						
1931	-12.92	-15.34	-24.11	-38.54	-41.29	-44.73					
1932	-9.67	-11.22	-17.88	-28.50	-27.06	-21.12	12.58				
1933	2.06	2.33	-1.81	-8.91	-1.77	14.29	64.36	139.95			
1934	3.85	4.32	0.96	-4.71	2.13	15.54	47.73	69.23	19.35		
1935	8.48	9.45	7.00	2.67	10.14	23.41	50.86	66.32	38.47	60.66	
1936	11.91	13.15	11.32	7.90	15.41	27.88	51.24	62.82	43.07	56.65	52.74
1937	5.35	5.83	3.58	-0.05	5.90	13.12	27.46	30.66	12.24	9.97	-9.02
1938	7.53	8.16	6.29	3.19	8.20	15.91	28.84	31.77	16.89	16.28	4.40
1939	7.27	7.83	6.08	3.25	7.76	14.51	25.42	27.37	14.61	13.69	4.27
1940	6.26	6.70	5.02	2.36	6.33	12.16	21.34	22.48	11.26	9.96	1.93
1941	5.31	5.65	4.04	1.53	5.06	10.16	18.03	18.65	8.65	7.20	0.21
1942	6.85	7.28	5.85	3.60	7.09	12.03	19.46	20.17	11.29	10.32	4.55
1943	9.34	9.91	8.70	6.74	10.31	15.25	22.53	23.48	15.54	15.13	10.43
1944	10.80	11.42	10.36	8.59	12.11	16.90	23.84	24.83	17.63	17.46	13.44
1945	12.94	13.66	12.76	11.20	14.74	19.50	26.26	27.38	20.84	20.97	17.59
1946	11.74	12.35	11.44	9.91	13.12	17.41	23.46	24.27	18.14	18.04	14.78
1947	11.16	11.71	10.82	9.35	12.33	16.29	21.82	22.47	16.72	16.52	13.44
1948	10.55	11.04	10.16	8.74	11.52	15.18	20.26	20.76	15.35	15.07	12.16
1949	10.98	11.47	10.65	9.31	11.99	15.50	20.33	20.80	15.72	15.49	12.80
1950	11.92	12.43	11.69	10.44	13.07	16.49	21.15	21.64	16.88	16.73	14.27
1951	12.07	12.57	11.86	10.68	13.20	16.46	20.89	21.34	16.83	16.68	14.37
1952	11.99	12.47	11.78	10.64	13.06	16.16	20.34	20.74	16.45	16.29	14.10
1953	11.42	11.86	11.18	10.07	12.34	15.26	19.17	19.49	15.40	15.20	13.09
1954	12.75	13.22	12.61	11.58	13.86	16.75	20.61	20.99	17.11	17.00	15.06
1955	12.99	13.46	12.88	11.90	14.10	16.89	20.60	20.96	17.25	17.15	15.32
1956	12.79	13.24	12.67	11.71	13.83	16.49	20.02	20.34	16.78	16.67	14.90
1957	11.83	12.22	11.64	10.70	12.68	15.17	18.47	18.72	15.29	15.11	13.38
1958	13.04	13.47	12.94	12.06	14.05	16.53	19.80	20.08	16.80	16.70	15.09
1959	13.12	13.53	13.02	12.17	14.09	16.49	19.64	19.91	16.75	16.65	15.10
1960	12.67	13.06	12.55	11.71	13.55	15.84	18.84	19.07	16.02	15.89	14.39
1961	13.10	13.50	13.02	12.22	14.02	16.26	19.18	19.41	16.47	16.37	14.93
1962	12.31	12.67	12.18	11.39	13.10	15.22	17.99	18.17	15.32	15.18	13.77
1963	12.48	12.83	12.36	11.59	13.26	15.33	18.01	18.19	15.43	15.30	13.94
1964	12.62	12.97	12.51	11.77	13.40	15.41	18.01	18.19	15.52	15.39	14.08
1965	13.00	13.34	12.91	12.19	13.80	15.77	18.31	18.49	15.91	15.80	14.54
1966	12.46	12.78	12.35	11.64	13.17	15.06	17.50	17.65	15.13	15.00	13.77
1967	13.23	13.57	13.16	12.49	14.02	15.89	18.30	18.47	16.03	15.94	14.76
1968	13.60	13.94	13.55	12.90	14.41	16.25	18.61	18.78	16.42	16.33	15.20
1969	12.69	13.00	12.60	11.94	13.38	15.13	17.37	17.50	15.20	15.08	13.96
1970	12.32	12.61	12.21	11.56	12.95	14.64	16.80	16.91	14.66	14.54	13.43
1971	12.47	12.75	12.37	11.74	13.10	14.75	16.87	16.98	14.79	14.67	13.60
1972	12.38	12.66	12.28	11.67	12.99	14.60	16.65	16.76	14.62	14.50	13.46
1973	11.30	11.55	11.16	10.54	11.79	13.32	15.27	15.34	13.24	13.09	12.05
1974	10.36	10.58	10.18	9.56	10.75	12.21	14.07	14.11	12.06	11.88	10.85
1975	11.21	11.45	11.07	10.47	11.67	13.12	14.98	15.04	13.04	12.89	11.90
1976	11.80	12.04	11.68	11.11	12.30	13.74	15.58	15.65	13.71	13.58	12.62
1977	11.75	11.99	11.64	11.08	12.24	13.65	15.45	15.51	13.61	13.48	12.54
1978	11.79	12.03	11.68	11.13	12.28	13.66	15.42	15.48	13.62	13.49	12.58
1979	12.19	12.43	12.10	11.56	12.70	14.07	15.80	15.87	14.05	13.94	13.05
1980	12.50	12.75	12.42	11.91	13.03	14.38	16.09	16.16	14.39	14.28	13.42
1981	12.38	12.62	12.30	11.79	12.89	14.21	15.88	15.94	14.20	14.09	13.25
1982	12.66	12.90	12.59	12.10	13.18	14.48	16.13	16.20	14.50	14.40	13.57
1983	12.99	13.23	12.93	12.45	13.52	14.81	16.44	16.52	14.85	14.76	13.95
1984	12.77	13.00	12.71	12.23	13.28	14.54	16.12	16.19	14.55	14.46	13.67
1985	13.04	13.27	12.98	12.52	13.56	14.80	16.36	16.44	14.83	14.74	13.97
1986	13.06	13.29	13.01	12.55	13.57	14.79	16.33	16.40	14.82	14.74	13.98
1987	12.79	13.00	12.72	12.27	13.27	14.46	15.96	16.02	14.47	14.38	13.63
1988	12.93	13.15	12.87	12.43	13.41	14.59	16.06	16.12	14.60	14.52	13.79
1989	12.99	13.20	12.94	12.50	13.47	14.62	16.07	16.14	14.64	14.56	13.84
1990	12.44	12.64	12.37	11.93	12.87	14.00	15.40	15.45	13.98	13.89	13.18
1991	12.80	13.01	12.74	12.32	13.25	14.37	15.76	15.81	14.37	14.28	13.59

1936	1937	1938	1939	1940	1941	1942	1943	1944	1945	1946
−45.81										
−13.68	37.49									
−8.18	19.52	3.89								
−7.87	9.96	−1.66	−6.91							
−7.89	5.18	−3.81	−7.44	−7.96						
−1.85	10.53	4.66	4.91	11.38	34.79					
5.43	17.80	14.21	16.95	26.19	47.76	61.97				
9.30	20.82	18.25	21.35	29.66	45.36	50.05	40.67			
14.22	25.35	23.74	27.39	35.64	49.46	54.69	51.17	62.46		
11.55	20.86	18.93	21.25	26.71	35.08	35.15	27.24	21.01	−9.86	
10.42	18.56	16.63	18.33	22.45	28.42	27.18	19.73	13.46	−5.18	−0.26
9.31	16.51	14.60	15.85	19.06	23.52	21.74	14.98	9.33	−4.19	−1.22
10.20	16.91	15.20	16.40	19.32	23.26	21.69	16.03	11.65	1.65	5.81
11.92	18.35	16.88	18.13	20.98	24.72	23.51	18.82	15.52	7.91	12.87
12.19	18.17	16.81	17.95	20.52	23.81	22.65	18.46	15.59	9.21	13.49
12.04	17.60	16.30	17.31	19.59	22.47	21.31	17.47	14.85	9.30	12.87
11.10	16.20	14.91	15.74	17.69	20.13	18.88	15.26	12.74	7.70	10.48
13.26	18.28	17.17	18.12	20.14	22.63	21.67	18.55	16.54	12.31	15.44
13.63	18.40	17.36	18.26	20.16	22.47	21.57	18.70	16.88	13.09	15.98
13.28	17.76	16.75	17.56	19.29	21.37	20.46	17.75	16.01	12.52	15.04
11.78	15.90	14.87	15.51	16.99	18.75	17.75	15.10	13.34	9.99	12.00
13.61	17.69	16.78	17.50	19.03	20.85	20.02	17.65	16.16	13.20	15.37
13.70	17.59	16.72	17.40	18.84	20.54	19.75	17.51	16.11	13.36	15.38
13.02	16.69	15.82	16.42	17.73	19.27	18.46	16.30	14.92	12.30	14.08
13.63	17.19	16.38	16.99	18.27	19.76	19.01	16.99	15.73	13.31	15.05
12.49	15.82	15.00	15.50	16.64	17.97	17.18	15.20	13.93	11.58	13.08
12.71	15.93	15.14	15.64	16.73	18.00	17.25	15.38	14.18	11.96	13.40
12.90	16.01	15.26	15.74	16.79	18.01	17.30	15.51	14.37	12.28	13.66
13.41	16.44	15.73	16.21	17.24	18.43	17.77	16.07	15.02	13.05	14.40
12.66	15.54	14.82	15.25	16.20	17.29	16.61	14.95	13.90	11.99	13.08
13.71	16.55	15.89	16.34	17.31	18.41	17.79	16.24	15.28	13.50	14.75
14.19	16.97	16.34	16.80	17.75	18.83	18.25	16.77	15.87	14.18	15.41
12.95	15.57	14.92	15.31	16.17	17.14	16.53	15.06	14.14	12.48	13.56
12.45	14.96	14.32	14.67	15.47	16.38	15.77	14.34	13.43	11.81	12.82
12.64	15.09	14.47	14.82	15.60	16.48	15.90	14.52	13.65	12.10	13.08
12.52	14.00	14.29	14.62	15.37	16.21	15.64	14.30	13.46	11.96	12.90
11.12	13.36	12.73	13.00	13.67	14.42	13.82	12.49	11.62	10.14	10.96
9.91	12.04	11.40	11.62	12.22	12.90	12.27	10.95	10.08	8.61	9.34
11.01	13.13	12.53	12.78	13.40	14.10	13.52	12.27	11.46	10.07	10.83
11.76	13.86	13.29	13.56	14.19	14.89	14.36	13.16	12.39	11.06	11.84
11.71	13.75	13.20	13.45	14.06	14.74	14.21	13.05	12.30	11.01	11.76
11.76	13.75	13.21	13.46	14.06	14.72	14.21	13.07	12.35	11.10	11.83
12.26	14.22	13.71	13.97	14.56	15.22	14.73	13.64	12.95	11.75	12.48
12.65	14.59	14.09	14.35	14.94	15.60	15.13	14.07	13.41	12.25	12.98
12.50	14.38	13.89	14.14	14.71	15.34	14.88	13.85	13.20	12.07	12.77
12.84	14.70	14.23	14.48	15.04	15.67	15.23	14.23	13.60	12.51	13.21
13.25	15.07	14.62	14.88	15.44	16.06	15.64	14.67	14.07	13.02	13.71
12.97	14.75	14.30	14.54	15.08	15.68	15.26	14.31	13.72	12.68	13.35
13.29	15.05	14.61	14.86	15.40	15.99	15.59	14.66	14.09	13.09	13.75
13.31	15.03	14.61	14.85	15.37	15.95	15.56	14.65	14.10	13.12	13.76
12.97	14.65	14.22	14.45	14.95	15.51	15.11	14.22	13.67	12.71	13.33
13.14	14.79	14.38	14.60	15.10	15.65	15.26	14.40	13.86	12.92	13.53
13.21	14.83	14.42	14.64	15.13	15.67	15.30	14.45	13.92	13.01	13.60
12.55	14.11	13.70	13.91	14.37	14.87	14.49	13.65	13.12	12.22	12.77
12.98	14.53	14.13	14.34	14.80	15.31	14.94	14.13	13.62	12.74	13.30

Table 30-1: Rates of Return on Investment in All Common Stocks Listed on the New York Stock Exchange with Reinvestment of Dividends (Before Commissions and Taxes)
Percent per Annum Compounded Annually (continued)

Bought as of Year End

TO YEAR END	1947	1948	1949	1950	1951	1952	1953	1954	1955	1956	1957
1948	−2.18										
1949	8.98	21.42									
1950	17.62	28.98	37.01								
1951	17.21	24.49	26.06	15.98							
1952	15.70	20.66	20.41	12.88	9.85						
1953	12.37	15.54	14.11	7.36	3.30	−2.87					
1954	17.88	21.60	21.64	18.08	18.78	23.51	57.07				
1955	18.19	21.43	21.43	18.53	19.18	22.46	37.50	20.38			
1956	16.88	19.51	19.24	16.51	16.61	18.37	26.43	13.44	6.90		
1957	13.30	15.17	14.41	11.50	10.77	10.96	14.71	3.31	−4.30	−14.32	
1958	16.90	19.01	18.74	16.64	16.73	17.92	22.58	15.22	13.54	17.02	59.84
1959	16.79	18.68	18.41	16.51	16.58	17.57	21.37	15.27	14.03	16.51	35.87
1960	15.26	16.85	16.45	14.57	14.41	14.99	17.80	12.29	10.73	11.72	22.05
1961	16.23	17.78	17.48	15.85	15.83	16.52	19.20	14.59	13.66	15.06	23.86
1962	14.03	15.28	14.82	13.14	12.89	13.20	15.14	10.76	9.45	9.88	15.48
1963	14.31	15.51	15.10	13.56	13.36	13.69	15.49	11.61	10.56	11.10	16.02
1964	14.54	15.67	15.30	13.89	13.73	14.06	15.73	12.25	11.38	11.96	16.32
1965	15.28	16.40	16.09	14.81	14.73	15.12	16.76	13.65	13.00	13.70	17.79
1966	13.97	14.95	14.58	13.30	13.13	13.37	14.72	11.76	11.00	11.42	14.73
1967	15.56	16.57	16.31	15.20	15.15	15.51	16.95	14.32	13.83	14.49	17.85
1968	16.22	17.22	17.01	15.99	15.99	16.38	17.79	15.40	15.02	15.73	18.93
1969	14.23	15.08	14.77	13.71	13.58	13.81	14.94	12.57	12.03	12.44	15.02
1970	13.43	14.20	13.86	12.81	12.65	12.81	13.80	11.54	10.97	11.27	13.53
1971	13.67	14.42	14.11	13.12	12.98	13.15	14.11	11.99	11.48	11.79	13.94
1972	13.46	14.16	13.86	12.91	12.76	12.91	13.81	11.79	11.30	11.58	13.57
1973	11.41	12.00	11.62	10.63	10.39	10.42	11.13	9.12	8.53	8.63	10.25
1974	9.71	10.19	9.77	8.76	8.46	8.39	8.96	6.99	6.32	6.29	7.65
1975	11.24	11.78	11.42	10.50	10.28	10.30	10.94	9.12	8.58	8.67	10.12
1976	12.28	12.83	12.53	11.68	11.51	11.58	12.25	10.55	10.11	10.27	11.74
1977	12.19	12.72	12.42	11.60	11.43	11.50	12.14	10.51	10.08	10.23	11.63
1978	12.24	12.76	12.47	11.68	11.52	11.59	12.21	10.65	10.24	10.40	11.74
1979	12.90	13.43	13.17	12.42	12.30	12.39	13.02	11.55	11.19	11.38	12.72
1980	13.41	13.93	13.70	13.00	12.89	13.00	13.64	12.23	11.92	12.13	13.45
1981	13.18	13.68	13.45	12.76	12.65	12.75	13.35	11.99	11.68	11.88	13.13
1982	13.62	14.12	13.90	13.25	13.16	13.27	13.88	12.58	12.30	12.51	13.74
1983	14.12	14.63	14.43	13.81	13.74	13.87	14.48	13.24	12.99	13.22	14.44
1984	13.74	14.22	14.02	13.40	13.33	13.44	14.01	12.80	12.54	12.75	13.90
1985	14.14	14.62	14.43	13.85	13.78	13.91	14.47	13.31	13.08	13.30	14.44
1986	14.15	14.61	14.43	13.86	13.80	13.92	14.47	13.34	13.12	13.34	14.44
1987	13.69	14.13	13.94	13.38	13.30	13.40	13.92	12.82	12.59	12.78	13.82
1988	13.89	14.32	14.15	13.60	13.53	13.64	14.15	13.08	12.87	13.06	14.08
1989	13.96	14.38	14.21	13.68	13.62	13.72	14.22	13.19	12.98	13.17	14.16
1990	13.10	13.49	13.31	12.77	12.69	12.76	13.22	12.19	11.97	12.12	13.04
1991	13.63	14.03	13.86	13.34	13.28	13.37	13.83	12.85	12.64	12.81	13.73

1958	1959	1960	1961	1962	1963	1964	1965	1966	1967	1968
15.50										
6.65	−1.52									
13.77	12.92	29.47								
6.47	3.62	6.29	−12.73							
8.81	7.20	10.28	1.78	18.71						
10.32	9.31	12.20	6.97	18.44	18.17					
12.77	12.32	15.31	12.02	21.74	23.20	28.63				
10.07	9.31	11.23	7.90	13.78	12.19	9.31	−7.10			
13.93	13.74	16.10	14.01	20.27	20.67	21.51	18.10	50.15		
15.47	15.46	17.78	16.20	21.88	22.53	23.64	22.03	39.86	30.27	
11.63	11.25	12.76	10.83	14.68	14.03	13.22	9.66	15.89	1.82	−20.42
10.33	9.88	11.09	9.21	12.32	11.43	10.35	7.02	10.87	0.21	−12.10
11.01	10.65	11.82	10.20	13.09	12.41	11.61	9.00	12.54	4.71	−2.64
10.83	10.48	11.54	10.04	12.62	11.96	11.21	8.92	11.85	5.45	0.02
7.55	7.01	7.69	6.05	7.95	6.93	5.75	3.19	4.75	−1.35	−6.69
5.02	4.36	4.79	3.10	4.54	3.34	1.97	−0.63	0.21	−5.42	−10.33
7.73	7.26	7.87	6.48	8.12	7.28	6.34	4.34	5.69	1.16	−2.43
9.54	9.20	9.91	8.72	10.44	9.83	9.16	7.54	9.13	5.32	2.56
9.54	9.22	9.89	8.77	10.37	9.80	9.18	7.70	9.16	5.74	3.31
9.76	9.46	10.11	9.06	10.59	10.07	9.52	8.17	9.55	6.46	4.33
10.86	10.63	11.31	10.38	11.92	11.51	11.08	9.92	11.35	8.61	6.83
11.70	11.52	12.22	11.38	12.90	12.56	12.22	11.20	12.64	10.18	8.65
11.44	11.26	11.91	11.09	12.51	12.18	11.84	10.86	12.18	9.87	8.44
12.14	12.00	12.65	11.91	13.31	13.03	12.70	11.88	13.19	11.08	9.82
12.92	12.82	13.48	12.81	14.19	13.97	13.76	12.98	14.29	12.36	11.26
12.43	12.31	12.92	12.25	13.55	13.31	13.07	12.30	13.49	11.64	10.57
13.03	12.94	13.56	12.94	14.21	14.01	13.82	13.13	14.31	12.59	11.62
13.08	12.99	13.59	13.00	14.22	14.03	13.84	13.18	14.31	12.68	11.77
12.49	12.39	12.94	12.35	13.40	13.27	13.07	12.40	13.43	11.85	10.96
12.80	12.71	13.25	12.69	13.81	13.62	13.43	12.81	13.81	12.32	11.49
12.93	12.84	13.37	12.84	13.92	13.74	13.56	12.97	13.94	12.52	11.74
11.82	11.71	12.18	11.62	12.61	12.39	12.17	11.56	12.41	11.01	10.21
12.56	12.47	12.95	12.44	13.42	13.24	13.06	12.50	13.37	12.05	11.32

Table 30-1: Rates of Return on Investment in All Common Stocks Listed on the New York Stock Exchange with Reinvestment of Dividends (Before Commissions and Taxes)
Percent per Annum Compounded Annually (continued)

Bought as of Year End	1969	1970	1971	1972	1973	1974	1975	1976	1977	1978	1979
TO YEAR END											
1970	-2.92										
1971	7.69	19.47									
1972	7.94	13.82	8.45								
1973	-2.90	-2.89	-12.45	-29.32							
1974	-8.16	-9.43	-17.42	-27.93	-26.52						
1975	0.94	1.73	-2.28	-5.62	9.07	61.89					
1976	6.35	7.98	5.82	5.17	20.06	53.47	45.49				
1977	6.74	8.19	6.42	6.02	17.33	37.14	26.22	9.50			
1978	7.52	8.90	7.47	7.30	16.65	30.93	21.99	11.71	13.95		
1979	10.02	11.56	10.61	10.93	19.58	31.81	25.21	19.10	24.21	35.38	
1980	11.77	13.36	12.70	13.24	21.13	31.65	26.32	21.94	26.39	33.11	30.87
1981	11.27	12.66	12.00	12.40	19.11	27.62	22.66	18.54	20.91	23.33	17.71
1982	12.58	13.98	13.49	14.01	20.23	27.86	23.62	20.31	22.60	24.86	21.54
1983	13.95	15.36	15.03	15.65	21.48	28.46	24.80	22.10	24.33	26.52	24.39
1984	13.02	14.26	13.86	14.33	19.44	25.38	21.87	19.20	20.66	21.81	19.26
1985	14.01	15.24	14.94	15.46	20.28	25.79	22.65	20.35	21.78	22.94	20.98
1986	14.03	15.18	14.90	15.38	19.81	24.79	21.88	19.74	20.93	21.83	20.01
1987	13.02	14.04	13.71	14.07	18.04	22.42	19.60	17.49	18.32	18.81	16.89
1988	13.49	14.48	14.19	14.56	18.31	22.40	19.80	17.87	18.66	19.14	17.46
1989	13.65	14.60	14.33	14.69	18.21	22.02	19.58	17.79	18.51	18.93	17.40
1990	11.94	12.73	12.38	12.61	15.73	19.06	16.65	14.84	15.24	15.35	13.68
1991	13.03	13.85	13.58	13.86	16.91	20.15	17.93	16.29	16.79	17.01	15.60

The data for this table were made available by the Center for Research in Security Prices, the University of Chicago Graduate School of Business, through the cooperation of Prof. Richard Leftwich and General Manager David Fialkowski. The data were compiled by Senior Research Analyst Peter D. Weinstein, with Senior Programmer Kenneth Kraus and Senior Research Analyst Joseph Bochenski

Bought as of Year End

1980	1981	1982	1983	1984	1985	1986	1987	1988	1989	1990
5.87										
17.12	29.57									
22.31	31.46	33.38								
16.53	20.31	15.94	0.77							
19.09	22.65	20.42	14.43	29.93						
18.29	20.94	18.88	14.40	21.89	14.36					
15.02	16.62	14.19	9.84	13.04	5.44	-2.79				
15.89	17.40	15.48	12.20	15.25	10.74	8.98	22.16			
16.00	17.32	15.67	12.95	15.56	12.22	11.52	19.44	16.78		
12.09	12.81	10.87	7.97	9.22	5.50	3.39	5.54	-1.91	-17.61	
14.30	15.18	13.68	11.43	13.04	10.44	9.68	13.03	10.15	6.97	38.89

compounded return tops +50%. And in none of these exceptionally high or low instances is the time span longer than five years.

(3) When the investment horizon extends at least 10 years (as in most planning for retirement, education, and similar objectives), the historic pattern is particularly encouraging. Of the 1653 10-year-plus periods covered in the table, more than 95 percent show an annual compounded return above 9.1%, 90% above 10.6%, and in half the periods the return was 13.6% or better. Indeed, in nearly three out of 10 instances, the return topped 15%.

(4) The worst period for longer-term investors to find themselves with a need to sell out was the mid-1970s (since the study began with 1926, there's no 10-years-and-longer data for the worst years of the depression). Especially for those getting out at the end of 1974, any all-stocks portfolios purchased in any year from 1949 on would have returned under 10% a year, and those purchased from 1959 on well under 5%. A key factor was the severe bear market of 1969–1970, followed by a weak and brief recovery in which the majority of stocks failed to regain the lost ground before the bears rampaged even more violently in 1973–1974. However, in 1974, as in nearly all years that would have left you with cyclically poor returns, those able to hold on for another two years before getting out would have seen a marked improvement in their average return.

The big table on returns does not consider the commissions paid to acquire the stocks. Fees paid to brokers will naturally lower your actual return, especially for short investment periods or for those who switch stocks frequently. For the steady long-term investor, however, the differences in the percentage yield are far smaller.

This is illustrated in Table 30-2, which takes investment periods of various lengths (but all ending in 1991) and compares the commission-free return with the equivalent return if $6 out of every $100 originally invested had gone for commissions or other transaction fees. No additional charges were computed for the reinvestment of dividends — but, then, many companies offer free automatic dividend reinvestment, as do most mutual funds.

Table 30-2: Impact of Commissions on Total Returns

Investment Period	With No Commission	Compounded Annual Rate of Return With $6 Transaction Fee per $100 Initial Investment
66 years	12.80	12.70
60	15.76	15.65
50	15.31	15.18
40	13.28	13.12
30	12.44	12.22
25	13.37	13.11
20	13.58	13.25
15	16.29	15.84
10	15.18	14.51
5	9.68	8.41
3	10.15	8.03
2	6.97	3.90
1	38.89	31.03

For investment periods ending December 31, 1991, based on acquisition of one share of each NYSE-listed stock and reinvestment of all dividends

For the full 66 years from 1925 through 1991, this charge would lower the average annual return only a tiny fraction, from 12.80% to 12.70%. The difference is still quite small at 20 years, and moderate at 10 years, but comes to more than a percentage point at 5 years. And for the single year 1991 (an excellent but far from unique year for the total market; it ranks 13th among the 66 one-year periods in the CRSP table), the pre-commission return of 38.9% is cut to 31.0%. That's because, in that brief period, you first had to earn $6 per $100 merely to get back the commission, before you could realize any actual income; also because only $94 of your $100 were available to go to work for you.

CRSP itself has no current data available that factor in commissions. However, an extensive study by Professors Lorie and Fisher covering the years through 1975 showed only minor differences for periods longer than 5 years. All this does not mean that commissions and other investment costs are immaterial; it simply indicates that you can take the comprehensive table as a pretty good guideline to the range of returns that have been available to the long-term investor.

The tables also do not take account of any taxes due on dividends received or on any ultimate capital gain. Of course, many investment earnings can accumulate in tax-deferred programs such as IRAs and 401(k)s. In any case, the compound interest rates paid on bank savings and the advertised yields on most other kinds of investment don't take account of taxes, either.

Eyeballing the big "Rates of Return" table, you may readily agree that, taking all stocks together, the investment returns over the years have been most impressive. "But," you may ask, "what about specific stocks, like the ones I might have picked?"

Well, CRSP did look into the question of how often and how much an investor might have gained or lost on each and every stock listed on the exchange from 1926 to 1960. While this study has not been updated, there is no reason to believe results would change materially.

The center computed results for every possible combination of month-end purchase and sale dates for every stock throughout the 35-year period from January 1926 to December 1960. This meant 87,000 monthly combinations for any one stock. For the entire group of NYSE stocks, it required tabulating more than 56 million possible transactions.

This study again assumed reinvestment of all dividends. But, unlike the data reported in our Table 30-1, it also took account of the broker-age commissions you would have paid on both purchase and sale.

The key finding: If you had picked a stock at random from the Big Board list, and then randomly picked a purchase and a sale date within the 1926–1960 period, you would have made money 78% of the time. The median return would have been 9.8% per annum compounded annually. At that rate of interest, money doubles in about seven years. In other words, during the 1926–1960 period, investors would have had a 50-50 chance of doubling their money every seven years with purely random selection.

The study also found that the risk of investors losing as much as 20% a year on their investment in any one stock was only one in 13, whereas their expectation of making as much as 20% per annum compounded annually was one in five.

And probably even more significant to any investor: by picking three or four stocks at random instead of just one, the risk of loss would have been considerably reduced, and the probability of a solid profit would have been considerably improved.

The advantage of relatively modest diversification is documented by another study conducted by CRSP a couple of decades ago. It sought to determine how large a portfolio has to be for an investor to be reasonably sure of matching the returns reported in the all-stocks table. The study, covering 1926 to 1965 and various interim periods, calculated results for portfolios, selected at random, that consisted of two, eight, 16, 32, and 128 stocks. By the time you expanded your portfolio to eight stocks, the study found, you should have been able to at least approximate the all-stock return in 94 cases out of every 100.

None of these studies guarantees anything about future investment success. But if you are willing to assume that the past is any kind of a guide to the future, their meaning is plain.

And since these studies cover all the stocks listed on the New York Stock Exchange, the results may be considered representative of what you might have expected to achieve, on the average, selecting stocks at random. This is sometimes called the dartboard method — figuratively, at least, you pin the stock table from the *Wall Street Journal* to the wall, and throw darts at it to make your picks. A fancier academic name for this procedure is *random walk*. The reasoning behind this concept is not that there's some extraterrestrial magic force that controls events, but rather that there's an *efficient market*. In essence, this theory holds that the price of stocks continuously reflects just about all the information obtainable as well as all potential investors' reactions to that information. It's the constant interaction and competition among traders and analysts, all seeking to maximize their returns, that makes the market "efficient." The corollary for the true believer is that it's difficult even for the well-trained professional manager to consistently outperform the market.

While there's debate about the validity of these concepts, the facts and figures of the random walk have been accepted in financial and academic circles as establishing the standard yardsticks against which various market theories can be measured.

The entry of scholars into the field of stock market research may not guarantee that someday the touchstone to investment success will be found. But it should go a long way toward disabusing the public of misplaced confidence in those who loudly proclaim the investment infallibility of their particular formulas.

In this connection, Professor Lorie, who long guided the crisp progress of CRSP, reiterates for today some observations made long ago:

"Many people have been beguiled by the possibility of buying wealth, believing that it is possible to buy information or formulas which will permit extraordinary high rates of return on capital. As evidence for my statement, one need only look at any issue of the numerous periodicals dealing with the stock market; they are thickly strewn with offers to sell for a few dollars the secret of getting rich. It should be clear that one cannot buy wealth for a few dollars, but this is not the same as saying that research on the stock market is without value or that it cannot provide the basis for the more prudent management of funds.

"For many years, it was probably true that formal and quantitative research was not very useful either because of its lack of comprehensiveness or its lack of rigor. It was very difficult to do comprehensive financial research before the availability of high-speed computers. Rigor was frequently or even typically lacking because research was usually the product of persons familiar with the financial markets under investigation but not the canons of scientific inquiry. . . .

"It is clear that much of the work done so far [at CRSP] has had the effect of discrediting beliefs — and even some relatively sophisticated ones — about the behavior of security prices. . . .

"For the businessman and investor, it is true that an awareness of ignorance is better than an erroneous belief, if only because it tends to eliminate buying the services of charlatans and attending to the insignificant."

Whatever the academic arguments, all the available statistics do seem to point to a common stock portfolio as a sound vehicle for *long-term* investment growth.

CHAPTER 31

Why You Should Invest — If You Can

WHY should a person who has extra money invest it in stocks?

The massive array of statistics in the previous chapter documented the impressive average return that long-term investors could have realized during almost any part of the past two-thirds of a century, if they bought and then kept reinvesting their dividend income. It's a truism that plowing back any income you receive is the best and fastest way of building up a nest egg — that, after all, is the magic of compound interest.

But what about those who can't or don't want to tie up the dividends they receive in a reinvestment program — who say, "Okay, we're ready to put this much money into stocks today, but we want to be free to spend the dividend checks as they come in." How does history show these people were likely to make out?

The table on page 303 (and the graphic rendering of this data on page 304) give an answer from their perspective.

First, you'd no doubt want to know, what would have happened to the capital you entrusted to the market — that is, how would your portfolio have fared over the years. That's told in the first column of the table and the white line on the graph. They show the movement of stock prices from 1926 to 1993, as measured by Standard & Poor's Industrials index. (Note that here we use the *average* price for each year rather than the *year-end* price. Also, the index is computed from the total market value of each stock, which means the stocks of big

Table 31-1: Market Movement and Current Income
Based on Standard & Poor's Industrials Index
Index Values (Market Prices) are the Average for Each Year

Year	Index Yearly Average	Yield %	Divd. Payout $	Year	Index Yearly Average	Yield %	Divd. Payout $
1926	10.04	4.86	0.49	1960	59.43	3.36	2.00
1927	12.53	4.73	0.59	1961	69.99	2.90	2.03
1928	16.92	3.93	0.66	1962	65.54	3.32	2.18
1929	21.35	3.61	0.77	1963	73.39	3.12	2.29
1930	16.42	4.84	0.79	1964	86.19	2.96	2.55
1931	10.51	6.40	0.67	1965	93.48	2.94	2.75
1932	5.37	7.74	0.42	1966	91.08	3.32	3.02
1933	7.61	4.06	0.31	1967	99.18	3.07	3.04
1934	9.00	3.37	0.30	1968	107.50	2.91	3.13
1935	10.13	3.52	0.36	1969	107.10	3.07	3.29
1936	14.69	3.39	0.50	1970	91.29	3.62	3.30
1937	14.97	4.83	0.72	1971	108.40	2.94	3.19
1938	11.39	4.96	0.56	1972	121.80	2.61	3.18
1939	11.77	3.87	0.46	1973	120.50	2.79	3.36
1940	10.69	5.51	0.59	1974	92.91	4.13	3.84
1941	9.72	6.62	0.64	1975	96.54	3.96	3.82
1942	8.78	7.04	0.62	1976	114.30	3.48	3.98
1943	11.49	4.76	0.55	1977	108.40	4.43	4.80
1944	12.34	4.69	0.58	1978	106.20	5.06	5.37
1945	14.72	4.13	0.61	1979	114.80	5.20	5.97
1946	16.48	3.81	0.63	1980	134.50	4.95	6.66
1947	14.85	4.90	0.73	1981	144.20	4.90	7.07
1948	15.34	5.47	0.84	1982	133.60	5.48	7.32
1949	15.00	6.63	0.99	1983	180.50	4.04	7.29
1950	18.33	6.69	1.23	1984	181.30	4.05	7.34
1951	22.68	6.17	1.40	1985	207.80	3.76	7.81
1952	24.78	5.88	1.46	1986	262.20	3.09	8.10
1953	24.84	5.86	1.46	1987	330.90	2.62	8.67
1954	30.25	4.92	1.49	1988	306.70	3.14	9.63
1955	42.40	3.97	1.68	1989	370.30	3.01	11.15
1956	49.80	3.95	1.97	1990	390.90	3.16	12.35
1957	47.63	4.18	1.99	1991	445.82	2.82	12.57
1958	49.36	3.87	1.91	1992	490.57	2.61	12.78
1959	61.45	3.11	1.91	1993	517.13	2.42	12.51

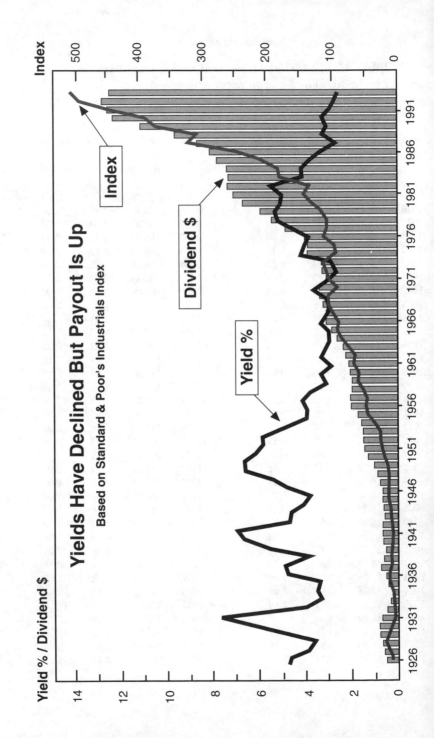

companies have much greater influence on the movement of the index.)

As you'd expect, the early going, through the calamitous Great Depression of the 1930s, was rocky. But from then on the trend has been decisively and often steeply up. Not that there weren't times when it was hard for investors to be enthusiastic about investing. It's hard to forget the October 1987 crash, when the market lost one-fourth of its value in two trading days. And during the sharp slump of 1973–1974, the Dow Jones Industrials dropped 45% and many individual stocks fared considerably worse.

All told, since the end of World War II there've been nine slumps in which the market lost at least 20% — all of them scary at the time, with investors wondering whether this marked a decisive turning point, whether the long line of progress in our economy would finally be broken, as had seemed to be the case in the depression. Each time there appeared to be good arguments for caution, for pulling in your horns — and, especially, for kicking yourself for having "missed the boat" by not having heavily invested during what you were now afraid was the last big bull market.

Of course, there can never be a guarantee as to what lies ahead, but the historical record so far shows that the market has always come back, and that in the long run common stocks have proved to be good things to own. Again, it's important to remember that the index measures performance of a large group, and results of specific stocks vary from much better to disastrously worse. However, if you held stocks that matched the performance of the S&P Industrials index, you can see that your portfolio would have multiplied 24-fold since the heyday of 1929 and more than seven-fold since the Kennedy inaugural in 1961, nearly quintupled since 1968 (when the long postwar bull market seemed to have topped out), and risen 3.8-fold since the start of the 1980s. All this, without the benefit of reinvesting your dividends, which would have substantially added to these returns.

Perhaps even more meaningful for the average investor is how you would have fared during specific time periods. If you had bought a stock that mirrored the S&P Industrials at its average price in 1968, 10 years later the value of your holdings would have been down slightly (1.2%), but if you held on for an 11th year, 1979 would have seen you 6.4% ahead. And in each and every other year throughout the postwar period, if you bought a stock matching the index, 10 years later you would have shown a gain. And that's in addition to the dividend checks you received.

So, now, let's take a look at the cash income you received while you were holding the stocks. The table's second column and the black line in the graph show the *yield* realized each year on the stocks in the index. You will quickly note that the figures jiggle a bit up or down from year to year, but, in general, the percentages in the past few decades seem to be stingier than they were early on. To be precise, the average yield between 1926 and 1955 was just over 5%; between 1956 and 1993 it averaged barely 3.5%.

Is that cause for concern?

No, it isn't. The yields are percentages figured by dividing dollar dividends by dollar prices for the stocks included in the index, and it's the *relationship* between the two that counts. Hence, a *decline in the average yield* can result *either from dividends being slashed* or omitted — as happened during the depression and World War II and, to a minor extent, in some postwar recessions — *or from a rise in the price of the stocks*. The latter explanation is clearly the one that applies to most of our experience of the past 45 years.

That's strikingly documented by the last column of our table and the bars that make up the shaded area of the graph. They trace the actual dividend payouts applicable to the index. Assume, for instance, that back in 1950, when the yield on the index came to a postwar high of 6.7 percent, you could have bought a share of stock exactly representative of the index for $18.33. That year your stock would have paid a dividend of $1.23. In 1993 you would have had to settle for a yield a mere two-fifths of what you enjoyed four decades earlier. But the value of your hypothetical stock had meantime risen to $517 and paid you a dividend of $12.51. That comes to just 2.4% of the current market value, but equals 68% of the $18.33 that was all you actually invested in that security. And that impressive result was attained even though the 1993 payout was down nearly 30¢ from 1992 (the first dividend decline in 10 years, largely due to massive restructurings by IBM and a number of other corporate giants).

There's an important distinction to be observed here between current and historic value and returns. Aside from tax considerations, it doesn't matter at what price you bought a stock when you are considering whether to hold or sell it. What counts is what price you can get for that stock today and how that compares in value with other investment possibilities — what it will give you in terms of earning power and income. Of course, you'll factor in not only today's earnings and dividends, but what you expect them to be in future. You're willing to pay more for a stock you think will double its earnings (and, especially for the income-minded, sharply increase its dividend payout) than for a stock with equal earnings and dividends now but whose future outlook is at best flat and perhaps downhill. That's why people are usually willing to pay a premium in terms of price/earnings multiples and to accept a lower yield for so-called growth stocks. In short, it's important to evaluate not only today but also the prospects of tomorrow.

And that offers a clue to the real significance of what these figures tell us. Because, after all, today is the tomorrow of yesterday. And simply matching the record of the S&P Industrials since the yesterday of 1950 would not only have multiplied the value of your stock 28-fold by 1993, but by now would be paying you close to 70% a year on the money you had invested. By contrast, if you had invested the same $18 in a savings account in 1950 (and similarly assuming that you withdrew your interest each year), today the account would still contain just $18, while your recent interest receipts would have run around 5% a year (and in 1994 most likely under 3%) on the amount you originally invested.

That's why, based on the historic record, stocks on the whole are attractive for those who can afford the risks and the cycles. Traditionally such investors could count over the long term on an increase in both the value of their assets and in their current income.

There's another persuasive reason for investing in stocks. We've become accustomed to the cost of living going up incessantly — it's only a question of by how much. As the purchasing power of the dollar declines, it obviously takes more greenbacks to buy the same amount of food, clothing, services, virtually everything. And, over time, that tends to include common stocks, which, after all, represent ownership of companies that produce these now more expensive goods and services.

This means that money invested in common stocks or other property is not as likely to lose its purchasing power as money simply set aside in a savings bank or invested in bonds that have a fixed dollar value. Not that anyone can guarantee inflation protection. And you shouldn't look for inflation and stock prices to move in sync. In particular, when inflation is at its most virulent, the stock market is apt to get discouraged and perform poorly. That happened soon after World War II, and even more strikingly in the early 1970s and around the start of the 1980s. But generally, once inflation settled down, the market got a second wind and moved briskly ahead. So, when all the results are in, it's hard to find a better hedge against inflation than common stocks.

For some powerful evidence, look at the data in Table 31-2, compiled by Ibbotson Associates of Chicago, which is led by Professor Roger Ibbotson, now at Yale, who is a veteran of Professor Lorie's University of Chicago seminars. It shows, decade by decade, the average annual compounded return (for these computations, we are back to assuming reinvestment of all dividends and interest) of several categories of equities and fixed-income securities. The principal common stock representation in this study is provided by the Standard & Poor's 500 index (or its predecessors), which, as we've pointed out, is dominated by America's corporate elite, the big-capitalization stocks. But Ibbotson also presented the results of an index of small-company stocks, made up of the 20% of NYSE-listed stocks with the lowest market value.

For the full 68-year period from 1926 through 1993, the small stocks, with an average 14.1% return, outperformed the biggies with their 10.6%. But the small stocks also were much more volatile. On a year-to-year basis their fluctuations were some 65% sharper than

Table 31-2: Average Annual Return over the Decades for Various Categories of Securities

	1926–1929	1930s	1940s	1950s	1960s	1970s	1980s	1990–1993	Total Period 1926–1992
S&P 500	19.2%	0.0%	9.2%	19.4%	7.8%	5.9%	17.5%	10.6%	10.3%
Small Company	−4.5	1.4	20.7	16.9	15.5	11.5	15.8	14.1	12.4
Long-Term Corp.	5.2	6.9	2.7	1.0	1.7	6.2	13.0	12.2	5.6
Long-Term Gov't	5.0	4.9	3.2	−0.1	1.4	5.5	12.6	12.8	5.5
Intermed-Term Gov't	4.2	4.6	1.8	1.3	3.5	7.0	11.9	10.9	5.3
Treasury Bills	3.7	0.6	0.4	1.9	3.9	6.3	8.9	4.9	3.7
Inflation Rate	−1.1	−2.0	5.4	2.2	2.5	7.4	5.1	3.7	3.1

Source: *Ibbotson Associates*

those of the big stocks. Over ten-year intervals (i.e., 1926–1935, 1927–1936), the small-stock volatility still proved some 40% higher — even though, by a quirky happenstance, the specific 10-year periods starting with a "0" year like 1930 and 1940 (the "decades" shown in our table) turned out to be no more volatile than the equivalent big-stocks results. (However, don't bet the farm — or your IRA — that when the "nineties" are done, they'll mark a similar exception to what by then will be a 75-year pattern.) In any case, for the long-term investor, the long-term results count far more than the interim fluctuations. All in all, weighing the historically higher return along with the higher volatility suggests that *if* you can afford somewhat greater than average risk and have a sufficiently long investment horizon, you might well consider putting a fair share of your money into the smaller stocks — perhaps through some of the index-type mutual funds that concentrate on such stocks.

The real importance of the table, however, is its demonstration that both groups of common stocks — both over the long term and in virtually every decade — far outperformed the other investment groups, and also were the groups that most consistently stayed ahead of inflation (with only a slight lag for the S&P in the 1970s and for the small stocks in the brief initial period from 1926 to 1929).

For all these reasons — for income, for a chance to see your capital grow, for the protection of its purchasing power — you may decide you want to invest in stocks.

But wait a minute. Remember, there is an inescapable factor of risk in owning stocks, even the best of them. Not only does the market go down from time to time, but even if stocks generally go up, your stocks may go down. That can be a risk well worth taking if you aren't going to be seriously hurt in case you lose some of those invested dollars. What's more, it's a risk that it has become well nigh essential to take in order to achieve some of your long-term objectives, especially for part of your retirement needs. But it's not a risk that a person should take with dollars that may be needed in case of some short-term emergency.

What if there were a serious and expensive illness in your family?

Are your savings and insurance adequate to meet that situation? What if you must look for new employment? What about the other expenses you may have to meet, including mortgage and credit payments, unforeseen repairs, and the like? What about enough life insurance to provide for your family if you're not there?

Once you can answer yes to these questions, you can, and probably should, consider putting some of your dollars regularly into common stocks.

CHAPTER 32

Can You "Beat the Market"?

ISN'T there any system to "beat the market," any system that will protect you against price fluctuations and virtually guarantee you a profit over the long run?

Regrettably, there are no foolproof systems. But there are methods that at least point up some important lessons about successful investing and that can significantly increase the odds of coming out ahead. Most prominent is the system called *dollar cost averaging.*

Dollar cost averaging simply involves putting the same amount of money — $200, $500, $1,000 — into the same stock, regardless of its price movement, at regular intervals — say, every month or every six months — over a long period of time. That was the basis of the New York Stock Exchange's original Monthly Investment Plan back in the 1950s and of the various stock accumulation plans that have come along since, including not only individual stocks but also the regular purchase plans available in most mutual funds.

Following a system of investing a fixed sum of money in the same stock at regular intervals, you could have made a profit on a significant majority of the stocks listed on the New York Stock Exchange over almost any period of five or 10 years you might want to pick in the postwar era.

Dollar cost averaging works by taking advantage of an elementary arithmetic principle. If you put up the same amount of money each purchase date, you get more shares for your money when the stock is low in price than you do when the price is higher, and that drives down your *average cost per share*.

Suppose you bought $500 worth of a particular stock when it was selling at $10 a share, another $500 worth three months later when it was $9, another $500 worth at $8, and so on, while the stock fell to $5. Suppose after that it rose gradually to $15, then settled back to $10. If you then sold out, you'd realize a profit of about 10%, ignoring both dividends and commission costs — despite the fact that the average price on the 21 days on which you made your purchases was precisely $10, and that's the price at which you sold. You don't believe it?

Don't bother to figure it out, because the proof is in the table on page 314.

To avoid the complication of fractional shares of stock, we assumed that at each purchase price level you put up a little more or a little less than $500 — whatever was needed to buy a whole number of shares.

All told, you paid $10,495, and your holdings at the end would be worth $11,510, a gain of $1,015, or almost 10%. Exactly the same end result — again exclusive of all dividends and purchase costs — would be achieved if the stock first rose steadily from $10 to $15, then dropped to $5, and after that came back to $10. Table 32-2 on page 315 shows the figures on this second scenario.

On the way, there'd be differences. If your stock drops first and then comes back, you'll show a loss after your first few purchases, but as soon as the stock reached $7 on its recovery path, you'd enter the profit column and stay there the rest of the way. If the stock rose first to $15, and then gradually slipped to $5, you'd have early profits but then start falling behind, and not catch up with the first scenario (or have a profit again) until the final investment in our example. However, all of the time in both scenarios, your average cost per share would be below the average of your purchase prices — or lower than if you had bought a fixed number of shares on each investment date.

Table 32-1: The Advantages of Dollar Averaging—Scenario 1

		Investing Same Dollar Amount Each Time						Buying Same Number of Shares Each Time					
Price per Share	Number Shares Bought	Cost of Shares	Number Shares Owned	Average Price/Share	Cumul. Cost of Shares	Total Value of Shares	Gain or Loss	Cost If 50 Shares Bought	Cumul. Cost	Cumul. Shares	Average Price/Share	Market Value	Gain or Loss
$10	50	$500	50	$10.00	$ 500	$ 500	$ 0	$500	$ 500	50	$10.00	$ 500	$ 0
9	56	504	106	9.47	1004	954	−50	450	950	100	9.50	900	−50
8	63	504	169	8.92	1508	1352	−156	400	1350	150	9.00	1200	−150
7	71	497	240	8.35	2005	1680	−325	350	1700	200	8.50	1400	−300
6	83	498	323	7.75	2503	1938	−565	300	2000	250	8.00	1500	−500
5	100	500	423	7.10	3003	2115	−888	250	2250	300	7.50	1500	−750
6	83	498	506	6.92	3501	3036	−465	300	2550	350	7.29	2100	−450
7	71	497	577	6.93	3998	4039	41	350	2900	400	7.25	2800	−100
8	63	504	640	7.03	4502	5120	618	400	3300	450	7.33	3600	300
9	56	504	696	7.19	5006	6264	1258	450	3750	500	7.50	4500	750
10	50	500	746	7.38	5506	7460	1954	500	4250	550	7.73	5500	1250
11	45	495	791	7.59	6001	8701	2700	550	4800	600	8.00	6600	1800
12	42	504	833	7.81	6505	9996	3491	600	5400	650	8.31	7800	2400
13	38	494	871	8.04	6999	11323	4324	650	6050	700	8.64	9100	3050
14	36	504	907	8.27	7503	12698	5195	700	6750	750	9.00	10500	3750
15	33	495	940	8.51	7998	14100	6102	750	7500	800	9.38	12000	4500
14	36	504	976	8.71	8502	13664	5162	700	8200	850	9.65	11900	3700
13	38	494	1014	8.87	8996	13182	4186	650	8850	900	9.83	11700	2850
12	42	504	1056	9.00	9500	12672	3172	600	9450	950	9.95	11400	1950
11	45	495	1101	9.08	9995	12111	2116	550	10000	1000	10.00	11000	1000
10	50	500	1151	9.12	10495	11510	1015	500	10500	1050	10.00	10500	0

Table 32-2: The Advantages of Dollar Averaging—Scenario 2

| | | Investing Same Dollar Amount Each Time | | | | | | Buying Same Number of Shares Each Time | | | | | |
Price per Share	Number Shares Bought	Cost of Shares	Number Shares Owned	Average Price/ Share	Cumul. Cost of Shares	Total Value of Shares	Gain or Loss	Cost If 50 Shares Bought	Cumul. Cost	Cumul. Shares	Average Price/ Share	Market Value	Gain or Loss
$10	50	$500	50	$10.00	$ 500	$ 500	$0	$500	$ 500	50	$10.00	$ 500	$0
11	45	495	95	10.47	995	1045	50	550	1050	100	10.50	1100	50
12	42	504	137	10.94	1499	1644	145	600	1650	150	11.00	1800	150
13	38	494	175	11.39	1993	2275	282	650	2300	200	11.50	2600	300
14	36	504	211	11.83	2497	2954	457	700	3000	250	12.00	3500	500
15	33	495	244	12.26	2992	3660	663	750	3750	300	12.50	4500	750
14	36	504	280	12.49	3496	3920	424	700	4450	350	12.71	4900	450
13	38	494	318	12.55	3990	4134	144	650	5100	400	12.75	5200	100
12	42	504	360	12.48	4494	4320	-174	600	5700	450	12.67	5400	-300
11	45	495	405	12.32	4989	4455	-534	550	6250	500	12.50	5500	-750
10	50	500	455	12.06	5489	4550	-939	500	6750	550	12.27	5500	-1250
9	56	504	511	11.73	5993	4599	-1394	450	7200	600	12.00	5400	-1800
8	63	504	574	11.32	6497	4592	-1905	400	7600	650	11.69	5200	-2400
7	71	497	645	10.84	6994	4515	-2479	350	7950	700	11.36	4900	-3050
6	83	498	728	10.29	7492	4368	-3124	300	8250	750	11.00	4500	-3750
5	100	500	828	9.65	7992	4140	-3852	250	8500	800	10.63	4000	-4500
6	83	498	911	9.32	8490	5466	-3024	300	8800	850	10.35	5100	-3700
7	71	497	982	9.15	8987	6874	-2113	350	9150	900	10.17	6300	-2850
8	63	504	1045	9.08	9491	8360	-1131	400	9550	950	10.05	7600	-1950
9	56	504	1101	9.08	9995	9909	-86	450	10000	1000	10.00	9000	-1000
10	50	500	1151	9.12	10495	11510	1015	500	10500	1050	10.00	10500	0

Incidentally, if you had bought exactly 50 shares (instead of $500 worth of stock) on each investment date, you would have done somewhat better than our dollar averagers for the first few investment periods, while the stock price went straight down (scenario 1) or up (scenario 2), but once these initial trends reversed, you'd quickly fall behind and all the rest of the way would show consistently poorer results than the dollar averagers. (You can see the detailed period-by-period results in the righthand portion of Table 32-1; the same pattern, with end result of $0 gain versus a $1,015 gain under dollar averaging, would apply with the second scenario.)

Thus, the tables drive home how dollar cost averaging works, and why it tends to work *for* you. The system can't guarantee you a profit, nor will sticking with it necessarily give you the best possible result (you'll note that, in the first table, if you had sold out after the stock fell to $5 and recovered to $10, you would have made a profit of $1,954, or about 35%, instead of the roughly 10% realized at the end). And, of course, no stock is likely to follow the neat, step-at-a-time pattern we used here for illustration purposes. But dollar cost averaging *will* lower your average costs and is an excellent way to turn the inevitable fluctuations of the market to your advantage — as long as you have confidence in the ultimate value of the stock.

So if the stock you buy drops in price and you have the confidence to believe that it will come back, as stocks — in general, though not necessarily in particular — always have, you would do well to continue buying it as it slides on down. This is called *averaging down*. It's a technique investors should keep in mind when they're worried about the decline in price of some stock they own. Indeed, true believers in dollar averaging should cheer (though it admittedly goes against the psychological grain) for the stocks they select to stay low or even decline in price during their early purchases, so they will have more shares with which to enjoy the long-term price increase that they expect.

One big catch to this system of beating the market is that you've got to have both the cash and the courage to buy the same dollar amount of your stock at whatever interval of time you've fixed on, be it every month, every three months, or every year.

And when it drops, you've got to keep right on buying, in order to pick up the low-cost shares that can later build up your profit. Unfortunately, when stocks are down, the average person's bank account may be down, too. So investors may not be able to afford to buy at just the time they should. And if you have to liquidate your holdings at such a time, it might even result in a loss.

More often, however, it's not lack of cash but simply a case of hesitation to keep investing when the climate has turned chilly — and that's the biggest threat to the success of dollar-averaging programs. You shouldn't ignore the risks, but, to repeat, the whole concept depends on buying more shares when prices are low. And most times, dollar cost averaging does work *over the long pull* because the long-term trend of the stock market has been upward.

Table 32-3 on page 318 shows how dollar cost averaging would have worked for 20 popular stocks over a 42-year period starting at year end 1949. It assumes an annual investment of $1,000 in each stock plus reinvestment of all dividends received during the year. The computer figured each share "purchase" to four decimal places (as is done in most stock accumulation programs), but to keep the table simple, we only show the end result to the nearest whole number of shares, and also leave out tax and commission costs.

Over the 42-year period, you would have multiplied your investment in each of the stocks. In the aggregate, the $835,000 invested in the 20 stocks (including the $37,000 put into RCA before it was acquired) would have grown to $19.1 million. However, the total market value at the end of 1991 would have ranged from barely over $200,000 for Union Carbide and USX to over $1 million for Consolidated Edison, General Electric, and IBM — and over $2 million for Exxon. A special case is Xerox, which was a virtually unknown company in 1949 (all the other 19 were established blue chips back then); thanks largely to fantastic growth in the late 1950s and 1960s, the $42,000 dollar-averaging investment in Xerox would have been worth over $8 million at the end of 1991.

Contributing heavily to the success of these regular-investment programs are reinvested dividends, which, with rare exceptions, kept

Table 32-3: Forty-two Years of Cumulative Investing

Company	Share Price	Shares Held	Ending Market Value as of 12/31/91	Dividends Rein-vested	Capital Appreciation	Ye u Neg Re
Alum Co of Amer	$64.38	5,564	$ 358,183	$ 118,121	$ 198,062	
Amer Tel & Tel	°	°	771,123	313,032	416,091	
Caterpillar Inc	43.88	10,047	440,809	241,217	157,593	
Consolidated Edison	28.63	40,459	1,158,147	504,879	611,268	
Dow Chemical	53.75	15,303	822,515	281,807	498,708	
Eastman Kodak	48.25	11,095	535,322	239,643	253,679	
Exxon Corp	60.88	33,627	2,047,014	671,648	1,333,366	
General Electric	76.50	14,233	1,088,823	232,020	814,804	
General Motors	28.88	12,374	357,288	336,264	(20,976)	
Goodyear Tire	53.50	15,537	831,246	294,798	494,448	
IBM	89.00	12,982	1,155,440	651,112	462,328	
Minnesota Mining	95.25	12,313	1,172,809	304,780	826,029	
Pacific Gas & Elec	32.50	25,474	827,907	374,541	411,366	
Philips Petroleum	24.00	30,699	736,785	283,762	411,023	
RCA Corp	°°	°°	666,440	327,171	302,269	
Sears Roebuck	37.88	10,153	384,543	205,695	136,848	
Union Carbide	20.25	10,269	207,950	135,804	30,146	
USX Corp	°°°	°°°	201,185	140,489	18,696	
Westinghouse Elec	18.00	24,543	441,780	215,581	184,198	
Xerox	68.50	121,971	8,355,014	3,843,557	4,469,458	
			$22,560,322	$9,715,918	$12,009,404	

° AT&T totals include value of regional telephone companies received in 1984 split-up o System. From 1984 on, assumes annual investment of $125 in AT&T and $125 in each of the "Baby Bell" companies.

°° RCA was acquired by General Electric in 1986 for $66.50 per RCA share. The 6,648 shares, worth $442,107, held as of then were assumed to be reinvested in Treasury bills until 31, 1989. However, no new annual investments were made. Thus, total investments in RCA $37,000, compared with $42,000 in all the other stocks listed.

°°° USX Corp in May 1991 issued 1/5 share USX-U.S. Steel Group for each USX share held, the USX shares themselves were renamed USX-Marathon Group. Table shows combined va the U.S. Steel and Marathon Groups.

growing significantly because each year there were more shares on which to earn dividends. For the entire 20-stock portfolio, dividends accounted for 43% of the total gains. Even so, every one of the stocks had a number of years with a "negative return" — in which the value of your investment went down because the dividend income that year was less than the decline in market price.

Indeed, in Xerox you would have fared even better had you dropped your investment plan at the end of 1972 when your holdings would have been worth $7.7 million. Subsequently, even with continued investment, you would have been down to $2.7 million in 1982; while a big jump in the Xerox stock price in 1991 would finally have enabled you to top the 1972 investment value, had you instead "cashed out" in 1972 and invested the proceeds in Treasuries, you would have been further ahead. And in IBM, your holdings would have been worth $400,000 more in 1985 than at the end of 1991. While the calculations for the table end with 1991, a spot check indicates the investor would have enjoyed moderate to substantial increases in 1992 and 1993 in the great majority of these stocks, especially when factoring in dividend reinvestment and the annual new investment of $1,000. The spectacular exception would have been IBM; however, your stock, worth close to $800,000 at the end of 1993, would still represent a solid long-term return on a $44,000 investment.

Actually, all this reiterates the key point about dollar averaging. You can't tell when a stock gets to its low and high, but if you keep on investing steadily, your consistency is apt to be rewarded even if your stock is not one of the most spectacular performers. Even in some stocks, such as Sears and USX, that have performed rather indifferently for a long time, the accumulation plan would still show positive results. Over the years you would have picked up so much stock that your total value would tend to be fairly substantial even when the price per share goes down.

The general rule is fine, but then there's always the chance you end up with one of the exceptions. How do you know whether to keep the dollar-averaging faith with a stock like Chrysler, which made a spectacular comeback after the government-assisted bailout in the late 1970s (and whose stock has roller-coastered several times since), or to bail out of a Penn-Central, whose bankruptcy in 1974 ended with old shareholders receiving but ⅕ of a new share, or out of some of the once well-regarded S&Ls whose stock turned totally worthless? Unfortunately, there are no sure signs, though it helps to stay well informed.

And even if you have limited funds, it's wise to diversify. If you have three or four stocks considered of good quality, the odds are strong that even if one fails, the accumulating gains in the others will keep you well ahead.

Also, a broad-based equity mutual fund appears well suited for a long-term accumulation program. You can be fairly confident the general market will come back, even if a particular stock doesn't.

If you had made a similar $1,000-a-year investment (plus reinvestment of dividends) over 42 years in a fund matching the Standard & Poor's 500 or its predecessor index, the $42,000 you put in would have grown to $960,000 by the end of 1991 — better than the growth attained by two-thirds the individual companies in our table. And sticking around for two more years would have lifted you to $1.1 million in 1993. The figures are based on the rates of returns for each year shown in the Ibbotson Associates' *Stocks, Bonds, Bills, and Inflation 1993 Yearbook*. The equivalent result for the Ibbotson "Small Company Stocks" group (consisting of the 20% of Big Board stocks with the lowest market value each year) would leave you with nearly $2.2 million at the end of 1991 and almost $3.3 million after 1993. Clearly, the small stocks offered a far higher total return over these forty-some years, but, as might be expected, they also were far more volatile. In 12 of the 44 years, this small-stock portfolio would have grown by more than one-third compared with only three such years for the S&P group. But the small stocks also had five years in which the portfolio value dropped more than 15%, in contrast to only one such severe down-year for the S&P group.

Table 32-4 on page 321, which reports these long-term results, also

Table 32-4: Cumulative Investing in Stock and Bond Groups

Results of $1,000 a Year Invested in Each Group at Year End from 1949 through 1993
with Reinvestment of Dividends and Interest

	Market Value as of 12/31/93
Common Stocks	$1,137,586
Small Stocks	3,280,086
Corporate Bonds	326,984
Government Securities:	
Long-Term	296,800
Intermediate-Term	343,614
Treasury Bills	217,871

Computed by Neil Hecht, CPA, based on Rates of Return as published in Ibbotson Associates *Yearbook*. Definition of each group as defined by Ibbotson, using S&P 500 and predecessor indexes as a proxy for common stocks, and the lowest quintile of market values of NYSE-listed stocks for "small stocks."

shows what would have happened to similar $1,000-a-year investments in various fixed-income categories. In short-term Treasury bills you would have enjoyed maximum safety and uninterrupted growth — but total growth would have been modest. Over the full 44-year period, long-term government bonds wouldn't have done much better for you, because the big upsweep in interest rates since 1950 would too often have driven down the market value of your holdings. In fact, in all the fixed-income groups, your return over the years would have been far smaller than for the equity groups. This just reemphasizes the basic investment finding: For most people it's wise to have some money invested in securities that promise you a fixed income, but your long-term security probably requires substantial dependence on equities.

Is dollar-averaging always better than making one large investment? Of course, you'd be better off by investing the entire amount at the low point for the stock — the only little problem you have is picking the right date.

On the other hand, if you have the entire sum at hand — if, say, you suddenly find yourself with a $100,000 inheritance, and decide to put $60,000 into stocks — it would be silly to parcel it out in $1,000 monthly purchases over a five-year period. But to avoid putting in the entire sum at what could prove to be poor market timing, you might well consider investing $5,000 or $10,000 each month or quarter, while temporarily "parking" the balance in short-term Treasuries.

Basically, however, because few people have large sums they can put into the market at any one time, and because most stocks fluctuate quite widely from time to time, long-term dollar averaging is a handy system — and one that has paid off for most people most of the time.

Another procedure that's sometimes mentioned as an aid to investment performance is *formula investing*. It's not so much a system for trying to beat the market as it is a mechanical means of enforcing prudence and caution. Essentially, it's a mechanical approach to *asset allocation*, or proportionate distribution of your investment assets among different categories, such as stocks, bonds, and cash.

Formula plans generally call for buying more bonds and selling stocks when the stock market rises — on the assumption that stocks become increasingly vulnerable as prices advance — and reversing the procedure when the market drops.

You may, for instance, decide to keep a 50-50 balance between bonds and stocks in your portfolio. Thus, if stocks go up and consequently come to represent a larger percentage of your holdings, you'd take some of your stock profits and put them into bonds to restore the desired 50-50 ratio.

The impact of thus reducing your exposure to common stocks as the market rises and increasing it when it falls is multiplied if you also adjust your allocation formula in line with market moves. Thus, you might start out on a 50-50 basis, but decide that you'd keep only 40% of your funds in common stocks whenever the market moved up 25% from your starting point. Should the market advance an additional 25%, you would cut back your common-stock holdings to 30%. On the other hand, if the market fell, you would reverse the operation, raising your percentage of stockholdings.

Assume (strictly for the sake of simplifying this explanation) that bond prices hold steady and that the stocks you hold move in line with the overall market. If you start with $10,000 each in stocks and bonds and the market then rises 25%, you'd now have $12,500 in stocks. To get back to 50-50, you'd switch $1,250 from stocks to bonds, giving you $11,250 in each category. But if, instead, your formula calls for now lowering your stockholdings to 40%, you'd sell $3,500 worth of stocks and use that money to buy bonds. That would leave you with $9,000 in stocks while holding $13,500 (60% of your portfolio) in bonds.

The premise behind formula plans — that surging markets tend to become increasingly vulnerable, while depressed markets can offer buying opportunities — is basically sound. And it also makes sense to decide first how much of your assets to put in each investment category before selecting specific securities.

But formulas don't always work out as well as you would hope. For one, with all their big cyclical fluctuations, stock markets have generally trended up. Consequently, such formulas would keep cutting your long-term commitment to common stocks — the investment that over the years has proven the best protection against inflation. This is what soured many big institutions on the concept. Also, there are always so many variables affecting the outlook that a rigid formula can turn into more of a straitjacket than an aid to investment discipline. Sage advice here — as in most investment decisions — might be: Don't flipflop with every whim, but do stay flexible.

Most major brokerage firms and investment advisers issue recommendations on asset allocation, based on their assessment of current market, economic, and political conditions. You can find various views in investment magazines, and the *Wall Street Journal* periodically tabulates the suggestions of leading investment strategists. These can serve as a handy guide, which you can adjust to fit your own needs and predilections. Quite obviously, a young professional starting on an earnings career is apt to favor investment allocations that differ from those of a couple nearing retirement. And you probably should shift your emphasis as your personal conditions change.

The professional strategists will usually recommend proportions of assets to be placed in equities, fixed-income securities, and cash. ("Cash" of course means money funds, CDs, Treasuries, or other interest-bearing instruments where the cash earns its keep.) Some also make recommendations for a specific proportion of funds to be put into other assets, such as gold, real estate, insurance, collectibles. And beyond the division into major investment categories, many strategists also provide recommendations for subgroups, such as how much of the bond allotment to put into long-term and intermediate-term bonds; and, in the stock sector, which industry groups should be heavily represented (*overweighted*) or largely ignored (*under-weighted*).

Is it practical for the typical individual investor to pursue an asset allocation program? The answer is both yes and no. An institution with hundreds of millions of dollars in the market may be capable of constantly adjusting its precise percentage of investments in different groups and subgroups — but, *no*, it would be far too costly, cumbersome, and unproductive for you to go out each week or month to buy a little and sell a little in an effort to keep your portfolio aligned with some allocation percentage. At the same time, *yes*, it does make sense to keep track of how your portfolio divisions compare with your current investment plan. If you regularly add to your investments, you can direct the new funds into the category in which you're under-invested. And, yes, periodically, when the variation between your portfolio and your allocation plan becomes too wide, you might contemplate a switch of some funds — especially when you feel you should get out of a particular stock or bond anyway.

Putting at least part of your investments into mutual funds makes switching among investment categories easier (but even if you have liberal switching privileges within a family of mutual funds, resist the temptation to "fine-tune" by excessive moving around). And you might even find some mutual funds whose stated investment objective may be a balance among investment categories that's adjusted for changing conditions and pretty much matches your own objective.

In sum, while you probably neither want to nor could follow some neatly devised, precise formula, you can profit by paying heed to the underlying precept:

Keep an eye on market moves and let them act as a brake on your buying enthusiasm as they rise, and on your investment despair when they sink. Remember, no bull market lasts forever. And neither does a bear market.

CHAPTER 33

How You Should Invest — If You Can

THE stock you'd like to buy, of course, is the one that just doesn't exist. You'd like a stock that is completely safe, one that pays a generous dividend, and one that's bound to go up.

Okay, you've learned there are no absolute guarantees, so you'd settle for a high degree of safety, a fat dividend that's considered secure and likely to grow, and a stock with strong prospects for substantial, prolonged price increases. Even so, you're not likely to find such a "one-stock-fits-all" ideal.

There are a lot of good stocks that will probably satisfy you on one of these counts. But meeting all three of your objectives at once? Hardly.

If you want safety in a stock, you'll have to give way on your hopes that it will increase sensationally in value.

If you'd like to see your money grow, you have to be prepared to take a considerably greater measure of risk.

Sometimes it's possible to find either a fairly safe stock, or one that seems likely to appreciate in price, that will also yield you a better-than-average dividend. But even here, as a general rule, you can't have your cake and eat it too. If you get a liberal dividend, it will probably be at the expense of one of the other two factors.

Hence, the first step in solving your investment problem is to decide on the one objective that's most important to you. Is it safety of capital? Or high dividends? Or price appreciation?

Oh, sure, you're not going to give up your *desire* for all three. But you should sort out your priorities and then seek out the proper balance.

By the same token, while you can classify stocks by their predominant traits into such categories as growth or income or stability, there are many fine shadings and gradations. Most stocks, to some degree or other, possess a variety of attributes. You may feel this faces you with a bewildering range of choices, but it also can give you more choices that match your particular set of objectives.

Also, don't ignore the function of price. Remember, at some price even the most promising stock becomes too expensive, while at some level on the down side, a great many (though certainly not all) stocks can become reasonable speculations.

And even when your main interest is safety and stability, don't forget to take a look at an industry's and company's future prospects. Remember, the carriage industry was a thriving business at the turn of the century.

One of the most successful investment managers of recent times, Peter Lynch, maintains that alert individuals often have a better chance than the professionals to spot promising investment candidates. When you or your family or friends find a company that offers a new service or product that people find attractive and seems to be able to do so in an efficient manner, it's well worth investigating. And when you hear that customers are no longer delighted, because service has deteriorated, or there's better or more economical competition, you have an early warning that it may be time to sell.

That's good advice. So are the suggestions formulated by Benjamin Graham, often considered the father of modern security analysis, who believed in careful study of a company's financial status and trends to find securities that are undervalued. You don't have to do all the detailed digging — but an understanding of basic investment ideas (which we hope this book has given you) should enable you to check out the ideas provided you by brokerage firms or investment advisers.

Basically, what you're really after is an appropriate *mix* of securities — appropriate to *your* specific circumstances — and subject to change as the market and economic environments as well as your own needs change.

To see how these various factors might influence your own investment selections, consider the following hypothetical examples of how people in various circumstances might approach investing.

Since individual employers' programs vary so widely, these broad-brush portraits don't try to specify which part of the investments are made in company-sponsored or tax-advantaged plans and which in regular investment accounts. As a general rule, it's wise to funnel as large a portion of your investment dollars as you can afford into plans where you can use pre-tax dollars (so more money goes to work right away) and can defer taxes on investment-generated income (to keep more money at work). Especially, to the extent you can afford, take advantage of programs where your employer matches part of your contribution, as in many 401(k) and 403(b) plans.

At the same time, you'll want to keep some assets in accounts you can tap immediately without withdrawal penalties for emergencies or major expenditures. And if company programs are primarily in the company's own stock, you must recognize the extra risk of having both your job and your investments heavily dependent on one source. You might then want to be more conservative in the rest of your investments — perhaps choosing an "index" mutual fund for the equity portion, while placing a larger percentage than you otherwise would into a quality bond fund and a short-term cache of money funds and CDs.

You should also, of course, be prepared to adjust for changing investment conditions. The final text of this revised edition is being prepared in spring 1994, while short-term interest rates are still near lowest-in-a-generation levels. People can't count on the ample returns on money funds and CDs to which they became accustomed in the 1980s. At this stage, you might want to keep only enough to cover your immediate needs (including some allowance for near-term emergencies) in money funds, and place more of your reserve funds in short-term (1–5 years) and even to a limited extent in intermediate term (5–10 years) Treasury or high-quality bond funds. These could still be turned into cash very quickly, and the risk that you might have to settle for a lower price when you do have to cash them in should be more than offset by the significantly higher yields you earn right from day one.

As a matter of fact — considering this risk/reward relationship and the well-established fact that no one can reliably foretell how interest rates will move — it could well make sense for many investors to keep part of their "ready access" reserves in high-quality short-term funds even if money fund yields turn more attractive again later in the 1990s.

While we've made some adjustments for current low interest levels in the examples below, we've tried to stick to scenarios that should be valid through a wide range of business and market conditions — and repeat our reminder that it's always important to take into account changes in both your personal situation and the market environment.

Because most of us who want to build up an investment nest egg can most readily do so by regularly setting aside relatively modest amounts, we're presenting these profiles mainly in terms of dollars per month. Actually, many of these investments might be made at different or irregular intervals, or there might be occasional lump-sum investments when more substantial funds become available. Either way, these rough guidelines for allocating investment assets may give you some ideas on planning for your particular situation.

- Bill Adams is a young professional, 27, single, earning $30,000. With few current obligations and solid career prospects, he is willing to take moderate risks to build a sound financial base and put a small amount at greater risk in search of greater long-term gains. After accumulating $10,000 in CDs and a money market fund, he recently switched half of this "ready reserve" into a short-term government bond fund. He is letting both the money and short-term funds grow through interest accumulation. In addition, he regularly invests $200 a month, of which he uses $50 to build the short-term fund up further, $100 for a good-quality growth mutual fund, and $50 for a more speculative or "aggressive" capital appreciation fund.
- Bill shares an apartment with Fred Wilson, another young professional. Fred's also investing $200 a month, but since he would like to buy a small condo in a year or two, he's channeling $125 into a money

fund to build up his ready cash supply and $75 into a growth mutual fund for a long-term nest egg.

· Bob and Mary Smith are a two-income family in their thirties, with combined earnings of $60,000. They are homeowners with a pre-school child. Their family responsibilities make them lean largely toward conservative investments, but they're willing to assume moderate risk in search of long-term growth, and in preparing for young Marilyn's eventual college costs. Since they depend on both incomes to maintain their lifestyle (not to mention coping with mortgage payments), they're prepared to pay for $50,000 term life insurance each, atop what their employers give them. They already have $8,000 in a money fund and try to let it grow by compounding, while investing $325 a month in stock and bond programs. Right now the $325 is broken down into $110 for two good-quality growth stocks, $80 for an "index" mutual fund based on the S&P 500, and $50 for an income-oriented mutual fund. The other $95 goes into a growth-type fund in Marilyn's name. And if there's a nice year-end bonus or other windfall, they're thinking of getting a zero-coupon bond for Marilyn's education. As noted earlier, the theoretical or "phantom" interest that builds up in "zeroes" is taxed each year, even though the investor gets no payment until the zero matures. That's a drawback in ordinary taxable accounts, since you must pay the IRS on income you have not yet received. But this can be an advantage for children, since this year-after-year tax obligation can often be covered by their exemption (or at least be taxed at minimum rate); then, when the bond matures and the accumulated proceeds are received, there will be little if any tax liability still to be met. (As of 1994, the "kiddie tax" provisions let children under 14 receive the first $600 of investment income free, and tax the next $600 at the bottom 15% rate, but anything above $1,200 is taxed at the parents' rate; however, once Marilyn turns 14, all her earnings will be taxed at her own instead of her parents' rate.)

· Lisa Swanson is a marketing manager in her forties, with no dependents. She earns $50,000, owns a condo, and has accumulated a $60,000 portfolio. In her situation, she feels she can assume higher risks with part of her capital in pursuit of above-average growth and to help her retire by the time she's 60. She's allocating $600 monthly or $7,200 a year to new investments. By now she feels she has the financial resources and the experience to do more of her own picking of individual stocks (a task she enjoys) rather than depending on mutual funds for her diversification. She puts roughly 20% into quality growth stocks, 40% into more speculative growth stocks, 20% into bonds (there she may use a mutual fund or a unit investment trust), and 15% into money or short-term funds (depending on relative yields for her tax bracket, these may vary between a regular and a tax-exempt municipals fund). The final 5% goes into a gold bullion accumulation program; she knows it earns no current return, but feels she'd like just a modest anchor to windward in case inflation gets completely out of hand.

· Tom and Kathy Brown are in their late fifties. He's a $75,000 corporate executive; she's a homemaker. Their children are grown. They look forward to an active retirement, supplementing Tom's good pension with their investment income. They're still willing to assume moderate risk in building up their assets, but also are eager to protect the $200,000 securities portfolio they've built up so far, in addition to a variable annuity now worth $80,000 (more about annuities, which can build up tax-deferred, in chapter 38). They're investing $800 a month, including $200 in an employee stock purchase plan at Tom's company. About $250 a month goes into good-quality stocks with good fundamental growth prospects as well as likely growth in dividends. These dividends are reinvested now but will be used for spendable income after retirement. The Browns also are placing $150 in a growth mutual fund and $150 into municipals. They also periodically add funds to the annuity contract. And in addition to their own investments, they faithfully put $50 a month into a growth stock fund for their two-year-old grandson in a Uniform Gift to Minors account.

· Finally, Jim and Betty Morton, both 69, are retired. The fruit of modest but steady investments over 35 years, added to their pensions and Social Security, enables them to live comfortably if not lavishly. Their obvious objective is to conserve capital, have ready access to their funds, and seek some protection against inflation. Their program calls not for new investment but for sound use of their present assets, as they gradually dip into some of their capital as well as current income, while seeking as much security as possible against inflation's erosion of their buying power. They're maintaining $10,000 in a money fund. They also held $10,000 in CDs, but as these matured, they placed the proceeds into a short-term bond fund. Their other investments include $12,000 in an intermediate-term bond fund and $18,000 in a bond unit investment trust, $20,000 in utility stocks that offer liberal dividends, $14,000 in a couple of conservative growth stocks, and $21,000 in a "growth and income" mutual fund. They've been liquidating some of the stocks they hold; whatever part of the proceeds they didn't need for immediate living expenses, they added to the mutual funds, which provides them with more flexibility as they make gradual withdrawals. Next year, when Jim reaches 70½, they will have to start making withdrawals from his IRA (including the 401(k) rolled into it when he retired). Again, to the extent the required withdrawals aren't needed for current expenses (including the tax on the amounts withdrawn), they plan to store the spare cash in their short- and intermediate-term bond funds, and — depending on interest rates and their own near-term financial needs — will probably also place some of it in their money fund.

While none of the profiles sketched above is likely to be a perfect fit for your situation, they can serve to illustrate the kind of sober thinking that helps investors decide what's right for their particular situation. Remember, there is no all-purpose security — no stock or mutual fund that fits ideally into every investor's portfolio. We all must diligently work out our own investment salvation.

That's why the best advice that was ever given is: "Investigate before you invest." And the investigation should properly begin with your own financial situation.

CHAPTER 34

When Is the Time to Sell?

THUS far we have been talking almost exclusively about buying stocks — about investing for the long run.

But just because a convincing case can be made that it is a good idea to have extra dollars invested, it doesn't follow that it is a good idea to keep them invested in the same securities forever.

Change is the common denominator of all life. And change can, and does, vitally affect the value of all investments.

The intelligent investor keeps in mind two broad kinds of change — change in one's personal financial situation, and change in available investment opportunities.

As far as the first is concerned, it is perfectly obvious that the kind of investment program that is well suited to a young person with no great responsibilities is not the kind of program that same young person should pursue when starting a family. And investments that are geared to that period of life when the heaviest load is being carried are not the kind to be made when the kids are through school and the investor is able — at the peak period of his or her earning power — to branch out again and try to build something of an estate before having to start thinking about retirement.

It is, of course, always later than we think. Changes in an individual's personal situation and financial circumstances often come very gradually and so fail to shock people into an awareness that it's high time for them to sit down and take a personal inventory of their situation —

where they stand now and where they are headed. Most of us are just too used to drifting with the tide.

This is particularly true as far as investments are concerned because of the strange, irrational attachment that many men and women seem to feel for the stocks and bonds they own. They may even feel a compulsion to talk up their investments to others, as a way of seeking confirmation from others of their own good judgment. In such circumstances, some proud owners might regard the sale of their stock as tantamount to treason.

There is another psychological reason why most people are loath to sell securities. Very often, the original investment decision — the selection of stock A over B, C, or D — was charged with emotional conflict. The investor doesn't relish the idea of fighting out the issue once again, weighing the comparative values of the purchased stock, this time against E, F, or G — or, for that matter, reevaluating it on today's terms against B, C, or D.

Nevertheless, there is the inexorable fact that investment values constantly change and what was a good buy last year may be an even better sale this year.

Investors owe it to themselves to take an objective look — as objective as possible — at their holdings at least once a year. And when they tackle that job, they should ask themselves at least one simple question about every stock on the list: "If I had the money, would I buy this stock at today's prices and outlook?"

If the answer is no, if you own a stock you wouldn't enthusiastically want to buy at that moment, you should *consider* selling it, even if you have to take a loss on it — or especially if you have to take a loss.

If you don't want to make the decision yourself, you may wish to seek your broker's opinion. Brokers are used to being asked for recommendations and suggestions, and in the main they do a remarkably conscientious job on them. They know that suggestions for changes that are made simply for the sake of building commissions are likely to backfire and result, eventually, in the loss of customers.

Of course, there are some investors who approach the job of evaluating their securities with enthusiasm and even enjoyment. These are usually the same stockholders who carefully read the annual and quarterly reports that they get from the companies whose stock they own and painstakingly compare performance with results in other years and other companies.

While only a trained analyst can get the real meat out of a corporate report, there are a few danger signals that every investor can look for — signals that might suggest the desirability of a switch to another stock. Of course, as we've tried to point out all along, it's wise to do your homework with annual reports and other available documents *before* you buy a stock as well as while you are a shareowner.

When looking at reports, it's natural to focus on earnings — the proverbial bottom line — but it's more important to see how those figures were reached.

First, there are the *revenues* — how much is the company taking in from its products and services? How do these revenues compare with those of earlier years and with the trend for companies in the same business? And what's behind these figures? Sales might be down because a division was sold, or up because one was acquired. Perhaps the company has a promising new product on the way, causing customers to slow their purchases of the old one. Or perhaps, sadly, the company has been losing market share to competitors, in which case you'd wonder what the chances are for a comeback, or if it would be better to abandon an unpromising line.

Obviously, the figures alone won't provide the answers — as regards revenues, or any of the other financial items. So it's important to look at all the available context. In the annual report's narrative part (usually near the front of the report) you can count on management placing the most palatable construction possible on the year's events; still, the basic facts should be trustworthy and you can expect a reasoned presentation of the company's view.

Then there's the *Management Discussion*, which the SEC now requires. Companies must discuss the key operating and financial condition figures, including comments (which, however, are often quite short) if these figures show significant changes over the past two years.

The financial statements themselves are accompanied by extensive

notes, which are mostly dry accountant's talk, but it pays to eyeball
them for any comments that seem out of the ordinary (if you've looked
at three or four different reports, you should have a fair idea of what's
ordinary).

Finally, there's the certification by the independent accountants
(auditors), which normally is strict boilerplate. If the certification is
"qualified" by any reservations, say, about the ability of the company
to refinance or some huge overhanging liabilities, that's a warning signal that at the least requires further investigation.

As a stockholder, you're also entitled to ask the company to send
you a copy of the 10-K report it filed with the SEC, containing more
detailed data on its operations and business. In most cases, however,
the additional material isn't worth it unless you want to make a highly
detailed and time-consuming study. For major companies, analysts
and the financial press will try to ferret out and publicize anything of
interest.

So, back to your look at the financial statements. After the operating
revenues come the *operating expenses*. How is their trend, and how
does it compare with the revenue trend? Obviously, if expenses keep
rising faster than revenues, the *operating margin* gets squeezed and
(absent special factors) the business of the company is getting less
profitable.

Then there are various *nonoperating* items, including investment
income on the plus side, and interest payments among the expenses.
Again, you'll want to know if these are one-shot items, or recurring
receipts and expenditures, and what the trend is. After the takeover
boom in the 1980s, many companies found themselves so heavily bur-
dened with debt that, even though they had good operating earnings,
they couldn't earn enough to meet interest payments.

You may also find any number of special items. They can range
from a write-off for restructuring expenses or the closing of a division,
to special gains (or losses) from the sale of a property or unit, to adjustments for foreign currencies (a major factor for many globally active
companies) to accounting adjustments (plus or minus), which occur

frequently these days because of continuous revisions of the standard accounting rules.

Some of these items may be included in the regular revenue or expense listings, some are stated separately, and some are shown as a special adjustment (again, plus or minus) to the reported earnings. If a business line or unit is closed or sold, its contributions will normally be shown as a separate line as "profit (or loss) from discontinued operations," with the accounts for the preceding year restated to put them on a similar basis.

Deducting all the expense from the income items, leaves you with pre-tax earnings. The provision for *income taxes* may also vary widely, because different income (including that from abroad) is subject to different treatment and there's a wide range of credits as well as adjustments from other years. There are *timing differences* when taxes are entered on the books in one year but paid in another; when tax rates change, these differences can vary dramatically in their impact on the income statement of different companies. The notes to the financial statements normally explain how the tax rate shown in the income accounts relates to the taxes actually imposed.

After deducting the tax provision, you finally come to *net earnings*, also shown on a *per share* basis, and often given for both before and after some of the adjustments.

Because of the many special factors, and their growing frequency, it is often difficult to derive a meaningful trend from the earnings figures. In fact, there have been many recent instances of companies reporting massive losses because of big write-offs connected with shedding a business, slashing employment, or otherwise getting various unpleasantries behind them — and being rewarded with a rise in the stock price by investors hoping they were now set for a brighter future.

On the other hand, sometimes a hefty reported earnings figure is based on some special bonanza or on some income credits or perhaps promissory notes from big but shaky customers that don't translate into ready cash. Shrewd analysts try to delve into the *quality of earnings*, looking for those portions that build up the corporate muscles.

Financial statements nowadays also carry a statement of *cash flows* for the three latest years. It starts with the reported earnings, adds such non-cash expenses as depreciation (a company has to write down the value of its plant and equipment each year on its books, but it doesn't spend actual cash), and makes adjustments for changes in inventories, and the bills the company owes or is owed. The result is the cash actually generated by operations. The cash flow statement also lists the amount invested in new plant and equipment (that's actual cash paid out), the money received from new financing (including any debt due on equipment), and the money paid to retire old debt. It also deducts the dividends paid out during the year. These figures, when studied in conjunction with the reported earnings trends, can give some indications of the company's financial health.

You'll also want to look at the key figures shown in the company's balance sheet. Check out the current assets and current liabilities, and the relation between the two. Current assets minus current liabilities represents a company's *working capital* — the money it has to grow on, the lifeblood of a business. Serious shrinkage from year to year in a company's working capital warrants careful investigation.

Of course, the makeup of current assets and liabilities is also important. On the asset side, you'd want to look into any big drop in the company's cash position (including *"cash equivalents"* such as short-term bank CDs, commercial paper, and Treasuries). Also, note any buildup in inventories, which might suggest a lot of unsalable merchandise on hand, but, on the bright side, it could reflect more work in progress to meet growing orders.

Among current liabilities, if accounts payable climb unduly, it could hint at problems in bills coming due to suppliers of raw materials, merchandise, or needed services. But in some cases it might represent a hardnosed effort to hold on to cash (and earn money on it) till the last legitimate moment.

Looking at long-term liabilities: Is the company piling up debt, and if so, why? And how readily should its earnings — and, more particularly, the cash the company generates — enable it to meet its *debt service* obligations? That's not just the current interest, but also principal repayments as they fall due. (A schedule of such debt maturities appears in the notes to the financial statements.)

In all these cases, the questions you raise may have explanations that range from the encouraging (e.g., the changes are triggered by strong expansion of the business) to understandable (the company did suffer some setbacks, which drained cash or built up inventories, but these should be temporary). In other cases, of course, the figures could be clues to more unpleasant surprises ahead. So the key point is: Don't panic, but do try to look for some answers.

Overall, reviewing the financial figures for the past couple of years, along with the commentaries you find in the report, should leave you better equipped to judge the quality and prospects of the company.

Another major question you should ask regarding any investment is: How good is the management? The annual report — both in how it's presented and what the results convey — can give a clue. So can impressions garnered from brokerage and press reports. But, at best, judging management quality is an inexact science and mysterious art.

You do want to have confidence in a company whose stock you buy or hold. But in addition, your decision must take the market price into consideration. A company with excellent results may have outrun the market to such an extent — say, the price/earnings ratio (P/E) for its industry is usually 1.5 times the P/E of the S&P 500 index, but now the stock is at 2.5 times the current S&P P/E — that you should consider selling at least part of your holdings. On the other hand, a company still in trouble, but with good survival prospects and a reasonably competent management, may be so cheap that you should certainly hold on to the stock and perhaps go out and buy.

In evaluating a company's reports and status, investors have the right to look for help and advice from their broker. Within reason, they can expect specific answers to their questions and reliable data on the basis of which they can make up their mind whether to buy, sell, or hold.

While brokers are frequently accused of stimulating customers to switch from one stock to another for the sake of building commissions, the blunt fact is that many don't suggest enough sales to their customers. In part, that's because they fear being accused of churning; in part, because their firms' research departments tend to have many more "buy" than "sell" recommendations; and also because they, like their customers, tend to weigh in on the optimistic side. For their part, the customers rarely solicit "sell" suggestions and are generally content to hold on to the same old stocks, even if that's not in their best interest. A New York Stock Exchange survey some years ago showed that a third of all people who owned stock had never sold any. They had just bought and held on.

The do-nothing attitude of many stockholders holding substantial profits is unquestionably explained by their reluctance to pay a capital gains tax on these profits, especially after 100 percent of such gains became taxable income for many people. It's understandable to hate having the IRS sharply reduce the amount of money left for reinvestment — and that should be factored into your decisions about securities held in a taxable account. But remember that, if you let your investment slide south instead, you may have far less left both to be taxed and to reinvest.

There's one other aspect of selling — when it's in response to a special invitation. For example, companies that have accumulated much extra cash (perhaps from the sale of one of their divisions) sometimes offer to use these funds to repurchase a number of shares at a specified price — usually a bit over the current market price — and without commission charges (rather, the company will pay a fee to the broker through whom you submit your shares). You'll get a formal *tender offer* outlining the terms and asking you to tender (submit) part or all of your shares. If the total number of shares tendered exceeds the amount the company has offered to buy, there is usually a *pro rata* allocation. Suppose our old friend Rod & Reel offered to buy 6 million shares and the holders submitted 8 million, then only 75% of each holder's tender would be accepted.

Many more companies have long-term repurchase programs under which they buy back a relatively small number of shares from "time to time" in the open stock market. (Also, sometimes a company will make a special offer to purchase back the stock of any holder of, say, less than 100 shares, in order to cut the administrative costs of serving many small stockholders.) In any case, all tender or repurchase plans must be filed with the SEC.

The chief argument for stock repurchases is that by reducing the total number of shares outstanding, there will be more earnings per share for each of the remaining shares. Or, as managements like to feel, "we haven't found any better place to invest spare cash than in the stock of our own company." A stream of stock repurchases can acquire stock for options or employee purchase plans without increasing the previous number of shares. Of course, managements are also conscious that a repurchase program can provide market "support" for a stock, and that, especially in large tender offers, encouraging outside holders to sell back their stock leaves a larger percentage in the hand of management and its allies.

This can be a potent consideration, since tender offers may also be launched by other companies or outside groups seeking a *hostile takeover*. Such efforts became especially active in the 1980s, when even the largest corporations found they were not immune from attack, often by far smaller outfits. In hostile takeovers the initial offer is usually at a price substantially above the current market for the target stock in the hope of quickly acquiring enough stock for control. As the eighties progressed, however, the first offer often simply put the target *in play;* often it was followed by offers from rival bidders, or management (once it considered further resistance useless) managed to persuade the initial bidder to raise its offer. And sometimes management was able to fend off the raiders by successfully taking the company *private* in a *management buyout.*

In any event, the acquirers (whether outsider or management) ended up paying a hefty price to the company's stockholders — paying for it with huge bank loans and issues of junk bonds. Such actions are called *leveraged buyouts* (or LBOs) because they balance so little equity against mammoth debt. The takeover operators often hoped to pay off these debts by selling major pieces of the company, utilizing any funds available in the old company (e.g., rearranging pension funds so as to free reserves that could be deemed excess), and, of course, from the operating profits of their leaner, meaner company. Unfortunately, many projections for fund and profit inflows didn't work out, leading to numerous spectacular bankruptcies, and (in milder cases) restructuring of big debts. At the same time, a goodly number of acquired companies did manage to survive (or have been revived); many of them have been *taken public* again with new stock issues.

And takeovers, hostile or friendly, are continuing, though at a slower rate and at more moderate prices. What should you do if you receive an offer to tender stock that you hold? As in all investment decisions, that has to depend on the particular situation — yours and the stock's. When you get an offer at or just above market, do you want to get out or do you believe the long-term values of the company will bring you a larger reward later — larger than an alternative investment? If there's a bid far above market, do you want to accept or hope for a higher bid or are you so enthusiastic about the company that you want to hold on if you can? (There's also a chance the bid may fail and the bidder withdraws, in which case the stock price may plunge.) And, obviously, if an acquirer succeeds in taking the company private, you have no choice but to accept the price — hopefully a fair one.

All in all, because the long-term outlook for American business remains a bright and promising one, no one wants to preach a doctrine of "sell . . . sell . . . sell." Nevertheless, if you think you can improve your investment position, it is ridiculous to stand pat lethargically, comforted simply by the thought that inflation and an expanding economy will rescue you from your own faulty judgment.

It is a truism of the stock market that there are sell orders to match all buy orders. There have to be. And it bears repeating: It's just as important to know when and what to sell as when and what to buy.

CHAPTER 35

The Folklore of the Market

THE cheapest commodity in the world is investment advice from people not equipped to give it.

Many a person who doesn't own a share of stock fancies himself an authority on the market. He's always ready and willing to deliver himself of an opinion about it on the slightest provocation. If he actually owns stock himself, chances are you won't have to ask his opinion. He'll tell you what to buy, what to sell, and what's going to happen to the market. And you can't stop him.

The more a person knows about the market, the less he or she is willing to come out with a flat prediction. The wisest of them all, old J. P. Morgan, when asked his opinion of the market, always used to reply, "It will fluctuate." He wasn't just being canny. He knew that was the only provable statement that could be made about the market.

Nevertheless, over the years a number of generalizations about the market and about investing have come to be accepted as gospel. Actually, these homespun axioms must be accepted as just that — little more than folklore. Like most folklore, each of them has a certain element of truth about it — and a certain element of untruth.

For instance: *"Buy 'em and put 'em away."*

This would have been a fine piece of advice if you had bought $1,000 worth of General Motors stock in 1923. In May 1994 the stock from that single $1,000 investment would have been worth more than

$82,000, and you would also have collected close to $125,000 in dividends. Of course, you could have realized about as much had you been foresighted — or, more realistically, lucky — enough to sell your General Motors way back at the 1965 high, before the road turned rough for American automakers. And had you been impatient before the recent GM recovery, you might have had to settle for under $25,000 (still well ahead of your cost) in 1981, or not quite $40,000 at the 1991 low.

Of course, in the early twenties the car company people were talking about was Stutz — not General Motors — and there was a great deal of speculative interest in Stutz stock. You might very well have decided to put your $1,000 into that. How would you have made out on that purchase? The answer is that you would have lost all your money, and, furthermore, you would never have collected a penny in dividends.

In short, there is a measure of sense in the axiom. If you start worrying about fluctuations of a point or two and try to buy and sell on every turn, you can needlessly pay out a lot of money in commissions and you may end up with less profit than if you'd "bought 'em and put 'em away."

Nevertheless, it's only good sense to remember that securities are perishable. Values do change with the passage of time. Industries die, and new ones are born. Companies rise and fall. Wise investors will periodically take a good look at all their securities — at least once a year, more often if there are big market movements. And they could do worse than to ask their broker to review their portfolio with them.

"You never go broke taking a profit."

In many ways, the other side of the "Buy 'em and hold 'em" maxim.

Obviously, the statement is literally true. But you can certainly be badly hurt. Suppose you had put $1,000 into Sears, Roebuck in 1906. By 1940, the stock that you had bought would have been worth $25,500 at its high for the year. That would have been a nice profit — and you might have decided to take it.

But look what you would have lost out on if you had sold. By 1954 your same holdings in that stock would have been worth about

$86,000, and in 1973 and again in 1987 well over $800,000. However, Sears (like GM) has had its share of problems, and in 1990 your investment would have been worth barely $300,000. Not bad for what started out as $1,000, but painful for those who remember the peaks — and even more painful if you sold then, since by early 1994 your investment would have topped $900,000.

For an even bigger long-term success (but, so far at least, less recent rebound than Sears and GM), look at International Business Machines. In 1914, $1,000 would have bought you about 36 IBM shares, and in just eleven years you could have sold out for $2,300. Certainly you can never go broke taking a profit of 130%.

But what profit you would have forgone. For as of spring 1994, your original 36 shares would have grown through numerous stock splits and stock dividends to roughly 105,000 shares with a market value of over $6 million. But despite the fabulous long-term gain, you'd no doubt be upset that your holding of this long-time blue chip known as "Big Blue" had shrunk from over $18 million at the all-time high in 1987 and $10 million as recently as mid-1992.

So there's no simple answer. Yes, a profit is always a nice thing to have. And you may prefer to have that profit in the pocket, not just on paper — unless, of course, you're worried about capital gains taxes.

"Buy when others are selling. Sell when they buy."

Don't confuse this maxim with that other folklore favorite, "Buy sheep, sell deer." Obviously, everyone wants to buy *cheap* and sell *dear*; the trick is to tell apart these market "sheep" and "deer."

In any case, that's not what "buy when others sell" is about; its theme is that it's often wise to go against the prevailing market wisdom. That's the gospel of the *contrarians*.

Their creed isn't necessarily based on the cynical argument that the majority is mostly wrong. Rather, to greatly simplify their concepts, the idea is that once everybody (or nearly everybody) agrees there's nothing to worry about, that all the portents are rosy, those "everybodies" will have put all their money into the market, so soon there'll be no place to go but down. And when just about everyone is bearish and has sold whatever they're prepared to get rid of, there won't be any further selling pressure, so the market will be receptive to an upward push. However, market movements are rarely simple, but an amalgam of many influences, so it's often difficult to figure out what's the true contrarian line.

Of course, as with most maxims, there's a counterpoint to "Buy when others sell . . ." In this case, it's "Don't fight the tape." That means, you may be perfectly right in your evaluation of the market and its underlying values. But when there's a strong movement in one direction or another, it's better to ride along with it, else you might be swamped long before you can prove you were right. Again, valid to a certain extent — but, inevitably, there'll be a time when that powerful wave has run its course.

The trick lies in anticipating the action of all the others — buying shortly before the crowd decides to buy and selling just ahead of them. Great for the magicians who can do it.

"Don't sell on bad news."

The reason's simple. Many unfavorable events — such as a strike, declining orders, problems with a major product, even a bankruptcy filing — are often long in development. By the time the actual news comes through, the stock is apt to have already declined. It may even advance once the news is officially out, as short-sellers "cover" (buy back) and others think the stock is now at healthier levels.

In the past few years, many companies have announced drastic restructurings, closings of major units, sharp personnel reductions, and abandonment of stale inventories. All this often required write-offs (at times in the hundreds of millions of dollars) and forced the company to announce a humongous loss for the year. Yet, in general, the market reacted by pushing up the company's stock — it figured much bad news (which was already widely known) was now behind, and the company could go ahead with more profitable operations.

And when there's really unexpected news that shocks the market, the reaction of the stock is often so swift that your sell order might well be executed at a panic level. It may be better to wait until the situation can be assessed further.

The same logic, of course, applies for good news. The stock price may already have risen to "discount" expected favorable developments, or may jump up wildly when a buy-out offer at a fancy price is announced. Again, it's important to assess the situation to see whether it's a good buy at the prevailing price.

"Don't overstay the market."

A fine piece of advice. But how do you know when to sell and take your profit?

Sometimes you can tell by watching those basic business indicators that show what's happening to production, distribution, and consumption of goods. But sometimes you can't, because the market doesn't always pay close attention to them. Sometimes business looks good and the stock market skids. Sometimes the reverse is true.

Remember, however, that the market prides itself on being a *leading* indicator — and generally that's held true — so, if anything, it's the *expectations* of future economic activity that count.

"Always cut your losses quickly."

Nobody wants to ride all the way downhill with a stock if the company is headed for bankruptcy, as Chrysler — a formerly well-regarded stock — seemed to be in 1981. At the same time you don't want to be stampeded into a sale by a price decline that may have no relationship to the fundamental value of the stock — or that may disregard reasonable prospects of the company being turned around.

Remember, the price of a stock at any time reflects the supply and demand for that stock, the opinions and attitudes of all the buyers and all the sellers. If a stock is closely held, if its *floating supply* — the amount usually available in the market — is limited, the price of that stock can be unduly depressed if one large holder sells a sizable block of it just because he needs the cash. Or, these days, if a big institution wants out for reasons entirely unrelated to the intrinsic value of the stock.

Even with the explosive growth of trading volume, the market on any given day is made by just a tiny handful of all those who own stocks. The quarter billion shares that may be traded on the Big Board on a typical day represent only about one-fifth of 1% of the 130 billion shares listed on the exchange. The 99.8% of shares that aren't being sold that day are being held on to by shareowners (individuals and institutions) who have some reason for holding on — or think they have.

Many institutions are quick on the trigger, ready to sell at any disappointment in a company or its stock. At the same time, there is some truth in the observation that unsophisticated investors tend to sell a stock too readily when they have a profit, but hang on grimly to a stock in which they have a loss, just hoping that it will come back.

"An investor is just a disappointed speculator."

This cynical observation has a measure of truth in it. Just about all stock buyers hope for a big, fat, fast profit, though they may not admit it even to themselves. So, when the market drops, they do their best to assuage disappointment by assuring themselves and everybody else that they never were looking to make a killing; in fact, they weren't even counting on any near-term gains. They were just investing on the basis of the stock's fundamental values, and would patiently wait for these values to assert themselves.

That's a psychological crutch leaned on by many small investors who, all too often, finally decide to buy only when the market is already too high. The supposed tendency of the small odd-lot investor to be late in buying and again in selling has been used by some professional traders as a contrary indicator. When the ratio of odd-lot buying to odd-lot selling rose, these traders began to anticipate a reversal of the upward trend. When more of the odd-lotters were selling, the worst of the market decline might be behind us. (Today it's more the views and actions of the professional advisory services and money managers that the contrarians watch for signs of how the market winds are blowing.)

In any case, over the long run, the small investors often have the last laugh. After all, the stock market has gone up pretty steadily since World War II. And as small investors are heavy buyers of the market leaders — the stocks that dominate the Dow Jones averages and the Standard & Poor's 500 — they made out pretty well over the long run, provided they were willing to hold on during the rough spots along the way.

On the other hand, many a big speculator has died broke.

"A bull can make money. A bear can make money. But a hog never can."

That's one to remember.

The desire to make money leads most people into the market. Call it ambition, or call it greed, but it still remains the prime motivating force behind our whole business system, including the stock market.

But greed is always dangerous. It's an engine without a governor. So you made a killing once in the market. Good. You were lucky. Don't think you can make one every day.

Or to use a baseball metaphor, when you come up to bat, try to get wood on the ball and concentrate on hitting singles and doubles. It'll build up your average and the score. If you manage to hit an occasional homerun, that's great. But if you regularly get in there swinging for the fences, you'll rack up a lot of strikeouts.

And on the playing field of the market, the advice given from the first edition of this book still holds good: If you own a good stock, one that's paying you a good return on your money and seems likely to go on doing so, it probably makes sense to hang on to it. Don't keep looking for greener pastures, bigger profits. And forget about the other fellow and the killing he made — or says he made. Maybe he can afford to speculate more than you can.

In short, if you're an investor, act like one.

CHAPTER 36

Who Owns Stock?

IF Wall Street didn't exist, it would be necessary to invent it. Of course, that's exactly what our forefathers did.

Why must there be a Wall Street?

Because in our economy, capital, like labor, must be free to work where it wants to. If you've got extra dollars, you've got the right in our society to say where you want to put them to work in order to make more dollars.

And that right would be a pretty empty one if there weren't some means for you to switch your funds from one enterprise to another whenever you wanted to, just as you might switch from one job to another.

Wall Street provides that means. It's a marketplace for money.

Especially since the end of World War II, it has played an increasingly important role in our economy. It has made it possible for millions of people to put their savings to work in American business. That has been good for them, good for business, and good for the whole country.

Time was when only wealthy people owned stocks and bonds, but that's no longer the case. For one thing, there's no longer the heavy concentration of large-scale investible wealth in relatively very few hands.

If business is to have the money it needs to go on growing, to build new and more efficient plants, replace old equipment, and finance vital research and development, it needs the broad base that can only be supplied, directly or indirectly, by the investor of moderate means. Sure, wealthy investors continue to furnish multimillions of capital. But to meet its ever-growing investment needs, business these days must also depend on the hundreds and thousands of dollars that each of millions of average Americans can put to work.

Much publicity and debate has surrounded the recent vast step-up of foreign investment in the U.S. There's nothing intrinsically wrong with permitting, indeed, encouraging, foreigners to invest in the growth of our economy, any more than Americans should be inhibited from investing abroad. The more open and unfettered the global marketplace, the better for all. But to properly meet the needs of the U.S. economy — to keep it competitive and us prosperous — will take billions and billions of dollars from the checkbooks and paychecks of ordinary Americans.

You may say that pension funds, mutual funds, venture capital funds, and sundry other institutions have taken on the role of major capital suppliers. True. And also true that many of these funds represent thousands of modest-income individuals — most likely including you. So, in one way or another, you can take credit for being an indispensable capital supplier. But, if you can, it's well worth considering direct participation as well.

Wall Street bears the primary responsibility for recruiting the investors, individually and institutionally, who must supply this capital. Wall Street and all its counterparts throughout America.

How's it doing? Better than you might think — but not nearly as well as it must.

Not until June 1952 did Wall Street know just how it stood on the job. Strange as it may seem, nobody could say how many stockholders there were in the country until the New York Stock Exchange got the Brookings Institution to find out. American Telephone & Telegraph knew it had 1,200,000 stockholders back then. And 30 other big companies knew they had 50,000 or more apiece. But nobody knew just what duplication there was in those stockholder lists. And nobody knew the grand total for all companies.

Brookings reported in 1952 that the total was 6,490,000 stock-owners, representing a little more than 4% of all the individuals and just about 10% of all the families in the country. One encouraging fact was that about one-fifth of the total had become stockholders in the preceding three years.

In 1956, the Big Board sponsored another census. It found a total of 8,630,000 stockholders in publicly owned corporations, an increase of 33% in four years. In addition, the study estimated that about 300,000 Americans owned stock indirectly through mutual funds, then still a tiny factor in the investment field.

Since then, the exchange has periodically conducted similar surveys (with equity mutual fund owners included in the count from 1959 on). Each showed a steady increase in share ownership, except for 1975 when (after the most severe postwar market slump) the census came up with only 25,270,000 shareowners. That was down 18% from 1970 and an even steeper 22% from a less-formal interim estimate of 32,500,000 issued by the Big Board in 1972.

By 1981 the tally was virtually back to that 1972 record estimate. And, reflecting the investment boom of the 1980s, the count reached 51,400,000 in 1990. While a goodly majority of these investors own stock directly, the mutual fund sector is responsible for most of the past decade's growth in the overall shareowner population. In fact, between 1985 and 1990 alone, holders of equity mutual funds multiplied from 11 million to 25 million, and that figure has no doubt continued to climb. There is of course lots of overlap. A study by the mutual fund industry's Investment Company Institute (ICI) indicates 55% to 60% of equity mutual fund holders also own stock directly. The vast expansion of retirement-oriented programs, which readily lend themselves to regular mutual fund investments, may well have helped accelerate this trend. The NYSE census showed 51% of all shareowners had an IRA or Keogh account, while the ICI study found mutual fund holders had a substantially higher 73% IRA participation rate.

Here's a portrait of the typical shareholder as drawn from the 1990 study. Men outnumber women by about five to three among adult shareholders, while children make up nearly 7% of the owners. The typical adult stockowner was a 45-year-old college graduate and owned three stocks worth a total of $11,400. About 40% held professional, technical, or management positions or were business proprietors. However, other occupations and educational levels were also widely represented. Typical household income was $43,800, which, not surprisingly, was well above the 1990 national median income of $30,000. About one-third of the shareowners acquired their first stock through a broker, another third began their investment through an employee stock purchase plan, one-eighth initially invested with a mutual fund company, and about one in nine was initiated into the investment world through gifts or inheritance.

The latest survey means that one out of every five Americans now own stock, a sharp gain over earlier levels. Still, what about the other four-fifths? Why don't more people invest? We may be the very bulwark of modern and enlightened capitalism, but millions of people still don't bother to understand stocks and bonds. And what they don't understand, they're afraid of.

Along with ignorance and fear, there's the fact that *successful* investing, even in convenient packaged forms such as mutual funds, isn't simply a "no-brainer." It does require thinking your own investment problems through to a logical conclusion. It means being willing to study the available facts about various investment alternatives — checking up on a stock or a fund both before you buy and after you buy.

That's not an easy task — but neither is it beyond the capabilities of any of us. Nor does it require excessive amounts of time — especially considering the returns that can normally be expected, and the needs all of us face. Periodically, newspapers publish stories of people who never held anything but modest-paying jobs, but who, through diligent investing (and, usually, also extreme frugality), amassed tidy minifortunes. Of course, few of us would care to pay their price in single-minded concentration and self-denial. But then most of us would be willing to settle for a more comfortable and moderate measure of success. And that kind of success, over time, seems well within reach, considering that the annual returns on stocks over the past two-thirds of a century, with all their big year-by-year and stock-by-stock variations, have averaged out to roughly 10%. What's more, it's a success that can be achieved not by luck, not by "inside tips," not by speculation, but only by prudent and intelligent investing.

CHAPTER 37

Stock Screens

IN this age of computers, Wall Street research firms are able to examine the total body of stocks available for investment in order to ferret out those that meet specified statistical criteria. Indeed, it's possible to program the computer to sift for an almost infinite number of combinations of different criteria — say, stocks whose earnings history and earnings forecasts, dividend record, cash flow, capitalization, and stock movement ("volatility") patterns all meet certain desired characteristics, making them potential investment candidates for certain types of stock buyers. What's more, the selection criteria can be quickly adjusted as business conditions or a client's priorities change.

These computer stock "screens" depend on extensive and complex databases maintained by major securities firms and research services. Institutional investors, money managers, and other investment professionals may buy access to these proprietary databases so they can run their own sophisticated analyses.

But most full-service brokerage firms also make numerous screens available to their retail brokers to help them advise individual customers on possible investments. Screens are also regular features in a number of advisory publications such as Standard & Poor's *Outlook* and Value Line's *Investment Survey*, and can be found periodically in many financial magazines.

And investors who subscribe to computer data services like Compu-

Serve can call up stock data from which they can construct some screens on their own home computers.

On the following pages are some examples of basic stock screens. They are presented here to give you some small idea of the kind of screens used by investors and the tremendous possibilities for statistical fine-tuning.

There are two vital points to keep in mind. First, we are demonstrating the *tool*, not presenting a list for current investment study. Because conditions change so rapidly, you should make sure any screen you use is based on fresh data — it can turn stale in a matter of weeks, and sometimes overnight.

Even more important, computerized stock screens can be a tremendous help in narrowing the range of potential investments for you to study, but *never allow the screen to make the final decision* for you. Stocks may meet any number of criteria you set, but still have other characteristics that make them the wrong investment, at least for you. One further cautionary note: While the databases on which brokers and service suppliers depend are very carefully prepared, occasional glitches do creep in, and every now and then a company passes the screen test based on faulty data. So, use a screen to identify candidates for your portfolio, then study these candidates carefully to find those in which you may actually want to invest.

Here then is a series of sample screens, courtesy of Merrill Lynch & Co. They are derived from electronic analysis of some 1,500 stocks actively traded in the U.S. markets and based on August 1992 data.

COMPUTER SCREEN #1

The first screen seeks out companies whose stock price is relatively modest in relation to earnings. Other things being equal, the less you have to pay for a dollar of earnings (that is, the lowest P/E) would of course be the most attractive. We asked the computer to pick out the companies in our 1,535-stock sample that had a P/E ratio under 10 — that is, the stock's price could be no more than 10 times the earnings per share for the latest 12 months; for comparison, the S&P 500

#1: **Stocks Whose Current Price-Earnings (P/E) Ratio Is under 10, and Price-to-Cash-Flow Ratio under 12. In Addition, the Company's Present Profit Margin Must Be above the Average for Its Industry, and Only Companies with More Than $1 Billion in Market Capitalization Considered.**

		P/E Last 12Mo	Mkt Val/ Cash Flo	Price 8/31/92	After-Tax Margin	Market Value ($ million)
Polaroid Corp	PRD	2.4	2.1	31.500	33.0	1526
Elf Aquitaine	ELF	3.9	3.7	33.375	4.9	16921
Northrop Corp	NOC	3.9	2.7	24.875	4.7	1174
Banco Bilbao	BBV	5.4	10.9	25.250	8.8	11665
Tiphook PLC	TPH	5.4	8.1	16.500	23.4	1798
Santander	STD	5.9	5.8	38.875	9.1	4325
St. Paul Cos	SPC	6.8	7.8	72.750	9.3	3103
Bankers Trust NY	BT	7.4	7.9	60.500	9.7	5014
Banco Central Hispano	BCM	7.5	8.8	15.500	6.2	5315
Boeing	BA	7.5	5.3	37.250	5.3	12725
Martin Marietta	ML	7.6	5.0	55.125	5.2	2676
Mellon Bank Corp	MEL	8.2	9.1	40.875	8.9	2091
Total	TOT	8.2	0.8	21.625	4.1	1796
IP Timberlands	IPT	8.3	7.0	26.000	63.3	1208
Kemper Corp	KEM	8.7	5.1	21.500	6.5	1042
Detroit Edison	DTE	8.9	5.2	33.125	15.8	4869
Empresa Nacnl Elec	ELE	9.0	4.2	33.625	13.4	8743
Western Mining Holdg	WMC	9.0	8.1	14.000	17.9	3291
Morgan (J.P.)	JPM	9.1	10.4	59.500	10.8	11326
Phila Electric	PE	9.2	6.5	25.750	13.4	5667
Supervalu Inc	SVU	9.2	5.9	25.875	2.0	1840
British Gas PLC	BRG	9.5	11.8	47.500	8.8	20244
Raytheon Co	RTN	9.7	6.6	44.500	6.4	5938
Golden West Fincl	GDW	9.8	10.3	41.250	10.6	2619
Humana Inc	HUM	9.9	5.5	20.500	6.1	3249
Nat. Australia Bank	NAB	9.9	11.4	26.875	6.1	6543
First Bank System	FBS	10.0	11.6	24.500	10.5	1930
S&P 500		25.6		414.03		

index had a P/E of nearly 26 at the time. But we also wanted to make sure that the company's operations generated a goodly amount of cash, so the 192 companies that met our P/E requirement were next put through a "sieve" or "filter" that demanded a price-to-cash-flow ratio under 12. That left us with 143 companies. In addition, we wanted only companies whose profit margin was better (higher) than the average for its industry; now we were down to 70 companies. Finally, we only wanted to consider companies that were fairly substantial, so the computer was ordered to discard any company with less than $1 billion in market capitalization (stock price multiplied by total number of shares). The end result of all this winnowing was a list of 27 companies that met all our criteria.

The investor must then investigate thoroughly the individual companies the computer has filtered out, to determine whether they fulfill his or her other investment criteria, whether they stand up under objective financial scrutiny, and whether there is any negative reason why these particular stocks appear to be statistical "bargains." For instance, while the screen's P/E ratio is based on earnings for the most recent 12-month period reported by each company, you would certainly want to know the outlook for future earnings.

COMPUTER SCREEN #2

Here we looked for two indications of dividend growth: dividend raises in at least three of the past five years, with an average annual increase of at least 15% — nearly double the S&P 500's five-year dividend growth rate of 8.1%. We also asked for a current yield (dividend as percent of market price) of at least 4%, significantly above the current 3% for the S&P. With this list of dividend-increase leaders at hand, the individual investor could decide whether to go for a company with a larger current yield or one that has shown the faster growth over five years.

Incidentally, the computer can readily be asked to churn out additional statistics — data not used as criteria in the selection process but that could be useful when taking a closer look at those stocks that the screen has picked out. For instance, on this screen we show the payout

#2: Companies That Have Paid Higher Dividends in Three of the Past Five Years, with Five-Year Dividend Growth Averaging at Least 15%; Current Yield Must Be at Least 4%.

		Yield %	Price 8/31/92	Divd. per Share Growth Last 5 Yr	Payout %
Great Northern Iron	GNI	8.9	67.750	16.8	100.0
Barclays PLC	BCS	8.4	23.375	29.0	172.8
Hanson PLC	HAN	7.8	19.250	54.0	92.0
Banco Central Hispano	BCM	6.5	15.500	21.4	48.3
Maine Pub Svc	MAP	6.5	26.875	26.2	61.1
Nat Australia BK	NAB	6.4	26.875	70.6	63.6
Aegon NV	AEG	5.5	39.000	47.4	46.5
Tasty Baking	TBC	4.8	16.750	19.3	59.3
Dow Chemical	DOW	4.6	56.250	15.5	146.9
Lockheed Corp	LK	4.5	46.875	15.5	40.8
Borden Inc	BN	4.3	28.000	15.4	53.6
Penn Central	PC	4.2	19.250	95.3	80.8
Bristol-Myers Squibb	BMY	4.1	66.625	16.2	67.8
First Hawaiian	FHWN	4.1	25.500	17.5	39.4
Upjohn	UPJ	4.0	34.125	19.5	44.6
S&P 500		3.0			76.7

ratio, the percentage of latest earnings that is being paid out as a dividend. A few companies are paying out more in dividends than they earned — which may happen when companies take a special charge or they encounter what they're confident is a brief adverse period — but it's one more item to be checked out.

COMPUTER SCREEN #3

This screen first looks for companies whose earnings have grown rapidly over the past five years — averaging at least 30% a year. But we also want stocks that can continue to grow at an above-average rate, even if perhaps not quite as fast as during the past five (it can get more difficult to sustain growth rates as a company gets bigger and

#3: Companies Whose Earnings Per
Share Have Averaged at Least 30% Annual Growth over
Past 5 Years and Are Expected to Average at Least 18%
Growth over Next 5 Years

		EPS Growth Last 5 Yr	EPS Growth Estimate Next 5 Yr	Aftr-Tax Margin	ROE 1 Year	% Held by Inst
Amgen	AMGN	140.5	27.5	14.3	21.1	62.6
Genzyme Corp	GENZ	118.7	30.0	10.2	6.3	71.6
Jacobs Engr Group	JEC	80.0	20.0	2.0	21.5	35.0
Costco Wholesale	COST	71.4	25.0	1.6	15.7	56.2
Interspec Inc	ISPC	62.5	20.0	13.8	52.7	24.3
Novell	NOVL	57.8	25.0	25.4	32.6	69.4
Microsoft Corp	MSFT	56.9	30.0	25.1	40.8	33.7
Sun Microsystems	SUNW	51.7	20.0	5.9	17.8	64.8
Symbol Technologies	SBL	50.0	23.0	7.1	9.3	77.7
Home Depot	HD	46.5	29.0	4.9	21.0	57.0
CBI Industries	CBH	42.7	18.0	3.8	11.6	70.4
United Healthcare	UNH	42.4	35.0	8.8	33.7	87.7
Medco Containmnt	MCCS	41.0	40.0	4.4	14.8	81.9
U.S. Surgical	USS	39.0	35.0	10.8	32.9	60.3
Cracker Barrel	CBRL	38.0	24.0	7.6	16.3	56.2
Elan Corporation	ELN	37.5	50.0	21.1	16.8	55.3
Plains Petroleum	PLP	33.7	25.0	28.4	20.6	58.5
Isomedix	ISMX	33.0	25.0	19.1	10.2	55.2

bigger). And when we get down to study the companies that have been found by our screen, we want to see how big a profit margin (after-tax profits as a percent of revenues) and a return on equity (ROE, or after-tax profits as a percent of stockholders' equity) the company earned last year. In addition, we're checking on how big an institutional following the company has. Of course, big institutional holdings can cut two ways — they show that the company has found some solid and presumably astute backers; but there's also the danger that these institutions may run away fast if a company fails to live up to expectations.

#4: Companies Whose Average Earnings
Growth Rate over the Past Five Years Is at Least 4
Times the Latest P/E

		Ratio EPS Growth to P/E	EPS Growth Last 5 Yr	P/E Last 12 Mo	Price 8/31/92
Polaroid Corp	PRD	20.71	49.7	2.4	31.500
Conseco Inc	CNC	12.96	70.0	5.4	25.375
Northrop Corp	NOC	11.51	44.9	3.9	24.875
Leucadia National	LUK	10.44	59.5	5.7	66.000
Dresser Industries	DI	9.40	190.8	20.3	20.875
Honeywell Inc	HON	8.56	101.9	11.9	65.250
Kuhlman Corp	KUH	8.47	101.7	12.0	15.375
Teradyne	TER	8.03	125.3	15.6	12.625
CSS Industries	CSS	7.59	52.4	6.9	25.500
Intelligent Electrnic	INEL	6.97	66.2	9.5	9.375
Air Products	APD	6.86	123.4	18.0	42.250
Esterline	ESL	6.49	59.1	9.1	8.375
Rorer (R.P.)	RPR	5.77	113.6	19.7	51.375
York Internatl	YRK	5.59	147.1	26.3	33.625
Fabri-Centers of Amer	FCA	5.08	51.3	10.1	11.375
Amer President Cos	APS	5.03	38.7	7.7	40.500
Primerica	PA	4.90	34.8	7.1	39.750
Cubic Corp	CUB	4.85	72.7	15.0	16.625
Mirage Resorts	MIR	4.59	82.2	17.9	25.250
Kennametal Inc	KMT	4.48	101.6	22.7	27.250
Humana Inc	HUM	4.38	43.4	9.9	20.500
Medical Care Intntl	ME	4.06	97.4	24.0	49.250

COMPUTER SCREEN #4

This type of screen is popular with some institutional investors who seek to identify what they call "strong growth available for good value." They look at the five-year earnings growth record (demanding an annual growth rate of at least 15%) and at the latest price-earnings ratio, but the key measure for this study is the relationship between the two: the ratio of the average annual earnings growth to the P/E.

#5: Companies Whose Return on Equity (ROE) Has Averaged at Least 20% over Past 5 Years. In Addition, Latest ROE Must Be above Company's Own 5-Year Average and Better Than Current ROE for Its Industry. Also, Latest Return on Capital Must Be at Least 20% and Debt Represent No More Than 30% of Total Capital.

		ROE Latest Year	ROE 5 Yr Average	Ret on Tot Cap	% of Debt to Capital	Price 8/31/92
UST Inc	UST	55.6	43.0	55.6	5.4	31.750
U.S. Healthcare	USHC	52.1	22.6	52.1	2.8	55.125
Merck & Co	MRK	48.5	46.2	41.7	12.0	48.625
Syntex Corp	SYN	47.7	44.8	40.8	21.0	28.750
Amer Home Products	AHP	46.0	42.4	41.0	3.0	72.625
Microsoft Corp	MSFT	40.8	38.6	41.2	0.0	74.500
GAP Inc	GPS	40.2	32.7	38.1	8.9	33.875
Coca-Cola	KO	39.5	35.3	36.8	24.4	43.000
Bristol-Myers Squibb	BMY	36.7	27.0	36.7	2.0	66.625
Abbott Labs	ABT	36.1	33.9	36.6	20.0	30.500
Tambrands Inc	TMB	33.5	24.6	36.9	7.2	62.250
Novell	NOVL	32.6	28.8	32.4	0.1	50.500
Upjohn	UPJ	32.4	23.4	22.7	21.0	34.125
Nike Inc	NKE	31.6	28.0	33.9	6.8	72.375
Lilly (Eli) Co	LLY	31.2	25.6	30.8	8.0	65.125
Gerber Products	GEB	30.0	26.0	25.0	18.3	66.000
Wrigley (Wm.) Jr	WWY	29.8	29.4	30.1	0.0	97.000
Johnson & Johnson	JNJ	27.8	27.1	24.9	16.0	49.375
Heinz (H.J.)	HNZ	27.5	26.9	27.9	16.3	41.750
Block (H&R) Inc	HRB	27.3	25.6	28.2	0.0	35.375
Reebok Internatl	RBK	25.8	25.3	25.2	19.6	27.750
Biomet Inc	BMET	25.6	24.4	26.0	0.0	20.750
Benetton Group	BNG	25.1	23.6	25.8	25.0	19.625
Schlumberger	SLB	23.0	16.5	23.6	8.2	68.875
Amgen	AMGN	21.1	8.0	20.6	12.3	63.375
Automatic Data Proc	AUD	20.9	19.2	20.7	7.4	43.125
General Electric	GE	20.5	18.7	26.7	15.7	74.000
Winn-Dixie Stores	WIN	20.4	17.8	20.8	9.0	51.125
Stryker Corp	STRY	20.2	19.0	20.4	0.8	34.000

COMPUTER SCREEN #5

This is an example of a screen using multiple criteria in search of financial strength and earnings power. First, it wants companies that have been able to earn at least 20% return on equity, on average, over the past five years. To guard against an unfavorable trend, we want the latest ROE to be better than this five-year average, and also better than the return earned by the average company in the same industry. We also want relatively low debt. And as another sign of financial strength, we want the return on total capital (equity plus debt) to be at least 20%.

The computer found 55 companies that met all these requirements. That made for a rather unwieldy list, so, with an additional computer filtering, we cut our roster to the 29 companies with more than $1.5 billion capitalization. Of course, some other potential investor might prefer middle-capitalization companies and have the computer select the companies with $500 million to $1.5 billion market value.

COMPUTER SCREEN #6 (page 364)

For those who want to concentrate on Blue Chips, this is the list of the very biggest U.S. companies, as measured by the value accorded by the marketplace itself. Multiplying the number of shares outstanding by the price per share gives you this total market valuation for the company. Of course, size by itself shouldn't determine your investment decision; it's still vital to consider such standard investment factors as the relation of the current stock price to the outlook and degree of risk the company represents. As one indicator of relative strength in various significant categories, we show the ranking among the members of this group in five-year earnings growth, return on equity, and price/earnings ratio (in P/E, the lowest is ranked #1).

Also, keep in mind that the standing of these market leaders shifts frequently; this list differs greatly from that in the last edition and will no doubt be much different again in the next edition. In short, this "Leader Board" changes as quickly as that in a golf tourney — only unlike in golf there's never a time when it reports final standings.

#6: The 30 Companies with the Largest Total Market Value

		Market Value ($Billions)	Number Shares (Millions)	Price 8/31/92	EPS Growth Last 5 Years		ROE for Latest Year		P/E for Last 12 mos	
					%	Rank	%	Rank	%	Rank
1 Exxon Corp	XON	79.8	1241.4	64.250	3.7	20	16.7	15	17.8	12
2 Philip Morris	MO	74.9	914.0	82.000	22.3	5	32.1	7	17.4	11
3 Wal-Mart Stores	WMT	65.6	1149.2	57.125	28.6	3	26.0	11	37.3	25
4 General Electric	GE	63.5	858.1	74.000	13.3	14	20.5	13	13.9	3
5 Coca-Cola	KO	56.8	1322.0	43.000	15.0	11	39.5	4	31.9	23
6 Merck & Co	MRK	56.2	1156.2	48.625	27.7	4	48.5	1	24.3	18
7 Amer Tel & Tel	T	56.2	1329.9	42.250	13.8	13	3.4	27	88.0	26
8 IBM	IBM	49.4	570.7	86.625	...	...	...	...	...	...
9 Bristol-Myers Squibb	BMY	34.6	518.6	66.625	13.9	12	36.7	5	16.4	7
10 DuPont (E.I.)	DD	33.2	672.8	49.375	-0.3	25	8.5	25	28.2	21
11 Johnson & Johnson	JNJ	32.9	666.3	49.375	36.5	2	27.8	9	20.9	15
12 Procter & Gamble	PG	31.8	678.5	46.875	18.6	6	27.7	10	17.9	13
13 GTE Corp	GTE	30.6	893.8	34.250	-0.9	26	15.3	17	17.1	10
14 Pepsico	PEP	29.7	792.1	37.500	18.3	7	20.7	12	25.3	20
15 BellSouth	BLS	26.1	488.9	53.375	-1.7	27	11.7	22	16.5	8
16 Abbott Labs	ABT	25.9	848.4	30.500	17.1	10	36.1	6	21.9	16
17 Mobil Corp	MOB	25.8	398.4	64.875	6.2	19	11.3	23	23.9	17
18 Amoco Corp	AN	25.7	496.1	51.750	10.2	17	8.3	26	126.2	27
19 Pfizer Inc	PFE	25.4	329.3	77.250	1.8	24	14.3	20	33.7	24
20 Chevron Corp	CHV	25.1	341.3	73.500	12.0	15	8.7	24	25.2	19
21 General Motors	GM	23.8	687.1	34.625	...	...	...	...	...	...
22 Amer Home Products	AHP	22.8	314.5	72.625	11.0	16	46.0	2	15.7	6
23 Minnesota Mining	MMM	21.6	219.0	98.500	9.1	18	18.6	14	18.5	14
24 Bell Atlantic	BEL	20.9	431.6	48.500	3.1	21	15.9	16	14.2	4
25 Amer Intnatl Group	AIG	20.4	212.0	96.250	17.6	8	14.5	19	12.7	1
26 Microsoft Corp	MSFT	20.1	269.5	74.500	56.9	1	40.8	3	30.9	22
27 Southwestern Bell	SBC	20.0	300.2	66.500	2.4	22	13.3	21	16.8	9
28 Ford Motor	F	19.8	485.5	40.750	...	...	...	...	...	...

#7: Companies with No Long-Term Debt and Latest ROE of at Least 15%, As Well As a Current P/E below the Market Average

		ROE Latest Year	ROE 5 Yr Average	P/E Last 12 Mo	Price 8/31/92
Thomson Advisory Gp	TAG	140.0	157.9	7.5	15.875
PCA International	PCAI	75.0	35.0	16.8	15.750
Great Northern Iron	GNI	68.4	57.6	11.3	67.750
Vodafone Group	VOD	42.2	53.9	18.6	59.375
WD-40 Company	WDFC	38.4	40.0	17.4	40.500
National Health Labs	NH	35.4	28.4	19.3	22.625
St Jude Medical	STJM	28.0	28.8	16.1	31.250
Centex Telemngmnt	CNTX	25.3	13.6	18.4	10.875
Altera Corp	ALTR	25.0	28.2	10.4	9.125
Acuson Corp	ACN	24.8	28.5	12.0	17.875
Edwards (A.G.)	AGE	24.0	16.9	8.7	21.000
Dun & Bradstreet	DNB	24.0	25.3	19.3	55.875
Rag Shops	RAGS	23.3	na	15.0	9.750
20th Century Ind	TW	23.3	25.7	11.1	24.375
San Juan Basin	SJT	22.4	15.4	16.0	8.000
Dames & Moore Inc	DM	21.9	na	18.8	17.500
Frontier Insurnc Gp	FTR	21.3	25.9	13.4	36.000
Phlcorp	PHX	21.3	2.2	8.1	23.250
TBC Corporation	TBCC	21.2	23.4	17.9	17.750
Metropolitan Fincl	MFC	20.8	14.1	3.7	13.125
Kasler Corp	KASL	20.1	14.4	11.0	7.125
Washingtn Fed S&L	WFSL	20.1	na	10.4	25.250
Diagnostic Products	DP	19.9	22.3	19.4	27.875
Apple Computer	AAPL	19.3	32.0	11.0	46.000
Family Dollar	FDO	19.0	16.0	18.2	17.250
Quick & Reilly	BQR	18.7	15.4	7.5	19.625
Logicon	LGN	18.0	14.5	8.5	15.250
Golden West Fincl	GDW	17.9	17.5	9.8	41.250
Sturm Ruger & Co	RGR	17.9	18.5	12.1	38.250
Anthem Electronics	ATM	17.3	16.2	15.6	34.250
Quantum Corp	QNTM	17.1	20.2	11.0	13.625
Coast Svgs Fincl	CSA	16.6	na	4.3	7.000
Morgan Keegan Inc	MOR	16.1	8.1	4.7	13.250
IP Timberlands	IPT	16.0	13.8	8.3	26.000
Roadway Services	ROAD	15.3	12.9	16.3	60.750
Transatlantic Holdgs	TRH	15.3	na	10.8	35.750
Berry Petroleum	BRY	15.2	16.5	17.0	12.500

COMPUTER SCREEN #7

With so many companies highly leveraged with debt, we are looking here for companies that have no long-term debt at all. At the same time they must have earned at least 15% on equity in their latest year (a five-year ROE record is also provided for us to look at). And we want them modestly priced in relation to earnings, by selecting only those whose P/E is below the P/E for the general market (20 at the time this table was prepared).

COMPUTER SCREEN #8

This screen illustrates a system used by a number of professional investors to develop a list of stocks for more detailed study. They realize that no stock is likely to be "perfect" in the sense of having all the favorable statistical characteristics they'd like. So, they set down their "wish list" of criteria and then ask the computer how many of them each stock meets, and then they concentrate their study on the stocks with the highest scores. They can assign extra points to characteristics they consider especially important (as we've done for strong earnings growth in this example). And, of course, they can keep changing the criteria or weights they use and add as many other factors as they like. And instead of just screening the Dow Jones Industrials, as we did to keep the example simple, they can ask the computer to score all the stocks actively traded, or over a certain size, or whatever else they're interested in. In short, this is an extremely flexible tool to help you zero in on the stocks you want to look at more closely.

Incidentally, you may note that as of August 1992 only one of the 30 Dow stocks reached even half of the maximum possible score of 13, and a handful did not meet any of this particular set of criteria. On a similar scoring screen run two years earlier, the typical score was a couple of points higher, but still illustrates that finding stocks that meet all or most of a wish list is a formidable task.

A number of the sample screens we've shown can be constructed, at least in modified form, on your home computer, if you're a subscriber

#8 Dow Jones Industrials Ranked on Point-Score Basis
Maximum of 13 Points Based on:

3 Points: EPS Growth Averaging at least 20% for Last 5 Years
2 Points: Stock Price No More Than Twice Book Value
1 Point Each for:
   Price/Earning Ratio for Latest 12 Months Being Below the
      Average P/E for Last 5 Years
   Debt No More Than 20% of Total Capitalization
   After-Tax Profit Margin Greater Than Average for Com-
      pany's Industry
   Lastest ROE at Least 20%
   Earnings up in Each of Past 5 Years
   Institutions Holding No More Than 30% of Stock
   Earnings Per Share up at Least 20% over Previous Calen-
      dar Quarter
   Risk Factor with a "Beta" Volatility Rating of No *More* Than
      2 (Beta of 2 means the stock's fluctuations — up and
      down — have typically been twice as large those of mar-
      ket as a whole)

		Score			Score
Merck & Co	MRK	7	DuPont (E.I.)	DD	2
Boeing	BA	6	General Motors	GM	2
Philip Morris	MO	6	International Paper	IP	2
Morgan (J.P.)	JPM	5	McDonald's Corp	MCD	2
American Express	AXP	4	Minnesota Mining	MMM	2
Coca-Cola	KO	4	Sears Roebuck	S	2
Disney (Walt)	DIS	4	Texaco	TX	2
Goodyear	GT	4	Union Carbide	UK	2
Woolworth Corp	Z	4	Westinghouse Elec	WX	2
Caterpillar Inc	CAT	3	Allied-Signal	ALD	1
Chevron Corp	CHV	3	Amer Tel & Tel	T	0
General Electric	GE	3	Bethlehem Steel	BS	0
IBM	IBM	3	Eastman Kodak	EK	0
Procter & Gamble	PG	3	Exxon Corp	XON	0
Alcoa	AA	2	United Technologies	UTX	0

to some of the popular data services (it may be a premium service subject to surcharges). CompuServe, for instance, enables you to screen over 10,700 publicly traded securities through 24 different filters ranging from price, earnings, and dividend trends to cash flow and the ratio of market price to book value.

However, while the CompuServe screening procedure is extremely flexible and simple to use — it enables you quickly to screen through any combination of criteria and tells you just how many companies are left after each pass through a filter — when you're ready for a report, the table listing the companies that met all your criteria will automatically show their stock price, dividend yield, and total revenues — for any other statistics (including those just used for the screening process) you have to call up other programs (a more flexible reporting program may become available in future).

COMPUTER SCREEN #9

To show how this works, in this final example, provided by CompuServe, we asked the computer to search first for companies with average five-year earnings growth of at least 35 percent; the 512 companies found were then screened for a current stock price between $5 and $15 (some people seek a moderately-priced stock but not one in the "penny" category); that left 169 companies which were then screened for a price-earnings ratio under 14; finally, the 81 that survived this cut were screened for a market-to-book ratio of under 1.0 (or, put the other way round, the company had a balance-sheet or book worth greater than what you would have to pay for it in the stock market). This left 18 companies that met all four criteria. For practical purposes, you are really left with 15 companies; the three with "D." in front of their ticker symbol are no longer traded in their major market; however, in response to some subscribers who want data on all companies available for historical study, CompuServe retains these "delisted" companies in their database, generating the Computer Screen #9 report.

#9: Companies with 5-Year Earnings Growth Rate Greater Than 35%, P/E Less Than 14; Market-to-Book Ratio under 1, and Stock Price Between 5 and 15.

Company	Symbol	Sales	Price	Yield
AEL Industries Inc	AELNA	140.11	6.000	.00%
Banister Inc	BAN	418.36	7.125	.00%
Collins Foods International Inc	D.CLM	559.33	10.188	1.96%
Dataflex Corp	DFLX	89.61	6.500	.00%
Federal Screw Works	FSCR	57.15	14.625	2.74%
Foxmeyer Corp	FOX	3077.70	12.250	2.29%
Health Mor Inc	HMI	60.79	13.500	5.04%
IPSCO Inc	IPSCF	538.66	14.750	3.25%
Manhattan Life Insurance Co	MLIC	69.49	5.000	1.20%
Maxxam Group Inc	D.MIN	2254.50	13.875	.00%
Nalcap Holdings Inc	NPHIF	57.82	7.750	.00%
Norex America Inc	NXA	60.49	7.250	.00%
O Okiep Copper Co Ltd	OKP	156.07	9.000	5.33%
Olympus Capital Corp	OLCC	42.99	5.250	.00%
Railroad Financial Corp	RF	45.05	10.000	.00%
Sierra Tucson Companies Inc	STSN	43.80	6.250	.00%
Silicon Valley Bancshares	SIVB	77.49	8.375	.72%
Southeastern Public Service Co	D.SCP	229.57	6.500	.00%

Courtesy CompuServe Incorporated.

In sum, screens — whether you get them from a broker, a service, or a magazine, or generate them yourself — can be a very handy investment tool. But, it bears repeating, a screen is exactly what its name says. It screens a vast number of stocks — but then it's up to you to examine the manageable few it has sifted out for you.

CHAPTER 38

Other Investment Areas

WHEN the first edition of this book was written in the early 1950s, stocks and, to a small extent, bonds were the only investments this side of low-yielding savings deposits that were readily available to most Americans. Succeeding editions have reflected the steady broadening of opportunities for the individual investor. To name but a few: mutual funds, which have become significant alternatives to direct stock investment, as well as Unit Investment Trusts and other forms of packaged investments; listed options in stocks, and then in other financial instruments; money market funds and central asset accounts that enable individuals to tie together their different investments in a single account, greatly enhancing their financial flexibility; all sorts of other securitized investment packages that make it practical for individuals to participate in areas previously open only to large institutions.

None of the momentous developments over these four decades has shaken our conviction that common stocks (held directly or through mutual funds) are the best long-term investment tool for the average American. They are truly "shares" in the tremendous accumulated wealth and promising prospects of this country's, and — to an increasingly significant extent — the world's, businesses. All the evidence indicates that, over time, common stocks outperform other types of investment and offer the most realistic hope for outrunning inflation.

In addition, as we've noted throughout this book, it's usually wise to keep a portion of your nest egg in safe fixed-income securities such as high-quality bonds, and some in ready (and interest-earning) cash reserves.

Beyond that, some of the other investment alternatives may make sense for you, depending on your overall financial situation, your stage in life, and your personal comfort level with different degrees of risk. Still others are probably unsuitable for nearly all individuals without very large resources, sophisticated understanding of all the elements involved, and the time to monitor their investments closely. Still, it's a good idea to be aware of the basic aspects of the various alternatives — if only so that you can say, "No, thanks; it's not for me," when some persuasive salesperson calls.

Many of the newer investment instruments have been discussed in prior chapters. In this concluding section, we are providing thumbnail sketches of some others which have attracted attention in recent years, and also pull together more concise portraits of some important areas (such as insurance and retirement plans) that have been mentioned repeatedly but peripherally in earlier chapters.

Life Insurance and Annuities

Since this book's first edition, readers have been cautioned to secure a layer of basic insurance protection before venturing into securities investments. This advice remains as sound as ever. In the intervening years, however, the scope of insurance programs has broadened greatly. You can obtain policies that combine the protection of traditional insurance with the appreciation potential or higher yields associated with securities, while the investment income accumulates on a tax-advantaged basis. Often there's flexibility to adjust premium payments, benefit levels, and investment strategies along the way. Marketing has changed, too. You're apt to find that your friendly securities broker will now also happily sell you life insurance and annuities. Most major brokerage houses sponsor insurance products and have the majority of their registered representatives also licensed for insurance.

Two basic product categories are offered: *life insurance*, which pays benefits when the insured dies; and *annuities*, which are generally designed to pay regular benefits (often to the policy buyers themselves), starting either immediately or at a designated future time, such as retirement. (Because of tax considerations, income from annuities is normally expected to be paid out after age 59½.) The distinction has become a bit fuzzy at the edges; for instance, annuities can be utilized to assure regular income to a survivor, while some new-style life insurance policies are bought more as during-life investment vehicles (with accumulated income tapped through policy loans), though the death benefit is in place as a convenient emergency safeguard.

All life insurance is based on (1) the relatively small risk that the insured will die in the immediate future, and (2) the certainty that, if the policy is kept in force, a death benefit must be paid eventually. It's the interplay of these two considerations — along, of course, with allowance for administrative costs, sales commissions, and profit — that underlies the premium charged on the specific policy you buy.

Concentrating on the first consideration makes *Term* insurance — where you pay strictly for coverage for a limited time period, with no build-up of future values — easily the cheapest form of immediate life insurance. It's particularly popular with young families because it enables them to buy larger amounts of coverage at a time when they need maximum protection. But premiums can rise steeply with advancing age, so they may also want to consider ways of coping with later needs.

Other insurance plans are premised on the need to set up reserves for an eventual benefit payment. Most traditional is *Whole Life*, where you pay a constant premium from the time you buy the policy. The insurance company invests the part of the premium not needed to pay immediate claims (and expenses) and this builds up the policy's cash value over the years — value you can use by borrowing against the policy, by getting some money back if you decide to drop ("surrender") the policy, or by arranging to have the policy continued in force for some years without paying further premiums.

The 1981 tax law change that permits property to be passed from one spouse to the other without any estate tax (and thus can postpone the big bite on large estates until the second spouse dies) has spurred a special wrinkle: *Survivorship Whole Life*, sometimes called "Second to Die." Since benefits are not paid (or needed) until both husband and wife have died, premiums on the policy can be substantially lower.

Newer insurance concepts link some elements of an investment account with traditional insurance by combining the risk and reserve components in different ways. *Universal Life* provides death protection on what is essentially a continuous term insurance basis, coupled with a tax-favored asset accumulation plan. The part of the premium not needed for pure (i.e., Term) insurance earns competitive money market rates, which are typically higher than what's offered in traditional Whole Life. You also get considerable flexibility. Within preset limits, you can vary the split between the insurance and accumulation portion and the amount of the death benefit, vary the amount and frequency of premium payments according to changing needs, and even skip an occasional payment, with the amount then subtracted from your accumulated cash value. When funds are needed for education, retirement, and so forth, you can borrow against cash value at attractive rates without tax liability in many cases. And the cost of Universal is usually cheaper than Whole Life.

Even wider investment flexibility is offered by *Variable Life*. While the investment portion of Universal is based on money market rates, Variable lets you invest in one or more of a variety of stock, bond, or money market funds. If the investments work well, both cash value and insurance benefit grow; but even if they falter, you are guaranteed a minimum death benefit. Again, there's a lot of flexibility in being able to change investment instruments, add payments to increase values, and take out policy loans.

Many variations are available. *Single-Premium Life* is bought through a single, up-front premium payment that buys significant insurance protection plus long-term asset accumulation. As is typical of insurance, the cash value can grow faster because the income generated within the policy is not subject to current taxation. Originally, this increased value could be pulled out each year through low- or no-cost policy loans — in effect, giving the holder substantial spendable tax-free income. However, in 1987 such withdrawals (but *not* the accumulation within the policy) became taxable on Single-Premiums; at least seven equal annual premium installments are required for the loan to be tax-free. Even so, Single-Premiums can still be attractive for established individuals seeking maximum accumulation to meet longer-term objectives.

There is a similar wide range of plans and investment setups for annuities. These policies can be Single-Premium or they may call for periodic payments, usually with considerable flexibility on how much you pay in, above a specified minimum premium. Payout can start immediately or at a future date (*deferred*). The value of deferred annuities may be built up at a *fixed* interest rate, or on a *variable* basis that depends on investment results, or by a combination of the two. Benefit payments can be for the life of the annuitant (and, if desired, continue for the life of a beneficiary), for a specified minimum period, or some combination.

Insurance companies have set up or contracted for a great variety of mutual funds into which policyholders can funnel the investment portion of their Variable life and annuity policies. Results of several hundred of these funds are periodically chronicled in major financial publications. However, if you're dissatisfied with the performance of the funds sponsored by your insurance company, you normally can't shift to another company's without surrendering your policy.

Most companies also issue *Guaranteed Investment Contracts* or *GICs*, which have been described as a kind of nonbank (and therefore not federally insured) CD. Though industry-funded protective arrangements (usually the result of prodding by the states) may provide some degree of help in case of disaster, this absence of federal backing makes it vital to look carefully into the strength and reliability of the insurance company responsible for payment. A GIC normally carries an interest rate guaranteed for a specific period, most often from one to five years. Sometimes subsequent renewal rates are pegged to some standard measure such as Treasuries or the prime rate. With others, the company is free to set its own renewal rate, though you may have some cancellation rights if the rate is unsatisfactory. In any case, since you presumably plan a long-term commitment, be sure to get all the details in advance.

What attracts many to the investment aspects of life insurance and annuities is that the investment earnings within the policies can grow tax-deferred at a much faster rate than equivalent earnings in an ordinary account where only after-tax proceeds are available for reinvestment.

As for the overall tax status, the general rule is that the beneficiaries of a life insurance policy receive the policy proceeds completely free of income tax, though the value of the policy itself is counted among the (taxable) assets of the policyowner's estate. If the policyholders themselves try to cash in during the life of the insured by surrendering the policy, then anything received above the amount of premiums paid in will be taxable. That's why a policy loan (mostly not subject to tax) is usually the better alternative to surrender.

For annuities, the tax deferral aspect means that the longer you invest, the more money you will have stored up for future income. When you start taking distributions, part of each payment is considered a return of principal and free of tax; the rest, derived from earnings, is taxable. The same rule applies if the annuity holder dies and the beneficiaries get the proceeds: the portion attributable to earnings is taxable.

In sum, life insurance and annuities can meet many needs, and today there are many more choices than ever before. But whether you opt for traditional insurance or newer-style policies — or quite possibly a combination of both — the basic rules for any investment apply. It's vital to understand just what you are buying, the costs (and how much of the fees, which may be sizable, is collected up front), how benefits are figured under various circumstances, what happens if you want to change or even abandon your policy, and how solid the company underwriting the insurance is.

Commodities and the Futures Markets

As we discussed in chapter 24, contracts on financial instruments now account for the vast majority of trading on the futures exchanges. Not that the exchanges have abandoned their original business: providing a forum where producers and users of farm and industrial commodities can cover their demand and supply requirements for a season or more in advance.

U.S. exchanges now host futures trading on some 30 such commodities. They have long included such American farm staples as wheat, corn, cotton, and soybeans, as well as hogs and pork bellies. There are some tropical products like cocoa and coffee; and metals like copper, silver, and gold. There are also more recent additions to the trading list such as frozen orange juice, broilers, and feeder cattle, as well as a slew of petroleum products like light sweet crude oil and unleaded gasoline.

A futures contract is a commitment to deliver (or accept) a specified amount and grade of a commodity at a designated time. It helps members of the "trade" — such as growers, warehousers, manufacturers — to *hedge* their operations; that is, protect themselves against some of the vagaries of the market while they wait for the crop to mature or a raw product to be gradually turned into finished goods.

But for the "trade" to be able to hedge their risks effectively, it requires *speculators* willing to assume the risks. Thus, speculators, ready to risk their funds in the hope of realizing substantial profits if they're right, can be not only an honorable but an *essential* part of the market. Which doesn't mean it's wise for most individuals to rush in and perform that function.

The bulk of the speculative interest is provided by professional traders on the exchange floors and others who can study intensely the factors affecting the commodity and are in position to react quickly to any breaking news. Such expertise and resources are hard for most people to match.

Also, don't overlook some of the special characteristics of futures. For instance, in securities, it's inherently more risky to hold a short position — when you've borrowed stock that you must sooner or later buy back — than a long position — where you've bought and now own a stock or bond. But in futures, your position is essentially just as risky whether you're long or short — whether you've entered the market by buying or by selling a contract. Either way, you've in effect simply placed a bet on the direction prices will move within a limited period of time — and, whatever your expectations, you know that price can just as soon go down as up. You don't own the underlying commodity — in fact, the last thing you'd want is to have either to buy or to deliver the wheat or pork bellies or gold in question, which for you would be an expensive and cumbersome process. Indeed, if you're determined to buy or sell futures, make sure that you close out your position (whether long or short) in ample time before the delivery period begins.

There's unquestionably a hard-to-deny appeal in the massive potential profit that a small initial cash investment can generate — in those cases where everything goes right. Commission charges are relatively low. A position (long or short) can generally be established with a margin payment of 5 to 10 percent of the market price of the commodity. But the margin is constantly marked-to-market, which means you have to ante up more funds quickly if the market price moves against you. Indeed, it's possible, if prices move adversely, that not only will your entire investment in the contract be wiped out, but that you'll be left owing money, because your contract couldn't be closed out fast enough. Against that tremendous risk, there's the hope that, if the commodity's price moves just 10 percent in your direction, you might double your money.

However, it's said that 90 percent of all nonprofessional futures traders lose money. And aggregate losses are six times aggregate gains. Even the best commodity traders lose money more often than they make it. They stay ahead of the game by taking small losses right away while letting their gains pile up.

For those with a strong urge to dabble in futures, the most prudent way may well be through a commodity fund (similar to a mutual fund or limited partnership). Individuals participate by buying units to create a pool of cash managed by commodities professionals. You pay a commission or load when you purchase the units, and the managers typically get a share of any profits (at times, in addition to an annual management fee) but, even after costs, the average track record seems better than that of individuals speculating on their own. And investors in such funds don't have the constant worry about sudden margin calls or the need to make trading decisions in markets that change from minute to minute. Also, you normally face no liability beyond the money you put up at the time of purchase. In fact, many funds provide that, should the fund's trading operations eat up more than a specified percentage of their capital (say, 50 percent), they will liquidate so that unit holders will be able to salvage at least a portion of their original investment. Some others put a portion of their initial capital into zero-coupon Treasuries, so investors can count on getting much or all of their principal back even in a worst-case scenario.

Thus, participating through funds can moderate the risks and give you the benefits of qualified management (but be sure to check both the qualifications and costs); however, keep in mind that any commodities speculation is only for those able and willing to undertake very substantial risks.

Gold and Other Precious Metals

Since the dawn of history, gold has been the world's most popular store of value. It's an internationally recognized medium of exchange, which, unlike paper currency, has an intrinsic value of its own. It's portable. In times of political or economic turmoil, people return again and again to gold — both to buy immediately needed goods and services, and to hoard against future uncertainties. This is why gold prices tend to rise whenever world peace is threatened or inflation gets out of hand. Overall, gold is a crisis commodity. It usually does well when everything else is doing poorly, or looks as if it is about to do poorly.

In the U.S., the Depression-era Gold Reserve Act of 1934 barred private ownership of gold bullion (bars or other bulk form), except for industrial purposes, and also set the Treasury's official price of gold at $35 an ounce (up from $21). From that point until 1968, as the price of everything else rose dramatically, the price of gold remained static. By 1968, world market pressures could no longer be resisted and the price of gold was set free. However, not until 1974 was the ban on gold sales to individual Americans lifted. By then the price of gold was already around $150 an ounce. In a series of dramatic spurts it soared to $875 in 1980. The subsequent retreat was also dramatic, followed by wide fluctuations. In recent years gold has been in the $325 to $450 range.

This history makes it plain that gold is not a sure-thing investment. Also, not only does a gold holding pay no dividends or other investment income, but it costs money to store and insure, and there may be an assay (inspection) fee when you're ready to sell it. And, since the 1986 tax act, you no longer can buy gold for an IRA or other retirement account. There may, however, be justification, in the opinion of numerous (but by no means all) investment advisers, for putting a small amount (perhaps 2% to 5%, or even a bit more) into gold for those who want an ultimate hedge against runaway inflation — and then you should hope it's a hedge that won't be needed.

There are five basic ways to invest in gold.

(1) Gold bullion. Aside from precious metals dealers, many large brokerage houses buy and sell the metal. Many will also store and insure it. Merrill Lynch offers precious metals through its Blueprint program (its successor to the Big Board's Monthly Investment Plan) under which you can place orders for as little as $50 worth of bullion at a time.

(2) Gold coins, both antique and freshly minted. The latter are bullion coins, in most cases exactly one ounce in weight, produced mainly for sale to those who want to hold gold in a convenient form. They usually sell for a little more than the price of the gold they contain. Their value as legal tender theoretically assures a minimum value, but it's so low (e.g., $50 for the U.S. Eagle, $50 Canadian for the Maple Leaf) that even a cataclysmic collapse of gold bullion is unlikely to approach that level. A few of the old coins, especially if in

good condition, may have a numismatic worth above the intrinsic value of their gold content.

(3) Gold futures, which call for you to buy or deliver a fixed amount of gold at a fixed price at a certain time. Like all futures contracts, they are basically short-term price speculations meant only for sophisticated traders.

(4) Gold stocks. Shares in gold mining companies naturally are impacted by changes in the value of their principal product. But their stock prices also heavily depend on the companies' production costs and capacity, the amount and quality of their ore reserves, and so forth.

(5) Gold mutual funds. They buy a wide range of gold mining stocks and may be a better way to participate in the industry — but, as noted, gold price is only one factor in the price of mining stocks. (However, mining stocks and mutual funds are eligible for IRA investment.)

A substantially lower-priced precious metal is *silver*, which is also available in bullion and coins, and is actively traded on the commodities markets. From New Deal days until the 1960s, its price was pegged at $1.29 an ounce, before it was freed to seek its market level. In early 1980, while gold was climbing to its all-time high of $875, silver was staging its own panic buying rally. Fueled by increasing margin buying by the Hunt brothers of Texas, silver shot up in a few short months from $10 to over $50 an ounce. Then the Commodities Futures Trading Commission stepped in and demanded that more cash be put into such speculative margin buys. The price of silver dropped even faster than it had risen, and by mid-1982 was below $5 an ounce. Since then, there have been substantial fluctuations. The metal's price in recent years has ranged between $3.50 and $7.

Silver has a wide variety of industrial uses — in electronics, photography, dentistry, and sundry manufacturing processes. (Gold, too, is used in industry, but this is overshadowed by its monetary and ornamental functions.) There's a chronic shortfall between annual demand and yearly production of silver, which may foreshadow long-range price pressures. But there are still massive stockpiles held by governments; also, heavy supplies of hoarded ornamental and coin silver seem to appear whenever prices move up.

The only other precious metals with a substantial world market are *platinum* and its sister metal *palladium*. They are essential in numerous industrial processes, some highly exotic, and also in demand for jewelry, and there are a few platinum coins. The metals are traded on the futures exchanges, but their use as an investment medium is very limited compared to gold and silver.

Collectibles

Headlines periodically proclaim the sale of an Old Master for millions of dollars or a prized baseball card for hundreds of thousands. And each time there's hype about the profit potential of collecting everything from crockery to comic books, not to mention another chorus of "diamonds [or sapphires, or opals] are the investing girl's best friend."

Actually, while new highs are still being set in some categories as well as in specific items that for one reason or another prove particularly attractive, the heyday of the "Collectibles as Prime Investments" boom appears past. In the inflation-plagued 1970s, when prices of everything but stocks and bonds seemed on an irreversible skyward course, various types of "hard assets" often were at the top of well-publicized "investments of the year" lists. The array of proffered opportunities was almost limitless: art, antiques, stamps, coins, autographs, rare books, antique cars, breeding horses, vintage wine, to cite just a few. But as the 1980s progressed, more and more collectibles investors faced disappointments. Not only did many items fail to appreciate further, often they could only be unloaded at a considerable loss. And for collectibles as a whole, the 1990s seem just as uncertain.

Among the realities to be faced even in times of strong collectibles interest: a large part of their value depends on their unique, or at least rare, qualities — which, in turn, means it's hard to determine a market value, and even experts can vary widely in their judgment. Also, you'll want to make sure you do business with a reliable dealer, both as regards price and the authenticity of whatever you buy. Most purchases are made through retail dealers or galleries, or at auction, particularly from the larger international auction houses like Sotheby's and Christie's, which started out dealing mostly in art but have rapidly expanded into every imaginable collectible area. Inevitably, because of the retailer's markup or auctioneer's fee, you need a big gain in basic value during the period you hold a collectible just to break even. Most states will also tack a sales tax on your purchase. And the IRS will tax you on a capital gain if you come out ahead, but probably treat your collection as a nondeductible hobby in case you sell out at a loss.

If you do want to get into the collectible market, prime considerations include: (1) knowledge — find out as much as is possible about your specific area of investment, and remember, the time you must spend on the learning curve could be tedious and almost certainly expensive; (2) passion — if you don't really care about what you're collecting, your time would probably be much more fruitfully spent investing in some less subjective area, especially in view of the just-noted learning curve; (3) quality — all experts agree that it is the better examples of any collectible that appreciate the fastest and the most; (4) knowing where to buy — in collectibles, prices and quality vary more widely than in any other investment area. And beware of "instant" collectibles — items newly created in "limited quantities" for the express purpose of marketing to would-be collectors.

Most fundamental: collecting stamps or coins (or many other things) makes a wonderful hobby — you can have fun, learn, meet interesting fellow enthusiasts — and if, in time, you find the collection you've built up is also worth a tidy sum, that's a delightful bonus. Similarly, if you find artwork you enjoy looking at and can afford, by all means hang it in your home and let it give you pleasure — and, again, perhaps you'll also get a nice capital gain. But unless you want to make it your business, it's almost certainly wisest to concentrate your investment efforts in more conventional areas. In short, collectibles make wonderful hobbies but iffy investments.

Real Estate

For most of the period since World War II, real estate stood out as an ideal investment. For buying your own home — provided you don't go in over your head with a mortgage you may not be able to maintain — it very likely still is. True, the fantastic boom that (with occasional but usually short-lived halts in one region or another) often doubled or tripled the going price of a house in a decade gave way near the end of the 1980s to a widespread and painful retrenchment. Still, the probabilities are strong that even most who buy near the top of the market, if they can hold out for a decade or so, will find the value of their house plus the tax advantages of ownership leave them ahead of the game.

For those dabbling in real estate as a sideline investment, however, uncertainties are far greater. Once you've bought a property, you may find it hard to sell, and, whether it's residential, commercial, or industrial, hard to find a suitable rent-payer. Meantime, you must meet carrying costs such as mortgage and real estate taxes as well as spending to keep the property in shape. And the ability to write off your operating losses (from both out-of-pocket outlays and such accounting items as depreciation) against some of your taxable regular income has largely vanished.

As discussed briefly in chapter 19, you can invest more indirectly through Real Estate Investment Trusts or REITs (similar to mutual funds, but in various aspects of real estate), through syndicated partnerships, or through other imaginative variations on investing in land and commercial and residential property that proliferated with the real estate boom. You do get professional management and don't have to concern yourself with the details of operation, but, as the record clearly shows, that does not guarantee success. Soured real estate investments contributed substantially to the problems of savings & loans, banks, and insurance companies, despite their presumed expertise in the area. In some cases, there was a matter of fraud, but more often it was simply poor judgment.

As in so many other investment areas, we must summarize: It's possible to go into real estate for income, but it's vital to assess the very real risks.

Tax Shelters

By strict dictionary definition, a tax shelter is any extension of a tax benefit, including municipal bonds, retirement plans, and (to a now lessened extent) capital gains. In common parlance, however, the term is used mainly for ventures undertaken and promoted primarily for their tax-saving potential — a potential often based on the venture's generating large early losses that can be written off against regular income.

One of the proud pillars of the American system is that no one should be expected to pay more tax than is legally required. The corollary is that it's entirely legitimate and honorable to organize your affairs so as to minimize the tax bite. And Congress has repeatedly authorized tax benefits to encourage socially desirable actions, such as investing in public housing.

But the system can also lead to abuses. Often one person's incentive is another's loophole. And some succumb to temptation to manipulate facts and figures (if not commit outright fraud) in an effort to qualify under shelter rules.

In any case, over the past 10 years the pendulum has swung the other way, with lower regular tax rates and fewer authorized ways to shelter income. And it is generally no longer possible to use operating losses from "passive investments" (ventures in whose operation you play no active role) to reduce your regular taxable income.

Thus, you are far less likely to find your mailbox or phone answering machine filled with tempting offers to join some limited partnership or other venture that promises to pay back your "modest" initial investment in the form of big tax savings. Nor is your trusted stockbroker likely to have many legitimate if quite speculative tax shelters to offer.

However, if any potential ventures do come your way and you are willing to undertake the risks, here are some rules to observe:

(1) Make sure you understand all the facts about the proposed venture, its operations, management, economic expectations, as well as what obligations you assume and how you can get out of the investment.
(2) Never go into a venture just for the tax advantage — if it's not economically viable, even a tax-deductible loss isn't worth it.
(3) Make sure the supposed tax benefits make sense for someone in your income and tax bracket.
(4) Have the whole deal reviewed by your tax adviser.

Retirement Plans

Retirement plans are not a specific investment instrument in themselves, but rather a special set of programs that permit you to utilize one or more types of investment in a tax-favored manner. That's why you've seen retirement plans mentioned throughout this book, as we commented on various specific investment categories as being well suited for use in such plans.

Since retirement planning is probably the most important aspect of the long-term investor's financial program, it's appropriate in this final section to pull together some of the key considerations regarding this subject.

We have repeatedly stressed that it's becoming more and more important for people to set up their own retirement program to supplement what will be available from other sources. Political realities, if nothing else, probably assure that today's earners can count on collecting their scheduled Social Security payments when they come due. However, it's also very likely that for anyone from the "middle-middle" income brackets up, these payments will cover a steadily declining proportion of living-standard maintenance. At the same time, ever-fewer workers can look to "defined benefit" corporate pensions pegged at a comfortable percentage of their peak salary period. More and more employers are switching to "defined contribution," under which they contribute a set amount to the plan each year and an employee's eventual pension depends on how well the investments in his or her account perform. Besides, with today's typical careers involving repeated job changes (voluntary or forced), many workers wouldn't build up the seniority needed to maximize "defined" benefits.

Do-it-yourself retirement programs got their biggest boost when Congress authorized anyone with earned income, whether covered by an existing pension plan or not, to set up an *Individual Retirement Account*. Under the IRA rules in effect for 1982 through 1986, up to $2,000 of *pretax* earned income per individual could be put into an account each year. (Separate accounts must be opened for husbands and wives based on their own earnings, but if there's a nonworking spouse a total of $2,250 can be apportioned between them.) And once within the IRA, the money can grow, fully sheltered from federal taxes, until you start taking it out. You must *wait* to do that till you are at least 59½ (or pay a penalty on early withdrawals) and you are *required* to take annual distributions once you reach 70½. These distributions are then taxed as regular income — fair enough, since no income taxes had yet been paid on either the money you had put into the IRA or any of the earnings on it.

The attractions of this fully tax-deferred IRA were clear, and its popularity overwhelming. For 1986 alone, some 15.5 million Americans put a total of $37.8 billion of deductible contributions into them. Starting with 1987, however, the law became considerably more restrictive. You can still make the same contribution as before, but you can do so with *pretax* dollars only if neither you nor your spouse is covered by an employer retirement plan or else if your adjusted gross income is under $40,000 if married ($25,000 for singles). There's a partial exemption for incomes up to $50,000 married or $35,000 single. Above that, your entire contribution must be made with *after-tax* dollars. However, the earnings (including capital gains) within the IRA will accumulate tax-free, so there's still a significant advantage. Once you start taking withdrawals, you get a credit for the after-tax money you put in; the computation isn't that difficult, but it's vital to keep careful records of your contributions to make sure you aren't taxed twice.

The restrictions have clearly cut into the IRA appeal. The latest available figures show that in 1991 only 4.7 million taxpayers made deductible contributions, totaling $9 billion. This decline in much-needed savings has added to the widespread efforts to restore the tax-free contribution rights. Some proposals go even further — for instance, they would permit penalty-free withdrawals for such socially desirable purposes as first-time home buying or college tuition. To date, worries about the momentous budget deficits have stymied action, but the possibility (some would say likelihood) of enacting modifications remains very much alive.

Among the IRA's appeal, even now, is its great flexibility. The money has to be invested through an IRS-approved trustee or custodian, but nearly all brokerage firms, mutual funds, banks, credit unions, and insurance companies have master plans that fit the bill. You can establish a self-directed brokerage account where you decide in what securities to invest; go with a mutual fund family that offers many different types of funds and permits you to move your money around among the various funds in the family; pick a bank and select from its CDs, other savings vehicles, and in some cases special mutual funds; or obtain annuities or some other investment instruments from insurance companies. You are free to move (roll over) your money from one trustee to another.

While IRAs are the most universally applicable plans, you may also be able to participate in others that can offer greater advantages, including much higher annual contribution limits. Many companies now offer 401(k) plans (named for the pertinent section of the Internal Revenue Code), while similar opportunities are open to many employees of nonprofit organizations or local governmental employees under Section 403(b) or Section 457. Employees can have a certain portion of their *pretax* salary placed into the plan, and part of this is often matched by an employer contribution. Participants usually designate one or more investment vehicles (typically some stock, bond, and money market funds or some long-term savings instruments) in which their portion of the plan is placed, and of course the earnings accumulate tax free; you pay tax only when you eventually withdraw funds. Like IRAs, most withdrawals before 59½ incur a penalty, but often it's permissible to borrow from your account.

For the self-employed, there are *Keogh Plans*, which permit funneling a percentage of your earnings into a tax-deferred account where you can exercise many investment options. If you have any employees, they must generally be included in the plan if they meet certain specifications. Keoghs can also be used if you are moonlighting or doing some free-lance work; you can shelter a part of that income regardless of how much you earn (and what retirement provisions you enjoy) on your regular job.

There are also *Simplified Employee Pensions* or *SEPs*, essentially employer-funded IRAs available to small businesses. The employer may put into the plan up to 15% (maximum $30,000) of the employee's compensation. SEPs can include employee-owners, even if they're the only employees.

Of course, when planning for the future, building a sound investment portfolio, even without special tax benefits, can prove richly rewarding. Doing so outside the tax-sheltered plans avoids restrictions and penalties should you want to apply the proceeds to pre-retirement uses. In any case, it's best to consider the formal retirement programs the foundation but certainly not the ceiling of your total investment structure. This said, to the extent it's possible to take advantage of any tax-favored opportunity — especially when it is supplemented by an employer contribution — it will generally permit faster and greater growth of your retirement dollars.

In conclusion, we pay tribute to the prescience of those who worked on the preceding edition. The authors then noted: "As this seventh edition is being prepared in February 1982, the Dow Jones Industrial Average has fallen to 833.80 [from 1002.76 when the sixth edition of this book went to press in June 1976]. In a 5½-year period, during which the price of almost everything else has at least doubled, the price of the average stock, as measured by an assortment of popular averages, has declined 15 to 20%. Publicly owned American companies are making historically high profits, paying out historically high dividends, and their prospects, in both domestic and international markets, have never looked better. Still, stock prices are down. This is not a condition that can continue for very long. We believe common stocks are the last bargain around, and that prudent investors who show their faith in American commerce by buying them now stand to profit more than participants in any other investment area — that is, as soon as the relationship of these stocks' value to their cost rights itself. As it always has."

This confidence was certainly well placed. Soon after these words were written, the market took off on one of the longest and strongest bull markets in history. The old highs were quickly shattered. In the spring of 1991 the Dow topped 3000 for the first time in history, and in early 1994 almost touched 4000. Virtually all the other indexes have also set repeated new highs.

Of course, this great upwelling of stock prices leaves us with a decidedly different perspective than in 1982. Stocks no longer lag the other economic indicators, near-term prospects for many companies are more uncertain, and by historic standards stocks are generally not undervalued in terms of earnings and dividends. So there's not the same occasion to expect the price-value relationship to soon "right itself." But there still remains the long-term lesson: Unless history completely reverses itself, we can count on persistent long-term economic growth and that growth will almost certainly be reflected in the stock market. Which leads to the familiar refrain: Over the long term, it's hard to find anything that beats common stocks.

Key Points to Remember

1. You can never avoid risk.
2. Often, the biggest risk of all is to do nothing.
3. Over time, common stocks have outperformed all other types of investment, and been the only group to consistently outpace inflation.
4. However, stocks also are very volatile, so you must be both willing and able to withstand these fluctuations.
5. The biggest market gains often take place in relatively short and largely unpredictable periods, so it's vital to maintain a sound investment discipline.
6. "Dollar cost averaging" — putting in the same dollar amount month by month (or quarter by quarter, or even year by year) — is one of the best ways to increase your chances for investment success. You get elementary arithmetic on your side.
7. Use tax-advantaged investments, such as an IRA or a 401(k), as much as you can.
8. Keep in mind the need for emergency funds when figuring out what is "as much as you can" sock away in long-term investments.
9. Municipal bonds and similar securities exempt from income taxes are a good idea IF, and *ONLY IF*, you are in a tax bracket that gives you a higher *net* yield than equivalent-quality taxable bonds.
10. Any investment should first of all make economic sense; any tax advantage should never be more than the icing.

11. Asset allocation (apportioning your total holdings among different investment groups such as stocks, bonds, and quickly-available "cash") is very important, and should be adjusted from time to time as your personal situation as well as overall economic conditions change.

12. You'll want a reasonable amount of diversification. But while you shouldn't put all your investment eggs in one basket, there's no need to overdo it — you don't have to be in dozens of securities.

13. Both selecting securities on your own and choosing packaged investments such as mutual funds are valid strategies.

14. Keep your eye on the long term. Watch your portfolio, and be prepared to make changes periodically, but, whether you are in direct securities or mutual funds, avoid rushing in and out of stocks too often. And steer clear of any advisers who urge you to make frequent moves.

15. If you can't understand an investment instrument or proposal, hold on to your money.

16. Judge all investment decisions in light of your personal circumstances and requirements — there are no "one size fits all" bargains.

17. Above all, keep in mind — *and practice* — this slogan: Investigate before you invest.

Index